They who laid the intellectual foundations of the Western world were the most fanatical players and organizers of games that the world has ever known.

—C.L.R. James, *Beyond a Boundary*

One plays *football, one doesn't* play *boxing.*

—Joyce Carol Oates, *On Boxing*

THE CULTURE OF BRUISING

THE CULTURE
OF BRUISING

*Essays on Prizefighting, Literature,
and Modern American Culture*

Gerald Early

THE ECCO PRESS

The Ecco Press
100 West Broad Street
Hopewell, NJ 08525
Published simultaneously in Canada by
Penguin Books Canada Ltd., Ontario
Printed in the United States of America

Designed by Nick Mazella

FIRST EDITION

Library of Congress Cataloging-in-Publication Data

Early, Gerald Lyn.
The culture of bruising : essays on prizefighting, literature, and modern
    American culture / Gerald Early.
        p. cm.
      1. Boxing—United States—Philosophy.   2. Pluralism (Social
sciences)—United States.   3. Afro-Americans—Social conditions.
I. Early, Gerald Lyn.
GV1125.C85   1994
796.8'3—dc20   93-39179
    ISBN 0-88001-310-9

The text of this book is set in Garamond 3

To Dan Halpern (boxing aficionado),
my editor
and
my friend

ACKNOWLEDGMENTS

I would like to thank some people in connection with the work in this volume: my wife, Ida, and my family; JoAnn Collins, who, I am sure, did some important work somewhere along the line for some of this stuff; Ellen Raben, a most extraordinary library assistant in Washington University's Interlibrary Loan Department; Hiawatha and Theo Broughton, who were instrumental in making the magic essay happen; and, finally, Dan Halpern, without whose aid, advice, friendship, and assistance there would be no one in the world who would have heard of Gerald Early.

CONTENTS

INTRODUCTION

Bruising, as Subject

. . . to look for the sake of seeing only was the freest, liberalissimum, of all pursuits.

—Hannah Arendt

Immediately after his first title fight with Roberto Duran on June 20, 1980, Sugar Ray Leonard said that their next fight (which took place five months later) would be a continuation of the latter rounds of the first. Leonard lost a close decision in their first fight, largely trying to box on Duran's terms: mauling, infighting, the sort of macho street war that suited both Duran's temperament and his ability. Despite boxing out of character, Leonard still nearly won the fight, and clearly dominated Duran in the closing rounds. As it turned out, Leonard was right. The second fight picked up where the first one left off and, of course, as all the knowing coves can tell, Duran quit in the ninth round.

This book is, in one sense, an exact continuation of *Tuxedo Junction,* my first collection of essays. *Tuxedo Junction* ended not with an essay of mine but with an essay by James Baldwin on the first Patterson-Liston fight. This book begins with an essay that first appeared in a much shorter version in the *Kenyon Review* and is, in some respects, the central thesis of a certain stage of my work: the black intellectual and the sport of prizefighting, or, more precisely, the black male intellectual and the culture of bruising. That essay opens a door to the exploration of the subject I would call, borrowing from Stephen Twitchell, "preposterous masculinity," and all the essays that follow in the boxing section deal with variants of that theme. It is followed by "The Unquiet Kingdom of Providence: The Patterson-Liston Fight," in which I

again engage Baldwin—I jousted with him on this essay in *Tuxedo Junction*—
on the very subjects of his essay that ends my first book: Sonny Liston and
Floyd Patterson, which is, moreover, an extension of the ending of "The
Black Intellectual and Sport of Prizefighting," as a discussion of Liston and
Patterson ends that piece. So there is a sense of intricate intellectual design
here, a pattern of critical purpose.

 Why boxing—or more broadly considered, bruising—attracts is so self-
evident to me that I sometimes wonder why it is not so to others. Modern
prizefighting is a remarkable metaphor for the philosophical and social condition of men (and, sometimes, women) in modern mass society. Launched
in eighteenth-century England, largely as a way of upper-class betting men
to amuse themselves at the expense of lower-class ruffians, prizefighting was
created in anticipation of mass industrialized society, where it has flourished
as a sport and, even more startlingly, as an aesthetic: namely, to watch without seeing. The prizefighter enacts a drama of poor taste (but not of absurdity, as the modern professional wrestler does) that is in truth nothing more
than an expression of resentment or a pantomime of rebellion totally devoid
of any political content except ritualized male anger turned into a voyeuristic
fetish. Boxing is a form of kitsch, which explains why so many intellectuals
have been attracted to it: The intellectualization of kitsch is a growth industry. But the boxer symbolizes even more than resentment and human-
struggle-as-kitsch; he symbolizes, in some respects, the individual in mass
society: marginalized, alone, and consumed by the very demands and acts of
his consumption. Bruising is a kind of dumb play of the human crisis of
identity in the modern society. (I must add that I do not think this explains
modern mass society in its entirety or that our contemporary culture, symbolically, is only this. But that boxing so self-evidently provides this representation suggests that seeing modern mass society in this way is not simply
a convention but a driving, obsessive mass need.) I explain this more fully in
my essay on Jake LaMotta and Rocky Graziano, which I have always felt to
be my best effort on the subject. But taken together, the boxing essays develop aspects and offshoots of all my basic ideas and assumptions about bruising. As *The Culture of Bruising* ends with essays about my daughters (two of
the best essays I have ever written or am likely to write), I have framed the
work with my undying interests: the meaning of masculinity and femininity.

 At first, this book was meant to be devoted entirely to boxing, but two
occurrences made such an endeavor impossible: first inattention, then im-
plausibility. After *Tuxedo Junction* was published, I began to lose interest not
in boxing precisely, but in thinking about it in as passionate a way as I had. I
could not focus on the subject very well, perhaps because contemporary boxing as a sport, as a business venture, as a sociological construct seemed terribly unfocused and without much direction or much compelling presence in

our culture after about the mid-1980s. I am still drawn to the subject as a historical/cultural narrative of American life but no longer as a current activity of which I could call myself aficionado. This antiquarian attraction disturbs me, makes me feel that my writing about the sport now lacks a certain emotional, even psychobiographical compulsion that gave my past writings on the subject the authenticity and power necessary to make the subject worth addressing for anyone who does not love boxing. But I will return to the world of boxing someday as a living place. In the meantime, I will continue to write a stream of essays on the subject (even as I write this, I am working on a new boxing essay), but I cannot, until I can focus more completely, write a full-length treatise on the subject.

Alas, writing a full-length treatise on boxing also became more implausible, and unfeasible, as boxing became more uninteresting to the general public. Boxing has suffered lulls of this sort in the past and has managed to resurrect itself, and I am confident that, for better or worse, this will happen again. Even in the best of all possible worlds for such work, boxing books do not sell well, and to produce a book on boxing in the current climate is to watch one's work sink without a trace. I felt it best to diversify this work. Moreover, *Tuxedo Junction* needs a companion volume that is more or less like it in its design and aspiration. It needs a sequel if for no other reason than to convince myself that collections of essays are not the wholly quixotic pursuits that sales figures would suggest. I became convinced that if I produced enough essay books, the public might stop expecting me to produce something else and read these works as the self-contained entities they are.

But, contrarily, in many fundamental ways this volume is not a continuation of *Tuxedo Junction* nor even a companion to it. If anything, this book is more ambitious but, paradoxically, less daring than its predecessor because I do not put myself "in the breach" for the reader as a conflicted and divided soul whose very contradictions give the writing its power, its intelligence, its energy, and its humanity in whatever degree it can be said that the book possesses these qualities. I think this book is smarter in its pursuit of the broadly engaged wit of a solidly professional essayist, but *Tuxedo Junction* is probably more profound in its unabashed pursuit of wisdom through confessing the author's folly. This book, despite the autobiographical passages in the "Life with Daughters" essays, feels less personal to me and will probably feel so to readers of *Tuxedo Junction*.

Most of the essays in this volume were previously published in places that have been very receptive to my work: *The Hungry Mind Review, Antioch Review, Kenyon Review, Kenyon Review,* and *Harper's.* My essay on baseball first appeared in *Openings: Original Essays by Contemporary Soviet and American Writers,* edited by Robert Atwan and Valeri Vinokurov. I have been asked by several people why I do not write about baseball more often as I have such an abiding love of the sport. I can say in response that baseball, despite my devotion to it, has never drawn me as an intellectual or as a writer the way boxing has. Indeed, this baseball essay was originally written as a baseball and boxing essay, and Bob Atwan wisely deleted the boxing sections to improve the piece.

Every piece in this book is what I call a pure essay, written with the full intention of being a wholly realized statement on a subject. Some, such as "Pulp and Circumstance" and "Black Herman Comes Through Only Once Every Seven Years," are massive, sprawling works, far from the tightly etched études of "Life with Daughters." Few essays here appear exactly as they were printed. Some are changed a little and some are altered a great deal. In most cases the alterations simply restore the essay to its original form. Some essays have endnotes; others, usually shorter, do not. The endnotes are not meant to give the essays any academic pretensions. The sheer stylistic exuberance and demands of the long pieces are such that endnotes are a necessary device to help make them cohere even as they are trying desperately to find the confines of format and break apart before the reader's eyes. This book is meant to be, unequivocally, an exploration and presentation of the art of the essay, including some of the most experimental and challenging essays I have written.

The three sections here are prefaced with poems, which are meant to thematically "place" each section, to unify it imagistically. Some were published previously. "Prizefighting and the Modern World" was highly and variously praised in some quarters when it first appeared in *American Poetry Review* several seasons ago—which means that it might even be, I hope, a passably decent piece.

It was most gratifying that *Tuxedo Junction* was recognized as a significant publication by both literary critic Hazel Carby and novelist Charles Johnson. (This is not to mention the praise heaped upon it by Stanley Crouch. I am eternally grateful to *Tuxedo Junction* if only for the simple reason that it gave me an introduction to Stanley Crouch, and knowing him has been one of the great pleasures of my life.) It is nice to be noticed by writers I admire, even nicer to be noticed by writers who had no reason to know I was alive. Yet this does not indicate a broad acceptance of my work among academics and writers. In fact, I fear that *Tuxedo Junction* has fallen between the chairs, being neither fish nor fowl: not theoretical enough for the lit. crit. scholars and probably a bit too lit. crit. for writers. That is symbolic of this writer himself: I have never taken a creative writing course, never studied the subject, and never wanted to. I do not consider myself a creative writer. But I am equally estranged from the current world of literary criticism where people sprout other people's theories and ideas because they are unable to think of any themselves or because obscure language makes them sound smart. The grid of gender, race, and class bores me as the only triptych in town. Nation, political system, religion, language group, and generation are just as essential to understanding human identity as gender, race, and class. The business of being a critic is not to sound smart but to sound necessary, not to be obscure but to be so vastly absorbed and awed by the humanness of enlightened discernment that one can only be plain in one's utterance in recognition that nothing is more demanding and nothing can better serve. (Remember, fancy is always dated and falls out of fashion, but the plain is enduring.) There scarcely seems a reason to write if one is interested only in "subverting" the very act of what writing means. This is not a sign of brilliance but of infantilism. I do not "do theory" (and the world of lit. crit. would be far better off if fewer people professed such a fanciful and self-indulgent preoccupation). I do not wish to subvert anything; I wish to engage. I have been equally influenced by good scholars and good writers. I wish to be both when I can, either when necessary, and a good writer only if that alone will serve the cause of my ideas (and the ideas of others) and serve the intelligence of my readers. One of the big disappointments of *Tuxedo Junction*'s critical reception was that some readers felt free to condemn a book that failed to do what it was never trying to do. *Tuxedo Junction* was not a sports book; it was not a jazz book; it was not an autobiography. It was a literary book, a certain kind of intellectual proposition or set of propositions. *The Culture of Bruising* is like *Tuxedo Junction* in offering a set of propositions. It is certainly neither a sports book nor a jazz book. For I am, finally, not interested solely in any subject because it engages me either as a fan (except as it gives me emotional entrance to the subject) or as a scholar (except as it gives me both knowledge and discipline to understand the subject) but as a critic in the truest and most old-fashioned sense of that term. It is not required that my books be classified in any camp. It is not required that I be called anything in particular. In my Emersonian moments, as I have said elsewhere, I refer to myself as Man Thinking, and in my Ellisonian moments I ain't nobody but myself.

I

PRIZEFIGHTING AND THE MODERN WORLD

PRIZEFIGHTING AND THE MODERN WORLD

Angelically turning his head,
He saw a girl's very indifferent eyes,
Heard the thin cry for his blood upon the floor,
From high and away, his blood on the killing floor;
And he turned his head another way and waited:
Falling down, alas, was the hardest of the two
And not getting up which, telling himself,
He did so quickly that he could not recall why he fell;
Get up, he told himself, and up he was, like that,
Losing again, staggering again, and waiting for the end
With the heroic benignity of a child watching the moon.
Easy like that it was to get up to get beat up again.
But the falling down was hard, a floppy descent from
Not grace and all that but maintaining, hanging on.
So long to go down and so sweet and peaceful.
He found it hard to believe that the rage that caused
His downfall could make him almost happy, succumbing
To a sleep that passes all understanding.
But he was up again like that: just like that,
Waiting, his face a battered thing, a mask like
The finest sort of perishing, waiting for the end.
No, not this ending: The fights come and go, and go again.
But that ending, some other ending where he could
Imagine Tom Molineaux, weak, spitting blood,
Dying in a dirty bed of filthy linen; other
Negroes in the filthy room come and go, muttering
About the foul end of the foul slave who could not beat Cribb.
And Molineaux angelically turns his head, absolutely
Not sorry to be a wretch, stinking, in the end,
Not praying to some dumb Damballah, not aflame with gnostic glory,
But turns his head to his window, the only window there,
And his indifferent eyes stare indifferently on the modern world.
It was, of course, the ending he always imagined
While gasping for air in appeal,

Benighted by shrouds of his own sweat, bored
And enfeebled by his shallow gallantry:
This one moment when the absolute showering
Opulence of certain positive thinking
Would anoint him with the assurance that
In the modern world everything counts but nothing matters.

THE BLACK INTELLECTUAL AND
THE SPORT OF PRIZEFIGHTING

A THEORETICAL PRELUDE

> *Once I saw a prize fighter boxing a yokel. The fighter was swift and amazingly scientific. His body was one violent flow of rapid rhythmic action. He hit the yokel a hundred times while the yokel held up his arms in stunned surprise. But suddenly the yokel, rolling about in the gale of boxing gloves, struck one blow and knocked science, speed, and footwork as cold as a well-digger's posterior. The smart money hit the canvas. The long shot got the nod. The yokel had simply stepped inside of his opponent's sense of time.*

The quotation is from Ralph Ellison's *Invisible Man,* a novel that makes a number of allusions and references to prizefighting. This quotation, it seems to me, resonates in a number of very crucial ways. It is, of course, the classic dialectic of boxing: the speedy, scientific boxer versus the artless puncher. But it is also the story of the tortoise and the hare, the con man and the homeboy, the country mouse and the city mouse, Brer Fox and Brer Rabbit.

Yet all those classical American metaphors of innocence and experience collapse into the image of the prizefighter's confrontation with his opposite, his nemesis, the very antithesis of himself. It was Mark Twain who wrote in his 1889 novel, *A Connecticut Yankee in King Arthur's Court,* that the world's best swordsman needn't fear the second best swordsman in the world; he needs to fear the man who has never held a sword. In this light, the world's best boxer needn't fear the man who is almost his equal but rather the man who could not possibly match his skill. In other words, the Trickster, inasmuch as he is represented by the slick accomplished boxer, does not need to fear another formidable Trickster; rather he needs to fear that which is the negation of the Trickster; for in the brutal pantomime of the prize ring the Trickster's technique masks the fact that he is the personification of anarchy. Thus, his technique is not a virtue but utter decadence, his paradoxical expression of the contempt for both virtue and technique. And his negation is paradoxically he who through the complete absence of technique wishes to rescue it from the Trickster's laughing and lurid display of it as a stunt.

Technique (and boxing since its inception in the bare-knuckle days of Broughton and Slack in England has been, in part, nothing more than the history of its own rationalization through the obsessive quest for more reified technique and rules) must always fear not other technique but the utter void of technique. It is no accident to speak of confidence games in connection with the metaphor raised by the Ellison quotation. Professional prizefighting, from its early brawling days in eighteenth-century England, has been the sport of the gambler and the gambler's romance; his dream, if you will, has always been to have the long shot come through as a sure thing. Variations on the theme of the victory of the yokel as a fixed fight can be found in such diverse sources as accounts by David W. Maurer of various fight store cons in his study, *The American Confidence Man;* in some of the boxing short stories of Charles Emmet Van Loan in *Inside the Ropes* (1913) and *Taking the Count* (1915), where, in that maddening fluidity of identity that has come to characterize the American, long shots disguise themselves as sure things and sure things masquerade as long shots; and in the actual history of American prizefighting itself: the halcyon days of New York's Horton Law (1896–1900), a historical period that yields many tales of sordid wheelings and dealings designed to rip off the unsuspecting public, or a fight such as the Billy Fox–Jake LaMotta middleweight bout on November 14, 1947, which LaMotta admitted, several years later before a Senate investigating committee, he threw on orders of members of organized crime so that the long shot—Fox—would win, which he did by a fourth-round knockout. This latter example is, of course, one of many riddling a sport that has problems with the honesty of its presentation.

The two most powerful, most staying images of the yokel and the prizefighter can be drawn from two entirely different realms of American culture, and both involve white fighters. The first is Francis Wallace's 1936 novel, *Kid Galahad,* which was made into a film on two different occasions: *The Battling Bellhop* (the original theater title was *Kid Galahad*), which was released in 1937 and featured Bette Davis, and *Kid Galahad,* a star vehicle for Elvis Presley in the early sixties. The fact that it has twice been made into a film nearly thirty years apart and that its basic theme—the good, incorruptible midwestern or southern country boy goes to the city, becomes a crude but effective boxer to raise money to buy the family farm—has been used in a number of other films shows how deeply the Galahad myth of male American innocence (e.g., Billy Budd, the American Adam) and inadvertent Horatio Alger–like success (humility and determination as forms of grace from Ben Franklin to Sylvester Stallone's Rocky) is ingrained in our national consciousness. Dubbed Galahad in the novel because of his purity of heart, the former bellhop, fresh from the Navy, is always the long shot in his fights and always knocks out his opponents with one punch. His opponents are always better boxers, better stylists in the ring than he is. The films tend to stress Galahad's ineptitude more than the novel does. Wallace, in the end, is ambiguous. Over the course of the book, the Kid learns to become a pretty good boxer/stylist and in his last fight—a grudge fight, as these confrontations usually are in novels and films—is actually beaten severely for the first several rounds because his manager, Nick, pressured by gangsters and affected by his own jealousy of Galahad, gives the wrong advice and has the Kid slugging instead of boxing. Eventually, Nick changes his mind and the Kid, through sly boxing, finally wins. Of course, at novel's end, the Kid quits boxing. He is, after all, not a pug and his mastery of boxing is not a sign of commitment but an indication of disdain. He does not wish to be tainted by boxing; it is simply the avenue by which he can seize the chance to remain stolidly agrarian, implacably at peace with a series of values that can scarcely be considered even conventional. His values are the gestures of folksy platitudes: He likes to eat, does not drink, likes to work in the open air, is by turns polite to and shy around women, believes in his country, and yearns for the family hearth. And the fact that he has become a decent boxer in the end is a sign that he might be corrupted by all this, might adopt another series of values that would allow him to dress fancy, go to nightclubs, chase women, and drink liquor.

In the Presley film, the necessity of this reactionary male purity is made clearer: first, by never having Galahad achieve any sort of prowess as a fighter; and second, by having his ultimate opponent be a Hispanic who is a slick and accomplished boxer. The element of race is never very distant in the novel, although none of Galahad's opponents there is black or Hispanic. The book is the sort of generally racist fare that one might expect from a bad novel written by a white writer in the early or mid-thirties. (This was, after all, the time when the radio serialization of "Amos 'n' Andy" was the biggest show on radio, and books such as *Bigger and Blacker* and *Dark Days and Black Knights* by Octavus Roy Cohen and other such comic denigrations of blacks, published just ten years earlier in the mid-twenties, were still quite popular. There were the Scotsboro boys. And the country was still segregated, as we know. We might safely characterize this era by paraphrasing what Katharine Brush called 1925: a Ku Klux Klan series of years.) The issue is always, in effect, Galahad's whiteness as being inextricably bound to his maleness and to his pious set of provincial American moral glitches. In this sense, Wallace's

novel and the films that resulted from it are nothing more than measured re-
finements of certain boxing novels by white male writers, both British and
American, that were written during the fifty years preceding *Galahad*'s pub-
lication: George Bernard Shaw's *Cashel Byron's Profession* (1886), Arthur
Conan Doyle's *Rodney Stone* (1896), Jack London's *The Game* (1905),
W.R.H. Trowbridge's *The White Hope* (1913), Jeffrey Franol's *The Amateur
Gentleman* (1913), and Robert E. Howard's *The Iron Man* (1930), this last being indicative of the type of pulp material serialized in *Fight Stories* magazine.
The one immediate concern of these novels is the presentation of boxing as a
symbolic discourse for a very hoary version of bourgeois morality: The white
gentlemen boxers here are all of royal blood or they all ought to be and, thus,
through these unlikely heroes the writers can rearrange the complex of ideas
specifically associated with economic class and make them a set of virtues
that are a kind of obtainable sensibility through some mysterious transfigura-
tion called culture.

Shaw's work is the most sophisticated of the lot, but even the preposterous and comic union of the prizefighter Cashel Byron and the rich heiress
Lydia Carew does not seem to turn class pretensions on their heads as much as
to expose a kind of hypocrisy that bourgeois society has always loved to churn
up because it is so minor a criticism of the assumptions that support it:
namely, that aristocratic snobbery cannot be condoned in a liberal democracy, and one can fancifully but conservatively undercut it by having cultured boxers fall in love with upper-class women. This explains why such
polished white boxers as Georges Carpentier, Jim Corbett, and Gene
Tunney—the last succeeding in living out the Cashel Byron fantasy by marrying an heiress—were quite popular with many white male intellectuals
during the eras in which they fought. They were all living evidence that the
prize of culture could transcend both class and profession. They were new
versions, liberal bourgeois versions, to be sure, of racial stereotypes.

The fact that these books, by and large, were metaphorical discourses
on the philosophical issue of the universe-of-force, on the sociopolitical issue
of Social Darwinism, and on the popular romance of American capitalism
simply highlighted their preoccupation with race. After all, boxing was simply the metaphorical demonstration of the late-nineteenth-century view of
the world. As Ronald E. Martin has argued in his literary study of the era of
Social Darwinism: "The theme of evolutionary racism is an important one in
the late nineteenth century. . . . the universe-of-force viewpoint was of a piece
with some of the Western world's most pernicious social practices and theories at the turn of the century. Force-thinking generally rationalized racism,
class superiority, imperialism, the acquisition of wealth, and the veneration
of the 'fittest.'" (Other scholars of this era, notably George M. Fredrickson,
Rayford Logan, and Richard Hofstadter have made this point as well.) The

good white fighter in these novels, who is not always inept in the technical sense, in the end symbolizes the essence of the "white civilization" that seemed to be standing at the brink of either an endless dawn of imperialistic lordship or the eternal night of nonwhite domination. It is the central myth of the central novel of Victorian America: Edgar Rice Burroughs's *Tarzan of the Apes* (1913), the quintessential blending of athleticism and racism. The power and popularity of this conjunction are revealed ironically in F. Scott Fitzgerald's 1925 novel, *The Great Gatsby,* in which Tom Buchanan, the powerful football player, talks about reading Goddard's *The Rise of the Colored Empires.* It is suggested too by Gatsby's reading of *Hopalong Cassidy,* a dime novel adventure with extremely lurid and racist portrayals of Mexicans. A book from the same tradition as the racist adventure Westerns of Johnston McCulley, the creator of Zorro—whose fascination with caballeros and hidalgos seems the equivalent of the white southerner's fascination with the cavalier (which helps to explain my belief that Gatsby is a reworking of a Western; in part, at least, a reworking of Owen Wister's *The Virginian*) and which ultimately produced the greatest masked avenger in this genre, Ben Cameron in Thomas Dixon's *The Clansman* (1905), essentially a little boy's adventure-romance about how white civilization must be rescued in much the same manner that a princess is rescued from a dragon. It is indeed quite striking how vigilantism and terrorism, both of which are rooted in the masculine and bourgeois mythologies of competition, contest, social mobility, and identity disguise, from Zorro to Batman to G. I. Joe, is the theme of much of male adolescent literature, is, in fact, the cultural cluster of themes surrounding the creation of the modern fantasy male American hero. Sanitized as a reactionary political literature, which, of course, it is, it simply becomes a little-boy genre for adolescent minds—adolescence symbolizing the state of innocence that the American male has always found both admirable and desirable.

An important historical conjunction was taking place between, say, 1870 and 1930—the period during which all of the aforementioned literature was written: Boxing was changing from a bare-knuckle, irrational sport of indeterminate length to a rationalized sport of gloves governed by time and weight classifications, and those changes helped to make it more popular; Social Darwinism in particular and popular science in general were now a part of mass culture; ordinary people thought about science in a positive way; and blacks were beginning to achieve notice in boxing, which meant that they were achieving notice in American popular culture itself through their image as bruisers. Boxing was the one sport, more so than baseball, pedestrianism, or jockeying, the other three professional sports that had a significant black presence in the late nineteenth and early twentieth centuries, that could produce an intense if vulgar fame, enough so that Corbett, Sullivan,

Fitzsimmons, and Jeffries, the important champions before Jack Johnson, had to draw a color line against black challengers during their reigns. Although boxing today is practiced with a vengeance in most Third World countries and in several of the countries that made up the former Soviet Union (indeed, Yugoslav boxer Mate Parlov was briefly light-heavyweight champion of the world during the late seventies), it is clear that the transformation of the sport from ur-prizefighting to scientific boxing took place during the ascendancy of the world's two major capitalistic societies—England and America—and that maturation of the sport coincides with the maturation of bourgeois culture. As capitalism became less raw and bloody, less laissez-faire, boxing became more and more self-conscious about masking its barbarism. In the oddest cultural paradox, just as when the black presence in basketball grew and the black player became the acrobatic, aerial wonder, the white player became the "truck driver" and the "enforcer" because he could not match the black's grace, so in boxing the black became, for the most part, the master technician for the most practical of reasons—he had to (in the early twentieth century his career was usually six to eight years longer than the average white boxer's)—and the white, with admittedly important exceptions, symbolized the purity of primitivism. (Perhaps the whole business started as early as 1810, during the golden era of the bare-knuckle, when the British champion, Tom Cribb, fought and defeated the black American, Tom Molineaux. By all accounts of their first fight, Molineaux was clearly the superior boxer and had in fact knocked Cribb cold, but through cheating on the part of Cribb's seconds he eventually lost the fight.) In other words, conditions in the late nineteenth century were such that professional boxing was metamorphosed into an American sport, serving a particular and powerful set of collective psychic needs. With the completion of its final stages of development, the recodification of the rules and the entry of the black, boxing was now ready to become the most metaphorical drama of male neurosis ever imagined in the modern bourgeois-dominated world. Out of all of this emerged the mythology of white male innocence, the complete articulation of the Kid Galahad persona.

This leads me to discuss another image of the yokel and the boxer, this taken from an actual prizefight. In April 1915, black heavyweight champion Jack Johnson defended his title for the last time against Jess Willard of Kansas in Havana, Cuba. Johnson, who had won the title on Christmas Eve in 1908 when he defeated Tommy Burns in Australia, had not had an easy time of it during his reign. A conviction for the violation of the Mann Act in 1912 led to his flight from America; by 1915 he had been abroad for a few years, was no longer lionized, and was in fact broke and possessor of a title that didn't mean much. It was a strange bout. Johnson always maintained that he threw the fight (he lost by knockout in the twenty-sixth round) in a deal to return to the United States and beat the Mann Act rap; yet right before the fight he was confident in his utterances in black and white newspapers and was telling all his black fans, including his mother, to bet on him. (Of course, black fighters had betrayed black sports in fixed fights before; fifteen years earlier, in December 1900, in Chicago, black lightweight Joe Gans threw a fight to featherweight Terry McGovern, and blacks on the South Side took a bath.) Despite his age—thirty-seven—and his lack of conditioning caused by an extensive period of inactivity and lack of strenuous competition, Johnson was favored to win because he was such an outstanding boxer, while Willard was not even the most distinguished of a mediocre lot of white hopes; he was, probably, the biggest. Johnson had been involved in a fixed championship fight with a white challenger before: On October 16, 1909, in Colma, California, Johnson fought middleweight champion Stanley Ketchel on the condition that he would carry him for the distance and not try to knock him out. When Ketchel tried a double-cross and knocked Johnson down in the twelfth round of the battle, Johnson arose and knocked Ketchel unconscious with an uppercut that broke off Ketchel's front teeth at the gum line. As a black fighter, Johnson knew all about faking fights with white fighters; it was a common practice at this time, and such notable black fighters as Sam Langford, Sam McVey, Denver Ed Martin, Joe Jeanette, and others carried their share of incompetent white fighters. But the fact of the matter is that Johnson, despite the claim in his autobiography and in the "Confessions" he sold to *Ring* magazine editor Nat Fleischer, did not throw the fight to Jess Willard. He lost in much the same manner that the slick boxer always loses to the yokel. He could not knock out Willard despite administering substantial punishment, he tired because of his age and lack of condition, and eventually, with the hot sun beating down, Willard was able to land the one punch that put Johnson on the floor. Willard's victory was the beginning of the glorification of the white yokel in boxing (although, admittedly, Willard himself was never very well liked by the white public). Johnson's claim for a fix served first, to make the white yokel's claim essentially ambiguous; and second, to make the fight between the white yokel and the black boxer a comic encounter.

Excepting Jack Dempsey and Gene Tunney, virtually every white champion has been, despite his style, a yokel: Sharkey, Braddock, Schmeling, Baer, Carnera, Marciano, Johansson, Coetzee. For all of these fighters, their most notable contests were against their significant black opponents, be it Joe Louis, who fought and defeated the first five mentioned; Jersey Joe Walcott, Ezzard Charles, Louis, and Archie Moore, who fought Marciano; Patterson, who became Johansson's alter ego; or Leon Spinks and Greg Page, who fought Coetzee. Jerry Cooney, whose chief black opponents were Larry Holmes and Michael Spinks, and Jerry Quarry, whose chief black opponents were Joe Frazier and Muhammad Ali, fit this mold although they never became champions. In their fights against black opponents, these fighters were not expected to win by guile or by ability exactly. They were expected to win as Willard had against Johnson: take punishment, then land the ultimate blow. To be sure, there have been black fighters known as punchers; Sonny Liston comes to mind as does former heavyweight champion Mike Tyson, though neither of these fellows would be considered nearly, to borrow from A. J. Liebling, as "gauche and inaccurate" as Rocky Marciano, who, along with Dempsey, is the most mythical of the great white fighters. (Liston, for instance, was so skillful at rope-skipping that during his championship reign he was often invited on such programs as the "Ed Sullivan Show" to demonstrate his abilities.) But the greatest black fighters in the twentieth century and the most famous and highly regarded by experts were Tricksters of style: Jack Johnson, Muhammad Ali, Sugar Ray Robinson, and Sugar Ray Leonard: indeed, Sugar, a title given to a fighter in recognition of the refulgences of his style, has never been given to a white fighter. Even Joe Louis, despite his reputation as a heavy hitter, was really a stylist, "as elegant as the finest of ballet dancers," said Ralph Ellison in an interview. Against black opponents the white yokels were not even really fighters; they were more like preservers of the white public's need to see Tricksters pay a price for their disorder. Liebling was right in the end: If the black fighter as Trickster sees the white yokel as nemesis, then the white yokel becomes Ahab and the black Trickster the ultimate blackness of the black whale, and the ring itself becomes the place where ideas of order are contested.

BLACK WRITERS AND THE SPORT OF PRIZEFIGHTING

Aside from the autobiographies of black fighters, the books by blacks such as Art Rust, Harry Edwards, Ocania Chalk, and A. S. (Doc) Young that may contain a section on boxing while discussing blacks in sports generally: former light-heavyweight champion José Torres's fine biography of Muhammad Ali and his more dubious effort on Mike Tyson; the sociological articles by Nathan Hare, a former boxer; and a book such as Al-Tony Gilmore's *Bad Nigger* on the trials and tribulations of Jack Johnson, there is only one full-length nonfiction treatise on the sport of boxing by a black writer on the order of A. J. Liebling's *The Sweet Science,* George Plimpton's *Shadow-Box,* Joyce Carol Oates's *On Boxing,* Thomas Hauser's *The Black Lights,* or Norman Mailer's *The Fight.* That is former *Sports Illustrated* editor Ralph Wiley's 1989 book, *Serenity.* Jeffrey Sammons's *Beyond the Ring: The Role of Boxing in American Society,* published in 1988, is the only academic study of the sport by a black. Indeed, the most complete though not necessarily the most accurate history of blacks in the sport was written by the Jewish editor of *Ring* magazine, Nat Fleischer, whose 1930s series dealing with that subject called *Black Dynamite* goes from Molineaux to Joe Louis. It must be mentioned here that James Weldon Johnson provided a capsule history of blacks in the sport in his 1930 study, *Black Manhattan,* thus making him the first black intellectual to consider at any length the cultural importance of prizefighting for Afro-America.[1]

No black mainstream fiction writer has written a novel using a boxing theme in the same manner as Leonard Gardner in *Fat City,* Nelson Algren in *Never Come Morning,* W. C. Heinz in *The Professional,* Budd Schulberg in *The Harder They Fall,* or numerous others. This is not to say that boxing is not mentioned in some black novels and has not, in fact, figured as an important image in a few, but there has been no black novel on boxing by a major black writer. (I must add here that there is a genre of black novels published by Holloway House in California called "novels of the black experience" generally characterized by potboiler plots and a type of effective if occasionally pornographic naturalism, less artistically accomplished versions of the works of someone like Chester Himes. The leading writers of these types of books are Iceberg Slim and the late Donald Goines.)

It is at least somewhat odd that major works, either fiction or nonfiction, by black writers on the sport of prizefighting have not been produced. Boxing figures quite prominently in the social and cultural history of blacks in America; indeed, one could argue that the three most important black figures in twentieth-century American culture were prizefighters: Jack Johnson, Joe Louis, and Muhammad Ali. Certainly, there have been no other blacks in the history of this country (with the possible exception of Martin Luther King) who have been written about as much and whose actions were scrutinized so closely or reverberated so profoundly across the land. We know from such books as Lawrence Levine's brilliant study *Black Culture and Black Consciousness,* and from William H. Wiggins's essay "Jack Johnson as Bad Nigger: The Folklore of His Life" that black prizefighters were important and celebrated personages in African-American folklore; indeed, these fighters were more celebrated in African-American folklore and in African-American life generally than other important black pioneers in sports such as Jackie Robinson, Jesse Owens, or Wilma Rudolph. Furthermore, prizefighting appears in important instances in other facets of African-American culture, ranging from Adam Clayton Powell, Sr.'s funeral oration for the African boxer Battling Siki to jazz trumpeter Miles Davis's fascination with presenting himself, in alter ego guise, as a prizefighter, an obsession that culminated artistically with the release in 1971 of his soundtrack album entitled *Jack Johnson;* from being mentioned in such significant black autobiographies as Maya Angelou's *I Know Why the Caged Bird Sings* and *The Autobiogra-*

phy of Malcolm X to Richard Pryor's routine about Muhammad Ali and Leon Spinks, and to rap star L. L. Cool J appearing on the back of one of his albums punching a heavy bag. Among the more important works by African-American intellectuals and creative writers on the subject of prizefighting are the following: Larry Neal's essay "Uncle Rufus Raps on the Squared Circle," which originally appeared in the *Partisan Review;* Jervis Anderson's "Black Heavies," which appeared in *American Scholar;* Eldridge Cleaver's "Lazarus, Come Forth" from his book *Soul on Ice;* Amiri Baraka's "The Dempsey-Liston Fight" from his book *Home: Social Essays;* Ishmael Reed's review of Muhammad Ali's autobiography, *The Greatest,* from his 1978 collection of essays, *Shrovetide in Old New Orleans,* "Boxing on Paper: Thirty-seven years later," an essay from Reed's 1988 *Writin' is Fightin',* and "The Fourth Ali," an essay from his 1982 collection, *God Made Alaska for the Indians;* Richard Wright's three journalistic pieces, "Joe Louis Uncovers Dynamite" and "High Tide in Harlem: Joe Louis as a Symbol of Freedom," both published in *New Masses,* and "And Oh—Where Were Hitler's Pagan Gods," which appeared in the *Daily Worker;* and John A. Williams's "Jack Johnson and the Great White Hope" from his book *Flashbacks.* They are not, taken as a body, the most important or impressive interpretative work by a black writer on the sport; the best would be Ralph Ellison's *Invisible Man* and three essays by former heavyweight champion Floyd Patterson: two mid-1960s *Sports Illustrated* pieces, "I Want to Destroy Clay" and "Cassius Clay Must Be Beaten," and a later *Esquire* piece entitled "In Defense of Cassius Clay." Taken together, however, they do constitute a kind of black anthropology of boxing, an important critical venture combining not only ethics and esthetics but tending toward a kind of political discourse of some real value in understanding some aspects of the black intellectual's heritage and range of concerns.[2]

Baraka's essay, written in 1964, and the Cleaver essay, which was published in 1968, deal fairly much with the same thing: the meaning of the phenomenon of having Sonny Liston, Floyd Patterson, and Muhammad Ali as the most powerful black presences in American popular culture of the sixties. In a sense, their articles are long-distance responses to James Weldon Johnson's critique of Jack Johnson in his book on the history of blacks in New York:

> Peter Jackson was the first example in the United States of a man acting upon the assumption that he could be a prizefighter and at the same time a cultured gentleman. His chivalry in the ring was so great that sportswriters down to today apply to him the doubtful compliment 'a white coloured man.' He was very popular in New York. If Jack Johnson had been in demeanor a Peter Jackson, the subsequent story of the Negro in the prize ring would have been somewhat different.

James Weldon Johnson did not dislike Jack Johnson; indeed, according to his assertions in his autobiography, *Along This Way* (1933), he was quite fond of the talented boxer: "It was easy to like Jack Johnson; he is so likable a man, and I liked him particularly well. I was, of course, impressed by his huge but perfect form, his terrible strength, and the supreme ease and grace of his every muscular movement; however, watching his face, sad until he smiled, listening to his soft Southern speech and laughter, and hearing him talk so wistfully about his big chance, yet to come, I found it difficult to think of him as a prize fighter."

But the comparison to Peter Jackson is made again inevitably: "Frederick Douglass had a picture of Peter Jackson in his study, and he used to point to it and say, 'Peter is doing a great deal with his fists to solve the Negro question.' I think that Jack, even after the reckoning of his big and little failings has been made, may be said to have done his share."

The assessment of Johnson in relation to Jackson is ambiguous; Jackson has become, to James Weldon Johnson, the icon of the era's most respected race leader, probably the most respected black leader in the history of Afro-America. In this regard, the praise for Jackson, who has been presented as something of a saint, is unqualified whereas the praise for Johnson is not. Part of this may be because Jackson seemed so much more the race martyr; he was unfairly denied the opportunity he merited, and he suffered with such dignity and grace in the face of it. Jack Johnson squandered both his achievement and the nobility of his ambition, bringing a good many of his problems on himself. In short, James Weldon Johnson's evaluation can be summed thus: Jackson was a great man and a gentleman; Johnson was a great athlete, and a fairly remarkable man, but not really a great one as he never quite reached the contours of tragic heroism that Jackson obtained. The center of Johnson's ambiguity is that one could not read his career and decide if it was tragic, comic, or simply unfortunate. Was he, alas, the wrong man at the wrong moment in history? Did James Weldon Johnson really wish that these men could have changed places, that Jackson could have become world champion and Johnson kept in the waiting room? By the sixties, the black intellectual was a good deal less interested in being a cultured gentleman himself than James Weldon Johnson was, or in the question of whether a black hero in American popular culture should represent any chivalric virtues; the very nature and essence of his blackness should make him unpalatable to whites. There were to be no more Peter Jacksons, no more tragic black gentlemen whom whites found to be spiritual mulattoes ("Black skin, White heart"). This is ultimately why both Cleaver and Baraka so vehemently condemn Floyd Patterson, for he seems to be someone who yearned to be, finally, the modern Peter Jackson. The sixties was the age of the reacceptance of Jack Johnson (in the guise of Muhammad Ali), who was, of course, the inevitable historical revision of Jackson. Jackson was the father against whom Johnson ultimately revolted just as Joe Louis was the father that Ali tried to overthrow. The sixties was not simply the age of overthrowing the father; it was the age that revered the denial of filiopiety as the exquisite affirmation of a sublime self. Filiopiety, in a real sense, was a bourgeois sensibility, more precisely, a bourgeois angst. No militant black intellectual of this day was really writing jeremiads. People were told to remember David Walker and Marcus Garvey, but only because they were not heeded the first time around. Return to the ways of the fathers whose ways were never adopted in the first place as history became the collaborative wash of the black middle-class sellout and the whites' oppressive revisionism. And who represented that collaboration to the minds of Cleaver and Baraka more pathetically than Patterson, and who were more effective refutations of it than the two black champions who followed him: Liston and Ali?

As Eldridge Cleaver wrote: "Muhammad Ali is the first 'free' black champion ever to confront white America. In the context of boxing, he is a genuine revolutionary, the black Fidel Castro of boxing." Or as Baraka wrote about the Liston-Patterson fight: "And each time Patterson fell, there was a vision that came to me of the whole colonial West crumbling in some sinister silence, like the across-the-tracks House of Usher." Indeed, in the sixties black intellectual themselves were rebelling against the idea of being "cultured" in the sense that James Weldon Johnson himself represented, which meant that they were rebelling against what engagement and commitment used to mean for the black intellectual. Black freedom in the sixties meant a Marxist-like, cultural nationalist critique of bourgeois culture itself and not simply a condemnation of the peculiar hypocritical Americanisms of race relations. The writing styles of both Cleaver and Baraka reflect this "new" enraged black intellectual: polemical, confrontational, and, in the end, obsessed with expressionistic style as the deconstructive aesthetic of a radical (essentially, nihilistic) black politics. Their discussion of the racial obsessions that underlie the design of American masculinity is essentially accurate although both tend finally to sound like Baldwin, who, as one critic once accurately put it, seems to think that the secret notion behind the pathology of racism is that all whites madly desire to sleep with any Negro they can find. What is strongest in both men's work is the observation that white bourgeois society fears a certain kind of mythology surrounding the black fighter, or the black male athlete generally; this fear and loathing reached a crescendo of paranoia and dread during stages of the careers of Johnson and Ali. But Baraka points out, for instance, the white bourgeois fear of Sonny Liston and the need to conjure up as a comparative antidote the great white mythic fighter Jack Dempsey, who was an aggressive knockout artist and a "savage brute" as was Liston during a stage of his career. Even during the height of his fame Liston was not, after all, thought by the white sporting establishment to have been as great as Dempsey. (The same comparisons were made between Ali and Rocky Marciano.) Consider, in the case of Liston and Dempsey, an early 1960s episode of the popular animated television series "The Flintstones," as reactionary an example of bourgeois values as anything ever broadcast on television, which featured a white fighter named "Sonny Dempstone," a curious attempt to superimpose Dempsey on Liston, to blunt the "bad nigger" image of Liston by giving the mass audience of the show the remembrance of a "bad white man." (It is intriguing how white bourgeois society becomes temporarily terrifically and obsessively aware of history whenever it feels threatened by black achievements in the realms of popular culture, an area of great historical passion in this society, particularly in the subject of sports history, because sports provides the comfort of nostalgia, the power of myth, and one of the few sets of sellable traditions that the mass public can be seduced into purchasing. For the white bourgeois mind, there is an undeniable necessity to have a white exist at some time who exceeds the claims of the black it is currently forced to deal with. Normally, of course, the white bourgeois mind is ignorant of history, especially about race and class, except through expressions of popular mythological distortions that serve as indications that white bourgeois society is indeed driven to be antihistorical about the very things that deny the luxury of its main need and desire: an undisputed, uncontested historical folktale.)

The discussion about boxing and American sport, on the other hand, is quite weak; Cleaver's ultimate summation of American sports as blood lust and competition is particularly the simplistic polemic of "leftist humanism" that was to characterize the analysis of later radical writers such as Paul Hoch in his *White Hero, Black Beast: Racism, Sexism, and the Mask of Masculinity* and *The Big Rip-Off.* Both Baraka and Cleaver endorse a schematic of Western culture rather similar to Hoch's alternating dialectic of the Puritan and the Playboy, an analytical grid limited by the very source of its appeal: its charming simplicity. It is a criticism that wishes to blame the current craze for sports in the modern world on the commercialization of athletics in bourgeois culture, an assumption that overlooks the craze for competitive sports in former Communist countries. There is not a shred of empirical evidence to support the idea that sports are any less competitive in Communist countries or that having sports run by the state results in a more "humane" or "holistic" concept of sport and play. Allen Guttmann has provided a thoroughgoing critique of both the Marxist and Neo-Marxist analyses of sports in bourgeois culture and has convincingly exploded this argument. Hoch, Baraka, and Cleaver also present a particular set of pathologies of the Western white male, some of which seem sound psychology, and some simply rhetorical. Moreover, the political deconstruction of the symbolism of Liston, Patterson, and Ali by Cleaver and Baraka seems actually to be based on the same set of assumptions about the critical reading of fights used by the whites they condemn. Liston, Patterson, and Ali represent the good, the bad, and the ugly in everyone's morality play; it is simply a matter of musical chairs when the time comes to personify the abstraction. While the Baraka and Cleaver essays are strong in making some points about the black fighter's relationship with white society, they are much weaker in talking about black fighters in relationship to one another in a way that future black intellectuals would find useful or even politically astute.

In this sense, I assume that Neal's piece, published in 1972, was meant to be a correction, an attempt to escape the previous politically motivated way in which the black intellectual read prizefights since the coming of Liston and Ali in the sixties. Neal's article is a strategic plea for reconciliation. Uncle Rufus, despite his scientific-mythical jargon, which sounds like nothing so much as Sun Ra in one of his more lucid moments, returns the reading of fights and of blacks in American popular culture to the framework of black folklore, which, for Neal, is the only trustworthy critical measure of black aesthetic conceptualization. ("I would say, therefore, that Frazier needs Ali's squares, and Ali needs Frazier's circles. I can't see it no other way.") In this way, the fight between Frazier and Ali is not simply dialectical war—the affirming self and the blank twin of its own negation—but rather the confrontation between two classic aspects of African-American style and being, a Ruth Benedict–like assertion of the Apollonian and the Dionysian ("Frazier is stomp-down blues, bacon, grits and Sunday church. . . . But Ali is body bebop."), a dialectical moralism that implies its own peaceful synthesis through the respectful admission of each for the other's necessity.

John Williams's essay, originally written in 1968 to serve as a preface for Howard Sackler's hit play, *The Great White Hope,* and which Sackler eventually rejected, is simply a sloppy piece of writing. A paragraph such as the following is really an inexcusable distortion:

> Having failed to dethrone Johnson in the ring, white forces, public and private, launched an attack on his personal life that drove his first wife to suicide and sent Johnson to Europe to avoid going to jail on trumped-up charges. He spent about two years in Europe. He went into show business, fought sparingly, avoiding other Negros as often as he could. Tutored by Belmonte and Joselito, he also fought a bull in the Barcelona ring. On the whole his life abroad was bitter.

The death of Johnson's wife was not really the result of any public campaign to get him. Williams fails to note the very salient point that Johnson's wife was white and committed suicide as much because of the difficulty a white woman faced socially at being married to a black man as for any other reason. Johnson was also notoriously unfaithful. His conviction for violating the Mann Act was a trumped-up charge only in the sense that the law might be argued to have been a trumped-up law. The conviction was valid enough. Johnson ran into trouble primarily because of his public association with several white women, a fact that Williams neglects to mention. Undoubtedly, it was shortsighted, cruel, and utterly reprehensible for society to have condemned him because he desired white women, but it is the height of historical disservice not to state the facts of the case because of a disdain of or distaste for them. "Bitter" is surely an odd word to use in connection with Johnson's life. Johnson probably felt a certain amount of bitterness about his exile, but he seemed to have made the best of it. Desperation might be a better word to describe Johnson in some stages of his life, for he was always the hustler looking eagerly for the main chance.

Jervis Anderson's 1978 essay on Louis, Ali, and Johnson, largely a historical descriptive piece in the same mode, is much better. When he speaks of Johnson as being full of "confidence (perhaps overconfidence), high self-esteem, a strong belief in his legal rights as a citizen, and a joyous obedience to what was dramatic and colorful in his character," he is much closer to the truth than Williams ever approaches. Admittedly, the ten-year delay made the writing of a piece on Johnson a great deal easier as it was not as necessary for it to be so politically charged or so politically self-conscious. Yet it is Anderson who reaches the more political, meaningful conclusion when he writes: "Yet there were at least two important characteristics that all three men [Ali, Louis, and Johnson] shared: each was superbly gifted as a boxer, and each desired very much to be himself." Obviously, there isn't really very much a gifted person could want to be but himself if he wants to be able to exploit his gifts at all; yet the statement compellingly reveals the true political importance of Ali, Louis, and Johnson: For a black public person to be both gifted and true to himself is first, neither automatic nor, one should say, axiomatic; and second, bound to be subversive by extending the scope and expressive range of black humanity in mainstream culture.

It is surely Ishmael Reed's hope to find the power of black humanity expressing itself in adverse settings that draws him to boxing, a sport about which he does not know a great deal. It is doubtless for this reason that he praises Ali's autobiography highly in his 1975 review. For Reed, the greatest adversity Ali overcame was not the hostility toward his religion or his stand against the draft but that he did not become the stereotype "entertainer for massa" that Reed describes in his opening paragraph, a victory for the black image over the white mind, a recapitulation of the glowing assessment of Ali by Baraka and Cleaver.

In his later essay "The Fourth Ali," Reed writes: "The Heavyweight

Championship of the World is a sex show, a fashion show, scene of intrigue
between different religions, politics, class war, a gathering of stars, ex-stars,
their hangers-on and hangers-on's assistants." Note that Reed is defining the
heavyweight championship and not a heavyweight championship match
which, for sake of pure accuracy, must be what he really means. Yet Reed is
speaking of a title, an athletic classification as, in effect, a cultural institution. It is not the actual performance of boxing that has meaning but the abstraction of its excellence signified by a particular boxer's signature—not by a
standard of accomplishment but by the possession of a consensus of opinion.
It is only in the sport of boxing that one finds the words "disputed" and "undisputed" bandied about with such undisguised relish in connection with
titles. And Reed, in his essay on the Ali-Spinks championship rematch
which took place in New Orleans in September 1978, hardly describes the
fight at all. At one moment in the essay, Ali is being mobbed as he approaches the ring for the fight, "the crowds pressed in for a souvenir of the
Greatest's flesh." The next moment Ali is at his postfight, victory press conference. "At the end of the 15th round there was no doubt in my mind that
Ali had won," Reed writes, "and so I headed for the dressing room without
hearing the decision." The basic assumption that underlies Reed's view of
boxing is that the myth of boxing lies in its intelligibility. For Reed,
boxing's "mythological trembling of meanings," to use Roland Barthes's
phrase, is not simply in its mere brutality and savagery or even in the ritual
of male expendability and contest but in the utterly bland objectivity of the
lurid, fantastic, nightmarish glitter of its unreality. "The Fourth Ali" opens
with a brief description of heavyweight boxer Ken Norton's two potboiler
movies, *Mandingo* and *Drum,* then moves to an account of Edy Williams, former wife of onetime soft-core porn moviemaker Russ Meyer and former girlfriend of Wilt Chamberlain, removing her clothes in the middle of the ring,
"revealing flesh the color of the hotdogs they were serving in the press
room." Throughout the entire piece, the general atmosphere Reed invokes is
that of a striptease or the making of a very bad movie. Reed soon enough sep-
arates himself from the white journalists who have written about Ali—
George Plimpton and Budd Schulberg—and most particularly Norman
Mailer, whose book *The Fight,* according to Reed, is about Mailer's "frustration he couldn't play the dozens with [the late Drew] Bundini [Brown,
one of Ali's trainers] and them; frustration that he couldn't be black." (The
number of white intellectuals who tried to fight or who trailed behind
fighters like star-struck teenagers trailing behind rock stars is remarkable:
Bernard Shaw, Ernest Hemingway, A. J. Liebling, Paul Gallico, Jack London, George Plimpton, Norman Mailer, Joyce Carol Oates.) In his review of
Ali's autobiography, written a few years earlier, he called boxing writing
"depraved," and perhaps he is implying that the depravity in the relationship

that is displayed between the white writer and the dark brute (whether Negro or not) results from the kind of inhuman psychological dependence and gratification that the white writer gets from being around someone so unlike himself. For Reed, the relationship must be akin to that, in Ellison's *Invisible Man,* of Norton the white trustee who wanted to have sex with his daughter, and Trueblood, the black sharecropper, who actually (or seemingly) committed the deed with his own child. The boxer is simply the consciousness of taboo violation for the white writer. Yet there is little to distinguish Reed's essay from the writing of one white boxing writer he does not mention: A. J. Liebling. It contains the standard and predictable bits on the people floating around the edge of a championship boxing match, the tasteless splendor of the surroundings, the writer-observer as a moral center traveling in an immoral world; this last point being most important as Reed makes it clear that he is not a neurotic groupie of the boxer as a romantic tough as is the white intellectual (i.e., Mailer). The essay becomes, in effect, what Liebling's pieces often tended to be: the boxing essay as a mannered miniature prose epic of the male's holy quest in popular culture's heart of darkness.

Reed's "Boxing on Paper" seems, curiously, to retract his earlier views in "The Fourth Ali." Indeed, Reed here sounds like a white writer of boxing, the very person he disdains, by expropriating the writer-as-boxer metaphor that white writers of boxing have found so attractive:

> I think that a certain amount of philosophical skepticism is necessary, and so regardless of the criticisms I receive from the left, the right, and the middle, I think it's important to maintain a prolific writing jab, as long as my literary legs hold up, because even during these bland and yuppie times, there are issues worth fighting about. Issues that require fresh points of view.
>
> It was quite generous, I thought, for critic Mel Watkins to compare my writing style with that of Muhammad Ali's boxing style. My friend the late Richard Brautigan even saluted me after the publication of *Mumbo Jumbo,* my third novel, with the original front-page description of Jack Johnson's defeat of Jim Jeffries, printed by the *San Francisco Daily,* 4 July 1910. This, too, amounted to overpraise. If I had to compare my style with anyone's it would probably be with that of Larry Holmes. I don't mince words, nor do I pull any punches, and though I've delivered some low blows over the years, I'm becoming more accurate, and my punches are regularly landing above the waistline. I'm not a body snatcher like Mike McCallum, and I usually aim for the head.

This fantastic romanticizing of boxing, the strange metaphorical obsession expressed here, is the result of two common infantile imaginative impulses of bourgeois writers, especially some males. First, these writers feel
inadequate about what they do for a living; it seems useless, indulgent,
overly cerebral, elitist. By creating the boxing metaphor, the embattled and
criticized male writer (blows coming from "the left, the right, and the
middle") now feels he is involved in a life-or-death struggle of some considerable relevancy for himself and his audience (for the essence of boxing is the
performance of the rite of enduring and overcoming adversity as a series of
obvious, even crudely melodramatic gestures). The writer becomes connected through metaphor with something that is working class or lower class
(Reed reminds us twice early in the essay that he lived in a housing project,
the sine qua non of the black working-class or underclass experience). He is
also connected with something that is technical, demanding discipline, and
even, in some blatant way, courageous. Boxing is—and this is important for
the writer caught between snobbery and enlisting the common cause—both
democratic (working-class and lower-class and plainly ethnic; Reed says at
the end of the essay that writing talent among blacks is common) and elitist
(involving vigorous and special training; Reed identifies himself with champion boxers and, in two instances, is told that he rates metaphorically with
the best black boxers of all time, Ali and Johnson). Second, the writer thinks
of boxing as conferring the gift of pure yet simplified competition upon the
realization and function of his work. He is engaged and enraged in one fell
swoop of undifferentiated passion. Professionally, prizefighting of course has
nothing to do with writing as the enterprise is an entirely contrived, commercialized representation of the degradation and reduction of the grandeur
of human conflict to the morality of an excessively reactionary and persistently preposterous theater. The mimetic politics of boxing as performance
are the politics of race relations in this country as engineered for the benefit
of the ruling class. Reed finds the metaphor attractive because he sees himself
as heroic in almost self-consciously adolescent terms, the idea of surviving
unjust attacks and the idea of prevailing and vanquishing enemies. But the
Reed of "The Fourth Ali" is of considerably more concern to us here than the
one of "Boxing on Paper."

If, for Reed, as he suggests in "The Fourth Ali," boxing is the analogue
for an underbelly catalogue of trashy and sleazy popular culture activities,
from gambling to confidence games to prostitution, all in the garish surroundings of casinos and luxury hotels—the American Xanadus; if, for Reed,
boxing is the cumulative negation of a series of negations where people, aping the contestants in the ring, simply prey on one another; then for Richard
Wright boxing was American popular culture as the grand critique of its
inanity. The Wright essays are an early indication of his preoccupation with

the tyrannical blandishments of American popular culture, an ambiguous preoccupation, to be sure, as his own major novels resembled so closely the pulp genre of the crime novel or, to borrow the term F. Scott Fitzgerald used to describe *Native Son,* "the pennydreadful." In his July 1938 piece in *New Masses,* "High Tide in Harlem," he calls both Joe Louis and Max Schmeling puppets, which implies that not only are they manipulated but their contrived gyrations are manipulating the public that watches them. He calls the second fight between Schmeling and Louis, probably one of the most famous sporting events in the history of sports on this planet, "a colorful puppet show, one of the greatest dramas of make-believe ever witnessed in America," and "a configuration of social images whose intensity and clarity had been heightened through weeks of skilful and constant agitation." Wright's fascination with popular culture would make itself apparent in such later works as *Native Son,* where Bigger Thomas would live in a world of newspapers, cheap magazines, and movies, where he would be literally entrapped by the images of popular culture when he takes over the room of the Daltons' former chauffeur, Green, whose walls were covered by pictures of "Jack Johnson, Joe Louis, Jack Dempsey, and Henry Armstrong . . . Ginger Rogers, Jean Harlow, and Janet Gaynor." Prizefighters and white Hollywood actresses, the kings and queens of American popular culture. (One is reminded of the scene in James Weldon Johnson's 1912 novel *The Autobiography of an Ex-colored Man,* where the hero enters the room of his "club" to discover pictures "of Peter Jackson, of all the lesser lights of the prizefighting ring, of all the famous jockeys and the stage celebrities.") Also, the pictures have political importance for Wright: Here is the way bourgeois society permits poor men and poor women—and white actresses were largely from impoverished backgrounds—to succeed mostly on the basis of the appeal and strength of their bodies and to allow their success, through a kind of sophisticated victimization, to become the role model for the poor. Bigger, who is not very articulate, never smiles, and seems sullen, bringing to mind the young Joe Louis, who was described by white sportswriters of the period as being sullen and who was once featured in a 1935 *New Republic* article entitled "Joe Louis Never Smiles." (It is an indication of his cultural importance and impact that a white national publication would print an article about a black fighter two years before he won the title. It was the same among blacks: Popular blues singer Memphis Minnie recorded an instrumental called "Joe Louis Strut" in 1935.) And the Louis career of the poor southern boy—without the presence of his real father, brought north to the big city by his family in search of employment and fresh opportunities—was the Bigger Thomas career and the Richard Wright career as well. (Incidentally, the last name Thomas was that of Joe Louis's character in the 1937 film *Spirit of Youth,* which starred Louis. Wright, a frequent though critical moviegoer and admirer of Louis during the 1930s, may have seen this film. In fact, it seems likely since Wright seemed so deeply fascinated by Louis. His admiration for Louis was to extend to songwriting. Wright wrote the lyrics to a song that honored Joe Louis for which Count Basie wrote the music and Paul Robeson supplied the voice. "King Joe" may have been, as Ralph Ellison pointed out, an unfortunate collaboration in an aesthetic sense, but it reveals the power of Louis's attraction for Wright. Moreover, Wright's eldest daughter has said that Wright very much wanted to do a biography of Louis.)³ In his autobiography, *Black Boy,* Wright's critique of popular culture continues in his depiction of his growth from *Riders of the Purple Sage*—a dime Western of the racist and adolescent male genre of fantasy and adventure and a sign of Wright's own juvenile entrapment in American popular culture—to H. L. Mencken. As Robert Stepto pointed out, Wright illustrates his own liberation from the snare of popular culture when, in *Black Boy,* he works at a movie theater but never enters to see the films. Bigger's life, in *Native Son,* is changed dramatically and unfortunately when he goes to the theater to see *Trader Horn* and *The Gay Woman.* The critique continues throughout Wright's works, in his conversation with the African boy who wishes to be a detective in *Black Power,* the depiction of the black woman desperately straightening her hair in *The Color Curtain,* the inescapable radio in *Lawd Today,* and the magazines read by the white women cafeteria workers in *American Hunger.* In all of these works, the machinations of popular culture are shown to be emotionally crippling, self-destructive escapism. The three Wright boxing pieces taken together reveal an essential ambivalence: Joe Louis is a product of American popular culture, its creation, in effect, and therefore is nothing more than the convenient bread-and-circus invention of white American capitalists; but Joe Louis is a hero of the black masses, a potential source of political mobilization because he can so deeply excite so many blacks. "It was, however," Wright stated in his 1938 essay "Blueprint for Negro Writing," "in a folklore moulded out of rigorous and inhuman conditions of life that the Negro achieved his most indigenous and complete expression." And it is how Joe Louis both touches and symbolizes the folk that attracts Wright. Louis is the stuff, the raw material for the black writer. In the same essay Wright continues, "How many John Henrys have lived and died on the lips of these black people? How many mythical heroes in embryo have been allowed to perish for lack of husbanding by alert intelligence?" Wright's pieces in the end are absorbed by this concern: how Louis affects large numbers of blacks. Each of his pieces is, in fact, more about how blacks in Harlem respond after a Louis victory than about Louis himself. Wright's ambivalence is not so much that of the Marxist trying to find an ideological way to tap an unreconstructed political resource as much as it is that of the black trying to find a psychohistorical way to tap the complexity of his own injured consciousness. The phrase "injured consciousness" is a moral fixation with Wright; in his autobiography, he makes use of the self-made man myth that is part of the tradition of both the male African-American and American autobiography, but he also emphasizes the abuse he suffered as a child. His life, at times, seemed nothing more than a series of injuries and batterings that he withstood when young and to which he stood up when he became older. In this way, his maturation process resembles that of the novice prizefighter who must learn to absorb punches, must learn to control and direct his aggression. Moreover, Wright came of age as an artist in the 1930s, the same decade that Louis came of age as a fighter. Could it be that Wright was drawn to Louis because the latter's struggles in the ring were so strikingly analogous to his own struggles as an intellectual in another arena?

But it is Ellison in *Invisible Man* who fully elaborates upon the ambiguity of the black in boxing that Wright suggests in his Joe Louis pieces. The battle royal scene at the beginning of Ellison's novel, one of the most famous fictional boxing depictions in all of American literature, is meant to conjure up images of turn-of-the-century black fighters who received their training in the sport as youths in just this way.[4] Nat Fleischer in his multivolume history of blacks in prizefighting describes black battles royal as commonplace. The black fighter Ellison particularly wants to suggest is Jack Johnson, who, as biographers Finis Farr, Al-Tony Gilmore, and Randy Roberts have made clear, in his youth was a frequent participant in the battle royal. In this way, Ellison makes allusions to the three most important black figures of early-twentieth-century America: The first is Booker T. Washington—the Invisible Man's graduation speech is in fact Washington's Atlanta Cotton Exposition Speech of 1895. The second is W.E.B. Du Bois—the Invisible Man is the tenth boy in the battle royal, thus a reference to Du Bois's concept of the Talented Tenth to which the Invisible Man would naturally feel he belongs. (According to Fleischer, normally nine youths participated in battle royal but, of course, any number could play.) The third allusion—by the battle royal itself—is to Jack Johnson. In a sense, the scene works out in such a way that each one of these evocations forms a palimpsest; the achievement of each man, dubiously rendered, is written over and merged, fused so that the misdirected rebel, the snobbish intellectual, and the pragmatic accommodationist become, by turns, subversive and submissive. One might imagine that Jack Johnson was much like Tatlock, the tough winner of the encounter. There has been much discussion about how the scene shows how white men used both sex (the white woman dancer with the flag tattooed near her genitals) and money (which is what, finally, the boys are fighting for) to manipulate blacks and to keep them divided. But black men are shown fighting each other throughout the book: The Invisible Man gets into a fight with Lucius Brockway at the paint plant; he and Todd Clifton fight Ras the Exhorter and his men in the middle of the novel; toward the end of the novel the Invisible Man, disguised as the confidence man, Rinehart, nearly has a fight with Brother Maceo; and he has a final confrontation with Ras. These scenes, in a vital way, all seem cognates of the original battle royal: Black men are fighting each other because of misunderstandings either instigated or exploited by some white or malevolent figure(s) of power. Note, in this regard, that the evil Brother Jack is described at one point as looking like "a toy bull terrier," which seems a bit too close to the nickname Toy Bulldog that the famous 1920s boxer Mickey Walker sported to be a coincidence.

For Herman Melville, the world may be described as a man-of-war, but for Ellison, the world is a prize ring. In truth, the battle royal scene works in much the same way as Wright's fight scene near the end of *Black Boy,* a fight instigated by white men who want to be entertained by seeing two black boys fight. The scene in Wright's book operates as an ironical comment on the near conclusion of Frederick Douglass's 1845 *Narrative,* which is his classic confrontation as a teenaged boy with the white slavebreaker, Covey. Wright, like Douglass, is the troubled black boy who cannot live under the system and who ultimately flees, but unlike Douglass, Wright, through his fight scene, asserts the utter impossibility of finding his manhood through any sort of direct confrontation with white men. That impossibility is symbolized when Wright is forced to leave the optical company after being trapped between two benches by a white man at either end. This probably explains why Wright, like so many blacks, was so deeply affected by Louis: Louis had the devoutly-wished-for opportunity that Douglass had, to confront a white man squarely with his fists. The charismatic power of that image cannot be denied; Ellison subtly frames his novel with images of black heavyweight champions beating white challengers. The first scene occurs near the beginning when one of the crazy educated blacks in the Golden Day gives a jargon-filled scientific analysis of Jack Johnson's knockout of Jim Jeffries; the second scene is during the riot at the end of the novel when a drunken woman drives a careening milk wagon down the street singing out in "a full-throated voice of blues singer's timbre": "If it hadn't been for the referee/Joe Louis woulda killed/Jim Jefferie [*sic*]." The anachronism is important (Louis never fought Jeffries) not only because Jeffries, the great white hope, becomes in the mind of both middle- and lower-class blacks—the demented and drunken of both the asylum and the street—every white fighter, but because Johnson and Louis are noted in the black communal psyche for having beaten white fighters, thus, having beaten white society. In that sense, as black heroes, Johnson and Louis become interchangeable. But the most telling part of Ellison's battle royal scene is when the Invisible Man suggests to Tatlock: "Fake like I knocked you out, you can have the prize." "I'll break your behind," [Tatlock] whispered hoarsely. "For them?" "For me, sonofabitch!" Louis was heroic, in part through the sheer accident that he was permitted to fight white men. Those fights resonated with meaning for both blacks and whites. But it was not Louis who determined his opponents or defined the meaning of his fights. Presumably, since Louis wanted to be a fighter he would have fought anyone, black or white. In the days when the color line was drawn in boxing, black fighters did get a chance to fight white fighters on occasion, but very often these fights were fixed so the white fighters would win. In most instances, great black fighters at the turn of the century spent much of their careers fighting each other; these tended to be their most viciously fought fights as there was little interest for one black fighter to throw a fight to another black. (For instance, the record for the number of knockdowns scored in a prizefight occurred in a fight between two black fighters, Joe Jeanette and Sam McVey, in April 1909. A total of thirty-eight knockdowns were recorded.) When the Invisible Man suggests that he should win the fake fight, he is putting himself in the position of the white fighter in the integrated fight. Naturally, Tatlock rejects this. Moreover, Tatlock wants to win because, freed from the fakery of the racially integrated fight, he can display completely his abilities as an athlete, as he asserts, not for the audience but for himself. This point concerning the epistemology of black male aggression and the meaning of black competition is quite significant. Randy Roberts, in his autobiography of Jack Johnson, *Papa Jack,* argues that the black fighter developed a passive defensive style when fighting white fighters, so as not to appear aggressive and to ease the effort of faking a loss. Obviously, this style went by the boards when blacks fought each other. Thus, the whole business of black male aggression, the whole concept of masculine contest for blacks, is more complex than Roberts's recapitulation of Lawrence Levine's arguments about the dozens' serving as an oral deflection of black male aggression. Levine sees the black fighter's defensive style as his masking extension and appropriation of the dozens for survival. But there is a really vital connection between oral culture, masculine aggression, and prizefighting. We know from Walter Ong's work on human contests that "oral cultures thrive on the challenge and riposte." So this feature among black males is more an indication of a highly combative oral culture than it is necessarily and solely a defensive response to racism. It is not necessarily true that males in such cultures do not contest in more violent rituals. We face, therefore, the real possibility that blacks fought each other as a real release of the aggression that they would have preferred directing toward whites but which, after a point, they began to enjoy directing at each other. The dozens did not save blacks from the hostile aggression of other blacks; it merely saved whites from it and thus, on one level, the folk game, praised by liberal scholars as a survival game, becomes reactionary politics. Among the lower class, orally oriented men generally, the art of the dozens—or oral contest—does not prevent the superimposition of the art of prizefighting; as we know from studying the history of prizefighting, it was common, from the days of Mendoza, the great Jewish fighter of the late eighteenth century, through John L. Sullivan to Muhammad Ali, for fighters to engage in elaborate rituals of bragging and challenging that greatly resemble aspects of ritual insulting in oral cultures. Such insulting did not prevent the fights themselves; indeed, it merely seemed to instigate them, to fuel the fighters emotionally.

What Ellison emphasizes with the battle royal is the paradoxical tension of white coercion on the one hand and the willing participation of the black boys in their own degradation on the other. The fight is not possible, no matter how much the fighter is a puppet in some aspects, without the fighter himself wanting to do it, without the fighter's seeing something of value in the ritual: hence, the term "prizefight." So the prizefighter, in the battle royal scene, in effect shows the impossibility of human solidarity, the metaphor for which in this case is racial group identity. As Ong writes: "The agon [agony, "the undergoing of pain or distress"] is normally a lonely struggle, from that of hercules beetles . . . to that of boxers in the ring." The ambiguity here that I think is a crucial issue for the black intellectual and prevents him from celebrating boxing in the way the white intellectual can is that boxing, finally, for the black fighter is an apolitical, amoral experience of individual esteem, which the black fighter purchases at the expense of both his rival's health (and often his own) and his own dignity. The black fighter is a figure of intense and aching symbolic adverseness, of the American black's learned self-hatred. For the black intellectual, boxing becomes both a dreaded spectacle and a spectacle of dread. Frederick Douglass becomes quite influential in this regard. In his 1845 autobiography he set the tone for the discussion of blacks and boxing in particular and blacks and sports generally. It was Douglass who derided his fellow slaves who spent their holidays "engaged in such sports and merriments as playing ball, wrestling, running foot-races, fiddling, dancing, and drinking whisky" or who spent the Sabbath "in wrestling, boxing, and drinking whisky." Connecting sport with whiskey drinking and the breaking of the Sabbath is certainly for the mid-nineteenth-century mind an apparent enough condemnation (and not simply a moral but a political strategy on the part of Douglass), although to many modern minds it may seem a puzzling equation, for we hold the athlete in somewhat higher regard. But it must be remembered that since the time of the Roman gladiators when the glory of Greek athleticism was made totally contemptible, the athlete has always been a suspect person in the Western mind—a hero to be sure, but a cheap and crude one. Doubtless, a black who was essentially a degraded, socially dead person could only further compromise himself in the eyes of other blacks by performing a socially degraded, or a non-ennobling, activity. Douglass's moralism has become the moralism of the black intellectual who looks at sports as the degradation of leisure, as the corruption of the work ethic, as heightening the black man's sense of irresponsibility, as in fact the creation of the white man to divert the black from the pursuit of his own humanity and dignity. Four years later in his novel *White-Jacket,* Herman Melville was to make a similar observation about the degradation of the black through combat sport:

> Head-bumping, as patronized by Captain Claret, consists in two negroes (whites will not answer) butting at each other like two rams. This pastime was an especial favorite with the Captain. In the Dog-Watches, Rose-Water and May-Day were repeatedly summoned into the lee waist to tilt at each other, for the benefit of the Captain's health. May-Day was a full-bodied "bull-negro" so the sailors called him, with a skull like an iron tea-kettle, wherefore May-Day much fancied the sport. But Rose-Water, he was a slender and rather handsome mulatto, and abhorred the pastime. Nevertheless, the Captain must be obeyed.

The description of the blacks at play on board the man-of-war follows an account of the brutal sport activities of the sailors generally on the ship, activities largely performed for the entertainment of the officers and as a diversion for the men themselves. The chapter ends with May-Day and Rose-Water being flogged for getting into an argument about their heritage and fighting among themselves, the Captain saying, "I'll teach you two men that, though I now and then permit you to play, I will have no fighting." Thus, Melville makes clear that the entire raison d'être for black versus black combat is to serve virtually as a racial gestalt for the white male mind which is, one supposes, what Kyle Onstott was trying to say in his use of prizefighting in his overwrought, poorly written slavery potboiler, *Mandingo* (1957). One recalls Freud in *Totem and Taboo,* Dr. John Langdon Down's writings about "Mongoloidism," and Dr. F. G. Crookshank's *The Mongol in Our Midst* (1924), also on "Mongoloidism," and the entire phenomenon of Negro minstrelsy in the nineteenth century—that the mental and emotional abnormalities and anxieties of the white mind are the normal, unalterable reality of the dark mind. The black, as always, is the white's secret, unsuppressed yet defective self.

So, the black fighter is only truly heroic for the black masses and the black intellectual when he is fighting a white fighter or someone who has been defined as representing white interests; this last, popularized during the era of Muhammad Ali, seems a bit dubious as every black fighter, sooner or later, represents white interests of some sort. When the black fighter fights another black how does he differ from Stackolee, the legendary black bad man who preyed on his own, or Brer Rabbit, the Trickster, whose victories are limited and short-term and whose motives are often selfish and shallow? Consider, in this regard, that in *Invisible Man* when the hero is dressed down by the college president, Bledsoe, he is called "a fighter," and "a nervy little fighter." The Machiavellian Bledsoe also tells the Invisible Man that "the race needs good, smart, disillusioned fighters." Of course, the compliments are ironic, and the advice ultimately proves false. Later in the book, Ellison brings this fight symbolism to a closure:

> I went across the room to a torn photograph tacked to the faded wall. It was a shot, in fighting stance, of a former prizefight champion, a popular fighter who had lost sight in the ring. It must have been right here in this arena, I thought. That had been years ago. The photograph was that of a man so dark and battered that he might have been of any nationality. Big and loose-muscled, he looked like a good man. I remembered my father's story of how he had been beaten blind in a crooked fight, of the scandal that had been suppressed, and how the fighter had died in a home for the blind.

The details resemble in some important respects the life of the great black boxer Sam Langford, the Boston Tarbaby, who went blind and died penniless in a charity home four years after the publication of *Invisible Man*. The story also alludes in general outline though not in specific detail to the lives of two other outstanding black fighters, George "Little Chocolate" Dixon and Joe Walcott, the Barbados Demon. But what is important is not that the tale is about the life of a great black fighter but that it is the archetypical life of the black fighter involved in a crooked game. Bledsoe himself is a prizefighter, as he tells the Invisible Man; "Your arms too short to box with me" is a paraphrase of the old black folk saying: "Your arms too short to box with God." And Bledsoe, like the black fighter, finds himself in a situation where he is in combat with his own people, where his victories come at the expense of the very people he is professing to help: "I'll have every Negro in the country hanging on tree limbs by morning if it means staying where I am." Perhaps Bledsoe can survive, but he will do so only through moral corruption, staying in the dark and pulling the strings, rather akin to the image of a little boy in a dark closet eating forbidden sweets or masturbating. It is either that alternative for the Invisible Man, to be made corrupt and perverted by playing the crooked game crookedly (and he is accused by Brother Wrestrum at one point in the novel of "working in the dark" like Bledsoe) or to be blinded and to die pathetically by playing the crooked game naïvely and in good faith. Ellison makes the latter point through the fate of Todd Clifton, who resembles physically and psychologically the tragic great black Australian fighter Peter Jackson. We know from the fight scene between the Invisible Man and Ras and his men that Clifton is a very good fighter: "Clifton's arms were moving in short, accurate jabs against the head and stomach of Ras the Exhorter, punching swiftly and scientifically." Yet it is the handsome, scientifically skilled Clifton who "plunges outside of history," an interesting phrase as it must obviously allude to the phrase used in the old bare-knuckle prize ring of the nineteenth century; the current term "to be knocked out" is a shortened version of the original telling phrase used when a boxer, under London Prize Ring Rules, could not come up to scratch, could not continue. That fighter was said to be "knocked out of time." So Clifton, the scientific boxer, like the boxer Ellison speaks of earlier who is knocked out by the yokel, is figuratively "knocked out of time," and he winds up on the corner selling Sambo dolls, which of course is a reference and a symbol for how the black men have been manipulated throughout the novel. Clifton is killed by a white policeman whom he knocks down on the street. And it is the white boy who, along with the Invisible Man, is witness to the scene who makes the final, horrifying tribute to Clifton: "'Your friend sure knows how to use his dukes.'" On one level, of course, the death of Clifton is just another stab by Ellison against the presumptions of science and reason: The science of industry is literally exploded in the scene in the paint factory, the science of boxing is quite inadequate against the white policeman's gun (or even earlier against Ras's knife when the Exhorter could have stabbed Clifton to death but didn't), and the science of Marxism as symbolized by the Brotherhood proves to be arrogant, dictatorial, and ultimately inhuman. Perhaps inhuman is the key word, for science in *Invisible Man,* the most impressive product of human reasoning possibilities, has failed to humanize the world. So Peter Jackson, too, was wrong when he said: "With the development of fistic science, the cruelty of [boxing] passed away." Modern boxing is only more efficient in its cruelty, in its expression of negation. It may have appeared less cruel to someone like Jackson, living as he was on the edge of the transformation of the sport from bare-knuckle to glove, because it is masked by professionalism and the rigidity of categories, classifications, and order. (In short, if we understand the influence of Dante upon Ellison's work, we become aware that science is heresy, a sin of such significance in the *Inferno* that when Virgil and Dante reach that circle of Hell they turn right instead of left, the only time they do so in the downward journey.) The Invisible Man's encounters with heresy in the form of science always involve a figurative turning to the left. Lucius Brockway, who makes the paint that is symbolically the whitewash of American culture, fears the narrator to be a spy for the union, "left" here being synonymous with the union's subversive solidarity. Clifton as scientific boxer must have a good left jab just as early boogie-woogie pianists like Jack the Bear, referred to several times in the novel and a favorite of the young Duke Ellington, had to have a good left hand; a left hand that ultimately fails Clifton who, as homo pictor—man as symbol maker—becomes lost in the labyrinths of competing symbolic realities in the world, falls before the policeman with the gun—homo faber, man as tool maker, or man submerged by his mechanical extensions. And the Brotherhood symbolizes the left as rigid subversive conformity, the failure of half-blind orthodoxy.)

The final message of concern for us is clear: For Ellison there are no real victories for the black fighter, for the prizefight into which the fighter is both coerced and seduced is itself an utter corruption and distortion of democratic values and American individualism.

It is interesting to note that virtually every heavyweight champion before Louis drew the color line and would not fight black fighters for the championship, including Jack Johnson, who fought only one black fighter during his eight-year reign as champion despite the fact that shortly before his last championship fight against Willard he designated another black fighter, Sam McVey, as his successor. Louis was the first true democratic champion of boxing to fight all comers. In a sense he had to, not only to make money but also to prove himself worthy of the championship. In short, his openness was, in part, the burden of his blackness. In exchange for acceptance from the white mainstream, he had to reaffirm constantly the validity of that faith, had to assure those who held it that it was not misplaced by refusing to take refuge in the luxury of resting on his laurels as other champions, especially white ones, had done. He had to confirm, with maddening consistency, his mythical stature. Nonetheless, he established a tradition in the very breadth of his daring the excellence that has produced a certain anxiety-of-influence in the black champions who have come after him. Floyd Patterson singled out his race heroes in his 1962 autobiography, *Victory Over Myself*. And note that those he names were not leaders of any race organizations; they are symbolic leaders by virtue of having been the first blacks to have achieved broad recognition and admiration in a particular endeavor:

> As a fighter, Louis's reputation and record were on a par with the best. As a Negro fighter, his importance was emphasized for me and every other person of my race. A Louis, Jackie Robinson, Dr. Ralph Bunche—these people hold a very special significance for Negroes that goes beyond the normal respect which must be paid to those who achieve distinction. They were all champions in their fields, but more than champions. They were men of history in the social progress of my people's fight for the dignity of equality.

The importance of the black fighter as a symbol, political and social, and as a kind of running commentary, critical and complimentary, in the whole matter of what it means to be a black American takes on a greater power, a more compelling insistence, with the black masses—both lower class and bourgeoisie—than the comparable instance of the white fighter for the white masses in defining meaning for the white American. Obviously enough, however, the conundrum of the prizefighter's presence is a crucial dilemma for both groups; otherwise prizefighting would not be the center of concern and debate, admiration, and condemnation, that it is and has been in our culture. The Patterson quotation resonates in a number of ways; probably importantly, Patterson ties together the issue of the meaning of being an American, the preoccupation of black achievement and status, and the whole business of heroism and male mythology. Cultural observers are wrong who say that Muhammad Ali was the most complex of all American heroes, although he was surely one of the most luminous; Patterson, during his days as an active fighter, was the most disturbed and disturbing black presence in the history of American popular culture.

THICK DESCRIPTION: THE BLACK FIGHTER AS INTELLECTUAL; THE BLACK INTELLECTUAL AS PRIZEFIGHTER

> *"At any time when you were down in that fight, did you recognize anyone at ringside?" "Yes," {Patterson} said. "I recognized John Wayne. I think it must have been the third knockdown, because there I was on the floor, looking right at John Wayne and John Wayne was looking right at me. I've never met him, but he's my favorite movie actor. I think I've seen him in every picture he's made. At first I couldn't figure out how I could be seeing him there at ringside. But I found out later he was plugging a movie during the broadcast of the fight, but all I knew then was that I'd seen John Wayne in person, and when I got back up I was still thinking of that and I was embarrassed that John Wayne had seen me down on the floor."*

—Floyd Patterson discussing his 1959 knockout loss to Ingemar Johansson

This brings us to Patterson's essays on boxing. It was Patterson, oddly enough, who continued the democratic impulse of Louis, not by the example of his career, which was pretty selective, but by the example of one fight.[5] He fought Sonny Liston, gave the ex-con a crack at the title in 1962 when neither blacks nor whites wanted him to have it. Patterson thought such an opportunity would change Liston, make him respectable and anxiety-ridden. It didn't. But it probably changed Patterson forever. That is to say, it made him even more insufferably insane about respectability and more anxiety-

ridden than any man has a right to be. In the end, Patterson made the mistake of thinking Liston was trying to overcome the same particular set of
neurotic passions that emotionally crippled him. But that simply is not very
likely. Patterson wrote about his childhood in this way in his autobiography:

> It struck me then how much of my life I have been frightened
> by one thing or another. As a child I was never at ease at home or
> in school or in the streets. I was embarrassed most of the time,
> shamed at other times, smothered in a feeling of inadequacy. . . .
> My mother tells me that when I became a little older I used to tell
> her over and over again as I pointed to the picture [a family por-
> trait] of myself: "I don't like that boy!" When I was past nine my
> mother came home from work one night and the picture no longer
> was the same. Over my own face and body I had scratched three
> large X's with a nail or something. I can't explain why now. I
> wouldn't remember it at all if my mother hadn't remembered it. I
> guess maybe I liked myself so little that I wanted to eliminate my-
> self completely from that photo. Or maybe the world was so hard
> to face that I wanted "out" from more than the picture.

To be sure, nearly every man who becomes a boxer is something of a
wayward deviant as a boy, and certainly every black who becomes a boxer
probably has been motivated by an intense feeling of inferiority: What else
am I good for? is the rhetorical question the boy in the ring poses for the
public and himself. Moreover, Patterson's struggles to overcome his pathological shyness and sense of inferiority as a boy—largely overcome through
his becoming a boxer and being forced, in order to succeed in that sport, to
become both aggressive and confident—is a vigorous testimony to a kind of
enormous strength that many lower-class adolescents possess. His becoming
an Olympic champion in the 1952 games was no small achievement. But few
boxers, and certainly not Liston, were ever quite the psychological conundrum to themselves that Patterson was. It is not very likely that Liston was
using boxing to try to overcome anything in himself or to try to understand
himself. Winning the championship was not psychotherapeutic achievement
for Liston as it was for Patterson. Liston, in his prime, simply seemed to have
enjoyed punching men out and getting paid for it. This is not to say that
Liston was only a brute, although it is undeniably the case that he was, in
part, a brute. James Baldwin did indeed speak a striking truth when he said:
"Liston seemed like he's lonely and he's been hurt. . . . To me, Liston is a
sweet guy." Liston, born in the South, dominated by his mother, one of
fourteen children of a poor sharecropper father who eventually abandoned his
family, beaten and ridiculed as a boy for being awkward, big for his age, and

stupid—surely Liston was indeed both lonely and hurt. But his response to that was more simplistic than Patterson's. He became brutal and cynical to a world that had been brutal and indifferent to him. To call Liston "sweet," a strangely effeminate term black men used to use with each other along with "baby," is to imply nearly a kind of masculine sentimentality that seems abruptly disarming when one considers how insistently uncharming and un-endearing Liston really was. When Liston said before the first fight with Patterson, "I intend to model myself after Joe Louis, who I think was the greatest champion of all and my idol," he was sincere. But the Louis he admired was a quite different figure than the one Patterson felt he had to emulate. Liston's Louis was a slick, tough black man who "got over" and made money. Liston saw Louis as a street hero; Louis knew the real world of white America and the code of survival for an uneducated, brawny black man in that world. To Liston, Patterson was simply weak and sniveling. When both Patterson and Liston, shortly before their first fight, appeared on a television show hosted by Howard Cosell, Patterson went on at great length and with colossal condescension about how Liston could be a great influence on the children of America and how Liston deserved a shot at the title. Cosell then turned to Liston and asked his opinion of the champion, Patterson. Liston responded with a chilling scorn: "I'd like to run him over with a truck."

Patterson must rank along with José Torres as one of the most thoughtful men ever to enter the boxing ring. Perhaps his constant reflection impaired his ability as a fighter; it is difficult to say. He was small for a heavyweight and this meant, all other factors being equal, that he stood little chance against either Sonny Liston or Muhammad Ali, his two archrivals, who together, through the sheer grandeur of their size, ushered in a new era in boxing. Patterson was fascinated with the man he called Cassius Clay or, rather, the man he refused to call Muhammad Ali. Perhaps he saw Ali as an alter ego. Perhaps Ali was the fighter that he, Patterson, always aspired to be. He expresses in two of the articles under consideration here the belief that if he had fought Liston the way Ali did, boxing and moving, he would have won. He probably wouldn't have, but isn't it pretty, for Patterson, to think so? These articles, especially the two that appeared in *Sports Illustrated,* were probably condemned by most black intellectuals of the time as the ravings of a particularly pathetic Uncle Tom. To be sure, Patterson did show a certain insipid naïveté and even wrongheadedness in his condemnation of Ali and the Black Muslims, expressing feelings akin to the outraged middle-class black who finds that his lower-class cousin has gone balmy over some sort of storefront charlatanism. But his basic instincts about the inadequacy of the Muslim response to American racism proved to be generally correct. But the importance of these essays is not what Patterson has to say about Ali, a man he hardly knows and still less is capable of understanding, but what they say about Patterson himself. And it is the subject of Patterson that most concerns Patterson. Despite his claims of loving the sport of boxing, one finds this hard to believe. Patterson complains that the sport has alienated him from his wife and children ("They know I'm their father and they all call me Daddy. They love me, I'm sure as much as I love them, but there's a kind of stiffness, a kind of unfamiliarity, almost too much of a politeness with which they treat me. I know children should be polite to their parents, and kids unquestioningly will do anything they tell them, but the easiness that should be in the usual relationship between children and father is not there in ours, and I'm completely aware that it's all my fault."). It has made him vicious against his opponents ("I never was as vicious in my life as I was the night I won back my title from [Johansson]. All I wanted to do was hit him and hit him again until I destroyed him"; "I was filled with so much hate [in the second fight with Johansson], I wouldn't ever want to reach that low again"), a viciousness he finds he must have if he is to win and to counter the complaint expressed by Ingemar Johansson that Patterson "is too nice."[6] He is forced to act out other people's hatred vicariously and publicly for money ("There is so much hate among people, so much contempt inside people who'd like you to think they're moral, that they have to hire prizefighters to do their hating for them. And we do. We get into a ring and act out other people's hates. We are happy to do it. How else can Negroes like Clay and myself, born in the South, poor, and with little education, make so much money?"). Despite this, Patterson feels deeply that being heavyweight champion of the world means something, a great deal. As he eloquently puts it:

> You've got to go on. You owe it to yourself, to the tradition
> of the title, to the public that sees the champion as somebody spe-
> cial, to everything that must become sacred to you the first time
> you put gloves on your hands. You've got to believe in what you're
> doing or else nobody can believe that anything is worthwhile.

In another passage he reveals his own sense of peculiar burden by virtue of having been champion:

> I do feel partially responsible for the title having fallen into the
> wrong hands because of my own mistakes. I want to redeem myself
> in my own eyes and in the mind of the public. I owe so much to
> boxing—everything I have, the security of my family, my ability
> to express myself, the places I've been, the people I've met. A man
> has got to pay his debts or he can't live with himself comfortably.

Of course, one is forced to ask how he can owe anything to a sport, however much he may have gained financially, that has demanded such emotional extortion, a sport that he acknowledges has degraded him. Is it related to how we see boxing, the ruthless irony that the poor men who become champions are still, in our eyes, degraded although they are also celebrated as well? The champion must be worthy of our admiration while we are deeply and secretly chilled by the very acts that make him admirable, chilled that he is willing to do it, chilled that we are willing to watch. And yet it is the urge to redeem and reform utter vice into complete virtue that motivates Patterson. It is the same urge, the same spirit that motivates Uncle Tom in Harriet Beecher Stowe's famous novel. Here I do not mean to use the term "Uncle Tom" pejoratively, rather merely to be descriptive of a psychohistorical mythology that has resonated for some time in American culture. It is the tragic heroic fate of the black American to bring humbly forth grand humanity from a social oppression that thoroughly contradicts the possibility of humanity itself: That, for Patterson, was the legacy of Louis, although Louis himself was never so self-conscious about it. Patterson, like Louis, reenacted the equivocal drama, the uneasy spectacle of Uncle Tom's stringent morality, a morality that James Baldwin rightly condemned in his reading of Stowe's novel as a "rejection of life, the human being, the denial of his beauty, dread, power, and in its insistence that it is categorization alone which is real and which cannot be transcended."

Patterson, like Ellison's Todd Clifton, becomes lost in a maze of symbols, finally, consumed and obsessed by the category he occupied: the acclaimed black prizefighter as accomplished black American. It is, incidentally, profoundly ironic that the noble Peter Jackson starred as Uncle Tom in a stage production during the era when the stage version of the novel was quite popular. After finishing his performance as humble "elderly" Tom, Jackson's manager would come on stage and announce that "Peter Jackson will box three friendly and scientific rounds to show how we will wrest the pugilistic crown from 'Gentleman Jim' Corbett." Only in America could one move with such ease, such psychic fluidity, from piety to punches. So, by virtue of his blackness, it is possible for Patterson to be participant in an extremely violent and aggressive profession while symbolizing a sort of self-effaced, nonthreatening, nearly transcendent masculinity, a quaint purity that brings to mind, ironically, the Kid Galahad myth of the white fighter. In this regard, Freud's ideas concerning taboo, which seem to have influenced Joyce Carol Oates's discussion of boxing, are germane in understanding how the boxer is objectified in American culture. Prizefighting, for most of the years of its existence in the Western world, has been either an outright illegal activity, as it was during the days of the Regency in England and the late nineteenth century in America, or an activity that bordered on both illegality and ill repute, performed only by socially outcast men; thus, its performers have always been associated with a taboo activity, which, by virtue of that association, has made them taboo persons as well. Taboo acts adhere to the people who perform them; this explains, for instance, why actors and actresses in hard-core pornographic films rarely make the transition to mainstream movies. But the complexity here is that the boxer breaks a taboo that we want broken; indeed, the very breaking of it has become a profound ritual and metaphor in the culture. In this way, the boxer becomes a totemic representation of masculinity. Oates's observation of the adoption of luridly macho nicknames by boxers is a penetrating one. This accounts for our intense identification with the fighter, how he comes to symbolize some tribal aspect of us, or comes to represent our fortune in the world through our betting on his performance—and gambling is, after all, the bridge that allows the nonfighting public to enter the world, the den of the boxer. So the prizefight is the ritualization of the triumph and defeat, the expression and the thwarting of—the sheer ambiguity of—masculine aggression. And the knockout is the ceremonial death of the totemic animal. The boxer symbolizes the same opposite tensions as our image of the spirit world: the place of devils, demons, and ghosts, on the one hand, but the place of ancestors and angels on the other. Ah, ambivalence! Ah, bruising!

In the end, Patterson condemns Ali because Ali does not recognize that any black champion must fight out of the Joe Louis tradition: He must be responsible and he must acknowledge the larger white society he is forced to represent by virtue of his position. Patterson flatly admits that boxing is ugly but thinks that it is the duty of the black champion to transcend the ugliness of the sport as a duty to his society. It is the black champion's burden and his honor. ("I am a Negro and I'm proud to be one, but I'm also an American." Alas, the whole business of the Du Bois-ian double consciousness rears its truthful head. What the black intellectual confronted in the sixties was his utter refusal to be both and the utter impossibility to be neither.) Probably because as a black living in the modern world it is so difficult to find an arena for its display, Patterson is obsessed with honor. It is no coincidence, then, that he was champion during the late fifties, the era of the Negro's proving himself worthy of integration: the pop-culture era of Sidney Poitier, who was the personification of black honor on the screen; of Sammy Davis, Jr., smiling in photos with his white "rat pack" friends—Frank Sinatra, Joey Bishop, Dean Martin, and Peter Lawford; of Nat "King" Cole and Louis Armstrong, playing segregated nightclubs with a fortitude that could scarcely be distinguished from a kind of cunning insouciance. Patterson was so disliked by the black intellectuals of the sixties probably because his position, as he defined it in the sport of prizefighting, was so similar to their own. They were part of a tradition that they were unable to denounce but were unable to embrace completely, torn by doubts not only about the nature of their ability but about the meaning of what they did in a society where their position is so precarious, shackled by a seemingly ignoble past that could only be lived

down by the pretensions of inhuman nobility. In this sense, the fighter becomes the displaced intellectual; the intellectual becomes the displaced
fighter. And indeed what has Ellison's novel achieved but to give us the
black intellectual as fighter in the ring? Patterson's quest is the dilemma of
the black American intellectual: caught between the urge for, to borrow Orlando Patterson's terms, existential solidarity and the need for ethnocentric
solidarity; and ultimately discovering, like Ellison's hero, the impossibility
of linkage, either real or contrived. If the Ellison hero is supposed to be
Promethean, it must be remembered that his stolen light (from Monopolated
Power and Light) is not given to anyone else. He uses it only for himself.
Patterson was a loner, the most marginal of the marginalized.

What Patterson ultimately hated about both Ali and Liston was that
both thought they could, through flights of escapism, avoid a dilemma that
Patterson thought was ineluctable and, unfortunately, character-building—
that is, ultimately, not simply a quest for moral order but for redemptive
piety. (Thus, Larry Neal was right: Patterson was "the first Hamlet of the
boxing profession.") Liston, through his defeats at the hands of Ali, simply
acquiesced in being what whites said he was. Liston, in essence and in fact,
quit. As Patterson wrote: "That's why that night when [Liston] refused to
come out for the seventh round I was so shocked. [In Liston's first fight with
Ali, then Clay, he supposedly injured his shoulder and discontinued fighting
after the sixth round.] It was almost as much a blow to me as being knocked
out by him. He, of all people! The unbeatable man, the press called him,
quitting on his stool. . . . I've seen fighters, even amateurs, cut up and bleed-
ing, but they'd go on and fight no matter what was wrong with them. I've
seen fighters who would try to hit the referee if he even indicated he was going to stop the fight. If you're the champion you fight on if you're faced with
permanent injury, even death. If Liston couldn't punch with one arm, what
was wrong with the other?" Liston accepted the blackness of blackness. Ali,
by becoming a Black Muslim, decided he wished to change the nature of the
terms, to escape the blackness of blackness by redefining the terms in his
own way. Liston accepted defeat as his lot; Ali denied its possibility; Patterson felt that the black champion, like the black intellectual, could do neither. For Patterson one could neither accept the terms nor redefine them; one
must heroically struggle with them, constantly defending one's rights to participate in the discourse. Although there may be several books in the future
by black intellectuals about prizefighting, it is easy to see why there have
been so few so far. Black people, in the final analysis, were never comfortable
with boxing for the same reason they were never comfortable with Patterson.
The answer for the black intellectual did not lie in someone like Patterson
making a response to boxing that was so much like Gene Tunney's in his autobiographies, *A Man Must Fight* and *Arms for Living,* a response of someone

who seemed to be a priggish Boy Scout. So much of Patterson's sentiment
seems summed up in this excerpt from an interview with Tunney in 1926 by
Katharine Brush:

> The interview proceeded. Mr. Tunney, leaning against a desk,
> talked. He talked about the mothers of America. He said he felt
> that the mothers of America were looking to him as an example of
> fine, clean young manhood, towards which they could point their
> sons. He said that he was no longer himself, that he no longer be-
> longed to himself.

It is all so corny yet so touching in about the only way a man, especially
an athlete, can be touching and romantic in American society: by being the
heroic son in Kid Galahad, in love with motherhood and displaying a perpet-
ual and sexless adolescence. But Patterson's hopes for the black fighter and
for himself were so bumblingly unreal, so terribly Victorian, so staunchly
and unquestioningly philistine. (The words of Peter Jackson are germane
here: "Boxing, I think, is a manly sport, and should be cultivated by the rising generation, not for the purpose of breeding a race of fighters, but for a
strong, brave, healthy race of men, no matter what occupation they follow in
life." The philistinism of Tunney and Patterson is, finally, rooted in the neurotic yet innocent nobility of black respectability.) We must be clear here in
understanding that Patterson was disliked by black intellectuals in the sixties. The fifties present us with other complexities, which may, in part, explain the disintegration of Patterson's reputation among blacks after his
losses to Liston. Someone like the great St. Louis fighter Henry Armstrong,
in his 1956 autobiography, *Gloves, Glory, and God* (a title quite similar to
that of John L. Sullivan's old-age temperance lectures, "From Glory, to Gutter, to God"), could write that "my victories in the ring were not my own
merely; they were the victories of a brown battler, a Negro, feeling pride in
other Negroes' achievements against great odds." Armstrong could also
write of his desire to be "God's champion" and express the black folk version
of the Messiah, chosen for greatness, going to a philistine extreme that Patterson never approaches. By book's end Armstrong is a broken-down alcoholic who manages to pull himself together and become a preacher. There is
in Armstrong's life a great sense of waste and of tragedy, of the far journey
out (he makes incredible pilgrimages from St. Louis to New York and then
from New York back to St. Louis and finally from St. Louis to California,
where with a new name he becomes a great champion), of the return home,
of great sin requiring great redemption. Patterson's life is never so richly dishonorable, so deeply adversative, nor his persona so brazenly egotistical. Yet
he felt the weight of messianic duty, too. He had to, emulating Louis as he

did, and Louis was this culture's most messianic sports hero until the coming of Ali. With Patterson one gets only that sense of faltering and slouching—finally, really an important aspect of respectable, bourgeois black life in white America at that time: an ungracious and graceless self-consciousness. It seems clear now why sociologist E. Franklin Frazier wrote his penetrating diatribe against black respectability, *The Black Bourgeoisie,* in the middle 1950s; it was an attack against everything Patterson symbolized, against the kind of mainstream acculturation that the bourgeois black wanted, a marriage to which he brought no cultural dowry at all except the confession that, of course, he did not and could not possess one.

On July 16, 1910, twelve days after Jack Johnson successfully defended his heavyweight title in Reno, Nevada, against great white hope Jim Jeffries, *The Washington Bee,* a black newspaper, ran an editorial condemning black celebratory interest in the fight: "What the colored people can find to go wild over *The Bee* fails to see." The editorial, interestingly enough, fails to note that the fight's result produced a number of race riots and that several celebrating blacks were assaulted and a few even killed by angered whites. Of course, it does imply that Johnson is a source of public disorder. The editorial particularly condemned the Elks for providing an entertainment for Jack Johnson and went on to remind its readers that it was men such as Dr. James E. Shepard, "Dr. [*sic*]" Booker T. Washington, and Dr. W.E.B. Du Bois who were "doing something elevating for the masses." This particular black middle class's censure of Johnson the pugilist as, in effect, a poor role model is obvious enough: It is the black philistine's cry for standards and achievements that whites would be bound to respect because the black philistine never wanted freedom for blacks, only the right and access to be absorbed by a massive white philistinism. Undoubtedly, they were partly right: it was a sign of the utter contempt in which they were held by whites that only a black pugilist who chased white prostitutes and drove fast cars could attract attention in mainstream culture. Jack Johnson received more white newspaper space by far than any other black of his era, including Booker T. Washington. Although other middle-class figures such as James Weldon Johnson were comfortable with Johnson, even admiring him, it was a standard opinion among many that Johnson's flaunting of his sex life made it hard on the race. (The business about his beating up white men for pay was a bit more ambiguous, because blacks, secretly if not openly, admired Johnson for that, although some victories were quite discomforting for some blacks in their ordinary intercourse with whites, as the post-Jeffries riots prove.) What the *Bee* editorial points out is the whole conundrum connected with "race pride." What blacks who achieve prominence in this culture should be admired? By the 1950s, when Frazier, a product of the black middle class, denounced that class, and when black intellectuals eventually, not immediately, turned away from Patterson, a critical attack was being articulated by middle-class blacks against some of the very elements that were part of the concept of race pride and social uplift, particularly against philistinism. It was not the beginning of the liberalizing of the idea of black achievement. That had, after all, been open enough in some circles for so long that virtually any black who did anything of note that was not illegal was bound to be praised for it in some black publication: It was this against which the philistines inveighed. But what the coming of Patterson, Liston, and Ali did was make blacks as a group examine to some considerable degree the epistemological core of black achievement, social uplift, and race pride. Not every black who achieves in this culture should be a symbol of race pride, and perhaps none should; but if there are to be such, then they should by their example tell us something remarkable about what being a black American is. Ellison in *Invisible Man* argued that the only standards are those that the individual forges for himself, not the totalitarian standards of the group. Whatever the validity of that, it is clear that by the 1950s black honor had become a national pop-culture icon, from James Edwards playing a kind of Patterson persona in the film *Home of the Brave* in 1949, the same year Sidney Poitier came to prominence playing a doctor in *No Way Out,* to Sidney Poitier starring in black playwright Lorraine Hansberry's paean to black aspiration, *A Raisin in the Sun* (1959). Some black middle-class intellectuals and nearly all of the black masses were thinking that what constituted black achievement ought not to be defined by what whites considered "a respectable Negro." (The numerous African references in Hansberry's play hint that something of this sort is, indeed, afoot.) This laid the psychological groundwork for the militant 1960s and, as I recall, one of the must-read books in those days was, in fact, Frazier's work on the black middle class; it was featured, for instance, on the reading list of *The Liberator,* the young militant black intellectual's organ. As long as Patterson's chief nemesis was the Swede Johansson (1959–1961), his aspirations were less troublesome to blacks. But by the early sixties, when his chief rival became Sonny Liston, a new awareness was born as a result of two such radically different black men confronting each other on the stage of American popular culture. Liston laughed at Patterson's pretension as if to say: "What do white folks care about your dignity; if they cared at all would you even be a fighter? Face it, chump, you're a bruiser just as I am, no better and no worse." That black cynicism blew like a harsh wind across the land, blowing through all black folks' windows and, to borrow a phrase, pushing the bad air out. The period of transition from the 1950s to the 1960s was symbolized by Patterson, Liston, and Ali, champions all, each the political supersession of the other, each challenging and, ultimately, redefining the type of black achievement, social uplift, and racial pride that mainstream culture would and could absorb.

Patterson lost twice to Liston (1962, 1963) and he lost twice to Ali as well (1965, 1972). He could never defeat the Satans (i.e., adversaries) of negation whom he said must be defeated in the end: Good did not triumph over evil for him. The beatific wonders of good citizenship and Catholicism lost out to a hoodlum enforcer for the Mob and an ethnically obsessed, showboating Muslim who had the grave misfortune, as it turned out, to be the greatest boxer in the history of the sport and one of the bravest men in his country during the sixties. His was the poignant, strangely heroic, completely nonsensical cry of black philistinism, of moral conservatism in the world of bruising culture in which one can only expect utter immorality. There was nothing good or moral for him to conserve, and so he must have realized. He was a product of the era of integration, coming to prominence right after the Supreme Court decision to desegregate public schools. He was the symbol of the black who wished to show himself ready and worthy to enter the house of white American manners, of white bourgeois culture, washed clean and bathed in a light that was as inhuman in its brightness as what it illuminated was strikingly yet childishly gallant in its debasement. As Oscar Wilde wrote, "For what man has sought for is, indeed, neither pain nor pleasure, but simply life." Patterson, trapped between affirmation and negation, unable, in defeat, to be himself, and unable in victory to be anything more than himself, seemed on the verge of denying life, because he so insisted on denying the possibilities of life in exchange for the imperative of his reality as a category and the conscientious comfort of his missionary morality. The true object of Patterson's heroism was the announcement and display of a virtue that only a Negro could possess or want to possess. In order to overcome his condition as an entrapped Negro, he must forever confess himself as something only an entrapped Negro could be. His career became, to borrow from Roland Barthes, "an ethic of vanity, an exoticism of endurance."

Whatever Ali and Liston were as symbols of negations for Patterson, they shared one affirming quality. After they had used up life—and local former heavyweight Wes Bascom described prizefighting in just that way, using up bits of yourself that could never be replenished—they desired greedily and incessantly only one thing: more life, whether pain or pleasure. How remarkable the majestic excesses of the Satans! How pusillanimous the ascetic tenacity of the Saint! Just as Patterson was never able to convince his children that his training headquarters was not his home, so it is doubtful he ever convinced himself—and certain that he convinced no one else—that his edifice of Negro rectitude was, at last, also the house black people really wished to live in.

NOTES

1 Black intellectuals such as Roi Ottley and J. Saunders Reddings have devoted chapters in certain of their nonfiction work to black prizefighters: *New World a-Coming* and *The Lonesome Road: The Story of the Negro's Part in America,* respectively. Also, West Indian scholar C.L.R. James mentions both Louis and boxing in his book on cricket, *Beyond a Boundary.*

2 A sense of gender consciousness is important here. Obviously, the aesthetic and moral terms of discussion and analysis here are masculine-oriented because men have so largely dominated the writing about sports and especially the writing about boxing. Black women have written virtually nothing on the sport of boxing, which is as striking as it is both predictable and regrettable. It is to be hoped that sometime in the near future, with so many black women now working at the writer's trade, that some treatises on the subject as well as on sports generally will appear. Their perspective on the subject, in addition to the very tiny body of journalistic and interpretive work by white women writers such as Nellie Bly, Katharine Brush, Sally Helgesen, and Joyce Carol Oates, is very much needed.

3 I think Wright was also fascinated by Jack Johnson. Certainly, his short story "Big Boy Leaves Home," in *Uncle Tom's Children,* can be quite persuasively read as an allegorical gloss of the Johnson career up to the point of Johnson's exile. It must be remembered that Wright was born in 1908, the year that Johnson became champion; by the time Wright reached his seventh birthday in 1915, the year Johnson finally lost the crown, it seems quite likely that he had heard much talk and folklore about him.

4 The great triple-crown winner Henry Armstrong of St. Louis describes the battle royal:

> I had my first amateur fight here in 1929, right here in St. Louis at the old Coliseum. I knocked out a colored kid in the second round at the old Coliseum. What they were usually doing at that time, and I wouldn't subject myself to it, they wanted the colored kids to get in there and fight in what they call a Battle Royal, where they put a black towel around your eyes and put five, six, seven guys in a ring and let them fight against each other blind and laugh at you. I wouldn't go for that. I was really too proud.

5 A. S. "Doc" Young, in his biography of Liston, *Sonny Liston: The Champ Nobody Wanted* (1963), wrote:

> Liston also revealed why he disliked Patterson. "I have a little dislike for Patterson, but it's not because he wouldn't agree to fight me for so long but because he hasn't fought any colored boys since becoming champion. Patterson draws the color line against his own race. We have a hard enough time as it is in the white man's world." Actually though this charge had been made against Patterson by others, in the Negro press even, it was unfair, at least to this extent: Patterson had defended the title against one Negro, Tommy (Hurricane) Jackson, whom he knocked out in the tenth round at New York on July 29, 1957. All others Patterson's title defenses up to his meeting with Liston, however, were made against white opponents, most of them regarded by many to be unworthy challengers, particularly so since such capable fighters as Liston himself, Zora Folley, Cleveland Williams, and, perhaps, Eddie Machen—all of these Negroes—were around, willing, and eager to meet the champion.

It is ironic, in this respect, that Patterson, who wanted to emulate Joe Louis, wound up resembling Jack Johnson. Johnson defended his title against only one black despite the number of good black heavyweights available during his era who, if they could not expect a title opportunity from him, could certainly expect it from no one else. Ali, on the other hand, who wanted to distinguish himself so much from Louis, defended his crown between 1964 and 1967 against Liston, Patterson, Williams, and Folley among others.

6 Cus D'Amato, Patterson's manager, had this to say about his young fighter during the early days of his professional career:

[Patterson] lacks the killer instinct. He's too tame, too nice to his opponents. I've been trying all the psychology I can think of to anger his blood up, but he just doesn't have the zest for viciousness. I have a big job on my hands.

THE UNQUIET KINGDOM
OF PROVIDENCE

The Patterson-Liston Fight

The world ought not to be a harmonious place.

—D. H. Lawrence, *Studies in Classic American Literature*

THE TEXT

On 16 August 1963, President John F. Kennedy issued executive clemency
on behalf of Hampton Hawes, a talented though erratic West Coast jazz pianist (decidedly not of the cool school as he sounded much like Hard Bop
monster Horace Silver) who had been incarcerated in federal prison for drug
possession and addiction. Hawes had served five years of a ten-year sentence.
It was not very surprising that Kennedy would do something of this nature.
First, Kennedy, as Billy Eckstine tells us, fancied himself something of a jazz
fan and he may very well have been familiar with the music of Hawes. Second, and more important, it was a profound gesture of liberalism, a sign of
the reformism that was the fashion of the country in those days. If Kennedy
was still, at this time, caught on the horns of the dilemma of the civil rights
movement, between needing white southern support for reelection and sympathizing with the ample justification of black claims for equality, here with
Hawes he could both recognize the talents of a black while sympathizing
with the conditions of his oppression in a broad humanitarian gesture that
would cost him nothing; after all, white southerners were not likely even to
have heard of a heroin-addicted jazz musician one of whose fondest memories
was the day, as a teenager, he permitted saxophonist Charlie Parker to drive
his new car and straightaway to strip the gears in the process. Kennedy realized it was not serving the interest either of Hawes or of society that Hawes

remain incarcerated. And he was aware that the public understood this as well; after all, the well-publicized deaths of saxophonist Charlie Parker in 1955 and singer Billie Holiday in 1959, both celebrated drug addicts, may have convinced most of the population that a black jazz musician was indeed the "sick" artist of American culture, more in need of pity than punishment. There was more than a little talk in enlightened circles in those days about treating drug addicts more humanely, about legalizing heroin and having physicians dispense it as was being done in England. Perhaps the heroin scourge that hit black communities nationwide in the 1950s made liberals think that *something* ought to be done about this problem other than to imprison or bury the users.

Kennedy's gesture was symbolic of an age that protested not repression but denial; and here the distinction is important because the concern of early-sixties reformism was not how institutions and cultures amassed their powers against those they were designed to serve but how the self was affected by external restrictions. So reform was seen not as politically or ideologically based but more as the psycho-romance of two types of rhetoric: populist male speeches about victimization (from Kennedy to King to Malcolm X, the successors to Depression-era reformers Father Coughlin, FDR, Huey Long, and Father Divine, to a whole generation of radical black and white speechmakers who went from the ramparts of late-sixties confrontation to the lucrative college circuit in the seventies; Louis Farrakhan and others even today show this sort of thing is far from being out of style) or the academic reading and re-reading of sociological data: the scientific tea leaves of American social engineering. (Sociology came into its own in the fifties not only as a discipline but as a pop culture newspeak as the whole nation was abuzz with talk of Levittown, the ghetto, the global village, the lonely crowd, why the poor pay more, Talley's corner, and why Johnny can't read.) In any event, some segments of white America had come to see racism and segregation particularly—among its most virulent forms of injustice—precisely as nightmarish repression. What had once been seen as something that properly endowed whites was now seen as an unfair deprivation for blacks. It was just this point that was made by one of the most popular books of the era: John Howard Griffin's 1961 classic *Black Like Me,* which went even one step beyond the sociological tracts since the author did more than study Negroes; he became a Negro. But racism was seen (and still is or else why the elaborate preoccupation with nostalgia on the part of whites for decades such as the fifties and the twenties unless to remember when the world was unambiguously white and when one could so touchingly relate to the nice, loyal colored woman who cleaned the house or the gentle, smiling colored man who swept the yard) as a sweetly vicious cheat gone bad, as something inherently orderly and gracious. Racism and the social system it spawned suggested among other things an idealism of such perversely innocent purity and such comfortable hypocrisy that its large-scale breakup in the fifties and sixties was almost a massive sort of heartbreak, and mad conservative Puritans, both black and white, Elijah Muhammad and George Wallace, issued antimodernist jeremiads on how lovely race consciousness truly is and what a disaster that children are falling away from it all.

The first Patterson-Liston heavyweight championship match (September 1962), which took place nearly a year before Hampton Hawes was released from prison, was meant, too, to be a gesture of liberalism. Kennedy had become quite famously associated with releasing blacks from prison: perhaps it was the symbol of the times, releasing the Negro from his psychic and actual cages. (If the image of the incarcerated black is one of the chief signs of American culture in the sixties, the liberal response to it changed over the course of the decade. In the early sixties, the image of the incarcerated black may have produced a sort of national meditation on unjust imprisonment, but it never produced questions on either the justification or justice of the white being responsible for the freeing of the black. In the late sixties, when the threat of black imprisonment or the actual fact of black imprisonment, specifically black *male* imprisonment, haunted not only the liberal imagination but the entire national consciousness—consider such figures as Ali, Amiri Baraka, Eldridge Cleaver, Huey Newton, George Jackson, Etheridge Knight, Iceberg Slim, and others—the question of the white's, particularly the white liberal's, *responsibility* to free the black was questioned. In the case of George Plimpton's discussion of Ali in *Shadow-Box,* published in 1977, the white liberal's *power* to free the black was questioned. But in this instance, if standard bourgeois liberalism was willing to admit its impotence, then the more radical aesthetic liberalism was more than willing to fill the breach in the late sixties by turning the imprisoned black male away from being a figure of pity or a figure in need of reformation to a charismatic figure of commitment and heightened political consciousness. Imprisonment now meant the black male was no longer victimized but engaged. Witness the transformation of Malcolm X as a cultural figure in the sixties: from the race demon in the early sixties to the American saint of the late sixties. Part of this is due to his departure from the Nation of Islam and his subsequent assassination. But the mythology of his imprisonment, popularized by the 1965 publication of his *Autobiography,* has no insignificant part in this changed perception.)

Kennedy won the election in 1960 against Nixon by, somewhat inadvertently, getting Martin Luther King released from a Georgia jail and thus assuring himself of the black vote, which had a powerful significance in such a close election. It is probably the sheer inadvertence of it, the very awkwardness of and uncertainty of the gesture in King's case, that will loom significantly as this essay unfolds, so it may be useful to summarize the event that helped Kennedy win the White House. The actual story of King's release is this: John Kennedy was asked by Sargeant Shriver to call Coretta Scott King to console her about the imprisonment of her husband on a charge of having violated probation for an earlier traffic violation as a result of being arrested for trespassing at a Woolworth's lunch counter. This call was placed on the afternoon of 26 October 1960. Either a day later or on the same day, Robert Kennedy telephoned De Kalb County Judge Oscar Mitchell, who had sentenced King to four months in prison, to request bail for King. The next day King was released on bail. It was later revealed by Robert Kennedy himself that he made the call only at the request of the governor of Georgia, who wanted pressure placed on the judge to release King so as not to ruin Kennedy's chances of carrying the state in November by a highly publicized King imprisonment at the hands of the local Democratic administration. Vice President Richard Nixon, Kennedy's Republican opponent for the presidency, had initially been approached by a frantic King family in an effort to obtain federal intervention for King's release. Nixon made no response to the plea. In his book *Six Crises,* Nixon explained that he felt that it was improper conduct on the part of a lawyer to try to influence a judge in sentencing a defendant by phoning him, and he berated Robert Kennedy for doing so. Nixon went on to say that he intended to have the Justice Department look into the matter to see if King's civil rights had been violated—the only real avenue he had as a federal official. Although Nixon was probably afraid that any overt action in favor of King would lose him white southern votes at a time when Republicans did not run well in that part of the country, his points are technically correct. Moreover, until Kennedy freed King from jail, Nixon had every confidence that he would run well in the black community. Despite the Roosevelt presidency, there were still a significant number of blacks at this time who voted Republican, in part because of southern segregationist Democrats (Adam Clayton Powell, a Democrat, endorsed Eisenhower instead of his own party's Adlai Stevenson in 1956 because he felt that Stevenson was not strong enough on civil rights) and in part because the black shift to the Democratic party was still not complete by 1960. Former baseball star Jackie Robinson, for instance, supported Nixon in 1960 and was a Republican throughout his postbaseball life. Robinson admittedly was disturbed by Nixon's lack of sensitivity and concern about racial matters and later regretted he had supported him. Frederic Morrow, the first black to work as a White House aide (he worked under Eisenhower), in his *Black Man in the White House* told how appalled he was by some of the crudely racist remarks of H. R. Haldeman and other Nixon staffers during the 1960 campaign. To be sure, this campaign firmly molded the identities of both parties for every subsequent election: Nixon's action made the Republican party

clearly the conservative party and, as far as blacks were concerned, the antiblack party. Republican presidential candidates would never do well with
black voters again. The Democratic party became the party of civil rights. (I
certainly do not wish to argue that Kennedy saw himself as a liberal. Too
many Kennedy specialists have asserted that he did not see himself as such.
Actually, Kennedy did not like liberals. What needs to be said is that because of Kennedy's close connection with Northern liberals and intellectuals
and because Lyndon Johnson, when he became president, was largely seen—
whether rightly or wrongly is of no concern here—as fulfilling Kennedy's
agenda, an agenda that became the most liberal and reform-oriented since
the days of Radical Reconstruction immediately following the Civil War; because of his apotheosis by many liberal intellectuals after his death, Kennedy
has become the shining symbol of liberalism in national American politics
before the tarnished undoings and fumblings of Johnson and Carter.)

Kennedy met heavyweight boxing champion Floyd Patterson shortly after Patterson beat Ingemar Johansson the second time in March 1961, and it
was through that meeting, a photograph of which figured quite prominently
both within the text and on the cover of Patterson's 1962 autobiography,
Victory over Myself, that Kennedy, quite unconsciously (since he felt, as Ted
Sorensen explained, that he was merely meeting a celebrity), legitimated the
creation of a public icon and thus revitalized the rhetoric of opportunity.
Certainly Patterson interpreted the meeting in that way when he wrote this
as part of the cutline for the photo with Kennedy: "Way back there [referring
to an earlier photograph of himself as a child] as a bedraggled youngster,
emotionally disturbed, with no talent and no outlook, could I ever imagine
it would some day be possible for me to meet the President of the United
States?" The photo that precedes the one of Patterson and Kennedy is one of
champion Patterson and Eleanor Roosevelt, the mother figure of modern
American bourgeois liberalism, at the Wiltwyck School for Boys, which
Mrs. Roosevelt helped found and which Patterson attended as a delinquent
child. Indeed, Patterson dedicates his book to the Wiltwyck School for Boys
(just as Claude Brown was to do a few years later with his black male delinquency autobiography, *Manchild in the Promised Land;* Brown also thought
Eleanor Roosevelt walked on water), the place that gave him an opportunity,
that saved him from becoming, horror of horrors, the black thug, the wayward black male; in short, the place that saved him from becoming his arch-
rival, Sonny Liston. Patterson thus gives us in his autobiography and in his
example as a public figure the incredible story of how a reform really did just
that: reform him; the incredible story of how his incarceration became his
freedom. The irony of this is the irony of American liberalism in the early
1960s, for if this was the age of freeing the black from his jail, it was, nonetheless, the heady and cheeky age that believed in the necessity of a black's

institutional processing so that he might emerge "normal." The photograph of the two young men together, both Catholic and both having won positions and acclaim by overcoming considerable odds, seems to speak of America as a kind of promise. Opportunity was alive and palpable, not simply a creed but an act of creation and re-creation. In this regard I must mention one last connection between Kennedy, delinquency, and the rhetoric of opportunity: it was under Kennedy that a federal commission on troubled teenagers, the President's Committee on Juvenile Delinquency, was formed in 1961; it was headed by David Hackett, a good friend of Robert Kennedy. Hackett had been deeply influenced by the Lloyd E. Ohlin and Richard Cloward classic 1960 study, *Delinquency and Opportunity: A Theory of Delinquent Gangs,* one of the most famous sociological treatises ever written, which argued, among other things, that the way to alleviate delinquency among underclass boys was to provide them with the opportunity that society at large kept denying them. The philosophic foundations of 1960s liberalism had been set; cultural cross-pollination of it had been generated. The rich white boy and the poor black boy, now both rich and famous, believed in an age of possibility that had, of course, made them possible.

If President Kennedy and Floyd Patterson, simply as public men who exemplified the magic of opportunity bestowed, were responsible jointly for intensifying the ideology that made the Patterson-Liston fight possible, Kennedy by himself, once again, quite inadvertently, influenced the making of the Patterson-Liston fight in another way: In December 1961, Kennedy joined millions of other fight fans who watched a televised boxing double-header in which champion Floyd Patterson beat Tom McNeeley in four rounds and Sonny Liston smashed Albert Westphal of West Germany in one round. It was Liston's showcase moment, as he had been campaigning for two years to fight for the championship. As reported in A. S. "Doc" Young's biography of Liston, *Sonny Liston: The Champ Nobody Wanted,* Kennedy casually remarked that the fights were mismatches and that Patterson and Liston should have fought each other. It was, oddly, that statement that made the Liston-Patterson showdown unavoidable for Patterson and inevitable for Liston. The idea that Liston should be permitted to fight for the title was strongly resisted by Patterson's manager, Cus D'Amato, and by most of the sporting press and some considerable segments of the public. Such a fight would be, it was argued by the more pious citizens, bad for boxing. Liston had been imprisoned for armed robbery and served time in the Jefferson City, Missouri, penitentiary. He had been arrested more than twenty times before on various theft and assault charges. If there seems a certain hypocrisy in the protestations of elements of the boxing establishment against a Patterson-Liston match (after all, boxing has always been a fairly disreputable sport with its share of jailbirds serving as active participants; in short, it is hard to

imagine anything that could be worse for boxing than boxing), it must be remembered that, first, such incorruptible figures as *Ring* magazine editor Nat
Fleischer really wanted to clean up boxing, especially after the Jim Norris–International Boxing Club scandal of the 1950s. And many of these res-
cuers of boxing were obviously ambivalent about a fight that might cause
more social aspersions to be heaped on the sport. However, many, including
Fleischer, felt that since Liston was the legitimate number one contender, he
ought, in all fairness to athletic merit, to be given the chance. Second, liberalism rears its head again in the guise of the rhetoric of opportunity and social uplift. Boxing offered poor boys a chance to get off the streets and do
something with their lives. This was what Patterson espoused rather naïvely
in his autobiography: the Gene Tunney belief that sport built character,
that, like exposure to art or receiving an education, this sport and sports in
general could make one a better person, a belief still commonly accepted in
some circles. (Ironically, this belief went counter to Ohlin and Coward's belief about delinquent boys and sports as an avenue of upward mobility:
"Studies have shown that some lower-class persons orient themselves toward
occupations in the field of entertainment and sports. People of modest social
origins who have been conspicuously successful in these spheres often become
salient models for the young in depressed sectors of the society. The heavyweight champion, the night-club singer, the baseball star—these symbolize
the possibility of achieving success in conventional terms despite poor education and low social origins. . . . But the dilemma of many lower-class people
is that their efforts to locate alternative avenues to success-goals are futile, for
these alternatives are often just as restricted as educational channels, if not
more so. *One has only to think of the many lower-class adolescents who go into the
'fight game,' hoping to win great social rewards—money and glamor—by sheer physical exertion and stamina. A few succeed, but the overwhelming majority are destined
to fail.* For these lower-class youth there seems no legitimate way out of poverty" (emphasis mine). As former New York State Athletic Commissioner
and amateur boxer Eddie Eagan put it, boxing is "the last outpost of the
under-privileged." That these series of assumptions underscored liberalism
in the early sixties simply reveals the basic Victorian and social gospel origins
of that era's reformistic impulse. If President Kennedy's endorsement of the
fight was inadvertent, then the stylish Harlem congressman and minister,
Adam Clayton Powell, Jr.'s was not: in reference to Liston he said, "I believe
that it is fundamental in our democracy that every man should be given a second chance."

That liberalism and prizefighting was tied together should not surprise
anyone knowledgeable of the history of the sport. As James E. Marlow has
suggestively argued in "Popular Culture, Pugilism, and Pickwick" (*Journal
of Popular Culture*, 1981), boxing, as it developed and reached its early es-

sence in Regency England, was surrounded and buttressed by ideals that were "egalitarian, technocratic, and humanitarian." Marlow considers its egalitarianism the fact that in the early nineteenth century the sport was popular among gentlemen who had spent fair amounts of both time and money to master it. In effect, it brought together different classes of men on an equal footing. Today the egalitarian quality of boxing, which did not exist during the time of bare-knuckle boxing during the Regency, is its division of weight classification and the fact that, unlike other sports, it permits men of all sizes to participate. The technocratic aspects remain the same as during the days of Regency: the sport is both an art and a science. Boxers learn techniques, practice maneuvers, need coaching and expert teaching, as well as special facilities and a special diet. Third, boxing was meant to be humanitarian in the nineteenth century because it replaced the duel, allowed men of all classes to respond to and defend themselves from masculine insult but prevented death (in most instances) because the contest involved no weapons. Nowadays boxing is considered humanitarian because it serves as a psychic outlet for the aggression of the lower-class male as well as an avenue of escape from his poverty, should he prove skilled enough to become a champion professional. In this way, prizefighting mirrors the ideals worshiped by liberalism: egalitarianism (all should be given fair opportunity; self-fulfillment of the individual), technocracy (ultimate progress in bourgeois democratic culture through ingenuity, invention, free markets, participation in political process, competitive jousting of ideas, the professionalization of culture that produced the culture of professionalization), and humanitarianism (eradication of human suffering, poverty; care for the less fortunate; progressive taxes; government entitlements). It is no wonder that professional prizefighting has reached its highest expression in the two most successful, liberal bourgeois democratic societies: nineteenth-century England and twentieth-century America.

And it was just this connection between boxing and liberalism that spawned the classist defenses of the sport by such people as Fleischer and Eagan, as well as the liberal defense of opportunity and reformism by Powell, that opened the door for Liston. Was he not a poor boy who needed a chance? And hadn't he been further victimized and discriminated against by Patterson's ducking him, as the young champion so obviously had done despite the fact that Liston had emerged for some time as a deserving and credible challenger? Hadn't he paid for his crimes? Certainly his supporters thought so. Although Kennedy had nothing to do with Liston's release from prison in the early 1950s (indeed, it was the work of a Catholic priest—of course, one is reminded of Kennedy's own lapsed Catholicism and how it became an issue in the 1960 presidential campaign and the general connection between Catholicism, injustice, and liberalism in the 1950s and early 1960s, running the gamut from the movie *Hoodlum Priest* to the aforementioned *Black Like Me,* which generally praised Catholicism as a progressive social presence in the South—of course, so did atheist Richard Wright in his 1945 autobiography, *Black Boy*), Liston *was* released largely under the assumption that a professional boxing career would reform him. When Patterson, a liberal Catholic, finally consented to the match he, too, began to mouth the rhetoric of opportunity and social uplift in connection with Liston that he had previously used for himself in such publications as his 1962 autobiography, *Victory over Myself.* "Sometimes," Patterson said in an interview shortly before the fight, "many of us get off to a bad start. Liston paid for his crimes. I met him at a boxing writers' dinner and I think he has a lot of good qualities buried within him. Should he be able to win the championship, these qualities will rise to the surface. I think you'd see a completely new and changed Liston." Look what boxing has done for me, Patterson was saying in effect, it might do the same for Liston. (All of this proves, in the end, that Norman Mailer was partly right when he called Patterson "a liberal's liberal.") He was now giving Liston a chance to prove himself and to be a model for the boys of America. He himself had been a wayward deranged black boy who had been healed, cured by competing for boxing honors; the maimed Liston could be therapeutically transformed to respectability. (That Patterson's remarks sounded terribly condescending was not lost on Liston, who responded in one instance to Patterson's drivel by saying, "I'd like to run him over with a truck.")

The fight between Patterson and Liston was supposed to be, for Patterson and for others, early 1960s liberalism's finest symbolic hour, the cross-section and cross-fertilization of two bourgeois myths: the white myth of denial renounced and the door of success and fame thrown open even to the least among us; and the black myth of blacks helping other blacks to rise, a black giving another black a break; and the fact that Patterson had fought, for the most part, white challengers for the title made this latter point quite significant in some quarters of the black community, certainly with Liston himself, who commented once that he thought Patterson was being racist by fighting almost exclusively white fighters. (It was cruelly rumored in some circles that it was only these mediocre white fighters whom Patterson could beat.) That this symbolic moment took place in the context of whites watching two black men trying to beat each other's brains out is both an essential expression of the irrationality of masculine contest and the sort of essential contradiction of good intentions and ignoble actions that the conjunction of American liberalism and American racism can produce; it is the typical American dilemma of the conjunction of good faith and hypocrisy. It might very well have turned out as everyone hoped if Patterson had won or had even been competitive. Liston won so easily that virtually all of white America and some segments of black bourgeois America were forced to think about not only the sheer volcanic force of the rage that was buried in the black underclass that Liston represented but the absolute inadequacy of liberalism and its rhetoric of opportunity to address or even comprehend the reality of it.

There was something about Liston that brought to mind the sheer rebellious depravity of Bigger Thomas, a character who, in his murder of the rich white girl, Mary Dalton, was defying opportunity in a novel that was obviously meant to be a critique of white American liberalism. Liston's effortless fury did not seem simply to resist bourgeois cure but virtually to belittle it. The title did not change Liston; he became the most hated champion since Jack Johnson; only Ali from 1964 to 1970 would exceed Liston as a publicly disapproved champion. In Liston's case, to paraphrase soul singer James Brown, opportunity won't change you. (Still, liberalism remains enthralled with its own cant word, "opportunity," and actually liberal activists enshrined it as a government office in 1964: the Office of Economic Opportunity created by the Economic Opportunity Act; and we encounter the Wizard of Oz–type hokum of the government dispensing opportunities in much the same way it dispenses patents and land leases. Liberals still talk about opportunity today; it's a way of saying down-and-out people ought to be given a break. They ought to indeed.) If the public discovered in the Emile Griffith–Benny "Kid" Paret welterweight championship bout that took place eight months earlier that one man could beat another to death over the issue of having his masculinity maligned, it discovered in Liston-Patterson that one man could, with cunning cruelty, effortlessly beat another in an open act of ridiculing of the opportunity he had been given. When Liston put his arm around the smaller beaten Patterson at fight's end it was one of the most condescending gestures in boxing since Jack Johnson flashed his golden smile while whipping white hope Jim Jeffries to a pulp in Reno, Nevada, in 1910, a kind of mocking masculine insult and a thumbing-the-nose at the audience in one sweep. Indeed, Liston's strength was made all the more pointed by Patterson's weakness. The fight was not merely a test of character for Liston but a test of manhood for Patterson. "I'm a man," Patterson said, in response to Liston's prefight taunts. "Any man can say he'll beat me, but no man can say I'm afraid of him." Patterson was a young champion—at that time he was the youngest man to win the heavyweight title, beating Archie Moore for the title in 1956 as a mere lad of twenty-one—and largely unproven (much like President Kennedy), having fought few fighters of any real worth. So in Patterson's mind, whatever else he symbolized in this drama of bourgeois liberalism, whatever else was at stake, what was most deeply personal for him that was being risked was his sense of masculine self-esteem. There have been few fights in American history—only the Jack Johnson–Jim Jeffries fight in 1910 and the Joe Louis–Max

Schmeling bout in 1938, both racially mixed fights, come to mind—where the personal honor of one or both of the fighters and the larger political and social issues they both represent have been so inextricably bound.

But if doubts existed about the worthiness of Patterson as champion based on his ability and youth, then it was an age of young cultural figures being scrutinized and measured in just that way by the public. It is perhaps because of Kennedy's own youthfulness that questions of foreign policy and national destiny and his own manhood and sense of personal destiny became so intricately interwoven. During the Kennedy era the country seemed more deeply *moved* by timocratic rhetoric than at any other time in the last fifty years. The Peace Corps was one public policy result of such rhetoric, the manned space program another; both were fostered by Kennedy. William Rust wrote the following in his *Kennedy in Vietnam:* "The Laos negotiations [Kennedy backed off a military intervention in Laos in 1961 and pursued a diplomatic solution] and the Cuban fiasco [the failed invasion that became known as the Bay of Pigs] raised doubts about Kennedy's leadership ability. Domestic critics charged that he lacked resolution in dealing with communism." It was just this sort of criticism, in which Kennedy's manhood and national policy seemed so intricately linked, that probably led to his aggressive stance during the Cuban missile crisis and his commitment to South Vietnam even after the assassination of the corrupt Diem and the impossibility of holding together an entity known as South Vietnam. Nor is there any evidence, despite Ted Sorensen's protestations, that had Kennedy lived he would have pursued a Vietnam policy markedly different from that of Lyndon Johnson. Kennedy no more wanted to be the first American president to lose a war than Johnson. (Kennedy may have thought that his youthful good looks and appealing image as war hero would have made it much easier for him to sell the war to the public. Certainly, the liberals and intellectuals would not have turned against him as quickly and relentlessly as they turned against Johnson, who, they felt, after all, was never really one of them but a rather boorish Southern hick.)

(One example of Kennedy's sometimes crude and immature sense of masculinity: Herbert S. Parmet in *Jack: The Struggles of J.F.K.* discusses how Kennedy could not understand Adlai Stevenson's appeal, particularly with women. Commenting on the subject to one congressional friend, "a bemused Kennedy said . . . 'he must be a switcher.'")

Norman Mailer was right, too, when he called Liston "Faust," for it is plain that Patterson desired to be *free* from his neurosis in order to be himself while Liston desired to be *empowered* by his psychotic image to be nothing but himself. Patterson-Liston was the first modernist fight specifically or sporting event generally in the era when black males began to overrun boxing and became a growing presence in a number of other popular American sports. It was the first prizefight between two blacks where the differences in personality and temperament, outlook and morality, were crucial to the public and crucial to the outcome of the fight. For the first time, two black men actually became distinctly unlike *selves*. They were charged political entities as a result of their differences, competing both literally and symbolically in a public arena.

SUBTEXTS

It is interesting to note that two of the principal writers of the early sixties, and two of the principal exponents of forms of intellectual liberalism, Norman Mailer and James Baldwin, both wrote about this fight: Mailer's "Ten Thousand Words a Minute" for *Esquire* and Baldwin's "The Fight: Patterson versus Liston" for *Nugget*. The articles appeared in March 1963.

Ironically, the relationship between Baldwin and Mailer, the two hot young male writers of the period, during these years seems to have taken on the overtones of a prizefight. The book by W. J. Weatherby that deals with their relationship has an adversative title: *Mailer versus Baldwin*. Mailer once said he was so angry at Baldwin that "I almost slugged him." And Baldwin said, "Norman and I fight too much. I don't even know what we're fighting about, you know." Baldwin, describing meeting Mailer in France, uses images associated with street fighting ("The Black Boy Looks at the White Boy"):

> I had heard of him, he had heard of me. And here we were, suddenly, *circling around each other*. We liked each other at once, but each was frightened that the other would pull rank. He could have pulled rank on me because he was more famous and had more money and also because he was white; but I could have pulled rank on him precisely because I was black and knew more that periphery he so helplessly maligns in "The White Negro" than he could ever hope to know. Already, you see, we were trapped in our roles and attitudes: *the toughest kid on the block was meeting the toughest kid on the block* [emphasis mine].

Mailer's essay is by far the more complex, largely because boxing means something to him while it meant nothing at all to Baldwin. Mailer's essay is also three times longer than Baldwin's. In essence, Mailer's essay is nothing more than a series of more or less virtuosic interpretative chapters about all the things a writer can possibly conjure up to write about a major prizefight: other writers of various sorts, the roles of the fighters, the setting, the training of the fighters, other fights, the fight itself, the aftermath. For Mailer, the focus of interest is, finally, always himself as he candidly feels that he is far more interesting than any of the people he describes, largely because he has the ability to describe people who cannot describe themselves. It is the uneasy possibility that his descriptions mean little or nothing to the people he does describe that creates the tension in the essay and drives Mailer to insert himself so shamelessly, in such an exhibitionist way, at the essay's end as he tries to usurp Liston's limelight at the latter's postfight news conference.

Mailer returns, as he always does in any essay he writes that involves race—and all of his boxing essays involve race because they all involve blacks—to his basic position about blacks, which he first expressed in "The White Negro" and reiterated as late as 1975 in his book on the Foreman-Ali fight entitled *The Fight*. A small portion of black outlaw, pathological experience becomes the essence and core of the black experience itself, although no evidence of either a sociological or psychological nature exists to support that the urban black hustler is the distillation of black American life. In essence, what Mailer is fascinated with is the invention of the male as rogue, as picaro-adventurer; and not only does he wish to observe what for him is a kind of spirituality in others, notably blacks, but he feels himself to possess this spirit as well, to be a rogue and outlaw. For Mailer ultimately sees blacks as his salvation, as his protection against not only a white, civilized life, but the end product of that life: a white, civilized death; this essay, like so many of his others, is filled with images of disease, particularly cancer and insanity, and their corrosive power, their plaguelike existences as curses, lesions upon the white man's life and culture. "[Mailer] still sees us as goddamn romantic black symbols," Baldwin said in conversation. "We still haven't been granted ordinary human status, the right to go to the bathroom. Until Norman sees us with no more romanticism than he views Jewish storekeepers, he'll never understand or be on to what's happening, *really* happening." What informs Mailer's vision is the intellectual assumption that Patrick Brantlinger describes in *Bread and Circus:* "Luxury undermines empires, which is another way of saying that civilization leads to the death of civilization." Mailer obviously believes that civilization leads to the death of itself. His fixation with disease imagery, diseases that he feels are a result of modern civilization and its way of death, so to speak, is proof of that. But Mailer also believes that blacks symbolize something like an antiluxury element in American life. He believes this for two reasons: first, because the lives of blacks have been, literally, hard, full of tension, and insecure; second, because blacks, having been shut off from white civilization, are not really civilized at all. What fascinates Mailer is not sports—a subject that apparently, beyond boxing and bullfighting, did not interest him a great deal—but the escape from the white, civilized death wish. Ironically, Mailer was drawn to sports such as boxing and bullfighting as a kind of life-force because the participants risked death in such a primitive and utterly astonishing way that it made the acts of living and dying mean something. And the blackness of boxing reinforced not simply its primitiveness (which it surely did) but the sheer poeticism of its paganism, the sense of its being not only before but beyond Christianity and its repression. For Mailer, boxing is the expressive rebellion against the modern civilized world's claim on the individual; against the nightmare of mass annihilation there exists only the lone virtue of an individual and individualized death.

The circus, to Mailer's mind, was the only antidote to the poison, the nausea, to borrow his term, of Christianity and civilized life, to its psychosis of being against the body and the ego. And boxing was the most profound celebration of the male body and the male ego in all the Western world. Boxing as circus was the ritual, the teaching sign of how man should learn to approach his death. In his way, Mailer was absolutely right; clearly boxing "belonged to the tradition of the humanist . . . it belonged to his ability to create art and artful movement on the edge of death or pain or danger or attack. . . ." Ironically, it is at this point, when Mailer is his most sentimental, his most neurotically masculine, his most neurotically white, that he approaches a kind of profundity: he does believe boxing to be an aesthetic and even a form of morality; and, most important, he does, no matter how confusedly, believe blackness to be aesthetic and a morality as well, which means he believes something more radical, perhaps more expansive and daring, than either Liebling (for whom boxing is not an aesthetic; only the act of appreciating boxing is) or Baldwin (for whom blackness is not an aesthetic but a condition). "The one weakness in Jimmy's [Baldwin's] vision," Mailer said, "is that he doesn't believe that there are whites who constructed their own moral universe by identifying with the rights of the Negro." But it is more than that: Mailer has constructed his own sense of himself by identifying not simply with the rights of the Negro but with the Negro's darkness.

Baldwin, in his article, which is not nearly so heady about boxing because Baldwin so disliked it while being completely bewildered by it, wrote about his preference for Patterson, "I just felt closer to Floyd." Baldwin, indifferent to sports, thought the young champion was the handsome boy saint. ("And we watched him jump rope, which he must do according to some music in his head, very beautiful and gleaming and far away, like a boy saint helplessly dancing and seen through the steaming windows of a store front church.") Patterson may have been Baldwin's handsome boy and Mailer's liberal's liberal ("The worst to be said about Patterson," Mailer wrote, "is that he spoke with the same cow's cud as other liberals . . . 'introspective,' 'obligation,' 'responsibility,' 'inspiration,' 'commendation,' 'frustrated,' 'seclusion'"), but he was also an ascetic and a devout Catholic, which reminds us that Patterson's quest for freedom was simply to find a new

kind of denial. (Liston sought desire, sought only to want what he wanted.)
In this sense, Patterson, oddly yet plainly, stands for a liberalism that was
quite distinct from that which Baldwin espoused in his commercially successful novel, *Another Country,* published in January of 1962, about eight
months before he met Patterson. (Baldwin may have been more than a little
disappointed when, on first being introduced to Patterson, the fighter could
not place him. Perhaps he had hoped to have been recognized as the young
firebrand black writer who had just set the literary world on its ear with his
latest novel.) We might call Patterson's a bourgeois, natural liberalism, and
Mailer's and Baldwin's an aesthetic, modernist liberalism. In the novel,
Baldwin wishes to explode the categories of black and white, heterosexual
and homosexual. As Norman Podhoretz explains in his essay on the novel,
the book asserts that anything that comes between the individual and love is
evil and must be done away with. Moreover, the book also preached the pri-
macy of the self. Podhoretz is half right when he states the message of the
novel, "a form of the standard liberal attitude toward life"; the first part of
the message about the individual is bourgeois, natural liberalism, and is
quite standard since the inception of bourgeois society; but the second part of
Baldwin's message about the self is aesthetic, modernist liberalism, which is
largely a post–World War I occurrence. It is especially the last portion of
Baldwin's message that found a vast popular audience in the 1960s. But this
was not quite Patterson's message although he too, like all Americans, believed in the individual and love. But Patterson, Catholic that he was and is,
did not believe in the self, and he certainly did not believe in the antinomi-
anism that Baldwin and Mailer preached.

Patterson was to attack Muhammad Ali vehemently in the mid-sixties,
an attack that was certainly to make him no longer the darling of the liberal
elite. But such an attack should not have surprised liberals; it was the out-
growth of all Patterson had said earlier. Indeed, Patterson was attacking Ali
in much the same way liberals had always attacked conservatives: Ali's ideas
were backward and they were not rational. Bourgeois liberalism could not
accept the undeniable moldy nature of its pronouncements. In short, the
liberal's misreading of Patterson was to prove as shortsighted as his or her
misreading of Liston and the upward mobility–reformism of American professional sports. And this misreading was largely the result of the growing
discomfort liberals felt with standard bourgeois liberalism, its sources and its
aims. (The central point here is desire, and so we return to Liston again: as
the sixties went on, Patterson fell into disfavor with liberals because he did
not want enough; Ali was loved by the liberals because he wanted more. Patterson wanted mere acceptance; Ali wanted transcendent worship. Patterson
wanted admiration; Ali authority. As I said, Mailer was only partly right:
Patterson was a liberal's liberal but he was also a liberal's conservative, which

is precisely what anyone who espoused bourgeois, natural liberalism by the mid-1960s became.) Of course, it must be remembered, too, that by June 1967 Ali had been convicted in Houston of draft evasion.

This mad conservative Puritan had, ironically and inadvertently, ushered in a new, more self-consciously radical phase of liberalism. And what makes this all the more complex is that the new, radical liberalism was, in fact, nothing more than a more intense articulation of the aesthetic, modernist liberalism of the self of Baldwin and Mailer. Ali did not become the prince of liberal politics; he became, in a kind of wild contradiction, the prince of liberal aesthetics. In the age of "black is beautiful," Ali ("I'm the prettiest") became the most beautiful of all blacks. In the modernist age of the self beyond the individual, Ali had become, merging the tragedies of Jack Johnson and Paul Robeson by combining both a black physical presence and racial political utterance into a spellbinding saga, the most self-conscious black man in history.

So we know that Baldwin's sentimental beliefs in homosexual and interracial love—the idea that if people (white, principally) were free to make love randomly across both sexual and racial lines they would be cured of their pathological behavior (racism and sexual repression)—mirror Mailer's sentimental beliefs in the hip, the Beat, masculine derring-do, and the aesthetic morality of blackness, all of which figure in his essay on the fight. What all of this means is that liberalism of aesthetics in the early 1960s was partly a kind of masculine sentimentality, or worse, a cult of sentimentality about masculinity. (In an era, paradoxically, where liberalism was the symbolic release from denial, women were horribly denied and belittled. What better symbolizes this than the women's clothing of the period—cone-shaped bras and spiked heels—the rise of *Playboy* magazine, the lonesome death of Marilyn Monroe—another major cultural event of the sixties connected with John Kennedy.) What else but masculine sentimentality could explain Kennedy's endorsement of Liston as a challenger for the crown when Liston's ties to organized crime were common knowledge and when Kennedy's brother as attorney general was supposed to be conducting a war on racketeering?

And here lies a tale worth telling: Robert Kennedy had made a reputation for himself as something of an organized-crime buster. His 1960 book, *The Enemy Within,* the cover blurb of which read, "A crusading lawyer's personal story of a dramatic struggle with the ruthless enemies of clean unions and honest management," tells the story of Kennedy's career as chief counsel for the Senate Select Committee on Improper Activities in the Labor and Management Field, which was largely the story of his confrontation with the Teamsters Union and Jimmy Hoffa. An interesting episode recounted in the book is the July 1957 trial of Jimmy Hoffa on charges of illegally possessing government documents and bribery. Kennedy tells (quite disparagingly, it might be added) how the jury of eight blacks and four whites acquitted Hoffa largely because Hoffa was seen very favorably by the black community and his lawyers took advantage of this during the jury selection process. Hoffa also hired Martha Jefferson, a black woman attorney from California, as one of his lawyers. She may have been hired merely for show, as Kennedy suggests, but she was a very good criminal lawyer and had a very successful practice in California. Joe Louis was also present throughout the trial. (Louis married Jefferson in 1959. Kennedy is incorrect when he implies that the marriage failed. Indeed, had he not married her, the last years of Louis's life would have been a great deal unhappier than they turned out to be. She provided him with a home and a stable environment as well as freeing him from the relentless harassment of the IRS. Martha Louis stayed with Joe until his death from a heart attack in 1981 and times were often trying: Louis suffered more than one mental breakdown, was addicted to cocaine, had affairs with other women, one of which produced an illegitimate child that Martha Louis adopted as her own, and was generally neither a good father nor a good husband.)

Kennedy writes:

> I have often been asked why we did not subpoena Joe Louis to Washington to tell under oath why and how he came to attend the trial of Jimmy Hoffa.
>
> To me, Joe Louis emerges as the most unfortunate figure in this whole case.
>
> When we looked into his connection with the Hoffa trial, we learned that it was Paul Dorfman, a friend of Hoffa with contacts in the boxing world (as well as in the underworld), who had made the arrangements with Truman Gibson of the International Boxing Club for Louis's appearance. (Gibson is presently under indictment in connection with the boxing scandal in California.) We learned that Barney Baker, Mr. Hoffa's roving "organizer" and ambassador of violence, had arranged for Louis's hotel reservations in Washington.
>
> Walt Sheridan went to Chicago after the trial to question Joe Louis. The former fighter was a lonely figure. Walt found him in a third-floor apartment, sitting in a chair and reading a newspaper, with both the radio and the television going. While he was there, Louis's former manager Julian Black, whom Louis made and who owed Louis everything, appeared at the ground floor doorway and called up to him. Louis went dutifully.
>
> Joe Louis had been one of my heroes when I was a small boy. I had requested Walt to ask for the former champion's autograph for

my son, whose name is also Joe. At the end of the interview, Walt made the request.

Louis said: "I'll give it to you for his son, but not for him. Tell him to go take a jump off the Empire State Building." I understood.

I do not believe that Joe Louis was aware of the seriousness of what was being asked of him when he came to Washington. He has made great contributions to this country. And he has been used again and again over the years by a long list of people he has encountered. Jimmy Hoffa simply joined that list.

All these feelings wrapped together is why Joe Louis wasn't called as a witness.

The passage reveals two things very clearly: that Robert Kennedy knew very well about the connection between labor unions, organized crime, and boxing. (One of Sonny Liston's jobs for the mob was as a union thumb-crusher and labor goon.) So one would have thought the Kennedys would have vehemently gone on record as being opposed to the 1962 championship fight between Liston and Patterson because of Liston's well-known and frightening mob connections. But the passage also reveals why the Kennedys never opposed the fight. Kennedy began to wax sentimental about Louis the childhood hero who had "made great contributions to this country," the poor ignorant black who continued to get used (and presumably screwed) by those around him. Kennedy's perception was a gross misunderstanding of Louis, who never felt as though he was used by those around him (and in some sense he gave as good as he got in the who-used-whom business: with the brief exception of his fling as a professional wrestler, Louis never worked a day in his life after his fight days were over; he always found someone who was willing to take care of him). Moreover, in the underground world of professional boxing, the fighters themselves usually feel quite comfortable being around underworld figures. Louis particularly felt no real concern about how the people around him made their money. Kennedy's condescending sentimentality is not only typically male, it is also typically bourgeois elitist. This attitude, coupled with Kennedy's early sixties belief in the connection between delinquency and deprived opportunity, may explain why the Kennedys never said anything about the Liston-Patterson fight.

(Incidentally, not all Democrats felt this way. Senator Estes Kefauver of Tennessee, who beat out John Kennedy to become Adlai Stevenson's running mate in 1956, and who chaired the Senate Subcommittee on Antitrust and Monopoly which, among other things, investigated boxing, starting in 1959, wrote an article about the Liston-Patterson fight entitled "Will Gangsters Be the Real Winners?" which appeared in *Family Weekly* in September

1962, shortly before the bout. Kefauver expressed genuine alarm over the possibility of a Liston victory because he suspected that Liston was not his own man but merely a creature of the mob. The article provides portions of Liston's testimony before Kefauver's committee.)

What else but masculine sentimentality could explain Baldwin's admiration for Patterson or Mailer's sickly sweet fascination with boxing itself? In other words, standard bourgeois liberalism and radical aesthetic liberalism spring from the same impulse; they are simply variants of the same hope. So, in the early sixties bourgeois liberalism and its rhetoric of opportunity bore within it the seeds of its own supersession with the late sixties' aesthetic liberalism. In short, Baldwin's homosexual and interracial love feast, Mailer's fascination with hip, masculine tests of courage and emotional attachments to the underworld and lowlife, and Kennedy's piercingly righteous and symbol-fixated rhetoric of opportunity were all expressions of the masculine sentimentality of early 1960s liberal idealism, a sentimentality that each tried to deny: Kennedy through his aggressive policies against Cuba and Vietnam showing himself to be the unflinching anti-Communist; Mailer through his acceptance of the death-daring rituals of boxing and bullfighting and his shrill condemnation of the death wish of modern Western civilization riddled with disease and decay; Baldwin through his insistent rejection of womanly sentimentality, a rejection that produced the essay "Everybody's Protest Novel," which condemned Harriet Beecher Stowe's *Uncle Tom's Cabin* in the same breath as it condemned Louisa May Alcott's *Little Women,* a condemnation made all the more stridently ironic because of Baldwin's feminized childhood fascination with Stowe's book. As he admits in two different books, *Notes of a Native Son* and *The Devil Finds Work,* published more than twenty years apart, he spent a good portion of his youth raising and nurturing his siblings and reading Dickens and Stowe.

And so we find, at last, liberalism's modern and modernist roots in such diverse but related psychocultural components as character building, upward mobility, the psychic welfare state of self-development, the virtuously psychoanalytic marriage of self-absorption and charity, guilt and innocence, empowerment and freedom, denial and opportunity—the very elements that not only characterize the racial dilemma in America and the menacing but often inept compulsion of our politics but are indeed the interlocking creeds from which it stems, the very elements that give our ritual of professional sports meaning and, finally, provide the matrices of Western self-consciousness and the modernist temper. Ah, how dark the liberal faith that lies in the heart of every American really is.

This should be said in the end, this: Sonny Liston remarked in 1961, after having been harassed from Philadelphia by that city's boys in blue, that he would "rather be a lamppost in Denver than mayor of Philadelphia." Perhaps he, too, had been affected by the liberalism of the times by so pointedly if humorously summing up his fate as alternative choices for the self. Of course, Liston was implicitly right: not only was it far more convenient for him personally to be a lamppost in Denver, it was, at that time, a choice that for any modernist was infinitely more charged with antinomian possibilities.

BATTLING SIKI

The Boxer as Natural Man

*Lonely? You don't know what its's like to be lonely. But I'll tell you:
You're waiting for the bell to start a fight. The seconds are out of the ring
but you're in there with a guy who wants to hurt you and a referee who
can't help you. Boy, you're lonely!*

—Jack Sharkey

*It is impossible to conceive of anything more hideous than the fate of the
unsuccessful boxer.*

—Trevor Wignall, *The Sweet Science*

The tragic African youth—and the pages of boxing history are littered with
the names of tragic men of color from Peter Jackson to Pancho Villa, from
George Dixon to Dick Tiger, from Hurricane Jackson to Sugar Ray Seales—
was born in 1897 or thereabouts in Senegal, then called French West Africa,
and was given the improbably European name of Louis Phal and the equally
improbable boxing moniker of Battling Siki. The name Battling Siki, unlike
Battling Levinsky (Barney Lebrovitz) or Battling Nelson (Oscar Nielson),
unlike even such adopted boxing names as Sugar Ray Robinson and Jack
Dempsey, is more than improbable; it is absurdly implausible. Siki, in the
end, wound up even more displaced than John Lardner's sensitive assessment
of his career implies: "He lived, as a man, without kin or country, roots or
guides, and that, it seems to me, is a hard way to do it." Even more important, Siki lived without a name, any name that possessed any meaning by
pointing either backward, forward, or inward. And that is the hardest way of

all to do it, a true stranger in a strange land. In a very lonely profession that constantly throws its practitioners back on the strength of all their inner and outer resources, Siki had to be the loneliest figure ever to play what Jack London so innocently and tellingly called "the game."

In Orio Vergani's 1930 novelization of the life of Siki, *Poor Nigger* (a work which indicates the degree to which Siki fascinated the white mind during his life and for some time after his death; he fascinated the black mind too, but more about that later), we discover that Siki, parentless, receives his European name, "George Boykin," from a French soldier who also gives him a red shirt as well when, as a small boy, he wanders up to the French army barracks. As Vergani writes later in the novel,

> Once he had had nothing but a dress shirt, and a necklace of red tape round his neck. Where was he? At the village: and he did not even know its name, nor the name of the river and the forest. He had known only the names of the Resident Officer, Sergeant Van Duren, and the soldiers, and his own name, George, which was given to him just because there happened to be a mark like a G on the shirt which was presented to him.

We learn that Siki does not know language at all, that in conferring the colonial gift of a foreign name, the French soldier has given Siki the "garments," symbolized by the shirt, of civilization itself. Vergani writes, "A little naked nigger boy has no pockets. Everything that he possesses he either holds in his hand or keeps tied around his neck." The shirt gave Siki his first pocket, symbolic of his first real lesson in making himself a receptacle by which he can gather and store and eventually evaluate his experiences: it is the equivalent of language, for the pocket symbolizes the possibility of private ownership, private property. It is the greatest, if misused and misunderstood, gift that the European colonialist can give the African boy; it is the gift that takes the boy from being a passive part of natural (i.e., nonwhite, animal) history to being an active part of human (i.e., white) history. It is, of course, all accidental: The letter G becomes his first name by whim, by circumstance and not by design. For Vergani, the African, a tabula rasa, is truly a nonbeing as the letter G or any letter, for that matter. He is simply European whim writ large upon the door post. Vergani's novel is, in fact, the story of how natural history and human history, natural history and salvation history, collide. And that has been, for the most part, the way most commentators have seen Siki's life: as an unfortunate collision with white civilization.

It is no wonder that this singular man, bereft of any identity, was found murdered on the mild night of December 15, 1925, shot to death in Hell's

Kitchen, another body in the gutter in a part of New York where, at that time, such sights, if not common, were certainly not unusual. He was, finally, just a "nigger corpse" as one of New York's finest was reported to have so expressively put it.

Unlike, say, Panamamian Roberto Duran (who stands as an intriguing and instructive counterpoint to Siki, both of them "mad" uncivilized alien boxers on our shores), a famed foreign boxer who has fascinated the Western mind, in particularly the American male mind, in recent years because of the sheer grotesque romanticism of his foreign-ness, Siki had no ethnic selfhood to protect or to use as protection in either France, where in 1922 and 1923 he enjoyed his only moments of true glory as a boxer, or in the United States, where his fall was as precipitous as his rise in Europe had been bizarre. Siki was, in all respects, a deracinated colonial, an absolute marginal man. His language, of course, was French, and he could speak or at least make himself understood in several other European languages as well. According to the *Chicago Defender's*—a black newspaper's—obituary, he could speak seven languages, and Ocania Chalk—a black scholar—in his book on blacks and sports, credits him with speaking knowledge of ten. On the other hand, the *New York Times* article on his death barely acknowledges Siki's ability to speak one. The *New York World,* in its editorial on Siki, said "he could speak nine languages, and his total vocabulary in all, it is said, was 157 words, counting profane expletives." There is something about Siki's essential marginality revealed in this informal debate about what he could speak, as well as something about his essential inscrutability. Siki was, no matter how fluent in speaking, illiterate; he never attended school, which in Western society, in the modern world, conferred upon him an even more lowly status than that of the marginal man: He was a socially dead person, possessing absolutely no place of legitimacy or even possibility in either Europe or the United States, and was treated as such. No wonder he wound up a boxer. What else could he have been?

Although the story of the French actress being so taken by him in his childhood that she made him her servant and took him to France is probably apocryphal (Vergani gives us "Madame Germaine," the rich widow of a French engineer who took "George Boykin" in because she needed someone to replace her "old negro [*sic*] Catholic . . . [who] could do little but listen to the discourses of her mistress and attend to the fire in the kitchen stove. A boy [was] really needed to do the marketing and to hold Madame's sunshade when she went out, and to sleep inside the front door, watchful and alert, like a dog")—it is a fact that by the time he was a teenager he was certainly living in France, tramping around, trying to make a way which is, ultimately, how he became a boxer at the age of either thirteen or fifteen. The story of the rich white woman patron mimics the typology of the benevolent paternalism that characterizes the relationship between black native and white master; it is, indeed, a minimalist's version of the "gift" of colonialism which explains the story's enduring appeal to whites. Siki's orphan state is a radical counterstatement to Roberto Duran's clannishness, so intense at one point that nearly the entire Latin world was his big extended family of fans, who worshiped him as a symbol of the glory of their manhood. One might say that Siki's stay in the West was nothing more than a series of adoptions by various audiences who enjoyed his ability and capacity to entertain, to be a "winning" child, so to speak. Duran was, in the minds of both Latins and Americans, someone's idea and even ideal of a man; Siki was never even *quite* a man but rather a being who *approached* being a man. Duran was primitive; Siki was both more and less than that: he was an inversion and a perversion. When he wore ordinary clothes, there was the shock of seeing the primitive strutting like a trained monkey, an imitation of a man. When he wore the trunks of the boxer, there was the shock of seeing the primitive reduce and distort the primitive dignity of a blood sport. Both Duran and Siki were natural men but not quite the same kind of natural man. This explains why both men's responses to their status as natural men are related but quite distinct.

Siki came to prominence in France after having served with honor in the French army during the First World War; in fact, he was a decorated war hero. As Lardner writes,

> His war record was distinguished; in fact, he is reported to have been the bravest soldier in his outfit, which saw action on several fronts and gave a strong performance generally. For heroism under fire, Siki won both the Croix de Guerre and the Medaille Militaire.

Louis Golding describes Siki's military career more imaginatively:

> "Ah! Louis Phall [*sic*]," the General said as his aide whispered in his ear. His voice drooped like his moustache. He picked up the bronze medal of the Croix de Guerre and fastened it to the Negro's tunic. "France is proud of you, my friend," he murmured. . . . Louis Phall marched mechanically out of the great World War and Battling Siki shambled awkwardly into history.

Siki's legs, apparently, bore the scars of shrapnel wounds. Vergani, although he mentions Siki's being in the war, does not detail his military career nor give any account of his heroism. It was this heroism that probably helped his boxing career; for Siki decided, as Lardner writes, despite having "his choice of a variety of ordinary civilian jobs," to go back to boxing. (What these job offers were Lardner does not make specific; the only job

other than fighting that Siki is known to have had was that of dishwasher in
Marseilles.) He was a fairly good fighter but a lazy one and, until his fight
with light-heavyweight champion Georges Carpentier, a Frenchman and a
war hero as well, he was considered nothing more than a journeyman—an ordinary fighter capable of providing an interesting and sometimes lively evening of diversion. Vergani described his style with some degree of accuracy:

> George's boxing exasperated the critics. They talked about wind-
> mills and street-fighting and a monotonous style. They kept on
> saying that he was ruining a magnificent physique, and that he
> was always obstinately gambling on a lucky break. He was not a
> boxer but a brute. They swore that more often than not he could
> not even see his opponent, and that he went on hitting at shadows
> in the hope that one of them contained a body. His punch was ter-
> rible but easily foreseen, his tactics were ingenuous and he wasted
> his breath in constantly jumping about from corner to corner. He
> expended ten times as much energy as was necessary.

The *New York Times* put matters more plainly in its obituary:

> With virtually no knowledge of ring science he displayed a will-
> ingness to take punches and mix it that made him popular.

And Louis Golding was flat-footed in his bluntness:

> Big, strong, and ugly, there was a terrific power in those long,
> pendulous arms of his which could be unleashed with devastating
> effect when he was roused. Skill and science were beyond the scope
> of his limited intelligence, but many a slogger has risen to the
> heights of the game.

Carpentier, at the time of the fight with Siki, was the most famous athlete in France. His knockout loss to Jack Dempsey on July 2, 1921, had done
little to tarnish his image, although his failure disappointed many European
intellectuals, including Bernard Shaw, who were under the crazy impression
that Carpentier might win. (Indeed, the Carpentier-Dempsey fight, held at
Boyle's Thirty Acres in New Jersey, ushered in the million-dollar-gate era of
boxing in the 1920s with promoter George Tex Rickard as the leading im-
presario and orchestrator. The Carpentier-Dempsey match was the first boxing contest attended by a large number of women. Carpentier was the popular choice of the crowd; the women were especially impressed by his good
looks.) When Carpentier fought and knocked out Ted "Kid" Lewis in Lon-

don in the spring of 1922, Siki fought in Amsterdam the same night against
an Englishman named Harry Reeve, whom he defeated easily. François Deschamps saw Siki defeat Marcel Nilles in Paris during the summer of the same
year and decided that he was a safe opponent for his fighter, Carpentier. A
French journalist said about the Carpentier-Dempsey debacle, "Georges
should not have fought Dempsey, he is a savage. George is a civilized boxer
who should box his own type." Siki was destined to be Carpentier's second
"savage" opponent, although Carpentier had lost fights to black fighters earlier in his career: to Joe Jeanette and, when a novice in 1911, to the famous
Dixie Kid, real name Aaron L. Brown. Dempsey, a Mormon from Colorado,
was the white western savage of the industrial world (dark and scowling, he
was called), whereas Siki was the dark child-savage of the jungles (black and
ugly, as he was seen). It was an open secret that if the Siki-Carpentier bout
was not fixed, it was at least "expected" by all parties that Siki would lose,
that Carpentier would knock him out in a few rounds. Siki was considered to
be a mere workout and not judged in boxing circles to possess Carpentier's
generalship in the ring. Perhaps it is true that it was common knowledge
that the fight, despite the experts' belief that Siki was not as good a boxer as
Carpentier, was a setup; that would explain, in large measure, why Frenchmen were not terribly displeased with the actual outcome. Fight fans, uni-
versally, loathe fixed fights and like to see the underdog win occasionally. It
convinces them that boxing, like all sports, disposes of its laurels in much
the same way that fate disposes luck in gambling: capriciously but demo-
cratically.

Golding describes the first encounter between the two fighters after
they entered the ring:

> Siki, his great black torso writhing with muscles, stared across at
> the Champion from under jutting eyebrows. The enthusiasm and
> the gigantic applause that had greeted Carpentier's entry had al-
> most stunned him. The idol of France, with his dazzling white
> skin, his fine profile, the detached contemptuous indifference of
> his handshake, destroyed Siki's confidence completely. The man
> was like a god . . . the impact of his primitive mind turned Siki
> from a swaggering figure into a badly scared coloured boy.

This, like most of Golding's accounts, is undoubtedly an exaggeration, but
Siki may have been intimidated, as a good many challengers are, by a very
popular and confident champion. (Duran, at the height of his powers, terri-
fied many of his opponents simply by staring at them. Sonny Liston and Jack
Dempsey were two other champions who struck terror with a baleful face.)
"The greeting to Georges was ear-splitting," read one account of the two

fighters' entrance, whereas "Siki was virtually ignored." That would be enough to unnerve a good many prizefighters, to be so utterly alone as that. To be a "badly scared coloured boy" was probably not a new act for Siki or any other black fighter boxing a white at that time; it must be remembered that it was not uncommon at all for interracial fights to be fixed in favor of the white boxer, if not arranged between the two managers of the combatants, then between the officials judging the fight. And it must be remembered that, when he fought Carpentier on September 24, 1922, in the Buffalo Velodrome in Paris, Siki was the first black fighter to fight for a championship of any division in seven years. It had to be, whether Siki was consciously aware of it or not, a momentous and even overwhelming occasion. He had to be thinking that he could, with some luck, become the first black champion of any division since the days of Jack Johnson.

Accounts of the fight differ in some minor details but a general consensus would read in this way: Siki did not fight well in the first three rounds, being knocked down in the first by a light blow and again in the third by a heavier, more legitimate one. In the middle of the third round, Siki apparently changed his mind about being a mere "opponent." A fit of "aroused innate savagery" suddenly surged in Siki, according to boxing historian Nat Fleischer. Golding writes of the fight, "His ugly, ape-like features were twisted with hatred; his teeth were bared in a savage snarl of anger. The black column of his body fell into a crouch, instinct with the savagery of a man-eating tiger." Vergani describes Siki's aggression as "the primeval savagery of his race, dormant since the dark and distant centuries." In any event, Siki proceeded to beat Carpentier all over the ring until the sixth round when, having knocked down Carpentier with a series of terrific blows, he became entangled with the fallen fighter's feet and fell himself. The referee immediately declared Carpentier the winner on a foul: His opponent had tripped him. This decision was not greeted with much relish; in truth, it was greeted with rage and disdain and, later, the decision was reversed by a boxing commissioner and Siki was rightfully given his victory.

The most vivid and probably most trustworthy account of this fight is provided by the black American prizefighter Bob Scanlon, in Nancy Cunard's anthology, *Negro* (1934). Scanlon was a friend of both Siki and Carpentier and had an eyewitness advantage over many others giving their accounts. The language is explicitly his own:

> So when the fighters was going to the ring a feather-weight by the name of Georges Gayer ask me if Carpentier was in good shape, and I not knowing, thinking him a friend of Carpentier's, I said naturally, No, he has not trained. So he said, Thanks, I'll get

my revenge because I have a grievance against [François] Deschamps [Carpentier's manager] since my match with Paul Fritsch so I am going to Siki's corner. So he did, and he told Siki: now is your chance to become champion of the world as this guy you are meeting is the light-heavyweight champion of the world—just look at the money you will make and the cars you will own and all the houses you can buy with the money you will make, everybody will be crying Siki, the president will invite you to dinner. . . . So Siki seen nothing but dough. So the fight started and Deschamps told me not to get into Carpentier's corner as it might have an influence on Siki so I sat by a neutral corner. Well, the first round Carpentier clipped Siki with a right. Siki went down for a count of 6, so after all feeling run high so I signalled to Siki to get up; being a colored man myself I didn't want to see him beaten in a way like that, so he got up to continue until the end of the round. The second round Carpentier sent Siki to the floor again for 9 seconds. After that Georges got careless and thought he had a cake-walk, to his sad mistake, as when the 3rd round started he began to play with Siki, pulling faces at him. So all of a sudden Siki caught Carpentier with a terrible left hook and poor Georges went to the boards for 9 seconds, and at that moment Siki saw his chance and he never left Georges. He fought him all over the ring and finally in the 6th round came the K.O. It was a left hook that done it, and as it was done in close quarters they tried to claim a foul by saying that Siki tripped Carpentier. So the referee gave the decision to Carpentier on a foul but the great crowd protested so strongly that the President of the Boxing Federation, Mr. Victor Bryer, got into the ring and at that moment you could hear a pin fall. So he said, Me as President of the Boxing Federation, I will not allow this injustice, Siki won fair and square, so therefore I reverse the decision, therefore I give the verdict to Siki. So the applause of the crowd was like a dozen machine-guns rattling, so they carried Siki on their shoulders all around the ring.

This passage, though it does differ somewhat from Benny Green's later detailed account which suggests that the influence of Blaise Diagne, the black Deputy of the Colonies (and, incidentally, a collaboration with W.E.B. Du Bois in the first Pan African Congress of 1 9 1 9), who happened to be present at the fight, was a significant factor in having the referee's decision reversed, indicates the difficulty in trying to ascertain what motivated Siki to win the fight. Siki may have "seen nothing but dough" when told the rewards of being champion, yet he did not fight the first few rounds as if he wanted to win. "For the better part of two rounds," one commentator wrote and all other accounts agree, "[the fight] was a travesty."

Were those rounds merely playacting on his part to lull Carpentier into overconfidence? Siki apparently knocked down Carpentier when the Frenchman had dropped his guard in either a show of bravado or disgust. Or were Carpentier's taunts in the third round what generated Siki's competitive fire? (In the case of Roberto Duran, another foreigner fighting a key fight on alien soil, in his second fight against Ray Leonard, taunting by Leonard made him quit.) It is clear that while the possibility of winning a championship was a spur, it was, by itself, insufficient motivation. Even if Siki were playacting, and there is some plausibility in the idea that he may have been, he did not strike until Carpentier began to insult him. He did not simply wait for the moment when Carpentier was overconfident and wide open for a counter, which opportunity was probably present before the third round; for Carpentier was quite supremely confident before the fight even started. Trevor Wignall described him as entering the ring "untrained, unfit and contemptuous of his black oponent." The admission that he did not train, which was common knowledge, was concrete evidence that he did not think Siki could beat him. Perhaps a fix was on to justify such reckless self-assurance.

The racist comments by most of the white observers concerning Siki's "racial instincts" can be dismissed as arrant nonsense, as it is certainly reasonable to assume that there was sure calculation and strategy behind Siki's actions. Moreover, it is equally possible that he responded when being insulted because he wanted to address, specifically and pointedly, the ridicule of the whites. It seems a reasonable conjecture to believe that Siki not only wished to be champion but that he wished, at some point in the fight, to beat and dominate an insulting, superior-acting white. If Scanlon could feel a certain sense of racial embarrassment of seeing Siki knocked down, why couldn't Siki himself have felt something like this during the course of the fight? In that sense, Golding was right when he wrote about the box-office potential of the fight: "Black *versus* white! The Monster against the handsome idol of all France!" The fight was as political as Johnson's championship bout against Jim Jeffries in Reno, Nevada, on July 4, 1910. Except in this instance the Frenchmen, at the fight's end, "demanded justice for the black man," as the *New York Times* reporter wrote, and so Siki was given the victory that had, at first, been denied him. Perhaps the partisan crowd turned against Carpentier because of his disappointing showing, perhaps because he hadn't trained and now had tried to avoid paying the price by trying to win the fight on a foul. Who can say?

For a time after winning the title, Siki was quite a celebrated figure in France and one could find him walking on the boulevards with various exotic pets, drinking absinthe, "more than is normal in the profession," as Lardner puts it, spending enormous amounts that he did not truly possess and generally having a good time in escapades that must have reminded the French of the early exile days of Jack Johnson when he, more or less, indulged the same fancies. Scanlon describes one incident with Siki:

> So a few days after the fight [with Carpentier] I was going to the gymnasium in the Faubourg St. Denis; at the corner of the Boulevard St. Denis I saw a great crowd of people assembled so a policeman called me and asked if I knew Siki. So I said yes. Well, he said, we don't want to arrest him so go and take him away. There he was with two big Great Danes and a revolver firing it in the air and trying to make the dogs do tricks, so I hailed a taxi and bundled Siki and the dogs in and myself.

It was apparently for doing these sorts of things as well as dressing in a gaudy fashion ("By day, ordinarily, he appeared in a high hat, a frock coat, red ascot tie, striped trousers, spatted shoes, and a monocle."), occasionally stopping traffic with his fantastic cane by pretending it was a baton, and brawling in public, that Siki was called in France and eventually in America "a natural man," "a jungle child," although there is not much that distinguishes him from, say, Babe Ruth or the white American boxer Mickey Walker or boxing manager Jack "Doc" Kearns, all of whom drank a lot, spent a lot, ate a lot, and whored a lot, generally acting like boys who have recently discovered the unutterable pleasure their mouths, hands, and genitals could provide. One writer describes Siki's activities a bit more ominously: "He wrecked night clubs, beat women, got involved in a narcotics ring." Yet, if true, even these doings were, however deplorable, not too ultra for certain celebrities in the twenties. There is even a dispute over interpreting Siki's behavior, since an article published in the *Chicago Defender* shortly after his death described him as "a cultured gentleman, with fine manners and deportment, and dignity beyond reproach." Of course, the *Defender,* a black newspaper, was expected to run articles of this sort, race pride, even when one has to make up the sources of it, being the thing to uplift the mighty race.

Siki lost his title on March 17, 1923, when he fought Mike McTigue in Dublin on Saint Patrick's Day. He had fallen out of favor to such an extent with the French that he could not defend his title there. It was rather like conceding defeat to fight to a decision with an Irish fighter in Ireland on that date. Siki could only hope to win by a knockout and McTigue fought too defensive a fight for that to happen. Wignall said this about McTigue: "Never a good or enterprising boxer . . . he is best described as a high priest of the re-

ligion of defence." But Siki probably would not have beaten McTigue if he
had fought him in New York, Osaka, or Tangiers. He simply did not fight
well. And Siki was never to fight quite as well again, either in Europe or in
America, as he did against Carpentier.

He came to America in September of 1923 in part because he could really no longer conduct a successful boxing career in Europe. He had publicly
testified before the French Boxing Federation that the Carpentier bout was
fixed in Carpentier's favor by his manager, Deschamps. He couldn't prove
his allegation and Deschamps was a very popular and well-liked man, as was
Carpentier despite the loss. Later, Siki was suspended by the Federation for
striking the manager of his man's opponent when he was seconding a fight.
But largely the intrigue that grew up around the Carpentier-Siki fight was
generated by a sudden revulsion on the part of a good many Frenchmen over
the fact that Siki was champion. He was virtually not permitted to fight in
France anymore until he lost the title; and, by that time, he was no longer
particularly marketable as a ring personality.

He fought quite often in America, winning more than losing but generally not distinguishing himself as anything more than an ordinary fighter
with an extraordinary lack of interest in the quality of his performance. His
record in America was 10 wins, 6 losses, 3 no-decisions, one draw, and one
no-contest. He lost his debut fight in America, a fifteen-round decision to
Kid Norfolk, a good black journeyman fighter. This inauspicious beginning
set the tone for Siki's considerably less-than-brilliant American career. Fans
came to see him for a time because he was erratic, which was precisely why
fans had ceased coming to see Duran during his two-year journey through
purgatory after the second Leonard fight. Siki's style was by turns either or-
nately screwball or simplistically crude—he had the amazing ability to throw
punches seemingly while his back was turned to his opponent—and this
made him, well, funny. Unlike Duran during his prime, Siki did not
frighten anyone nor was he held in awe by the public, although Scanlon
writes that he "quit sparring with Siki after a few days . . . he was very young
and strong and very brutal so I suffered a great deal from his onslaughts." Although, like Duran, he had an aggressive style that, according to Nat Fleischer, "was guided by one simple rule—to slug, slug, and keep slugging from
bell to bell, until either he or the other fellow dropped for the count," it was
not a particularly effective style. But if, in the end, both of them were more
aborigine ideals of men than real men, it is because each symbolized an important aspect of the primitive in the modern world: the comic and the dangerous, the clod and the cannibal. For to the mind of the modern world, is
not primitive man by turns either comic because of his naïve ineptitude or
awe-inspiring because of his savagery and pride?

Siki, during his spare time, continued to dress extravagantly, drink heavily, walk around with exotic pets, stop traffic, and brawl in the streets, where his most vigorous training sessions were conducted. (He claimed to have trained on liquor and late hours and it is acknowledged that he was never in good condition for any of his American fights.) "It is characteristic of some boxers that as they lose their ability in the ring, they swing their fists more frequently outside it, as a sort of blurred insistence on the claim that they are as good as ever," writes Lardner. It is a sign that a professional fighter has become at least somewhat unhinged when he begins to fight in bars and gutters for free, returns to the venues where, as a boy and youth, he learned the instincts and rudiments of the manly art. No sane boxer would remotely consider, no matter how severe the provocation short of actual physical endangerment, fighting in a common street brawl: it is felt to be degrading, foolish, and dangerous. One might say, of course, that Mickey Walker, a popular fighter at the time, was noted as a street brawler, having fought his return bout with middleweight champion Harry Greb in front of a nightclub on the same night he lost the first one with Greb in the ring, and having punched out, in Popeye fashion, half the members of a college football team in a hotel room. Although these episodes have their comic overtones, it must be remembered that Walker, by his own admission, was an alcoholic during these days and engaged in these fights while in a drunken state.

Siki's career was going downhill: he lost to Paul Berlenbach in March 1925 (the headline in the *New York Age,* a black newspaper, says it all: "BATTLING SIKI LETS PAUL BERLENBACH BEAT HIM IN MADISON SQUARE GARDEN BOUT") and he was disqualified for clowning in his fight with Joe Silvani in August. There is some confusion, depending on which record books one consults, over the last days of Siki's career: He lost either to Lee Anderson on November 13 ("razzed because of his clown antics," according to the *Chicago Defender*) or to Young Marullo. On November 27 he drew with Frank Kearns in Syracuse and on December 4 he lost to Jack Burke in Brooklyn. Siki had no money and he was deteriorating physically as a result of not keeping himself in any kind of condition. He kept getting into trouble with the police. As late as December 9, 1925, just one week before his murder, the *New York Amsterdam News,* a black newspaper, ran the following headline: "MONSIEUR BATTLING SIKI CONTINUES TO RUB ELBOWS WITH THOSE DEAR GENDARMES." There were indications that Siki might even be deported. Siki gave the impression in the last two years of his life, which he spent in the United States, of being used up like a broken-down thoroughbred; he seemed a Dostoevskian jade. One could sense that something was about to happen to him.

Perhaps the most intriguing aspect of Siki's life was the discussion of the significance of it as a result of the way he died. The views held by blacks were more complexly wrought than they appeared on the surface. Siki was, according to a writer for the *Chicago Defender,* "the victim of a white man's civilization"; that is, "the career of Louis Phal, known throughout two continents as Battling Siki, was a striking commentary on the hypocrisy of the white man's civilization." These statements are not particularly clear in any sense except that they were probably fueled by a flood of general rage or dismay about things racial in the United States at that time. Moreover, the same article asserts the prevailing view of the white press that Siki "was a child of the jungle." (Although this distinction must be noted: black commentators did not ever liken Siki to an ape or any other animal, as white writers commonly did. These degrading comparisons were made about many black fighters, including Jack Johnson, and in the pre–World War II accounts of Joe Louis. It was especially inevitable with Siki not only because of the times but because he was an African; as historian Winthrop Jordan writes, "If Negroes were likened to beasts, there was in Africa a beast which was likened to men. It was a strange and eventually tragic happenstance of nature that the Negro's homeland was the habitat of the animal which in appearance most resembles man." This explains, in part, scenes that occur in two of the most popular American novels written in the early twentieth century: Thomas Dixon's *The Clansman* (1905) and Edgar Rice Burroughs's *Tarzan of the Apes* (1913). Burroughs's work gives the reader two scenes where apes appear to be on the verge of sexually assaulting a white woman—Jane Porter when rescued by Tarzan escaped "a fate worse than death," the reader is told—and in both one wonders if the villains are apes or black men or darkness and chaos made anthropoid. In *The Clansman,* when Gus, a black man, rapes Ben Cameron's sister, he is described as if he were an ape. So the association between black men and apes was not only on the minds of white male writers but a very dominant image in turn-of-the-century American popular culture.) The *New York Amsterdam News*'s article on December 23, 1925, a few days after Siki was killed, seemed willing to dismiss him in a surprisingly patronizing way:

> The "Jungle Boy" has moved on—his going speeded up a little by two shots in the back of unknown assassins. And now that he is gone, the wonder is not at his going, but the length of time it took him to go. Siki survived dozens of brawls, numbers of encounters with the police, and the World War, any one of which might have brought him to his end.
>
> Siki challenged civilization, civilization accepted his challenge, they fought a good fight, and civilization won.

Its editorial in the same issue elaborated this position:

What a monstrous fellow was this Battling Siki, who has just been bumped off in so lamentable a fashion! Here was the brute primeval, musing on him, one could conceive him as the ancestor of the whole human race. . . . But he had the soul of a god . . . We have had a walking image of our beginnings among us and did not know it. Let us praise and admire ourselves. If we had such an ancestor, we had something of which to be proud.

It is unclear whether the pronoun "we" used at the end of the article was meant to refer to all of humanity or to blacks. If the former, then the effect of the piece is clearly meant to be satirical; if the latter, then the piece becomes a strange, ambivalent effort at finding sources of racial pride, of reclaiming Siki from white ridicule and belittlement, not by redefining him but rather by reabsorbing the already standard definition of him. This is the sort of cultural revisionist assertion that most black publications of the time, understandably, were obsessed with making. What is unfortunate is that the nature of the revision is so modest, so timid, being more quaint than seriously engaging.

Subsequent articles in the *Defender,* the black newspaper most fascinated by Siki, make clearer the source of black rage as a specific and protest-oriented interpretation of Siki's life begins to emerge: "Siki dared to demand his just rights as any other so-called white person in this country," was a statement in one article published on December 26, 1925, a week after Siki's burial, although there is no evidence of Siki's ever having done this or having any sort of political awareness of himself. He did, it is true, receive a Muslim's burial, as it was learned that he had apparently practiced Islam, but not very much of a political nature can be made of this, although American blacks may have been very impressed by this as it was played up quite a bit in the black press. The title of the quoted piece says everything: "SIKI MISUNDERSTOOD AND MISJUDGED BY AMERICANS; WAS LINGUIST, SOLDIER, BOXER." Siki could not join the pantheon of acceptable, bourgeois black heroes: Douglass, Allen, Washington, Du Bois, James Weldon Johnson, Forten. Much the same sort of thing was done in some black newspapers to reconstruct the reputation of Jack Johnson during his salad days some years earlier—he was a musician, knew foreign languages, etc. The editorial in the same edition makes the interpretation even plainer: Siki was not a savage innocent but a political innocent, a victim not of his own primitive background or the mores and demands of the modern world, as the whites asserted, but the more comprehensible victim of racial injustice:

Siki died a violent death and was a victim of the civilization he espoused [*sic*]. His highly eventful career was ended abruptly, almost before he could grasp the significance of things about him. They say he died of too much civilization.

And perhaps they are right. Siki did die of too much civilization—the civilization as dished out to him by white America. His primitive mind could never grasp the vast difference between civilization in the countries of his earlier and happier days, and in these United States. In his home of St. Louis in Senegal, Siki knew nothing of civilization. He lived a carefree, happy life of contentment. The land furnished him and his people with plenty, and he was wise enough to accept without question what was given to him.

In Senegal there was no race problem. In France, whence young Siki spent his childhood days, there was no race problem. He grew to look upon all the world as his kin. He grew accustomed to the freedom that is the heritage of all men. . . . Everywhere he was accepted on his accomplishment in his chosen field.

Then he came to America. On the way over he must have felt a change, but being a man accustomed to freedom of body and soul, he could not realize that the sinister influences of American civilization, encouching race prejudice of the most revolting type, were already taking effect. Being inured to hardships he immediately set about trying to overcome the new ones facing him in this country. But he failed.

There is something deeply disturbing, deeply distressing about this interpretation of Siki, nearly as much as Adam Clayton Powell, Sr.'s eulogy which asked "the people of the civilized world . . . for better treatment of the next mischievous boy of the jungles who comes to live among us." Surely Siki was not a juvenile delinquent. But the racial oppression, if one ultimately wishes to entitle the forces that killed him as such, was, doubtless, of a more ominous and powerful kind than was implied or stated in the *Defender* editorial. Siki was not a wayward boy, nor was he a prelapsarian innocent coming to the New World in much the same way that a slave, fresh from the West African coast, might be thought of as an "unspotted" arrival-turned-detainee. He was an exiled colonial. The irony of the article is that blacks themselves came to believe and to shape the idea that Siki was a natural man. The ironical questioning of primitive culture versus modern civilization is effective to some degree; it is certainly typical of African-American social protest writing, the basic aim of which has always been to reveal the moral contradictions of American culture as being hypocritical, iniquitous, and self-evident. But the naïve assumptions made about Siki's childhood in Africa as "happy and carefree" are unjustified at best. No evidence of colonial life in French West Africa would support this and the assertion is nearly as ludicrous as the opening of Vergani's novel, which describes Negro babies as having "large heads and shriveled legs," with "the black button of their eye the most mobile thing in their whole bodies." But at least Vergani does not make Senegal any less racist an atmosphere than either France or America.

It has always been an unfortunate misconception on the part of American blacks to think that any other group of white folk that blacks anywhere in the world were forced to live with or, more precisely, under, had to be better than the group they were stuck with; thus, the myth that Europeans are more understanding and tolerant of blacks than American whites. W.E.B. Du Bois, as early as 1903, in his *Souls of Black Folk,* showed his grasp of the horrors of colonialism by saying, in effect, that American black nationalists could not hope to find a homeland anywhere in Africa as there was virtually no independent country on the continent. Presenting Senegal and France as being free of racial prejudice not only blunts the satirical force of the protest element of the piece but reveals what is truly a more deeply fixed problem: the inability of the African American, at this time, to understand the scope of the problem of his own oppression by failing to understand the life of his African brethren or the ambiguous and psychologically complicated nature of his own marginal acculturation to American bourgeois standards and the seductive though racist ideals of the modern world. It is clear that long before Alex Haley's *Roots* the African American needed to envision Africa as an Eden, a place where "the land furnished plenty" and where "there is no race problem." Siki as natural man in the black mind is simply the personification of the ancestral myth, the historical greatness that emerges from living in harmony with nature. That is, it is a historical greatness only inasmuch as it is a seduction for the modern Western world. If, for the white mind, Siki as natural man was either the beast out of the jungle or a "Black Candide, thrown suddenly into the thick of the best of all possible worlds, and found society both violent and larcenous," then for the black mind, Siki as natural man was the Adam the African American felt he never had, he was what blackness was imagined to be before the coming of the impurity of the white man and the modern world.

At last, one is not surprised when Nat Fleischer, great boxing writer, founder of *The Ring,* and sympathetic liberal in matters of race, simply throws up his hands in the end and writes that Siki was "the most fantastic, most incredible creature the boxing world ever has known." But the *Defender* editorial merely rephrases the same sentiment, which is not an analysis of Siki's tragic innocence but a gloss of the African American's own willful innocence: Siki was the most fantastic and incredible innocent American racism has ever slaughtered. The horrible realization that never occurs to the blacks of the day is that America and the modern world, far from wishing to kill Siki, would have loved to have kept him alive forever. His presence as a socially dead yet culturally prominent figure was comforting, a positive proof of the correctness of their own asumptions about the world. He was the ideal sign: prophecy made self-evident.

Nobody knows who killed Siki and, suffering from a namelessness that afflicts so many victims in the modern world, nobody really cared very much. One wonders if his wives really cared, what they felt about him. He was married to two different women at the same time in different countries, which made him either a bigamist or a polygamist depending on how one looks at it. One wife, a Dutchwoman named Gertrude Amphier or Appletern, bore Siki a son. Incidentally, both Vergani in his novel and Golding in his book, which purports to be nonfiction but seems highly colored, give episodes of Siki's relationship with white women. In Vergani, Siki is a sexual innocent, presumably a virgin, who "knew little of women" when he is seduced by the wife of his first manager: ". . . the discovery that the world contained this secret of white warmth, living and submissive, and so white that he could see it, even in the dark, merely by the reflection of the moonlight, this gentle warmth that one only feared to hurt. She was white, she was white, something inside said to him: white as the day, as the line of the horizon, as the under part of a bird's wing . . . he leaned his forehead upon her warm shoulder, and murmured, 'Mistress . . . mistress' . . . For this was the only word of love he could find" (ellipses mine except following the word "mistress"). Golding was more general: "the young African, with his simple and brutish mind, was lonely. He would stand at street corners and watch the white folks with a puzzled intensity. Young girls passed by, laughing gaily, and he would hover near them, fascinated by the scent of their dazzling white skins, like a bee drawn by the honey in a flower. They ran from him with a thrill of terror, he was so physically repulsive." Later, after Siki beat Carpentier and became the toast of Paris, Golding writes, "He was a strutting gorilla in a fantastic loud suit, glittering with diamonds. Mincing by his side, or hanging on his arm as he entered an expensive restaurant, would be some delicate Parisian blonde, scented and sheathed in silk and with dazzling white skin. Why not? Wasn't he the Champion of the World?" There may be some accuracy in the description provided by Vergani and Golding—Siki may have been impressed with European women simply because they were white and he may have thought them to be superior to him—but much of it seems more about the white male obsession concerning relationships between white women and black men. Siki was, from all accounts, blessed with a magnificent body and he was also a champion athlete. He was also not nearly as ugly as white commentators at the time said he was. (There is a boyish whimsy about his face that probably would have made him quite appealing to a woman of any race.) His attitude toward women would have been no different than one would reasonably expect from a successful athlete. He was a very emotional and unpredictable man, so it is probably safe to say that his sexual relationships were stormy ones. His second wife, Lillian Werner, described as "an octaroon" by the *New York Times,* was from Memphis, Tennessee, and was living with Siki when he died. She said he was killed over a dispute about a $20 loan. He was nearly stabbed to death just a few months before he was shot, although the wound must not have been too severe as he was able to return to the ring just a few weeks after the incident. He was, it would appear, hanging out with a tough crowd in tough dives and speakeasies.

"Deprivation of identity," writes Erik Erikson, "can lead to murder." It can also lead, as in the case of Siki, to a special sort of victimization that can lead one to being murdered. It can be ascertained what Siki was to both the blacks and whites around him, but what is more important is what Siki was to himself. What was he to himself beyond being a boxer, a trade he worked with, in oxymoronic terms, a desperate indifference? Being both an African and a boxer, Siki represented in the minds of both whites (European and American) and blacks a series of, to use a phrase, negative capabilities, all of which revolved around the modern world's unease with and attraction to sensuality and orality. Siki was a black man and a boxer, a socially dead person in a socially disreputable profession, so he garnered the double attraction of being the personification of a double taboo. He was symbolic of warmth, indolence, ease of manner and gait, and sexuality because he was from some place that was understood only as being a tropic or a jungle, which meant that it was the landscape of lotus-eating, the landscape of human beings who remained forever something like fetuses, undeveloped mentally and all appetite. (Vergani captures the atmosphere of Senegal more accurately than most at the time; for him it was a sort of wasteland, a desert, which is, in fact, closer to what Senegal and West Africa generally is like, a demanding landscape.) Siki's essential sensuality was emphasized even by white racist writers who thought him to be an ape, for the ape was not an animal in the white mind but the unleashing of sensual drives. It is, therefore, not surprising that these same writers should constantly mention the muscularity of Siki's body. Even the *New York Times* in its obituary seemed obsessed with Siki's great frame and with the need to undercut or belittle the power of its magnetic presence, to make it a castrated body: "The autopsy also revealed that Siki, for all his magnificent physique, was suffering from adhesions resulting from pleurisy and from a general anaemic condition." (These findings are not surprising considering how much Siki drank.) And to think of Siki's appetites is to think of oral gratification through eating, through sex, through talking (since Siki was not literate). Siki was, in symbolic terms, the "not Me" writ large in the Western mind but he was also symbolic of the body and darkness (i.e., the dark body, its interior being dark and mysterious, and the major diseases of the time—the flu, TB, and cancer, being those of white fluids or masses of cells that weakened that body), and thus was thrust into the very center of human consciousness. Is this ultimately what whites meant when they would patronizingly compliment a black by saying that he or she was "white inside"? (Peter Jackson, the great black heavyweight of the late nineteenth century, comes to mind right away as someone who was always complimented in this way by white sportsmen.) Is it the tragedy of the black in the Western world that within the dark body there rages a disease of consuming whiteness that will ultimately kill its host?

This still does not answer the question of how Siki saw himself: as Man Friday, Sambo, or Caliban, the secretly deranged dark men of the modern world? It is, of course, a question that is impossible to answer and, after all, the deranged dark man of the Western world as we have come to understand him is a white invention. If Siki was deranged, it was perhaps something quite apart from how the white mind had categorized blackness in the past. One black fighter, Gypsy Joe Harris of Philadelphia, once said, "I'm scared. I been scared all my life. . . . I even became a fighter 'cause I was scared." Adam Clayton Powell, Sr., in his eulogy of Siki, said, "To the group he represented we say beware of his example." But what group did Siki represent? Being an African, he did not truly represent black Americans in the end. And if he is to represent Africans of some variety, it is not clear, being the exile that he was, how he does so. Siki was, finally, alone. To imagine Siki being as alone as he was, one must think that he was afraid too, and being a prizefighter, that most lonely of professions, was, paradoxically, the way for a very frightened man to come to grips, from time to time, with that core within himself that makes him afraid by confronting someone who is just as lonely and afraid as he is.

WORKS CITED

Bromberg, Lester. *Boxing's Unforgettable Fights*. New York: Ronald, 1962.

Burroughs, Edgar Rice. *Tarzan of the Apes*. New York: Ballantine, 1983.

Chalk, Ocania. *Pioneers of Black Sport*. New York: Dodd, Mead, 1975.

Dixon, Thomas. *The Clansman: An Historical Romance of the Ku Klux Klan*. New York: Triangle, 1941.

Erikson, Erik. *Childhood and Society*. New York: Norton, 1963.

Fleischer, Nat. *Black Dynamite: The Story of the Negro in the Prize Ring from 1782 to 1938*. Five volumes. New York: C. J. O'Brien, 1938–1947.

Golding, Louis. *The Bare-Knuckle Breed*. New York: Hutchinson, 1952.

Green, Benny. *Shaw's Champions; G.B.S. and Prizefighting from Cashel Byron to Gene Tunney*. London: Elm Tree, 1978.

Jordan, Winthrop. *White Over Black: American Attitudes Toward the Negro, 1550–1812.* Baltimore: Penguin, 1973.

Lardner, John. *White Hopes and Other Tigers.* New York: J. B. Lippincott, 1951.

Scanlon, Bob. "The Record of a Negro Boxer." *Negro: An Anthology.* Ed. Nancy Cunard. Newly ed. Hugh Ford. New York: F. Ungar, 1970.

Vergani, Orio. *Poor Nigger.* Trans. from the Italian by W. W. Hobson. Indianapolis: Bobbs-Merrill, 1930.

Walker, Mickey. *Mickey Walker: The Toy Bulldog and His Times.* New York: Random House, 1961.

Wignall, Trevor. *The Sweet Science.* New York: Duffield, 1926.

Various issues of the following publications: *The Chicago Defender; The New York Times; The New York World; The New York Age; The New Amsterdam News; The Ring; Time; Newsweek.*

THE ROMANCE OF TOUGHNESS

LaMotta and Graziano

Interviewer: Why don't all men eat bull's balls? Why aren't they twice their weight in platinum?
Mailer: Because very few people are ready to receive them.

—Norman Mailer, "The Metaphysics of the Belly"
from *Cannibals and Christians*

I wanted to kill them all.

—Rocky Graziano

I go to the Fifth Amendment on the grounds my answer may tend to incriminate me.

—Jake LaMotta, testifying before the Senate Subcommittee
on Antitrust and Monopoly in the summer of 1960

This is what Norman Mailer called Joe Frazier in his 1971 *Life* magazine account of the first Ali-Frazier fight: the war machine. There, it was almost a term of masculine endearment, Mailer's homoerotic kiss on the sweaty brow of sheer indomitable will. Mailer got the order of deterioration wrong when he spoke of fight metaphors in his essay: *first,* they go military, *then* they go sentimental. His own use of them is an example of that. Nothing could be more strangely sentimental and filled with longing than his description of an imagined bout between Frazier and Rocky Marciano, the last great white heavyweight; and nothing could be more military than the smashing of

Tonka toys: "If those two men had ever met, it would have been like two Mack trucks hitting each other head-on, then backing up to hit each other again—they would have kept it up until the wheels were off the axles and the engines off the chassis." So boxing really is analogous to industrial culture confronting itself in fits of masculine nihilism: how the machine can be made primitive again; how, instead of denying the aboriginal origins of the Western self, it might, in fact, reinvent them.

One can think of at least four great fighters—Marciano, Jack Dempsey, Harry Greb, and Roberto Duran—to whom Mailer would have applied the phrase "war machine" with the same poetic and aesthetic implication and nuances as he does to Frazier: "... hard and fast, a hang-in, hang-on, go-and-get him, got-him, got-him, slip and punch, take a punch, wing a punch, whap a punch. ..." But applied to Jake LaMotta it can only be a term of mere fact, a description of a state of mind and not the design of the mythic heroic. It becomes the meshing of the wheels of an individual dementia with a collective, cultural dementia. LaMotta was not a hero; he was and is at best a survivor. He fought savagely in the ring not because he wanted to impose his will upon his opponent, nor out of respect for his opponent's skill; he fought savagely because he did not want his opponent's will imposed upon himself and because he respected nothing but feared everything (the dilemma of everyone living in the modern industrial world: having to bear the faith of the absolute inability truly to believe anything): in short, he suffered from the disease of dread.

LaMotta was one of boxing's few real war machines, if it is possible to apply that term to a man, especially a boxer whose one and only appeal, after all, is that he is a nostalgic reminder of the atavistic humanity or *human closeness* of war before the march of technology. (Indeed, one might say that war is and has been nothing but the march of technology, that war has been nothing but the history of making machines out of human thought and human bodies. In essence, war and peace are now expressed in the scientific imagination of men. War is, alas, not science fiction but the romanticism of science.) It is the very irony of the metaphor "war machine," the strangeness of naming an athlete after an invention that his presence and profession are supposed either to supersede or predate, that is indicative of the complexity of our society's, of the modern industrial world's, response to boxing, to the primitive made flesh in its midst. We have no idea, when we watch a boxing match, whether we see our past or our future, or merely a contemptible, insignificant present. We have come, in our eroding irony, as Mailer calls Frazier "the human equivalent of a war machine," to saying "war machine" when we mean something like "natural man." It is further complicated, this strange ontological business about the fighter as war machine, by the fact that we do not respond to all boxers who would bear that appellation in the same way.

Rocky Graziano, a contemporary of LaMotta, is a case in point. He was a war machine who, in an odd counterpoint to LaMotta, wound up a very interesting kind of hero.

Simply put, the horrific story of Jake LaMotta cannot be examined alone; it must be considered side by side with the story of his old friend, Graziano; for if LaMotta's autobiography is the darkness of the ethnic boy's quest for fame and success, Graziano's is the same tale told in the light, the horrid made happy, how Edgar Allan Poe met Horatio Alger. Graziano was the bad boy who became one of the most beloved athletes and personalities in America during the forties and fifties. LaMotta was the bad boy who simply became a hated figure, booed at his fights, denounced by sportswriters. Here, for instance, is an excerpt from *Newsweek,* July 24, 1950: "Last week Jake (Bronx Bull) LaMotta insisted, with a fearsome scowl: 'I like people.' But he wasn't kidding himself about how people like him. In a year's time, he knew, he had become more hated than any two other boxing champions." This is from *New York Times* sports columnist Arthur Daley: "Jake LaMotta, who falls several light years short of qualifying as one of nature's noblemen. . . . He wouldn't add to the decor of a room even if stuffed and placed over the mantelpiece." And this is from *Time* magazine, June 27, 1949: "Most hard-boiled boxing fans thought the I.B.C. [International Boxing Club] deserved to lose a lot more than $4,000.00 [in promotion] for allowing the likes of LaMotta to have a shot at the title." LaMotta was, in the end, the bad boy who grew up and became a bad man.

The similarities between Graziano and LaMotta are striking; yet they have become the Cain and Abel of American popular culture. Both were born in 1922 in New York City where they were raised (LaMotta in the Bronx, Graziano on the Lower East Side); their fathers were both immigrant Italians; they both wound up in reformatories where they met (Graziano's stay in these youth institutions was longer and both men were to have penal stays of a very serious nature: Graziano was imprisoned by the United States government during the Second World War and given a dishonorable discharge from the Army, and LaMotta was to go to jail after his ring career ended on the charge of promoting prostitution); and they both, for short periods of time, became middleweight champions. Both have had autobiographies (LaMotta's *Raging Bull,* published in 1970, and Graziano's *Somebody Up There Likes Me,* published in 1955) made into major, Academy Award–caliber films starring two of the finest and handsomest leading men in Hollywood. (Paul Newman portrayed Graziano in the 1957 film *Somebody Up There Likes Me,* directed by Robert Wise, and Robert DeNiro, a bit grimmer looking, played LaMotta and earned an Academy Award for best actor in 1981 for the Martin Scorsese film *Raging Bull.*) They were both rugged, unpolished fighters, "war machines" who were unable to beat the most polished, consummate boxer of their day, Sugar Ray Robinson. LaMotta lost five of six fights with the Harlem Flash, as the white newspapers called him, while Graziano was kayoed in the third round the only time he met Robinson. And both men became, after their ring careers, second-rate comic actors, Graziano succeeding at this more than LaMotta.

Yet the titles of their autobiographies and the books' coauthors reflect the vast difference between the men: *Raging Bull,* cowritten by LaMotta's childhood friend Peter Savage (real name: Rick Rosselli), who is, indeed, a major character in the text since the basic plot is about how two male friends broke up and, after a period of years, found each other again, implies the angry, the heathen, the sexually threatening (LaMotta, in his sequel autobiography *Raging Bull II,* tells how he wanted at first to call *Raging Bull,* "The Ice Pick and the Gloves," and how co-writer Rick Rosselli, influenced by the then current film *Becket,* wanted to play up the male friendship angle). *Somebody Up There Likes Me* was cowritten by professional writer Rowland Barber, hired simply to do a job—and a very competent job at that, since the book nearly won the Pulitzer Prize the year it was published; the title refers in a colloquial manner to the grace and favor of God and providence or perhaps to the grace and favor of the American power elite in the business of sports who can promote some athletes by their own strange designs of inscrutable salvation. In short, the title seems to say, "Aw, ain't I a lucky stiff," the sort of folksy modesty that appeals to Americans: because it is so obviously corny, therefore, it must be, by right, sincere. Consider the story Graziano tells in a later book, *Sombody Down Here Likes Me Too,* of how he and Barber serendipitously came up with the title for the autobiography:

> One day when we working [*sic*] on remembering things he says, "You know, Rocky, nobody every fought the way you did to make it to the top, and nobody ever had so many obstacles thrown in the path."
>
> I says, yeah, I guess somebody up there likes me. The guy jumps up like I just stuck him a needle and he's yelling, "That's it, Rocky. That's it."
>
> That's it what? I want to know, and he says, "You just give me the title for the book—Somebody Up There Likes Me."

So the way the title came to be is an example of the magic of the title at work—indeed, is an example of what the title means: the luck of being an American, one supposes, or the sort of luck that could occur only in this country. LaMotta's title indicates he never stopped being in the public mind of seeing himself privately as a sort of psychopath; Graziano's psychopathology was simply a phase that was the result of youth and poverty—he did finally settle down, for instance, to marry his childhood sweetheart, nearly, if not quite, the girl next door (she was Jewish) and stayed married to her; LaMotta had a very stormy marriage to his second wife, Vicki, and has not stopped marrying women yet—and the final result of Graziano's psychopathology was that he became a comic actor on the Martha Raye show, a major pitchman in commercials in New York, and the inspiration for a new generation of actors in the fifties such as Marlon Brando (whom Graziano knew well for a time), Paul Newman (with whom Graziano worked closely when making the film about the fighter's life), and James Dean (who had originally been signed to play the lead in the bio film). All of these actors, in effect, wound up aping on screen the kind of mannerisms of the misunderstood, antisocial youth that Graziano had cultivated in real life: Brando in *The Wild One* and *On the Waterfront;* Newman in *Somebody Up There Likes Me* and *The Left-Handed Gun;* and Dean in *Rebel without a Cause.* Graziano became a kind of pathetic pop gestalt of the bad white urban kid turned establishment hip. Graziano had the ineluctable charm of an unlettered but gallant rogue; LaMotta, telling dirty jokes in strip joints, was the profundity of the devil.

To examine the lives of Jake LaMotta and Rocky Graziano is to answer one question stated two different ways: not what is the metaphysics of the belly, to borrow Mailer's phrase, which is close to the point, but what are the mechanics of the male belly or, put another way, how did the champion become not *deus ex machina* but *homo ex machina?*

JAKE LAMOTTA: AMERICAN CALIBAN

> *You taught me language, and my profit on't is,*
> *I know how to curse.*

> —Shakespeare, *The Tempest*

> *"Write a book? Are you nuts? I'm lucky if I can spell my own name!"*

> —Jake LaMotta to wife Vicki, *Raging Bull II*

Jake LaMotta, once the fighter and the ex-fighter whom a score of years ago most people loved to hate, who was called by sportswriter Jimmy Cannon during his active days as a fighter "the most despised man of his generation," is now on the threshold of becoming a kind of "grand old man" or "good gray poet" of American boxing. He was, in 1985, thirty-one years after he retired from fighting, elected to *The Ring*'s Boxing Hall of Fame, a mere twenty-three years after the election of Marcel Cerdan, the Frenchman LaMotta beat decisively to win the middleweight title, and a mere fourteen years after the election of Graziano, who lost the middleweight title in his very first defense. "Some of the guys in the Hall of Fame," LaMotta said in an interview, "I could have fought two or three of them on the same night. And beat them." So, for him, this election was less an honor than an overdue tribute of justice to a fighter whose worst sins in the ring racket were his part ownership of two boxing clubs—Jerome Stadium and the Park Arena—when the rules of the New York State Athletic Commission forbade a fighter from having a financial interest in a boxing club; and throwing a fight to a young black light-heavyweight named Billy Fox, who was being backed by the mob, in exchange for a title fight. The cynical may think this to be shrewd business practice among thieves or what else is new. LaMotta was also connected with gangsters Blinky Palermo and Franki Carbo, who, along with Jim Norris, millionaire businessman, ruled boxing through the fifties.

In recent years, LaMotta has come a long way from being the overweight ex-pug who beat his wife and was supposedly a pimp for a fourteen-year-old girl, an allegation that resulted in his serving six months on a Florida chain gang. During the summer of 1985, LaMotta awarded the ESPN heavyweight championship belt to Jesse Fergueson, winner of the cable sports network's boxing tournament. In the early and mid-sixties, LaMotta found it difficult to attend a prizefight, much less to be recognized at one. Whenever the crowd knew that LaMotta was there, he was roundly and rudely hooted out of the joint. He could not set foot in Madison Square Garden, the scene of some of his greatest fights, for many years. When Madison Square Garden gave Ray Robinson a retirement party in 1965, four former middleweight champions Robinson defeated to win the crown on various occasions—Randy Turpin, Bobo Olson, Carmen Basilio, and Gene Fullmer—were invited. LaMotta—the man who fought six incredibly tenacious bouts with Robinson and who, in effect, made him famous—was not allowed to participate.

Martin Scorsese's adaption of LaMotta's successful autobiography to film is very much like the one that LaMotta envisioned about his life when he wrote his book: a grainy, surreal reworking of *The Champion, Body and Soul,* and Robert Wise's *The Set Up* and *Somebody Up There Likes Me,* the black-and-white classics of this genre of film noir:

> Now, sometimes, at night, when I think back, I feel I'm looking at an old black-and-white movie of myself. Why it should be black-and-white, I don't know, but it is. Not a good movie either, jerky, with gaps in it, a string of poorly lit sequences, some of them with no beginning and some with no end. No musical score, just sometimes the sound of a police siren or a pistol shot. And almost all of it happens at night, as if I lived my whole life at night.

As a petty, violent criminal during his teenage years, as a main-bout fighter during his young adult years, and as a nightclub owner and comedian during his retirement, perhaps LaMotta could be right in his observation (it is certainly perversely funny enough, to say that one's life is like an amateurish home movie), perhaps he has lived his whole life at night. There is certainly a great sense that he lived a good part of his life in a kind of unrelieved darkness, culminating in the beginning and the end of his autobiography with the darkness he endured while placed in solitary confinement in a boys' correctional institution and in a Florida prison (the whole life becomes the hole life), a darkness greater than any moral or intellectual benightedness that may have afflicted him: it was the darkness of being a war machine, embattled forever in a compulsive way, fighting his family, his opponents in the ring, legal and illegal authority, schools, churches, his wives, and finally himself. LaMotta engaged in a war against life itself, raging like a crazed Manichean, raving that only the devil could have made this world in this way and made him to live in it. Boxing historian and former *Ring* editor Bert Sugar put it succinctly: "To LaMotta, fighting was a personal statement." Of what? one wonders.

Many think that LaMotta was one of the few true psychopaths ever to fight well professionally. I wonder about that and feel it more accurate to say that LaMotta was one of the few truly obsessed Manicheans ever to fight well professionally. It remains my contention that the true psychopath cannot become a good professional fighter because he is unable to delay gratification over a period of years to train hard in expectation of achieving the goal of champion. The recent example of Texas middleweight Tony Ayala, a brilliant prospect several years ago but now serving thirty years in prison for rape and robbery, is a good one to illustrate the point. Ayala was clearly psychopathic. In other words, there is very little difference, in one sense, between climbing the corporate ladder and working to become a champion athlete: one must constantly place carrots of motivation before one's face. Indeed, in either instance, the very idea and ideals of motivation and achievement become a religion that consumes the soul. That is why, finally, the professional athlete is as obsessively boring a personality as the average, single-minded hustling stockbroker, burrowing with all the grace and tenacious Faustian drive of a mad squirrel toward the epiphany of some truly profound irrelevancy. Historian Allen Guttmann was right when he called sports "one of the most extraordinary manifestations of the Romantic pursuit of the unattainable." For what is sport but the traumatic romance where complete rationality of aspiration meets the utter irrationality of act? Or perhaps it is the other way around: irrational aspiration, rational act.

LaMotta's reputation rests in large degree on the fact that the public certainly thought that he possessed a psychopathic personality, that he fought like a deranged man, a man who could kill. As boxing writer Barney Nagler describes him: "LaMotta was an outstanding middleweight renowned for his incredible stamina. He was less than five feet seven inches tall, but his torso was constructed along the lines of a tank. He was relentless in attack and apparently impervious to pain." LaMotta has said recently in a curious kind of understatement that he fought with "that devil-may-care attitude"; perhaps "devil take the hindmost" would be a bit more accurate. Still, in the mellowing of old age, LaMotta describes himself almost as if he were a swaggerer. However, I think it correct to say that LaMotta fought like someone who felt he did not deserve to live. There was desperation, an ugly desperation, in LaMotta's dramas of survival in the ring that somehow must have touched something in the crowds, reminding them of their own private desperation, their own inarticulate fear, their own inchoate rage, that made them dislike him. The fight crowds like the swaggerers-cum-war machines like Dempsey, Duran, Greb and, significantly, Graziano, who I think merits this distinction; they like these fictive psychopaths. But they do not like desperadoes like LaMotta, the bitter Manichean, who seemed so much like a true psychopath. Duran, Greb, Dempsey, Graziano were the stuff of romance; LaMotta was the absence of romance. The demons of Duran, Dempsey, Greb, and Graziano were as thrilling and as unreally heroic as giants and dragons, and they all seemed to bestow upon the crowd the light of the beatitude of male daring. (Think of the Dempsey–Jess Willard fight in Toledo in 1919 or the Dempsey-Firpo fight a few years later, which produced boxing's and indeed all of sport's most famous art work: Bellows's illustration of Dempsey being knocked through the ropes, which appeared in the *New York Evening Journal;* or the first Duran-Leonard fight in Montreal; or the first Harry Greb–Gene Tunney fight when Tunney suffered his only ring defeat and sustained a savage beating; or the last Greb-Tunney fight when Tunney turned the tables and beat Greb mercilessly.) LaMotta's demons were all too real, the virulent visions of madness and masculinity of the lower-class, ethnic-immigrant American boy, and he bestowed nothing upon the audience except his own enormous experience of trauma. In his way, he simply showered the audience with deafening yet silent, barbaric curses. It almost goes without saying, though, that Bert Sugar is wrong; LaMotta was no "throwback to the barge fighter"; he was no primitive, and that subliminal realization on the part of the public made him even more hated. He was the perfect embodiment of the male temperament in post–World War II, industrial society. He was the prizefighter *par excellence* of the modern world.

Of course, LaMotta hated his father and this hatred explains virtually everything and nothing about him. What Italian boy would not hate a Sicilian father, an uncultured peddler and immigrant, a typical "wop" who, naturally, would shame his son because he was so ethnic; a father whose only legacy to his son was an ice pick with the instructions to use it on the kids who bothered him at school:

> He yelled at me, "Here, you son of a bitch, you don't run away from nobody no more! I don't give a goddam how many there are. Use that—dig a few of them! Hit 'em with it, hit 'em first, and hit 'em hard. You come home crying anymore, I'll beat the shit outta you more than you ever get from any of them! Ya understand?"

LaMotta's father beat his wife and children regularly and finally returned to Sicily where he could be, at last, what the son terms "a big man." Many years later, after the father's return to New York, and long after LaMotta's salad days as a boxer, LaMotta, in his second autobiography *Raging Bull II* (1986), describes a meeting between father and son in the father's house. LaMotta, broken and broke, is asking his father for $400 for the birth of his child and the father, in disgust, gives him a ten dollar check:

> "Is this all I'm worth," [Jake] asked, his eyes glued to the check. "ya know, Pop, how soon they forget . . . the good times, the money—all the money I made, and I helped everybody. I supported the whole family. And most of all I helped you. What were you, Pop? What the hell were you but a cheap little peddler? You dragged the family from one slum to another, and pimped me off to fight every kid in the neighborhood. Did ya forget all those nickels and dimes I made you? And this is your answer—a lousy ten bucks. How heartless can ya be? Look at yourself—you're a broken down old man with nothin' but broken memories. . . . What do ya want from me—another championship? I'm an old man, too, now. I come to you begging for help, and you give me a kick in the ass like I was still eight years old. Why did you always hate me, Pop? All those beatings, and for what?" [ellipses LaMotta]

We see that LaMotta's assault on Harry Gordon, the local bookmaker whom for so many years he thinks he has murdered because that was what he read in the papers; this assault, which opens the autobiography, is nothing more than his attempt to slay the father by killing or maiming or cursing all appropriate surrogates. Those surrogates ranged from the godfathers of the mob to the divine in the person of Father Joseph, who introduced him to boxing when LaMotta was incarcerated in Coxsackie, a boys' reformatory:

> One day, just as I was finishing a sparring session, I heard Father Joseph call me.

"Hiya, Dad!" I said.

He made the same face he always did when I called him that and said, "If I've told you once I've told you a thousand times that you don't call a priest 'Dad.' You call me 'Father Joseph.'"

I gave him the innocent look I always did. "Yeah, and I've asked you a thousand times what's the difference and you ain't come up with a real good answer yet."

Concerning the godfathers of the mob, the aforementioned Palermo and Carbo, LaMotta said, "What was I going to do, fight the mob for the rest of my life? This was the establishment. What they say went. I'd been fighting them for four years and where had it gotten me?" Ironically, his revolt against mob control earned him only the nickname of "the policeman": "In boxing a 'policeman' is a top fighter who, for one reason or another, can't get a crack at the title. So the only fights he can get to make any money are with the real tough kids on the way up—the ones the champ himself would just as soon duck." In essence, within the world of professional boxing, LaMotta's revolt against authority garnered him the title of authority in a derisive way. In general, his revolts against authorities of various sorts, which in tone range from the smart-ass to the tiresome to that which is pleaded in a self-serving way, seem only to intensify the reader's feeling of dread, and perhaps LaMotta's own sense of dread as well. None of it ever seems heroic or appealing, although one can never be absolutely sure if LaMotta were not exactly wishing that it were so, hoping that it could be seen and felt that way, as heroic.

We see his discovery, oddly on the night when he won the middle-weight championship, that Harry Gordon is not dead but has, indeed, over the years been one of his staunchest fans. This knowledge makes him lose his *raison d'être* as a boxer in an irony that is so contrived—although I am not suggesting that it is make-believe—it seems almost a master stroke of sick humor:

> I was so stunned I couldn't think of what to say. I couldn't say any-thing. Then, finally, I said, "Harry . . . Harry . . . you're dead. You're dead, you son of a bitch. I saw it in the paper myself! You're dead!" . . .
>
> It was like what I had always dreamed of, that I would get to the top of the heap, and something like this would happen. And right here and right now.
>
> Except it couldn't because here was Harry Gordon, but he was alive . . . and he was laughing at me. I mean really, literally, laughing. . . .
>
> And suddenly I figured I had to get outta there. I thought

maybe I was going nuts. Here was the greatest night of my life and
all I could think of was all the things wrong with my life. . . . I
could see myself on that street in the Bronx trailing old Harry as
he was going home, hitting him with the pipe, pushing him into
that vacant lot, hitting him again, taking his wallet and running
off, throwing the pipe down the sewer, seeing the police car coming. . . . Shouldn't I be happy, out there drinking and having a
good time? Instead of which I was wracked by all this.

And then comes the moment of final assessment: "I think that the moment I
discovered I was not a murderer, I also stopped being a killer in the ring."
We might see this as an ironic maturity on LaMotta's part, that by slaying
the father or *thinking* that when he slayed the father he was burdened with
the instructions of his father forever: attack before you are attacked and respect nothing for fear it will make you a sucker: "I never let go of that ice
pick after that. I carried it with me in a leather case hung on my
belt. . . . Until the ice pick, I was always the kid getting it in the ass. If it
wasn't my old man belting me around, it was these kids after me, or a
teacher slapping me silly—always someone asking me what right I had to be
alive. The ice pick showed me what it felt like to make the other guy as
afraid as I had always been." And he tried to kill his surrogate father, the
other father figure in the form of Harry Gordon, the local bookmaker, by the
very terms of thuglike, primitive protection and aggression that his father
created for him. By discovering that Harry still lives, LaMotta is freed from
his father's instructions, from his father's oppressive self, at last. Harry Gordon's laughter is as revealing as the fact that he is alive: His father, in the
end, had played LaMotta for a chump. He had gotten the sort of left-handed,
self-mocking advice from his father the Invisible Man received from his
grandfather in Ralph Ellison's novel. When he discovers that Harry Gordon
is still alive, his fighting career goes down the drain. As I have said, this explains everything about the man without really explaining anything. It does
clarify that the book's struggle with the heroic is a struggle with the credible, with unreal naturalism.

In LaMotta's statement, "I think that the moment I discovered I was
not a murderer, I also stopped being a killer in the ring," why does he distinguish between "murderer" and "killer"? Or perhaps the question is how does
he distinguish those terms? Does he mean that the moment that he discovered that he was not a murderer in one life, he could not be a killer in another? Is his act of murder something that defines him in his real life, and is
his role of killer something that defines him in his fictive, unreal life? After
all, while he may have thought himself to be a murderer in real life, why
should he think himself a killer in the ring? Despite his uncompromising,

roughhouse style, he never killed anyone in the ring, unlike Ray Robinson, his nemesis, indeed his antithesis, and perhaps the greatest artist ever to don boxing gloves. Robinson killed Jimmy Doyle in 1947 when he defended his world welterweight title for the first time. Despite that fact and despite Robinson's ability to punch harder and more accurately than LaMotta, he was never known as a killer; he was simply and honestly the best boxing stylist in the history of the middleweight division. LaMotta, in fact, had more wins by decisions than he did by knockout, an unusual feat for a middleweight champion. So, LaMotta's role as killer, within his own mind so contingent upon his act of murder in real life, was acknowledging a fictive series of acts in a fictive life. In truth, LaMotta condemned himself or felt himself condemned to the actual darkness, the true darkness of this world by his murder of Harry Gordon; but he was also condemned to the fictive darkness of being a killer in the ring, hated by the fans and fueled emotionally only by the guilt and the rage that he felt made him an actual murderer and fit only to be something subhuman for the public: in short, a prizefighter, the benighted, well-conditioned freak of the modern world. For what is the true freak as Leslie Fiedler describes him but precisely what the prizefighter is: that which "stirs both supernatural terror and natural sympathy"? In the end, how was fighting before a crowd that is, as LaMotta put it, "crazy to see some guy get his brains knocked out" very much different from fighting for survival on the streets? When Father Joseph offered LaMotta boxing as a way out of the darkness of solitary confinement, had LaMotta really escaped the darkness? LaMotta knew the values of the society in which he grew up: "Like I read the old Romans had bread and circuses, we had home relief and boxing." Darkness was everywhere.

But LaMotta also knew the path he was following in the ring would assure that he would be just what he was as a kid: ". . . a bum and I lived like a bum in a bum neighborhood." "So here I was at thirty-five, right back where I was at fifteen—in the can. Except this was worse. Back when I was fifteen, who the hell ever heard of Jake LaMotta? Now everybody in the world knew that Jake LaMotta, once the world's middleweight champion, was a real bum. A first-class bum." He was, at last, the very thing he described his father as being in the beginning of the book: "an old bum" who beat his wife. Indeed, we now see that the prizefighter of the modern world is no longer even the déclassé warrior but simply an all-purpose monstrosity made less hideous by the very mediocrity of his deformities. The prizefighter, like the poor boy, is really a bum (a common term in boxing parlance for the has-been fighter or the fighter who never was). LaMotta's fictive darkness of his fictive life was not a penance for sin but an acknowledgment in his Manichean mind of the necessity of sin in a world where one's survival is contingent upon the perishing of another. In that one sentence about murderer and killer, LaMotta realized that the Manichean struggle is twofold: (1) It is not about the war between light and darkness but about the interrelationship between true darkness and fictive darkness; (2) and it is about the mad series of contingencies that keep human beings alive, certainly without dignity because we are willing to survive at nearly any cost and possibly without purpose since we cannot answer the question, What is the point of surviving at all costs? We realize, in the end, that the biggest irony of LaMotta's career is that rage failed to *empower* him, and that is the only thing a boxer can symbolize in any honorable way, for they are the only reasons—the rage and the symbol and allegory of rage in the ring—that would attract the poor boy psychically to boxing to begin with. Rage merely kept him alive.

I think what may have troubled LaMotta most was not quite the paradoxes he may have encountered but the ambiguities that arose from them. It was not the fact that the terms of his being a natural man-cum-war machine were meant both to honor and to execrate him by turns that caused him dread. What truly distressed and bewildered him was the unfathomable meaning of the simultaneous duality inherent in his being a natural man *and* a war machine. Consider the passage from the autobiography when LaMotta discusses his nickname, the Bronx Bull:

> There was a strange thing about me and the broads. There were times, sometimes months on end, when I'd be impotent. Sometimes I felt I'd go out of my mind about it because it would happen all of a sudden, without warning, and it seemed like no reason at all. I couldn't figure any reason for it, physical or psychological, and then after I was about ready to commit suicide, I'd be all right again.
>
> What made it ironic was the nickname that was hung on me early in my fighting career, and the one that a lot of people can remember, even today, was "The Bronx Bull"—"The Bull of the Bronx." That was because of the way I fought—charge out of the corner, punch, punch, punch, punch, never give up, take all the punishment the other guy could hand out but stay in there, slug and slug and slug. But the Bull, of course, is also a symbol of sexual prowess, the all-conquering male that can handle a whole herd of cows.

The passage resonates with the true alternatives of the war machine; for LaMotta is right: his impotency is caused neither by the physical nor the psychological. It is, in fact, what he is as a physical and psychological being that is caused by his impotency, by the fact that he is, in his words, "a bum." His receptiveness to his father's advice, his street crimes as a youth, his fights in the ring, his life outside the ring as an adult seem quite clearly to have been motivated by that sense, not simply of inferiority (although he thought himself ugly enough) but of true social impotency. The most striking example of this is his rape of Viola, the girlfriend of his best friend, Pete (i.e., Rick). He discovers that the girl is truly what she says she is: a virgin. And his guilt after the act is both predictable and enormous. He apologizes to the girl profusely, then leaves the room and takes a ride in his "fully paid for Cadillac convertible," a sign of his growing success as a prizefighter. Thus, we have a scene where the twin symbols of his manhood—sexual conquest and conspicuous consumption—fail him, are proven illusory, are the matrices of his degradation: "Never in my whole goddamned life had I felt so goddamned bad. Never." Thus, he is caught between the girl who will not give up the goods and the goods that will not give him status: the dilemma of male social impotency.

LaMotta refers to himself as a bum at least a dozen times during the narrative. The cultural implications of the acute awareness of impotency, almost to the point of amounting to self-psychoanalysis, are these: as a natural man, through the very simplicity and rhythm of his actions and desires, he can become, paradoxically, a machine, a contrivance, a programmed wonder, a predictable response to stimuli. LaMotta, ultimately, does not possess the psychotic's excessively high-strung nervous system, but the Manichean's sheer dread of a relentlessly dualistic world, a world that, at length, dehumanizes one's responses by reducing them to an action and its opposite, the strophe and antistrophe of the song of the machine. The bull itself is dualistic in many ways of which neither LaMotta nor those who conjured up his nickname were consciously aware; yet that stuff of universal myth exists relevantly and subliminally, the collective symbols of common human experience: the bull is the symbol of both the sun and moon cults; it is an animal both tame and wild, and its fecundating wetness is that of both the male and the female. So LaMotta was caught between the charge (boxing) and discharge (sex) of his role as the bull, not two related activities but actually two antithetical recreations, so reduced and pressurized by insistent cultural and critical concentration not on aesthetics but on the mere mechanics of performance that the very functions must produce dysfunction. And what is applauded in LaMotta's performance is the windup, toylike ability to respond almost masochistically when stimulated. Punch, punch, punch, take, take, take, screw, screw, screw: what will finally make the poor boy less threatening is when his actions are made more predictable. Here are some comments from sportswriters about various LaMotta fights:

> Not until the ninth round did LaMotta flash any of the bullishness for which he is noted. . . .

Often LaMotta fired his wallops with the piston-like steadiness and precision, while on other occasions when Mitri signified a readiness to step in and trade, the champion flailed away savagely like the Neanderthal man without a club.

Not far from the fragrant Chicago stockyard, the Bronx Bull took a ferocious slaughtering and his courageous tenacity in holding to his feet evokes a certain admiration.

Jake LaMotta, the hard rock from the Bronx, never has been deemed a pugilistic pinup boy. Yet there was something admirable about the way he absorbed Ray Robinson's raking cross-fire the other night.

Or as LaMotta himself put it: "Hit 'em first and hit 'em hard, stayed with me. It was the only good thing I ever got from my father, and later it always seemed to push the right triggers at the right time in my brain." His impotency, which was the cause of his being, was also the humanized response to the pressures of dumb performance. Ironically, inconceivably, and probably unbelievably for LaMotta when he finally became aware of it, the source of his lifelong trauma, being a bum, was also the humanizing solution to his trauma.

LaMotta was hated by the American sporting public because he was precisely the sort of war machine, precisely the sort of natural man that a technological society, a liberal welfare state, could truly produce. He was what the society sought, desired, and deserved; for he was both the extension and the invention of the technological mind and industrial culture, as indeed modern prizefighting since its inception in industrial, eighteenth-century England has been. LaMotta was not the embodiment of passion but rather the sign of the modern world's quest for passion, for a heightened sense of self, through the "base" instincts of survival, war, and sex, through the artifices of game and sport. Of course, in its quest for passion, modern society has only inaugurated a new age of slavery and an age of love of force, a slavery that reduces everyone to the dualistic choices of either/or (a far cry from Kierkegaard and the passionate doubt) and that worships the absolute nihilism of absolute mindless, responsive action, simply a new form of obedience. What was LaMotta the fighter, ultimately? Not a rebel but a clockwork orange: the natural man as robotized instinct. The dream of the clarity of behaviorism—which as a critique of psychoanalysis has its points—becomes the nightmare of ambiguity both for LaMotta and ourselves: Was LaMotta the fighter a feeble protest against death and evil or was he a feeble symbolic reenactment of them? His style of fighting, his anger, and Manicheanism may very well have been his own expression of the rejection of this world as it is, but his entrance into the prize ring was his acceptance of the impossibility of the necessity to escape it. We hated him and desperately needed to see him perform because his trap was our own. We live in a culture that could protest its innocence without truly believing in it anymore, that no longer desires virtue or aesthetics but simply wishes for a frantic escape from boredom; in such a culture the only real quest left is for the outsized emotion of furious passion being playacted in the most dramatic pursuit of the most meaningless possession imaginable: the ephemeral kingship of the hill.

ROCKY GRAZIANO: A WALK FROM THE WILD SIDE

Life is a cinch if you take by the inch;
It's hard when you take it by the yard.

—Nelson Algren, *A Walk on the Wild Side*

That is the mission of the proletariat: to bring forth supreme dignity from supreme humiliation.

—Albert Camus, *The Rebel*

Graziano's autobiography *Somebody Up There Likes Me* is almost twice as long as LaMotta's *Raging Bull* and covers less chronologically—it has to, since the subject of the latter book was a good deal older when he decided to take pen to paper. The difference in length indicates tales of vivid contrast, although both book describe a sordid and disordered male life of the underground. Graziano's books is perhaps the most detailed nonfiction narrative of the education or miseducation of a wayward ethnic boy written by an American with the possible exceptions of the *Autobiography of Malcolm X* and Claude Brown's *Manchild in the Promised Land,* both written by black males who had, one supposes, even more horrors to tell and, by virtue of their skin color, every right to tell them. (As Richard Wright once stated: "We have in the oppression of the Negro a shadow athwart our national life dense and heavy enough to satisfy even the gloomy broodings of a Hawthorne.") The tremendous piles of description of people and places in Graziano's book, descriptions mostly of white slums and youth penal institutions in New York that are heaped upon the pages like bales of dirty laundry might bear witness that the story of being white and poor is horrible enough. But it is the book's huge commitment to description that makes it, ultimately, a less ambitious work than LaMotta's because it is so much less psychoanalytic and less self-aware. *Somebody Up There Likes Me* is the American success story, structured rather like all American autobiographies of the bad youth who finds himself in

young adulthood. *Raging Bull* has no truck with any of that and certainly
never trades in the "only in America" or "I'm lucky to be an American" type
of currency that Graziano never hesitates to take to the bank of unquestioned
loyalty—which because of his dishonorable discharge from the service during
"the good war" he obviously needs to mint, especially during the paranoid
fifties when the book was published—and the stock exchange of good sales.
Raging Bull is a story of utter absurdity. Graziano's is the story of human reclamation; LaMotta's is the story of human waste, the absolute impossibility
of achieving true human reclamation. LaMotta's moral is that we must learn
to live with ourselves. Graziano's is that we can learn to be somebody else.

No autobiography by any fighter has come close to Graziano's in repli-
cating the speech patterns, the slang, the expressiveness of lower-class white
language, not even LaMotta's, which does this sort of thing very well. Indeed, so singular was the feat on the part of Graziano that he was destined
never to repeat it. His second autobiography, *Somebody Down Here Likes Me
Too,* is a shallow, show-biz narrative, written with a new coauthor and filled
with the sort of name-dropping that could be gotten away with if the book
aspired to be nothing more than a poor imitation of a newspaper gossip column. In this book, the zest of the unlettered and informal linguistic leaps
and tale loops of the white underclass becomes simply a zany patois of Brook-
lynese (Bronxese) slang, the nonsense that has made Graziano something of a
character these days because he sounds like a bad Groucho Marx, a Lower
East Side Italian trying to sound like a Lower East Side Jew. In the later
book, Graziano's speech is just a parody of what his speech had been as a
youth, and not a very interesting parody at that. Liberal use of the all-
purpose Saxon intensive "fucking" (as in "You're fucking right" or "You bet
your fucking ass") does not a vital slang make. The glossary at the end, filled
with such words as t'rew, wanna, winta, and nevva, seems as contrived an attempt at something picturesque as Cab Calloway's dictionary of jive that
closes his autobiography, *Minnie the Moocher and Me.* There are two ways to
state an important corollary here: old, self-conscious jive *is* jive, or language
is not meant to be considered cute; those who try to make it so are in immi-
nent peril of being bigger fools than the inadequacies of language make us
all. What Graziano wrote about language in his first book has a great deal of
importance:

> Of all the guys in the Tenth Street mob, I was the one fooled
> around the least with broads. I don't know, I never found it very
> easy to talk to them. In fact it was never easy for me to talk to any-
> body. Unless you come from the East Side and knew me good for a
> long time, you probably wouldn't understand what I said at all.
> Years later, when I had been around a little bit and had to make

public appearances and take bows at banquets, I took more trouble
to talk good. Up until then I didn't really talk East Side or Italian
or anything else. Like one of the sports writers said, I talked pure
Graziano. In the older days I guess it was pure Barbella I talked.

The identity split that resulted from changing his name from Barbella to
Graziano will be discussed later. The essential fact illustrated in this passage
is that Graziano isolated a core part of his being through the speech act,
through his ability or lack of ability with discourse. Clearly, his inability to
talk to anyone except those quite close to him insulated him, made him the
nearly closeted provincial that most urban street boys really are. This was, in
some measure, an act of self-protection, to keep away the unhip outsider, but
it also hindered his sex life and made psychological growth difficult. His
hampered discourse explains, in part, his antisocial behavior as a youth. He
found out that when words could not speak for him, his fists could. But the
passage also indicates that Graziano was self-conscious about his speech from
the time he was quite young. (Growing up in a bilingual household and suffering a bout with deafness as a boy intensified this preoccupation with language and expression.) And he clearly measures his later success when he becomes a main-bout fighter with his adoption of "good" or standard English
to some degree and his ability to talk to people beyond those who live on his
block in the Lower East Side. It is a perfect example of how greatness in athletics serves to mainstream the wayward, ethnic youth always in his imagination and sometimes in real life.

Graziano obviously was a more interesting personality and a more compelling presence on the scene of American mass culture when he was a fighter
and before he so blatantly sold his poor-boy mannerisms and speech as a
packaged commodity to be used as a foil for a talk show host or as the modal-
ity of a convenient "wise" dummy, a low-grade Casey Stengel or Yogi Berra
in comic drag, one might say. But the fact that he was able to sell himself, so
to speak, to sell what he, in essence, was, shows that at some point
Graziano's self-consciousness became a quite detachable persona; that is to
say, he found a way to make people laugh at malapropisms without laughing
at *him*. This method of overcoming an inferiority complex—and throughout
his youth Graziano desperately felt the need to overcome his inability to express himself well and in a way that outsiders could appreciate—is important
in our consideration of his autobiography. He found a way to make those beyond the pale of the ethnic, white slum tribe comfortable with what he was,
comfortable with his tribalness, largely by making his audiences feel superior
to it without really being threatened by it. So it is not such a big jump from
the prize ring to the comic stage. The boxer, the comedian, and the fool have
a great deal in common: to make the utterly humiliated and the utterly taboo

the source of some partial dignity. Read Peter Heller's book, *In This Corner,* a series of interviews with fighters from different eras: retired fighters always sound funny and somewhat sad in what might be perceived as the same sort of honorable way as the vanishing Native American might. Old fighters *sound* funny and sad because they *are* funny and sad.

Graziano's book opens and closes with his last fight, his attempt to win back the middleweight title from Sugar Ray Robinson in Chicago in 1952. He had every right to consider Chicago his lucky town, as he put it; it was there, after all, that he won the middleweight title from Tony Zale in 1947 with a sixth-round kayo. Graziano was thirty now, which meant that he was actually a year younger than Robinson, but he was truly a spent fighter. Those who fight in Graziano's all-out, incensed style usually do not last in the fight game for very long unless they possess an extraordinary iron-man constitution such as Rocky Marciano's or Jake LaMotta's. Graziano belonged and did not belong to that class of white fighters that Mailer described so well in his 1971 essay on the Ali-Frazier fight:

> Okay. There are fighters who are men's men. Rocky Marciano was one of them. Oscar Bonavena and Jerry Quarry and George Chuvalo and Gene Fullmer and Carmen Basilio, to name a few, have faces which could give a Marine sergeant pause in a bar fight. They look like they could take you out with the knob of bone they have left for a nose. They are all, incidentally, white fighters. They have a code—it is to fight until they are licked, and if they have to take a punch for every punch they give, well, they figure they can win. Their ego and their body intelligence are both connected to the same juice—it is male pride.

Graziano certainly had male pride: "I used to think them older guys were really tough. Now I knew that all they had was reputation. I still had the balls. Reputation you can buy for cash, but not balls." And he had the style and the anger:

> All I kept thinking was, *He's opening up.* With every punch he wound up wider and wider, and was a fatter and fatter target. O.K. O.K. Voom! Voom! Blam! He's giving me all he's got and it's nothing worse than I ever took from the cops up in the detectives' room or the screws in the Hole. He can give me all he's got. Just keep opening up, *just keep opening up.* I can take every punch he's got.
>
> . . . every punch I landed, every cut I opened over some guy's

eye, was like a shot of good wine to me. It put springs in my feet
and made me sing to myself sometimes.

But Graziano never had the stamina of, say, a LaMotta. In most of his fights,
he either won quickly or lost quickly. Graziano was surely more intense than
most white fighters but not nearly as durable. And his intensity was great
only when compared to phlegmatic boxers such as Chuvalo, Fullmer, and
Basilio. He was probably no more intense in style and bearing than Mariano
or LaMotta. And it is in this point of style that white fighters seem to differ
from black ones. Graziano gave every impression in the ring of being the
emotional equivalent to jazz drummer Gene Krupa in performance, stamp-
ing and sweating and seemingly possessed by something, if nothing more
than the overwhelming desire to will possession's look. And to black swing
drummers such as Jo Jones and Chick Webb, Krupa was not "cool," he
seemed to be just another "frantic white boy" who had no real style and no
real grace. Styles do make a fight, as Angelo Dundee is wont to say, and with
the Robinson-Graziano bout one wonders if this was just another instance of
the frantic white boy up against the nonchalant black: anti-style versus style
beyond style.

Inevitably, Graziano's style of fighting meant that one is bound to absorb much punishment which tends to tear down not only a boxer's physical
reserves but his concentration as well. Boxing is the sort of game where, after
a certain point, the mind begins to wander, as it does during the sex act.
Graziano was no longer interested in boxing when he made the fight with
Robinson. He *wanted* to be interested in fighting, and he surely wanted to be
champion again. But his mind was on other things, such as what he would
do when fighting became impossible. As he wrote, "I had to stop kidding
myself. I had been through for a long time, but never would I admit it." Besides, Graziano's three fights with Tony Zale had left him with little. Moreover, most experts question whether he could have beaten Robinson even had
he been at the height of concentration and condition. Ultimately, Graziano,
a man with other things on his mind, went into the ring against Robinson
and was knocked out by one blow that was delivered with such finesse, such
utter nonchalance, that one would have been willing to bet the house that
Robinson was surely thinking of something else when he threw the blow.

It was fitting for Graziano to frame his book with his last fight since
this autobiography deals with his youth and his fight career only—
predictably enough, considering it was written a mere two years after the
Robinson fight and there was very little beyond that fight for Graziano to
deal with. But there is another important thematic reason for the book to
open and close discussing the Robinson fight. It seems appropriate for the
poor ethnic white boy to fight his last battle against the poor black boy. All

of Graziano's wanderings in and out of jail and in and out of trouble and courts during his entire youth have finally brought him face-to-face with the only true nemesis he could feel no ambiguity about: the black boy with whom he shares the social workers, the sociologists, the courts, the cops and their brutality, the welfare system, the reformatories, the jails, and the streets. The white ethnic boy's inexorable shadow, his redoubtable double, is of course his most hated enemy; for it is against that black face or those black faces, as the case may be, that he can finally feel some sense of solidarity with something that gives him a sense of worth, that ends his sense of alienation and blind rebellion. Robinson felt something like this, as he writes in his autobiography, *Sugar Ray,* about the prefight introductions:

> Graziano was different. He had fifty-two knockout victories, and damn if Zale wasn't rooting for him. During the introduction at the Chicago Stadium, their bond was obvious. Zale, his blond hair clicked back above his hard Slavic face, took a bow, then strolled over and touched my gloves. He did it quickly, unemotionally, the way hundreds of other fighters had done to me.
>
> When he got to the other corner, he grabbed Rocky's gloves and held them for several moments. Then he made a fist with his right hand and clenched it in front of Rocky's face as he spoke to him. I never learned what Zale told Rocky, but his gesture seemed to be saying, "hit him like you hit me." Whatever he said, Rocky smiled and tapped him on the jaw with a playful left jab.

Robinson remembers nothing as clearly about that fight, not even the knockout punch he delivered in the third round, as he does Zale's blond hair and his hard Slavic face wishing Graziano well. The fight was symbolically the war machine, the white natural man, against another type of natural man, the noble savage made American slick. Fictive psychopathic rage against fictive animal cunning. The white-heated heart of white civilization against the wily (Rine)heart of darkness. Graziano states twice within the space of two pages that he cursed Robinson during the fight: "We clinch. I'm cursing him, every filthy name I can think of. . . . I yell at him, needle him, curse him, but he stays just out of reach of my right." And Graziano has every right to curse at that which symbolizes everything he is not and everything he is, that which he fears and that which he covets. A man as self-conscious about his ability at making discourse as Graziano certainly had to understand the significance of cursing an opponent, particularly a black opponent. He wrote about an earlier black opponent, Billy Arnold, in this way: "He is the enemy. I am going to destroy him. Only his dark figure stands between me and everything that is big and good, everything that everybody says never could belong to me." It is not that Graziano did not feel the same way about his white opponents; it is just that the darkness that black fighters represented was so much more the very darkness that was within him. (It might also be mentioned that Graziano wanted to beat Robinson because LaMotta, his old prison buddy, had done it once, and there was a real sense of playful rivalry between the two men.)

The essence of the Graziano story lies in the fact that he had to change his name. It was the only way he could escape his father and his life of juvenile crime and antisocial behavior. As he writes, "I didn't realize it then, but I realize it now. Every time I got in the ring I was fighting the East Side and I was fighting Rocco Barbella, who come up out of the East Side gutter." This admission means that Graziano has arrived at fairly banal and ordinary wisdom of being a male and a son in this society (or perhaps any other, for that matter). But it is the very commonness of the wisdom that makes the fact that it was so hard earned so impressive and its triteness glitter with a certain lucid profundity: How I got my name, writes Graziano, is how I got my freedom and how I got my living. The autobiography, in effect, answers the two main concerns posed by male autobiography in America since the middle of the nineteenth century: how to free oneself from one's father and create one's own name (Frederick Douglass), and how to make a living with the Yankee ingenuity of exploiting not one's strengths but one's limitations (Henry David Thoreau). The pattern and the meaning of the book become clear; for *Somebody Up There Likes Me,* like LaMotta's *Raging Bull,* is a story about resentment, what Camus called "an autointoxication—the evil secretion in a sealed vessel, of prolonged impotence." And the origin of this resentment is the hatred of the father. Graziano begins his fighting career by changing his name; he is on the lam from the authorities, AWOL from the United States Army, and, ironically, he must adopt the name of someone who is not in trouble: Rocco Barbella becomes Tommy Graziano who becomes a professional fighter, the very occupation that his father had. As Rocco Barbella he remembered that his father wanted the older son to follow in the path of prizefighting and would allow him to use young Rocky as a punching bag. When Rocky finally beat up his brother and freed himself from the beatings that his drunken father, frustrated over his failed career, would initiate, it was meant to be resentment turned to positive use: "I grabbed him under the chin and pulled him back up and smashed him one again. The Future Champion!" The cycle of the positive channeling of resentment (which is, in truth, the real and homely moral of this tale) is finally completed after a long series of petty, violent acts and wars against all nature of authority by Graziano taking his brother's place in the father's hopes and wishes and becoming a fighter (which was truly an instance of turning one's limitations to advantage since Graziano had only a terrific right-hand punch to hold him in good stead in that profession: "I could be a boxer if I wanted, but I wasn't a good boxer and I knew it"). In effect, by becoming a fighter, which his father surely did not expect, Graziano not only freed himself from his father's oppressive humiliation of failure by living out the daydream of every second son (beating the ambitions of both the father and the first son), but he also freed himself of the negativity of resentment. In this freedom, at the end, he could be generous to his father:

> My father—for the first time I begun to feel sorry for him. He only had a taste of what fighting can do to a poor kid coming up out a the streets. Only a taste and then he had to quit and try to scratch out a dollar breaking his back on the docks. No wonder he had his heart set his son should be a boxer. No wonder him and his pals used to sit around the wine jug and fight over the old fights and get drunk and think they're back in the only good days they ever knew.

And it is when resentment becomes, in this instance, a kind of condescending sentimentality, the kind of sentimentality we are all likely to blanket our parents with in order to make their presence bearable, that Graziano is able to think about approaching his father again, which really occurs only when his father dies. So it is apparent from the opening scenes with the Robinson fight to the final scene of the death of the father, that the curse of Graziano's wild youth was not resentment but rather resentment misplaced or resentment unwilling to become sentiment, lush, laden, and leaden.

What makes this autobiography so powerful is its simplicity and its determination not to be what the later LaMotta autobiography turned out to be: the tale of youthful male resentment as psychoanalytic critique of the modern world, the tale of immature dread, fear, and trembling. Graziano also avoids the trap of social protest, something which LaMotta, because of his own dark humor, is a bit more ambiguous about. But it is certainly the sheerest nonsense to propose that the terror on the streets can be ended by selling it as performance in a prize ring, always the self-serving argument of those of the modern world who wish to find some redeeming social worth in the sport without quite having to resort to the idea that it is the only way a poor, brutal, and brutalized kid could make a great deal of money, if he is very lucky. "I had to be a fighter to live this long and keep my place in the world," Graziano writes without irony, and the meaning becomes clear for all of us; for it is the argument of social redemption that the Graziano book ultimately supports and tries to legitimize through the vigorous example of its formidable subject. It is simply just another book—albeit a good one—about the romance of the male belly, about the mechanics of its hunger and the holy excesses of its flatulence. It is a book about the justification of the existence of the male belly and that the growl, the barbaric yawp of resentment, is its natural expression. If we denounce the conditions that make male resentment and create a world of dread, we might begin to foster the idea of the impossibility of male resentment as a constructive expression of anything instead of seeing it as a possible practical alternative of temperament in the culture of bruising.

II

HABITATIONS OF THE MASK

LAWRENCE TALBOT: KING OF THE B MOVIES

(for Lon Chaney, Jr.)

Imagine the difficulty of waking up:
Without shoes on the dark, cold moors, the howling sound,
The rain in a mist, the wet, lank hair, the hot, white face like
The light that kills the moon that kills the civilized;
Waking to face the silly gypsies, a fair rich girl, a bungled life.

Imagine the difficulty of remembering:
Another vaudeville script, the set made of occasional paper,
The unfooled children at matinees, the drunken director, miscasting,
The minstrel makeup that simply makes a beastly nigger of you, Beat
Ravisher madly buckling up the bungled absurdity, the bungled nothing.

Imagine the difficulty of escaping:
To skitter across the wet, sharp rocks; the dogs in pursuit—
To slither into the damp, lightless caves, to stamp across marshes,
O Princes of Faces! The lone howl, acrylic, like an atonal notation
Acknowledging the sleep that lies in the bungled habitations of the mask.

TWO NOTES TOWARD A
DEFINITION OF
MULTICULTURALISM

AFFIRMATIVE ACTION AND THE WORD

*The plight of the Negro in America is not that he is different, rather that he
spends so much time in painful contemplation on the meaning of the
difference. . . . He is more completely American than anyone else in this country,
not because, as some say, he has been here so long, but because the American
culture is the only culture he knows.*

—William Melvin Kelley, "The Ivy League Negro"

Despite all our protestations and wishes to the contrary, questions about
race—those strange spectral hybrids of politics and ethics, morals and economics, superstition and science—unceasingly haunt the American soul and
to this day remain an inescapable subject of conversation. Race has become
for us Americans our own peculiar inscrutable oxymoronic mysticism: a subject we are infinitely tired of thinking about but which provokes us even in
our weariness, even as it depletes us in its boringness. And contrary to what
many people think, especially whites, blacks too are exhausted by the subject; they are simply more trapped by it.

The latest round in this ongoing, comically tortuous, and extremely
self-dramatizing dilemma was the announcement in March 1991 by Assistant Secretary of Education Michael Williams that race-based college scholarships that use federal or state money are illegal. This announcement should
have come as a surprise to no one, as Affirmative Action judgments by the
Supreme Court since the mid-seventies' Bakke and Defunis decisions clearly
disallow such scholarships. Indeed, the conservatives are right: The 1964

115

Civil Rights Act prohibits them. But while everyone, including the "law en-
forcement folks" at the Department of Education, as Mr. Williams called
them, is aware of this proscription, it has apparently been ignored for a number of years even by the Department itself, as it instructed universities and
colleges to carry government-funded scholarship programs.

These scholarships would seem on the whole to be too minor a thing for
the current conservative regime to challenge. Besides, at least for some
people, they seem to have achieved a great deal of social good. (Of course,
that is debatable. It seems the major problem critics have is that these scholarships go, by and large, to middle-class blacks. Never are the poor invoked
so piously as when conservatives wish to trash Affirmative Action as ineffec-
tive, although most authorities admit that the black middle class is an extremely precarious economic group.)

Moreover, declaring race-based scholarships illegal opens the door for
many other restricted scholarships funded with government money to be declared illegal for their implicit "quota" possibilities. Indeed, virtually all
scholarships are given to specific categories of people. If there are a thousand
other categories from gender (women-only scholarships) to genes (athletes),
from nationality to disability, from service in the armed forces to social uplift
for welfare mothers to skiers from Scandinavia that constitute sufficient reason to pay someone's way in college, why not race?

In the *Wall Street Journal,* columnist Paul A. Gigot argued vehemently
against using this line of reasoning to justify race-based scholarships: "Race
is especially combustible. No one riots over scholarships for piccolo players
or Daughters of the American Revolution; the U.S. fought a war over the
rights of blacks." But it is the very combustibility of race that in some measure justifies these scholarships; the fact that blacks have had to die and to
suffer enormous indignities over the course of their history in this country
simply to enjoy the privilege of education is telling and should not be forgotten. What makes blacks different from piccolo players or the descendants of
the Daughters of the American Revolution is that they have been barred by
law from their rights as citizens. Their entire struggle in this country has
been to exercise citizenship in a culture that prides itself on conferring citizenship so freely and easily.

What has angered blacks over the years has not been the demand from
both conservatives and liberals that they assimilate (for some strange reason
conservatives have lauded Shelby Steele for arguing that in his book, as if
blacks historically, by and large, have ever really wanted to do anything
else). Rather, it has been the unrelenting demand that blacks assimilate and
assimilate and assimilate, as if climbing rungs on an endless ladder of respectability; the demand that blacks bear the burden of integration by making themselves appealing and tolerable to whites, as if they must apologize

for the phenomenon of their being. *This* has made blacks angry and depressed, as they see the entire social mode of integration as a new concerted effort to tell them that they are inferior.

We may wish to have a color-blind society but we haven't earned the right to it yet. (Remember: This is still a society that sells its popular music by race, worships by race, buries it dead according to race, beautifies itself by race, generally educates its young by race, and socializes by race.) Blacks remain the only Americans who have to prove constantly their right to be Americans, usually through the demands of continual acts of sacrifice (to counteract the image that blacks are, as a race, opportunists who want things without earning them), as if they must symbolize in our culture both social penance and social atonement. Nothing about this is particularly brutal or extravagantly harsh; simply put, to be black and striving for middle-classdom in this country is to experience pledging for a fraternity or sorority as a lifetime job. Racism is far from dead, and blacks are right to remain skeptical of the idea that they would have what little they have gained by way of new bourgeois entry if Affirmative Action did not exist. Besides, since the Negro has had to endure decades of the conservatives' separate but equal social engineering, why not try the liberals' version? While it is not guaranteed to be better, one can hardly imagine it being worse.

Aside from the issue of social justice, race-based scholarships are awarded in order to provide cultural diversity to white campuses, on the assumption that the Negro adds not only mere local color, so to speak, but also an entirely new cultural perspective of some sort. This process of diverse blending is called "multiculturalism," but even in this instance blacks get the bad end of the deal. Multiculturalism cannot possibly be the goal of Affirmative Action because blacks have no distinct culture. They have no distinct cuisine (excepting the malnutritious diet of the poor for the poor among them); they have no language except the slang and patois that some liberal educators have tried to define as a discrete language; they have no separate art. It is true that blacks have had an undeniable and an incredibly rich and deep influence in the shaping of this culture, but, Afrocentricity notwithstanding (and the fictive concept of a nationalized black political culture as a kind of psychic savior of the ravaged and defiled black personality is at least two hundred years old in this country), blacks have had to do this shaping in the absence of any rooted sense of an alternative nationality or culture available to them. Here we have simply the confused white American view of the black and the blacks' confused view of themselves as being caught between assimilation (which the opportunity of higher education is supposed to represent) and a kind of cultural otherness (which is the reason the Negro is on the white campus). Affirmative Action does not in this respect free the black from the racial dilemma; it intensifies blacks' specialness in ways that make them utterly helpless in making the experience intelligible except as opportunism or sheer disgruntled cynicism. Affirmative Action in this respect is neither good nor bad; paradoxically, as a social engineering project it does for blacks what blacks have been doing for themselves for a good while: It reminds them that they are black so that they can forget that they are black. It is at least a step above segregation, which wished to remind blacks that they were black so that they could never forget it.

For his ruling, Williams endured attacks from the civil rights wing of the black leadership and from black liberals which seemed, at times, excessive and emotional; perhaps this is because Mr. Williams is black and fellow blacks are always quick to seek out and denounce even the taint of perceived betrayal. Among those who defended him was the famous black conservative economist Thomas Sowell, also in the pages of the *Wall Street Journal*. Unfortunately, Mr. Sowell does not limit himself to the issue at hand but attacks all manner of black liberal opportunism:

> If preferential policies start to erode, what is to become of minority business set-asides, which have allowed individuals with greater average net worth than most Americans to raise their net worth still more through government largess? If the charade ends, what is to happen to those minority professors who get appointments they could not earn, at salaries they could never command in a free market, because the pressure is on for racial body count rather than scholarship? Most important of all, what is to become of all the lawyers, activists, organizations and movements whose skills have become specialized in extracting concessions from white authorities, rather than doing something about the tragic patterns of self-destruction in minority communities.

Mr. Sowell accuses the liberal, civil rights blacks of being opportunists, but if it were not for the race issue he himself would not be enjoying his considerable income and fame. After all, he is known for his books about race and Affirmative Action, not for his work on Marx. Moreover, his opinions would scarcely be heeded by conservatives if he were white. They only have importance because he is a black who espouses something that is far from new in white political circles. In short, one could accuse him of the same opportunism of which he accuses liberal blacks.

Furthermore, why Mr. Sowell feels a need to attack minority set-asides in business, as if minority business people were the biggest leeches in human history and this minute expenditure by the government were something of the magnitude of the S and L scandal or of the waste in the defense department, is beyond me. Why he feels a need to imply that black professors get ahead by trading on race and not scholarship is beyond me as well. The reason *good* black professors (no self-respecting school wants mediocre black professors; they have enough white ones to fill that bill) sought is that there are so few of them and, using the principles of the free market (contrary to Mr. Sowell's assertion), they take financial advantage of their scarcity just the same as left-handed free agent pitchers in baseball. Moreover, Mr. Sowell's scholarship is often not as thorough as it should be; he wrote a book on the history of the rise of ethnics in America and never once in the entire text mentioned the word "union." One might argue that that omission blatantly forces scholarship to become the handmaiden of ideology. Whether Mr. Sowell is a better-than-average economist or social historian is open to question, but his endless stream of articles in newspapers and popular magazines assures his position as a brilliant polemicist, which places him within a tradition of black intellectualism that he, paradoxically, finds himself committed to denouncing.

Finally, if blacks use Affirmative Action as a kind of political patronage, this is no different from how other ethnic groups have risen in America. The fact that blacks have needed active government intervention on their behalf to help invent a form of patronage where race would serve as an advantage is simply further proof of how powerless blacks really are.

Despite the considerable shortcomings of Affirmative Action, football coaches put it best: Take what your opponents give you.

MULTICULTURALISM AND THE SIGN

> *Democracy, in a word, is meant to be an aristocracy which has broadened into a universal aristocracy.*

—Leo Strauss, *Liberalism Ancient and Modern*

Nowadays, Americans talk so much about cultural differences that it is becoming difficult to imagine what holds us together as Americans, as virtually any disparate group is now a "culture." There are of course cultures for every racial minority as well as a woman's culture, a culture of poverty and a culture of wealth, a culture for the pathological and a culture for those who live in the Midwest, a culture of a classroom, a profession, or an institution. Nearly any group now has a sufficient system of signs, rituals, language, beliefs, and customs to be called a culture. Twenty or thirty years ago, these groups may have been referred to as "subcultures." But no one today wishes to be so identified because, first, the term implies the existence of a dominant culture—white, Christian, Protestant, Eurocentric, male-dominated, take your pick—which has become distasteful to us. Second, no one wants to be a tributary when one can be the mainstream, and that is exactly what all this multiculturalism, on one level, is all about.

If the only way we Americans can understand diversity and value is to exaggerate all group differences to the status of cultures, so be it. Diversity is in fact part of the American myth; we are probably the only country in the world to make such a big deal over the fact that our culture, like everyone else's, is a synthesis. The problem with multiculturalism today, the paradox it presents, is that the more we see diversity, the harder it is to discover synthesis. In short, the more diversity, the more divergence. Afrocentricity, radical feminism, and Christian fundamentalism, for example, exert their claims through a kind of insistent exclusivity; but their very existence, the very intelligibility of their claims can only be realized by understanding them as singularly American and particularly as synthetic moral gestures of bourgeois wishes. Multiculturalism has this distinct purpose from the liberal perspective: It is the liberal's intellectual assault against the stigma and anonymity of mass culture. There is now no mass culture because, simply, there is no mass. Multiculturalism means in effect that everyone can be granted an ethnicity and a set of traditions, intellectual and otherwise, associated with this ethnicity. Cultured people are now those who know their own culture, which we have specialized to the extent that it is, of course, impossible for a person not to know it, impossible for a person not to be cultured, impossible for a person not to have a mind, impossible for a person not to know something special. We are all members of a cognoscenti. Culture itself has become vulgarity.

Here's the upshot: During this past summer the County Council of St. Louis County (a distinct and decidedly whiter entity than St. Louis City) debated whether a support group for gays and lesbians should be permitted to participate in its adopt-a-highway program that allows virtually any group—companies, civic groups, political clubs, and churches—to "adopt" a stretch of county road and keep it clean. In exchange for this volunteerism, a sign with the group's name marks its part of the road, lest do-goodism go unrecognized; self-promotion is an integral art of civic duty. Because of the sign, several objections were raised to the participation of Parents and Friends of Gays and Lesbians. Some thought this would open the door to such groups as the Klan and the Nazis wishing to participate in order to advertise themselves. Others thought this legitimatized homosexual life-style, while still others thought that the sign would encourage opponents to vandalize that stretch of road.

The real threat homosexuals pose for the heterosexual community is not dissimilarity but a frightening similarity. (Why is it, I wonder, that liberal commentators always refer to heterosexuality as "culturally conditioned" but never to homosexuality in this way, when, of course, it is just as clearly so?)

As someone once said, whenever people raise a ruckus over the promiscuous sexual practices of others, they are largely motivated by envy rather than disgust. With abortion and birth control now common, the heterosexual can no longer make a superior moral claim to sexual practices because procreation no longer looms over the act as a kind of adumbration of ethical and spiritual endowment. Procreation provided the sex act with a materiality that suggested something eternal. Heterosexuals now engage in sex for the same reason as homosexuals: the aesthetics, the pure recreation of it. What frightens the heterosexuals is their subconscious realization that over the centuries they were tending toward a time when sex could become purely an art form, which the homosexual always had. This is why, in this hardy Protestant and Catholic country, the homosexual has been a put-upon, marginalized person to some significant degree. The homosexual secularizes and dematerializes sex, democratizes it while, ironically, making it a purely aristocratic function freed from necessity. There is a pure degeneracy in this, not due to the so-called homosexual's pathology, but in our general misunderstanding of what sex and morality are.

By the early fall, the County Executive approved the participation of the gay and lesbian support group. So, as one drives through the streets of St. Louis County, among the plethora of signs for the Kiwanis, the Girls' Club, United Missouri Bank, and all the other advertisements of volunteerism— the final and perfect expression of multiculturalism in the land: a sea of billboards that denigrates the land even while announcing our efforts, jointly but separately, to beautify it; a sea of billboards about our collective self that announces our aristocracies as a democracy that anyone, after all, can join— there stands among them a sign for Parents and Friends of Gays and Lesbians, a landmark showing how far we've come and how far we've yet to go.

THE AMERICAN MYSTICISM
OF REMEMBRANCE

AN INSTANCE OF STORYTELLING

And the day came on which I was actually to be freed of this profession of rhetoric . . .

—St. Augustine, *The Confessions,* Book IX, Chapter 4

For any thinking black person, one of the more remarkable, if not comforting, features of the month of February in recent years (with the celebration of black history being something of the rage in an otherwise gloomy season unless we have a Persian Gulf war going on) is not only that one is reminded of the race burden with more force than usual but that one is also forced to deal with the burden of an untenable history, a common American preoccupation. There is something about Black History Month (now at least six weeks long, as Martin Luther King's birthday celebration in mid-January gives us an early start on the festivities) that seems alternately depressing, even crushing and (at least in some small way) strangely moral and necessary—although the ethical imperative of this quaint American institution can barely justify the sheer pedestrian and mediocre insistence of its being. One is always caught between taking it too seriously and wanting to laugh at it as something of a very bad joke that can be funny only in America, where the "punch line," so to speak, is both so obvious and so pathetic. There is only so much of this sort of dementia, so much of this rampant intellectual trivialization generated by guilt, that this culture can stand.

My earliest memories of Black History Month are from the late 1950s and early 1960s, when I was an elementary-school student. Then it was Negro History Week, so named by its inventor, the black historian, Harvard Ph.D., and committed "race man," Carter G. Woodson, back in 1926, about ten years after he founded the Association for the Study of Negro Life and History. My black teachers (I attended a nearly all-black grade school), nearly all of whom were products of black schools like Cheney State, Morgan State, Hampton, Fisk, and the like, taught us, predictably and sanctimoniously, about two Negroes and only two Negroes: Booker T. Washington and George Washington Carver. I left elementary school associating Negro History with the founding of Tuskegee and a scientist who did a great deal with peanuts. I heard something vaguely about Frederick Douglass and something even more vague about Mary McLeod Bethune (who, one of my grade school friends said, after seeing her photograph, looked like a black monkey, for which the teacher, overhearing the remark, promptly slapped him with the yardstick), but I don't recall being taught much of anything about any other Negroes, famous and accomplished or not.

Perhaps how I felt about this as a boy might best be summed up by a particular experience I have never forgotten. In the fifth grade, I was among several students asked to do reports on famous Negroes to present during Negro History Week before the entire school at a special assembly. I was assigned Phillis Wheatley, the noted black colonial poet. We were each "to tell a story about a famous Negro," as our teacher put it. I never did the research for the report. To this day I am not sure why I dawdled, why I did not do the work. I was a conscientious, if not especially brilliant or remarkable student as a boy. Indeed, it was the absolute assurance the teacher felt that the assignment would be done that landed me the job to begin with. I had no problem doing reports of this sort, and earlier in the year I had completed long reports on Johann Sebastian Bach (when our class did "The Great Composers") and zoology and was quite proud of my work. I felt no greater affinity for either of these projects: I had heard the music of Bach neither before nor during the time I worked on the report and, indeed, was not to hear his music until I reached high school. Zoology, like all sciences, left me indifferent. At the time, my imagination was inflamed by the film *Lawrence of Arabia*, and I would have much preferred doing a report on T. E. Lawrence or the Bedouin than on Bach, zoology, or anything else. I was reading about Lawrence and the Arabs incessantly. Yet, when I went to the library to do the report and found nothing on Wheatley in any encyclopedia, I decided not to search any further or seek the help of the librarian. I simply packed up and went home, puzzled yet benignly at ease with this unaccustomed inertia. I might add that I was not daunted by the prospect of speaking before the school assembly. I had done this on a number of previous occasions, having read the Bible before the school many times. (During my first six years of public schooling, it was not illegal to have Bible reading or class prayer on the premises, nor was it illegal for teachers to practice corporal punishment. Typical of the anxiety of both my age and the era, I was constantly praying not to have an Atomic Bomb dropped on our neighborhood and not to have some bullyboy beat me up!) When Negro History Week finally arrived and our special assembly was called, I was either second or third to give my presentation. There were several white adults in the audience, visitors who came to see us perform, and our white principal was beaming in the light of this demonstration by the school's best and brightest students. Already, knowing I hadn't done the report, I felt a creeping sense of panic within my loins as if at any moment—as I was wont to do when seized by uncontrollable fear and shame—I was going to cry and wet myself. But I also felt a growing sense of defiance and a strangely deepening sense of myself as a person distinct from all the others around me. I realized that I never did the work because I did not want to tell this woman's story or the story of any other Negro.

Those who preceded me were sufficiently parrotlike, reciting with all the indigestible grace of someone who had just swallowed bad medicine after a bad meal. When my time arrived I stood before the audience and said in a very clear, loud voice: "Phillis Wheatley was a famous Negro Poetess." (I thought poetess sounded a bit more learned and correct than poet. I refused to call her a Negress, as black women were referred to in some books I had read. That term seemed insulting to me even then.) "She lived a long time ago," I continued. "She's . . ." I was silent for a long time, having nothing more to say. My teacher, who was particularly depending on my successful performance because I was given one of the more obscure Negroes to report on, seemed visibly concerned with my stumbling. Finally, I concluded, ". . . been dead a long time." I was promptly ushered from the stage amidst a gale of giggles and guffaws. My teacher grabbed me backstage and startled me with a look that seemed a numbingly helpless combination of fury and utter befuddlement.

"Why did you embarrass me and yourself like that? I had been telling the other teachers that your report in particular would be a good one. Why didn't you prepare your report? If you had trouble finding information on her, I would have helped you," she said to me angrily.

"I guess there was some information. I didn't look for any," I said sullenly.

"You what?" she said, genuinely stunned by my acknowledgment that I had not even tried to prepare the report.

For some reason, despite feeling embarrassed and even feeling great pity for my teacher and real guilt about the entire situation, I was glad I hadn't done the report. It occurred to me just at the very moment that I hated Negro History Week, hated it with a vehemence and a contempt that left me speechless and shaking. It seemed to me even then that Negro History Week took "Negro achievements," whatever they were and whatever that meant, and belittled them even more. Everything about it seemed patronizing and inferior. All Negro History Week reminded me of as a boy was that my people had no history worthy of being shared alongside Washington, Jefferson, and the immigrants. It was just a bunch of disembodied names that some other inferiority-afflicted Negro adults told us about so we might know, and be so much the better for the knowing, that Negroes had done things in this world. I hated these little stories that were supposed to make us aspire and wish to achieve. What did Phillis Wheatley or Marian Anderson or anybody else mean to me? I looked up at my teacher and wished she would hug me, but she simply stormed away in disgust. I knew I had grown up a little that day, because I did not cry and I did not wet myself.

PRISONER OF RACE

> *. . . from which in my mind I was already free.*

> —St. Augustine, *The Confessions,* Book IX, Chapter 4

Now, I can hardly shut up during Black History Month. I find myself, noted black professor, on a very modest circuit, speaking before various groups— from black children in run-down schools to upper-middle-class white women at university teas—about the achievements of blacks with, more or less, a sense of performing a necessary and even privileged public service. For one month, after all, this subject—the history of the life and culture of African Americans—takes on the sainted secularity of a kind of Eve of St. Agnes where we might imagine not an understanding of the past, but a utopian future of the races as bridegroom and bride going off to a beatific conjugal bed of neighborly love. Perhaps it is this burdensome yet false weight of history as American civic piety that makes Black History Month, in many respects, such a literally sickening experience for me. After one recent lecture, I went to the rest room immediately and felt the sweat oozing through my clothes, my stomach heaving: Good grief, I thought, how I hate this, how I hate all this besooted and benighted race talk! But why the hell am I doing this?

Woodson dreamed up Negro History Week in order to give black people pride by reminding them of the greatness of their past, a thesis, nay, an obsession that was hardly unique to Woodson and hardly new in Woodson's time. That because of the identity-obliterating force of several hundred years of New World slavery blacks would be inordinately concerned about both their history, which was denied them by the "master race," and their pride in their peoplehood is not surprising and is quite understandable. Blacks would be a strange people indeed if, under such circumstances, they had any less interest in creating a heroic history than any other group. It was apparent to black people for a long time, even during the age of slavery, that they needed a national identity and a national sense of character, in short, a popular history, and these can only be achieved through convincing people that history is not a tragic burden of sin (as Nathaniel Hawthorne taught us) but a set of simplified myths demonstrating the eschatological meaning of adversity and suffering as millennialism: History was not the fall of Adam but the coming of New Jerusalem. But it is probably the stifling "Parson Weems" stylization of black history that gives it an air of being virtually insufferable and in some real way practically useless, the persistence that after all history, in a popular sense, must be heroic and grand if it is to be anything at all. Even during slavery in the nineteenth century, blacks and whites, to create a more redemptive national myth, had already reinvented the Negro: no longer a character without a past, but as Lydia Maria Child, Richard Hildreth, Theodore Parker, William Ellery Channing, William Wells Brown, Ethiop, Forten, Delany, McClune, and others made clear, a character whose grand past presupposed a grander chiliastic and ontological restoration. It is with something like this assumption that Woodson created Negro History Week. This idea of the psychotherapeutic, metaphysical redemption of the Negro has been enlarged to make this week a month and has had bestowed upon it, much to the guilty pleasure of many liberal whites, an intensely Afrocentric and chauvinistic dimension, the seeds of which are also present in what, in truth, is nothing more than a monumental confession that the African American plays out as a national ritual a painful drama of psychic exile, identity confusion, double consciousness that is forced to stand apart from the double consciousness, the psychic exile, and the identity confusion that afflicts this nation, forcing the African American's trauma from its central position as *the* double-consciousness of the nation. And even Afrocentricism cannot retrieve what, in fact, no one wishes to have retrieved: the undeniable fact and the undeniable tragedy of slavery, which made us— Africans, black folk, people of color—Americans and westerners at such a terrible, terrible yet deeply profound cost. It is this profundity of utter and absolute exile and shame, heroic because of its absolute defilement and nihilism, to which the Negro can lay claim as being at the heart of Western history and at the heart of American history: and it is this profundity that ultimately is swallowed up in a mediocre vat of antiintellectual racial, heroic virtue that makes Black History the failure that it is in reimagining African American national identity and reconfiguring the extent of African-American character or in forcing Americans, black and white, to deal with the true burden of their common history. For in Afrocentrism we have the ultimate tyranny that the black person's history must not simply be asserted as actually having meaning in this world but must be seen as the source, the origin of all meaning in the world. In its search for empires, world domination, genetic superiority, and ultimate psychological wholeness and goodness in all things black, this view does nothing more than ape the unimaginative cultural priorities of the Eurocentrism that it claims to despise but in truth secretly worships in its imitation of its paradigms. This makes the burden of our history, American and Western, beyond the ability of anyone to bear because it does not force us to confront our contradictions but seeks to deny they exist. The real limitation of the creed of Afrocentrism of Pan-Africanism (as with Pan-Germanism or Pan-anything that insists upon the special racial destiny of any people) is that it denies any idea of human transcendence not rooted in race. In short, African Americans find themselves, by their own invention, trapped in a prison of race that is no more liberating than the prison of race whites constructed for them and that, indeed, offers them no transcendence at all. Like the white Americans, who, facing the horror of national "mongrelization" and a cultureless void without history, imagine Europe as the source of the history and the culture to which they aspire, so black Americans, recoiling from the degradation of a brutish and forced "mongrelization" and a cultureless past, look to Africa. Yet the deepest disappointment is black Americans' failure to recognize that they are something remarkably different and, in many respects, remarkably *more* than the African to whom they now genuflect in confused wonder.

Of course, the African American's Afrocentrism is just another American ethnicity project (despite the vaunted internationalism of its Pan-African implications) that makes history untenable by suggesting that a true historical consciousness is unbearable and offers in its stead a false one that circulates between the poles of a morally aggressive *j'accuse* against the whites (who were colonizers and imperialists, robbers and rapists, after all, by their very nature). This denunciation of whites as morally and genetically inferior, paradoxically, aggrandizes them through the sheer infinitude of the African Americans' need to have whites' self-evident demonization match their justified outrage, in a kind of 101 appreciation course of "what the Negro has done for modern civilization" that supposedly will make us all better people, as 101 appreciation courses in anything from opera to chemistry are advertised to do. Afrocentrism, in short, has all the worst uplift elements of a typical American moralistic enthusiasm and so, alas, does Black History Month.

WHAT I SAW AT THE GATE

So it was done. You rescued my tongue as you had rescued my heart.

—St. Augustine, *The Confessions,* Book IX, Chapter 4

And what as a boy did I know of history? A few weeks ago, during Black History Month, I was in Philadelphia for a Black Writers' conference. I went down to the old neighborhood in South Philadelphia where I grew up, down around Fifth and Fourth streets and Washington Avenue, Carpenter, Christian, Montrose, Fairhill, and Randolph streets, and I found it older and more shabby, more broken than I could ever remember it having been. The neighborhood, frankly, was filthy: trash-filled empty lots, broken-down homes, the squalid housing projects. "The rock has destroyed this neighborhood," I was told by an acquaintance, meaning the rampant addiction of so many to crack cocaine. One very warm and sunny day, hardly a February day at all, I stood before Sunshine Playground on Christian Street between Fifth and Sixth and remembered how my friends and I played there many years ago when we were children. When I was young, both boys and girls played on the swings and slides, but as I got older, I hung out with the teenaged boys who shot baskets and played baseball. The playground was overgrown with weeds as high as small trees and littered with trash of all sort, broken bottles, cans, little empty plastic vials that were probably crack cocaine containers; the green bars of the gate were rusted shut and padlocked. As I stood there I tried to think of Alex Haley, the grand African-American storyteller and mythmaker who so shrewdly exploited the image of the griot when *Roots,* the book that gave blacks a mythic origin in an Edenic Africa and an immigrant history of overcoming adversity through the story of a great and enduring family, was at the height of its popularity. His sudden death had just been announced a few days earlier, and I had written an op-ed piece on him for the *St. Louis Post-Dispatch.* With both *The Autobiography of Malcolm X,* about a black leader who based his ideology on being both race conscious and theologically non-Western; and *Roots,* one of the grand American stories of race and slavery and the national character, Haley's achievement (despite questions about the authenticity of the authorship) is daunting and probably not as fully appreciated as popular culture events of some magnitude as they ought to be.

But I really was not thinking about Haley at all at that moment. The only person I could think about was an overweight boy with a gimp leg, a few years older than myself, whose name was Poppy and whom we sometimes called the Fatman. He was the best storyteller I ever knew, the best curser I ever knew, the best teller of pornography I ever knew. ("Y'all niggers want to talk about fucking," he once said to us disdainfully during a sex bragging session. "If you ever saw a woman's wet, quivering pussy, you'd run for your lives.") He couldn't play ball like the rest of us, so he was our champion checker player. ("We playing 'touch a man, move a man.' You touch that motherfucker, you gotta move 'im. You ain't no jury, so don't be doin' no deliberatin'," he told me once when I sat down to play him. He then proceeded to beat me in a blizzard of moves that positively blinded me. "Next chump?" he called after I was humiliated.) The Fatman was also our resident rhetorician and storyteller, telling long, elaborate jokes about the black man, white man, and China man, politically incorrect ethnic stories that made all of us boys laugh uproariously. Sometimes in the jokes, tales really, the black man would be the goat and at other times he would be the hero, but the jokes were equally funny either way. Sometimes, they were virtually lessons.

"Once upon a time, there was a white man, China man, and a black man and they each get a thousand dollars. The white man say, 'I'm gonna invest this money on Wall Street in stocks and shit,' and off he go to invest his money. The China man, he say, 'I'm gonna get my relatives and open me a Chinese restaurant in a nigger neighborhood 'cause I know them niggers love Chinese food and I'm gonna make me some money.' The black man take that money, look at it real close to make sure it's real. Then he say, 'I'm getting me some Ripple wine, some women, and I'm gonna lay back and enjoy myself on this here fine day.' Who you think did the best thing with the money?"

We would argue this back and forth. Some of the boys would say that the white man did the smartest thing by investing the money on Wall Street. "That's how white people get rich," one of us would say. Some would think the China man was the smartest for starting a restaurant and running his own business. "That's what black people need to do: start they own business in the neighborhood," one of us would say. No one picked the black man as the smartest.

"I didn't ask you niggers who did the smartest thing with the money," the Fatman said. "I asked who did the best thing with the money. And the answer is the black man."

"Aw, man, that's a lot of bullshit. That's what white people want us to do with money. Go around and spend it and have a good time," someone would answer disgustedly.

"What the white man gonna do with that money but go gamble. And why he wanna gamble? To make more money so he can do what the black man wanna do: have a good time. What the China man wanna do? Make more money by selling shit so he can have a good time. The black man wanna do the best thing 'cause he wanna have a good time and he don't want to have it at somebody else's expense. He don't want to be making more money off people being greedy and shit when he can have a good time with what he got. Besides, the white man invest in Wall Street and lose all his money; the China man's restaurant gets burned down. So, what them motherfuckers got to show for the money. Nothing! So, the black man doing the best thing with the money but not the smartest thing." As a boy, I think these jokes, these stories which the Fatman told us, were the real and only black history for which I felt anything, the only American history that meant something to me, that reverberated in my being as something profound, wise, inspirited, crafted, joyous, yet tragic. Those boys, that playground, those stories, were the only real racial solidarity I have ever known, the only real racial consciousness I have ever felt. Standing at the gate, I did not long for its return, but only for an understanding of what it was and what it meant. Perhaps, as I entered my middle age as a black man in America, the Fatman, at that moment, may have been able to help me understand what I felt and what I was destined to feel. "Sometimes you ain't a fool but most of the time you are, sometimes you dream lucky, but most of the time you don't, what the hell else is there to say? That's life in America and every fucking place else," he was fond of telling us boys. As I stood by the gates of Sunshine Center, I suddenly missed the Fatman a great deal, missed those stories more than I thought possible. The Fatman died more than a dozen years ago from acute alcoholism, but when I last saw him, thin, sick, and very drunk, when I was a graduate student at Cornell visiting Philadelphia one summer, he told me, "Happy [one of my nicknames because I always looked so serious and sad], I'm glad you made it off the block." Off one block and onto another. That's what I wanted to tell him, in the end. There's always a block one is trying to get off of. And for any black person in America the word "block" resonates historically and culturally: Is it true, finally and at last, that there is, in the words of that old black spiritual, no more auction block for me?

As I sit in front of my home in an all-white, affluent neighborhood with my golden retriever, with my children who speak in the white patois using such terms as "rad," "gross," and "super," with my wife who drives a Chevy van, the car of the white housewife as it is called, although my wife is neither; as I sit and look across the street at a house for sale and the people, all white and all presumably middle class, who go through examining it on a unseasonably warm early March afternoon, I notice that some wave at me, some are indeed quite happy to know me, some ignore me, a smaller number look at me oddly as if to say, "Oh, blacks live here, too." I sometimes think that the wide expanse of Sunshine Center is no whit wider than the sides of this street on which I live. As I sit here I would like to ask my friend, the Fatman, did I do the smartest thing or the best thing?

HOUSE OF RUTH,
HOUSE OF ROBINSON

*Some Observations on Baseball, Biography,
and the American Myth*

*The most marvelous gift of sports is its faculty for making heroes of underdogs, of
lifting the downtrodden up to solid ground.*

—A.S. Young, *Negro Firsts in Sports*

*For they had much rather see us engaged in those degrading sports, than to see us
behaving like intellectual, moral, and accountable beings.*

—Frederick Douglass,
Narrative of the Life of Frederick Douglass, An American Slave

THE INEFFABLE NATIONAL PASTIME;
THE EXPRESSIBLE NATIONAL CHARACTER

The following tableaus are about baseball, one of the sports I know best, and
one that (along with boxing) perhaps defines and reflects the complexities of
American culture better than any other. There is little here about the sport
itself. The examination is centered on baseball's political, social, and cultural
meaning. I leave it to wiser and more scholarly heads than mine to talk about
sports as philosophy, as play, as performance, as economic enterprise, or in
relation to American history.

It is one of the persistent ironies in our culture that athletic endeavor,
such a speechless act, should generate such need for narrative, for language,
for story—from the coach's pep talk to the sportswriter's column; from the
television sports announcers who describe actions readily seen to sports talk
shows and "open lines" that discuss events which, for the most part, are set-

tled on the field of play. What is remarkable about the rise of professional sports in America (beyond the increasingly exacting specialization among athletes themselves) is that the popularity of athletics would not have been possible without the progressive technology of endlessly reproducing discourse about it: newspapers, radio, television, VCRs. The far-reaching varieties of discourse about sports signify not only our commitment to athletics but also our commitment to language as metaexperience; once the athletic event has ended, the discourse about it displaces the event. The event becomes the shadow.

Everyone knows, for instance, that as a young man Ronald Reagan worked as a baseball announcer. He was a very good one, describing games he himself did not see, simply embellishing stark summations he received off a ticker tape. There he sat at the microphone, speaking threads and threads of narrative, shaping drama like a blind Homer. It is fitting that this collective fantasizing should revolve around baseball, which promotes a gamut of fantasies from old-timers' games and daydreamers' camps to card and board games, from professional sports' most publicized All-Star Games to computer match-ups. What Reagan did as a broadcaster is what most rabid baseball fans do: namely, work backward from the facts and statistics and reconstruct the entire narrative structure of ball games, for ball games are insistently and relentlessly narrative. One must not simply *know* baseball, one must *tell* it. Baseball is one of two sports that seek to be an omnipresent—and sometimes ominous—metalanguage. (Boxing is the other.) It is in this maze of fantasy that the hero of Robert Coover's *The Universal Baseball Association, Inc., J. Henry Waugh, Prop.* (1968) finds himself. Our enjoyment of baseball, and of sports generally, is inextricably bound to story, to rhetoric, to conversation, to dialogue, to pure fussing about how the event actually was and how it should be told. The Greeks were right: in a fundamental and timeless way, sports are about our being human, about our being what we are. Only a barbarian would hate sports.

"Sports give people things to talk about other than the inadequacy and unhappiness of their lives," someone once told me. Sports do even more: they give people, specifically men, a language *in* which to talk as well as a language *about* which to prate. Often, sitting in the company of older men during my boyhood, I wondered what would there be to talk about if professional sports did not exist. Discussion and argument were bountiful and eternal about all sorts of questions athletic: how big were Sonny Liston's fists; which was the better local high-school basketball team, West Philadelphia or Overbrook; which records did Wilt Chamberlain set at Overbrook High; were the Washington Redskins a racist team; why did the Philadelphia Eagles trade Sonny Jurgenson; who was the better Eagle running back, Timmy Brown or Tom Woodeshick; why could local light-heavyweight Harold

Johnson never beat Archie Moore; why could local middleweight Bennie Briscoe never win a title; who was the better center, Bill Russell or Wilt Chamberlain; why was Joey Giardello a pretty good fighter "for a white boy"; who was the better baseball player, Hank Aaron, Willie Mays, or Roberto Clemente; why were the current crop of black ball players (circa the early and middle 1960s) not as good as the old Negro league players; why were current black ball players better than current white ball players: why were old-time Negro league players better than old-time white players; who was the best fighter, Jack Johnson, Sugar Ray Robinson, or Joe Louis?

Around and around the talk went, swirls and eddies, torrents and streams, which, as a youngster, I found both fascinating and enriching, foolish and funny, learned and exhibitionist by turns. "Dammit, nigger, can't you get it through your thick head? Wasn't no way on earth Louis was gonna beat Lil Arthur! Ain't nobody was ever born who was a better defensive fighter than Jack Johnson. Johnson could be hitting you all upside your head and peeling a grape at the same time." "I knows I'm right, man! Josh Gibson got better numbers than Babe Ruth and you can look it up. I got the book at home, man. The book don't lie." "I don't care what nobody say. I *know* that Satchel Paige, in his prime, was a better pitcher than Bob Gibson 'cause I seen 'em both pitch. I know what I'm talking about." "It take about five white guys to bring down Jim Brown excepting maybe Sam Huff. You got to give the devil his due there. That Huff is a bad white boy." "How come ain't no colored middle linebackers is what I wants to know. Some colored boys out there be badder than Huff if they give us the chance."

But I was shaken once when, sitting around with the cronies in the local barbershop, one of the guys, Raymond, I think, jumped up and shouted. "Why y'all always sitting around talkin' about these goddam sports? Why don't you talk about something natural that a man is supposed to talk about—like a woman, or a bottle of scotch, or how the world ain't treatin' you right? All this here talking about these jocks and these games ain't natural; it ain't a natural way for one man to talk to another." The fact that the vast majority of athletes experience defeat more commonly than they do victory is why the mystical insistence on unnaturalness is sport's great fascination and great virtue. Alas, the athlete replicates a holistic yet puzzling human experience by giving us the male (and some females) whose vocation and condition are identical. There are two explicit and distinct memories I have of baseball and language.

As a child I remember never discussing baseball with my grandfather, a native of the Bahamas, a short, stern, very black man who, I was told by other family members, was, in his youth, a follower of Marcus Garvey, although I never heard him utter a political word in his life and he has seemed a particularly accommodating man around whites. I recall one incident I was told several times: during the Depression, in order to feed his quite large family, my grandfather, in desperation, tried to steal some sausages from the local white grocer by stuffing them in his pocket. Such ineptitude made his discovery nearly inevitable. It was painfully embarrassing for him to have to plead his case to the white grocer because my grandfather has always prided himself on being an honest man and on being able to feed his family. The grocer knew my grandfather well and times were hard for everyone, so he did not have him arrested. He simply sent him home. Family members tell the story with a great deal of good-natured humor, although he has never found it funny. I do not recall ever having a real conversation with my grandfather during my entire life, certainly not during my entire childhood. I was too afraid of him.

Yet despite the silence of our relationship he took me to professional baseball games every summer as he was an ardent fan of the sport; in fact, in a way, he introduced me to the sport. I remember many a sunny Sunday afternoon (we always seemed to go on a Sunday after church), sitting in Connie Mack Stadium's bleacher section, watching the Philadelphia Phillies play: Johnny Callison making grand catches in right field; Art Mahaffey and his curious windup; Don Demeter fouling balls off his left foot; Dick Stuart, old "Dr. Strangeglove," hitting a homer; the voice of Byrum Saam and Bill Campbell, the Phillies sports announcers, on radios around the park; Frank Thomas having a racial run-in with Richie (later Dick) Allen; the colorful southpaw Bo Belinsky, who once dated Mamie Van Doren and who, along with pitcher Dean Chance, was, if not one of the playboys of the Western world, certainly one of the most publicized playboys of professional baseball; the less colorful southpaw Dennis Bennet, who never made it; the deadly way Wes Covington cocked his bat before swinging; the two great years Jack Baldshun had as a relief pitcher before being traded away to mediocrity and obscurity.

I hated the Phillies as a boy; virtually every black person I knew felt the same, recalling how the team had treated Jackie Robinson when he first broke into the National League. My grandfather, however, silent and strict-looking, handing out the sandwiches and drinks for our lunch with his usual authority, liked the Phillies a great deal. Perhaps that is why we never spoke to each other about the games. Once, during a twilight double header against the Dodgers (in which Sandy Koufax pitched the first game, winning 6 to 2), he bought me a Phillies yearbook. This was unusual for two reasons: First, we almost never went to night games, and second, he almost never bought anything at the ball park. I had ambivalent feelings about the book; I felt especially treated because my grandfather bought it for me, yet I remember always intensely disliking the *smell* of it. The book always smelled new, even after I had had it for several years. I never read that yearbook; I do not recall even opening it except while standing before my grandfather a few moments after he bought it. I thanked him profusely for buying it. My grandfather bought the book because he knew I liked books about baseball. In fact, I liked them almost more than I liked the game itself.

The books that most readily come to mind from my childhood are Dr. Seuss's *The Cat in the Hat;* L. Frank Baum's *The Wizard of Oz;* Edward Ormondroyd's *David and the Phoenix;* and seemingly miles of juvenile baseball biographies. I would occasionally, if only for the sake of variety, read the biography of an athlete from another sport—the lives of Red Grange, Oscar Robertson, Bobby Hull, A. J. Foyt (if one can consider him an athlete), Benny Leonard, and others. But the baseball biographies were my favorites, and having such books written for young boys was, I suppose, a very profitable market for publishers. Henry Aaron, Willie Mays, Babe Ruth, Lou Gehrig, Joe DiMaggio, Ty Cobb, Walter Johnson, Cy Young, Grover Cleveland Alexander, Felipe Alou. Mickey Mantle—all were presented in ghost-written, antiseptic volumes that were simply longer versions of articles in *The Sporting News* or *Boys' Life.* (Many of the books were autobiographies, but I made no distinction as a boy between self-narrative and reportorial narrative; since all were ghost-written and all were, in some essential ways, fraudulent works, their core attraction was their *narrativity,* not their authenticity. Or let me say that the books' authenticity was located in something far larger and much more gripping than the normal consideration we give to the nature of biographical writing.) During my boyhood and adolescence, my love for these books was so intense that I once had a fistfight with my friend William Bradshaw over a Warren Spahn biography he had been given. I knew he was not interested in baseball and I wanted him to give the book to me. In fact, I demanded it. He refused to give it to me, so we fought. He, being both stronger and bigger, easily beat me. What is so surprising and dismaying about this in retrospect is that I was very shy and timid as a boy. It is still hard for me to comprehend how I could have been so aggressive about something that did not belong to me.

I learned a certain sort of factual information from these books, the sort of information that a boy who loved baseball would want: year-by-year statistics, career statistics, teams played for, best games played, and the like. But it was not for this information alone that I read these books, information that, after all, was condensed on the back of the baseball cards I sometimes collected. It was the sheer redundancy of the paradigmatic lesson, the comfort of knowing that each player's life was like every other player's, that producing the odd oxymoron of dull, rooted inspiration. You had to work hard to succeed, the books taught incessantly. You had to be single-minded and dedicated. You had to live a pure, clean life. You had to marry your teenage sweetheart. If you worked hard, you would be rewarded sooner or later. The books became better, infinitely more interesting than watching the games themselves in which I could see many of these athletes play. The games began to seem in my youthful mind, like the end product, although I still enjoyed them a lot. It was far more vital to learn the story of how a man became an athlete. Once he achieved success, his story was finished. There was something like the Ben Franklin father-to-son story in all of this, and something that reminded me, years later, of F. Scott Fitzgerald's Jay Gatsby writing out his day's schedule, as a boy, on the cover of *Hopalong Cassidy.* I did something similar, writing out a schedule for success when I was about thirteen, on the cover of a juvenile biography of Roy Campanella.

It did not occur to me until I taught *The Great Gatsby* and Hemingway's *The Sun Also Rises* in a freshman English class that the connection between sports and literature is central to understanding what sports are and why they exist. On one level, those books are about the very imposture of our national character and our national myth: blacks, Jews, and Catholics as athletes and sportsmen in *The Sun Also Rises;* the fake-yachtsman, fake-polo-player Gatsby, whose name-change resonates with ethnic overtones; the rich, hard, Yale football star, Tom Buchanan, self-centered and racist; the woman's golf pro Jordan Baker, who cheats and feels no responsibility for her recklessness. These books are the absolute unraveling (unwriting and rewriting) of the American myth through sports. (It is surely no accident that these books were published in the 1920s, the golden age of American professional and amateur sports, both in terms of mass popularity and the production of mass sportswriting in newspapers.)

Obviously, reading those baseball biographies as a child gave me a very usable mythology of male heroism, much more usable than, say, Greek legends or tall tales of the American frontier. The books also provided me with an orientation toward the culture I was to live in as a man, an orientation that was valuable, if not always honest or harmless. Indeed, the true value of the books as cultural orientation may center in the fact that they are dishonest—one must learn, in some ways, to negotiate their simplistic moralizing, which so distorts the real issues of real life. That I never read sports *fiction* as a child is also quite telling: for me, nothing could be made up that was more exciting than the re-creation of a real athletic career. And the re-creation of that young man-career became, over and over, simply the recitation of games, the story of games. We know that sports are an essential part of our cultural history and social fabric, but it is my contention that the sheer narratability of sports, or, at least, our fixation with their narratability, is, whether we are sports fans or not, the incessant reinvention of ourselves as males in relation to our national myth. The meaning of sports biography (and autobiography) is indelibly tied to its narrative dramatization of our national character as a rite of beautiful young manhood.

About two years ago I saw my grandfather while I was revisiting Philadelphia. It has never been easy for us to talk, but I felt very genial, possibly because my children were with me. I remember turning the conversation to baseball, after he had asked me about living in St. Louis. I talked about the Phillies and was in fact eager to show that I still kept up with the game and even with the local team. When I asked him about their chances that year he gave me a curious, almost childlike look, a wan smile, and said, "Oh, I don't know," as if he hardly thought about baseball anymore. I felt momentarily nonplussed. But his eyes seemed almost sad at my discomfort as our conversation fell away, almost as if he felt sorry for me, as if, in the calm center of wisdom, he knew, always knew from my childhood and before, what I would only come to know years later: What is there to say about games anyway?

BASEBALL AND THE HOLLYWOOD MYTH

In 1952, Ronald Reagan starred as pitching great Grover Cleveland Alexander in *The Winning Team,* a film of some tepid social significance as it dealt with a player who was both an alcoholic and an epileptic. (It was Reagan's second film of "social statement" in the early 1950s. The other, *Storm Warning,* was about the Ku Klux Klan as an organization that terrified helpless women.) Nonetheless, *The Winning Team* was part of the series of whitewashed Hollywood biographies about ball players made in the forties and early fifties: *The Pride of the Yankees* (the Lou Gehrig story, 1942), *The Babe Ruth Story* (1948), *The {Monty} Stratton Story* (1949), *The Jackie Robinson Story* (1950), and *The Pride of St. Louis* (the Dizzy Dean story, 1952). These movies are montages of bathos and incoherence, displaying the kind of shimmering sentimentality that appealed to moviegoers and baseball fans of the day. And Reagan, the former baseball announcer, has always stood in the middle of that cultural muddle, an actor who both blunted and intensified the politics of his art.

Most of these films, incidentally, were made at a time when baseball was undergoing changes both from within and without. A post–World War II boom had reinvented it as truly the national pastime. Toward the end of the 1950s, Major League baseball expanded to include the West coast, and racial integration had radically altered professional ball by enriching the major leagues while simultaneously destroying the Negro leagues. By serving as historical romances, the films undoubtedly permitted both the baseball establishment and society at large to cope with these drastic changes. Even *The Jackie Robinson Story,* with its cameos of a Tom Sawyer boyhood, Washington, D.C., the flag, and the Statue of Liberty, comforted audiences with the reassurance that, after all, the game was still the same. Perhaps baseball provided a refuge from Communists and overbearing women, the twin towers of totalitarianism for the white American male.

It goes without saying that these popular films have little to do with the

actual biographies of their subjects. Indeed, the lives of these great players
are reduced to the insipidity attendant upon a schoolboy morality, a knight-
errantry once removed. Here is the Hollywood fantasy, the chivalric code of
human sexuality as the life cycle of virginity, monogamy, and, finally, a heroic death without the taint of guilt or sin. But what these films are really
about is not morality but morale. They are about the overcoming of adversity, which is, after all, the national creed of American life and what passes
here for a reasonable facsimile of morality. The films remind the viewer of
American individualism, determination, team spirit, fair play, and resource-
fulness. In these films, the baseball player is not simply *good*, he is *inventive.*

But getting back to schoolboy morality, there is something insistent in
the perennial boyishness that baseball has successful palmed off on the public
as a sense of history and tradition; it is this quality that has attracted so many
white male intellectuals to the sport: it does not *remind* them of their childhood so much as it *transfixes* it. In that sense, baseball is nothing more than
another symbol of the American's quest for eternal innocence. Witness, for
example, the 1984 film *The Natural,* loosely based upon Bernard Malamud's
excellent 1952 novel. In the film version, Roy Hobbs ultimately becomes
the golden boy who hits the homerun to win the championship instead of the
jerk who both sold out and struck out. This revision conflates the celebration
of mythical baseball with the celebration of the clichéd Hollywood baseball
film. *The Natural* comes close to being one of the worst baseball films ever
made.

And these clichéd virtues, celebrated so unabashedly in baseball films,
are precisely the virtues that baseball itself wishes to celebrate, not about
American life per se, but about itself. Baseball has always been preoccupied
with itself as a cultural image, a set of signs that indicates an underlying
rhetoric of rectitude: the green fields; the bats and balls; running the bases;
the sunlit air; the communing crowd. This partly explains the excessive use
of signs in baseball: the third-base coach sends signs to the runners on base
and to the batter; the manager sends signs to his coaches and players; the
players in the field signal one another about plays; the catcher signals the
pitcher while guarding his signs from the view of the batter or the runners on
base, because, in this plenitude of silent instruction, one must always be
wary of an enemy who is constantly on the prowl to intercept and steal them.
Baseball is a game that loves the labyrinths of its own encoding. Baseball has
become, in essence, its own Hollywood film, self-reflexively celebrating its
own faked bourgeois myth. It must be remembered that baseball is a tough
game, "It's no pink tea," as Ty Cobb once said.

But as a bourgeois myth, baseball has certainly become its own sign
whose signification is clear to everyone. The self-evident nature of baseball's
simplistic (and largely fictional) integrity has made it an appropriate image

to be exploited by presidential candidates. We remember, for instance, Jimmy Carter's regular softball games with the press in Plains, Georgia, when he was candidate in 1976. In the 1988 presidential campaign, staffers for Democratic candidate Michael Dukakis made sure that newspapers across the country ran a picture of him dressed in a baseball uniform (presumably he played Little League) in a blatant appeal to all those Little League, American Legion, sandlot league parents and former players who could recall the sunlit glory of those bygone days. It was also part of the immigrant drama of Americanization that Dukakis tried to reenact, if somewhat clumsily, before blue-collar voters. In her essay "Insider Baseball," Joan Didion, trailing Dukakis on the campaign beat, describes a ritual Dukakis seemed particularly to enjoy: donning his glove and playing catch with someone during a campaign stop. I suppose it was meant to conjure the image of both the beginning and the end of *The Natural,* where Robert Redford's character is first the son playing catch with his father, then the father playing catch with his son. Perhaps there was something strikingly Midwestern and folksy about this ball-catching stuff, just as there is about baseball itself, although its origins are neither. But, like Dukakis himself, it never quite caught on with the public. The symbolism just did not work in a campaign where both candidates were searching for some chord-striking image with the desperation of hungry alley cats in quest of food. Dukakis's ball-catching just seemed a dumb stunt. He did not know the Boston Red Sox, as some Boston reporters complained. (He apparently did not know the Boston Celtics, either, virtually a capital offense in basketball-crazy Beantown.) He really did not know baseball. Some Republican presidential candidates have understood baseball much better.

BASEBALL AND POLITICAL AUTOBIOGRAPHY

Nixon at the Bat

Reading Richard Nixon's first book, *Six Crises* (1962), is a bit like walking in an unrelieved twilight. The truths and lies blend so compellingly and compulsively that the book manages to avoid twisting by turns from self-revelation to nonsense and back. The work *is* self-revelation as the nonsensical pathology of self-defense. The "crises"—the Alger Hiss case; the slush fund scandal when he was selected as Eisenhower's running mate in 1952; Eisenhower's heart attack in 1955; Nixon's violent reception when he toured Latin America as vice president in 1958; meeting Khrushchev; and his first campaign for the presidency in 1960 against Kennedy—are really nothing more than a series of Nixon's public victimizations: character "smears" (a word he uses constantly), adversarial relationships as the hallmark of character-testing, the endurance of unjustified physical outrage. It is one of the extraordinary ironies of the book that its writer should be so obsessed with character when he seemingly possesses so little of it; and, moreover, that the book should so persistently argue that character (perhaps politics itself) is a profound psychological formation resulting from emotional overload.

This mentality, I suggest, results from Nixon's absorption of the ethics of sports. Here was a poor, uncoordinated boy who could not play football but who, at Whittier College, as Fawn Brodie writes, "took a vast amount of brutal punishment for four years," trying to make the team. Trying to make the college football team was, in fact, Nixon's first real crisis and his real public victimization. He grew to love football because it possessed what he saw as the real meaning of sport: crisis management and physical endurance. He believed the old saw that sport builds character. That is why he allowed the stuffing to be knocked out of him every day in the fall for four years during football practice.

Although Nixon makes metaphorical references to a number of sports in *Six Crises,* including boxing, football, track, and gambling (if one can consider gambling a sport; Nixon was a skilled poker player), I find intriguing two specific allusions to baseball, both made in reference to Soviet Premier Nikita Khrushchev, with whom Vice President Nixon had his famous "Kitchen Debate" in Moscow in 1959.[1] The premier is characterized as the consummately canny player:

> I even had the benefit of a preview of what I might expect from Khruschev when Mikoyan and Kozlov, who occupy the next to the top rung on the ladder of the Soviet hierarchy, visited Washington in the period just before I left for Moscow. They threw some pretty fair fast balls and a few curves in the long conversations I had with each of them. But meeting Khrushchev, after talking with them, was like going from minor to major league pitching. He throws a bewildering assortment of stuff—blinding speed, a wicked curve, plus knucklers, spitters, sliders, fork balls—all delivered with a deceptive change of pace. (236)

But Nixon is up for the game:

> This was the moment for which I had been preparing myself for many months. I was on edge with suspense as I entered Khrushchev's office shortly after 10:00. He was toying with a model of Lunik, the satellite which the Russians had shot off toward the moon several months before. It looked like an oversized baseball in Khrushchev's chubby hands. (250)

Obviously, Khrushchev is the pitcher and Nixon the batter, in the most stark and lonely diagram of adversative contest that Nixon can imagine—a baseball game without fielders, without umpires, without teams, simply the repeated existential wonder of confrontation between a pitcher and a batter, each with an instrument that is meant to be the destruction of the other but is also the other's reason for being, for neither instrument has any meaning without the other or apart from the other. It is the perfect analogy to the theory of "the balance of power" and "mutual deterrence, the theory of the cold war." Moreover, because Nixon sees his confrontation with Khrushchev as an individual-within-a-team (or individual-in-an-embracing-ideology) encounter, the baseball analogy is apt, for baseball is the one team sport that perfectly isolates the individual's drama against the background, or scrim, of the team's fate. Football would not have worked, as Nixon knew. Football is the reenactment of the sweep and boredom of war and conquest; baseball is conflict as the mediation of possibilities, the contemplation not simply of action, but the challenge and the inevitability of fate.

But Khrushchev is no ordinary pitcher. He has an impossible assortment of pitches that no real pitcher has ever possessed. Whoever heard of a knuckle-ball pitcher who could also throw a good fastball? What pitcher ever existed with the blinding speed of Nolan Ryan or Steve Bedrosian or Herb Score and the "junk" pitches of the aging Tommy John or Rick Mahler or Satchel Paige? They are, indeed, nearly mutually exclusive stages in the development and maturation of a big-league pitcher. Khrushchev is, in effect, both a youngster and a veteran simultaneously. He is not, in Nixon's mind, simply a pitcher, but a symbol of the implausible perfection of the perverse potentialities of pitching. Khrushchev's skill is not the zenith but the absolute corruption and debasement of pitching. And of course the cagey Khrushchev possesses the illegal spitter, as one would expect: the ultimate subversive man should be master of the subversive pitch. (Fairness, playing by the rules, and the subversion of the rules to win are ever on Nixon's mind. Consider this metaphor from boxing describing one of his encounters with Khrushchev: "I felt like a fighter wearing sixteen-ounce gloves and bound by Marquis of Queensberry rules, up against a bare-knuckle slugger who had gouged, kneed, and kicked. I was not sure whether I had held my own.") It is this utterly impossible array of pitches, all thrown by a pitcher who has uncanny, unnatural control ("change of pace"), that Nixon must face as a batter. No batter has faced a more daunting task, and no batter has succeeded more admirably than Nixon in the face of batting's adverse odds (a pitcher is expected to get a good hitter out 70 percent of the time).

Khrushchev, in Nixon's second allusion, is toying with a model of a Russian satellite in his hands, "like an oversize baseball." Nixon has enlarged the stakes of the game, for the pitcher is seen as a monstrous Soviet leader, a giant who has to be slain. The satellite symbolizes what is at stake: technology, science, indeed, all higher learning as a free human expression. The battle with communism has always been an ideological struggle over who will control not knowledge itself, but the nature of how one knows anything. (The science-fiction films of this era, for instance, were about who should control the industry and proper political limitations of knowledge.) Nixon's preoccupation is, in fact, with epistemology. Consider that during Nixon's years as vice president and as president he never expressed interest in any body of knowledge or in technical expertise. Nixon is neither philosopher nor intellectual. His sensual being throbs like a star in nova for the visceral reality of mass political manipulation, much like an athlete's for competition.

Observers are wrong. Reagan was not the first actor as president. Nixon was, because he was the first president since Theodore Roosevelt to think of himself in such purely athletic-turned-moral terms. (Nixon also had some amateur acting experience.) To be sure, Roosevelt, taking boxing lessons from Mike Donovan and writing about the strenuous life, was more self-consciously the performer, as was John F. Kennedy, who needed to present a robust public figure to hide his poor health. In connection with the Kennedy and Roosevelt myths, both men were president during the peaks in the popularity of football; Roosevelt, when college football was king; Kennedy, when professional football had caught on with the public in a big way. But Nixon was more truly *absorbed* by the power of athletics, by its power as metaphor, or to borrow one scholar's phrase, by "the inseparability of ideals and action." And so the series of confrontations with Khrushchev was, for Nixon, his great moment of truth, his ultimate test of character; it is what the athlete lives for, the proof of his greatness in the challenge of a pressured performance: "... the moment for which I had been preparing myself for many months."

It is crucial, in understanding Nixon, to note his singular use of baseball metaphors for his most important confrontation with America's most powerful enemy (as he saw it) during the period of baseball's expansion, across both geographical and racial (i.e., political) lines. During baseball's great expansionist era, a young politician wishes to make a reputation as the heroic loner standing up to the expansionist politics of the Soviet Union. There is an odd self-reflexive quality in this cultural moment. He does not invoke an image of baseball as romantic or pastoral. His image of baseball, as with his other sports references, mirrors the frenzy and desperation of the man himself. For those writers who have most promoted the romance of the sport, baseball's pastoral myth conjures up images of harmony and natural bliss. How striking that in the vision of Richard Nixon, baseball becomes the central metaphor for the widest political and philosophical schism that he could imagine.

Bush and the Bush Leagues

Looking Forward, George Bush's 1988 campaign autobiography, written with Victor Gold, reminds the reader of Ring Lardner's *You Know Me Al* (1952), the epistolary novel about a bush league pitcher with a modest career for the Chicago White Sox who thinks himself a great deal more talented than he truly is. But there is an underlying folksy modesty to it all; the brilliant colloquial language makes one unsure how much this young pitcher really knows about himself. Is he a jerk, a fool, an egomaniac, or just a sweet kid?

One asks those questions about Bush as one reads his autobiography, for, although it is not as colloquial as Lardner's novel, it exudes the same folksy modesty, the same plain, unassuming American speech, and the same lack of any real definition of its subject. "Looking forward," the author notes, "reflects [a] philosophy," but of course this is not true. The phrase, taken from the book's epigraph, a statement by Senate Chaplain Edward Everett Hale, is not remotely connected to a philosophy but rather is the clichéd summation of a bourgeois Christian mood—the sort of maxim or self-motivation jingle that might have been created by Norman Vincent Peale or the Jehovah's Witnesses or the boosters for a university's multimillion fund-raising campaign. It might characterize the attitude of a minor league pitcher who hopes for the big time, or a mediocre politician who hopes to be president.

Bush's book is a story about a self-made man but not a man who is pathologically driven. Though Bush was shot down as a fighter pilot during World War II, he was not dramatically injured as was his Republican rival, Kansas Senator Robert Dole. Bush's heroism seems routine. He is wealthy but he still enjoys backyard barbecues with friends. He started a business that was moderately successful, and his political career has been successfully moderate. That is to say, he has been appointed to a good many important jobs without having to do much to get them other than assure the people who appointed him that he would not do much while he occupied the post. Bush has the type of ambition that reassures his supporters because it does not accompany any particular drive for personal achievement. In this, he is rather like the company man who wishes to experience life as a series of painless promotions that come not because of one's talent but because of one's loyalty. Loyalty is worth a great deal more in politics than mere talent. It is both more durable and more profoundly exacting: it forces the fulfillment of promises and it withstands temptation.

Bush went to Yale, where he majored in economics and earned a Phi Beta Kappa key. He also played baseball there, and this seems as essential as anything he mentions in his book. One can hardly imagine a better way to reacclimate to mythical America after fighting in a war or to reinvest in the hypnotic comfort of the American dream than by going to an Ivy League col-

lege and playing baseball. The entire baseball section of the book is sand-
wiched between two legendary players: Lou Gehrig, Bush's hero, "a great
athlete and team leader," "nothing flashy, no hotdogging, the ideal sportsman," who died several years before Bush came to Yale; and Babe Ruth, who
visited Yale in 1948 when he was dying of cancer. Bush, then captain of the
Yale baseball team, met Ruth during a ball field ceremony in which Ruth
donated the manuscript of his autobiography.

None of this is without political or autobiographical significance: The
passing of Ruth and Gehrig signified the end of an era in the conservative's
vision of the American dream, the death of pastoral innocence; after all, 1948
was the year after Jackie Robinson had integrated Major League baseball.
Inasmuch as conservatism was, for such a long time in this country, an expression of white male privilege, baseball, by this time, was no longer its
suitable icon. Conservatism had to reassert its values not through icons and
athletic heroes but through a new text. It is not surprising that, in his baseball section, Bush mentions William F. Buckley's *God and Man at Yale*
(1951), the book that is credited with regenerating conservative thought in
America or at least attaching it to something that was intellectual (Yale)
instead of merely sentimental (baseball). Paradoxically, of course, despite the
intellectual veneer of its argument and even its continued relevance as a critique of certain aspects of academia and undergraduate education, Buckley's
first book is in fact a sentimental work. How seamless American culture is
for Bush! Into the vaults goes Ruth's autobiography of a hero of the American dream and out, three years later, comes Buckley's lament that the American dream is no longer taught at Yale.

Bush played first base at Yale and improved from being "good field, no
hit" to being "good field, fair hit." Bush quotes an article in the *New Haven
Evening Register* that describes him as a "classy first baseman" who happened
to be hitting .167, or what a professional ball player would call "a buck and
some change." He received some advice about his hitting which in effect told
him to be more aggressive at the plate, and he slowly improved as a hitter
until by his last game he was hitting .280. Although he admits mild envy of
his teammate Frank Quinn, who became a professional ball player, and con-
fesses he would like to say that what took him to Texas was "a fat contract to
play professional baseball," one feels fairly sure that Bush did not really want
to be a professional player. He would have lost all sense of himself as being a
true sportsman, and sport itself would have lost its essentially upper-class appeal for him.

As titans of the American dream, Ruth and Gehrig (though Gehrig
went to Columbia) located their mythic power in the fact that they were
working-class men. Professional sport for them was upward mobility. Bush's
own upward urges could not be satisfied by a professional sports career. Bush

had a boyish and typically American worship for his baseball heroes, and Gehrig and Ruth, especially Gehrig, made particularly suitable heroes. Ruth was the orphan boy who made out well when it was discovered that he could play ball. Because of his outsized sensual appetite and his expansive personality, Ruth was a Rabelaisian boy wonder. Gehrig was more puritanical and driven. Perhaps their nicknames tell the whole story: the Babe for Ruth; Iron Man for Gehrig. Gehrig was the hardworking son of an immigrant, a mother-obsessed boy who was, as baseball historian Donald Honig writes, "the perfect son, the perfect husband, the perfect ball player, the perfect Yankee... one of the game's few inviolable saints." His going to Columbia was part of his upward mobility. His mother wanted very much for him to get a college education, the immigrant parents' dream of a better life for the offspring. And we are reminded in the literature on Gehrig how long a social stretch going to Columbia was. Consider, for example, this passage from Robert Rubin's juvenile biography, *Lou Gehrig: Courageous Star* (1979):

> Lou was not a typical Columbia freshman. Most of his classmates were from well-to-do homes. They dressed smartly and were used to comfortable living. Lou was poor and looked it, going about campus hatless, coatless, his pants and shirt patched and worn. Many of his more fortunate classmates looked down on him because his parents were immigrants who worked at menial jobs. (52)

But, like the typical jock, Gehrig never finished his architecture studies at Columbia, signing a contract with the Yankees after having completed two years. This too is part of the myth, as he supposedly signed to help his parents financially. But George Bush, the son of Prescott Bush, was meant for a different career, which he well understood, and to have become a professional ballplayer himself, if it were possible, would have been out of character.

That Bush omits writing of two crucial instances in his life when he received help from his father, Prescott Bush, Sr., a successful businessman and a United States senator from Connecticut, is not surprising. In fact, it is probably central to understanding not only how and why he is drawn to using Gehrig and Ruth but also the importance of their myth to him as a patrician politician. Omitting to mention his father's help is understandable, since he wishes to present himself as self-made. Moreover, we can see a kind of symmetry between his connecting of Ruth's working-class autobiography to Buckley's privileged, intellectual "education" book, and his use of the myth of Ruth and Gehrig in relation to his own myth as privileged scion of the upper class. Bush wants to bridge a social gulf in America through the image of sports while, paradoxically, not bridging it at all.

The first assistance Prescott Bush provided was a substantial loan so that young Bush could get started in the oil business in Texas. The second was securing for him a key committee appointment when Bush was first elected to Congress in 1966. Yet, despite his admiration of Gehrig and Ruth, Bush does wish to make clear that his father's career is the paradigm for his own. His father attended Yale, fought with the field artillery during World War I, and did not join his own father's firm but went first to St. Louis and then to Tennessee to make his way in business. Finally, he returned to Connecticut to start his political career. It is nearly identical to Bush's own career with the noted exception that Bush did not return to New England. So, after all, it is better to have simply fantasized about a baseball career and thus be like many other boys.

Playing professional baseball is one version of the American dream, which in most cases it is better to have dreamed than to have fulfilled. The aspiration has a certain juvenile gentility that transcends class. Indeed, sport is one of the cultural instruments in America that makes class distinction bearable among men and ultimately gives them something to talk about. But the professional sports career, its pursuit, is, finally, nothing more than another class quest for identity and the shape of a career. And that is why Bush would have gone to Texas to enter the oil business without the contract, even if the professionals would have had him (which of course they wouldn't have because he could not hit, and it is easier to teach a good hitter to field than to teach a good fielder to hit). It was time to put away childish things.

But if, with the coming of social integration of the races in the 1950s (or at least an official government policy so stating), baseball could no longer be the same sentimental, childish locus of white conservatism, it did not become something much different. The black player was absorbed, albeit uneasily, into the myth and the tradition.

THE BLACK ATHLETE IN OUR TIME

Jackie Robinson and Willie Mays

In 1964, at the height of the civil rights movement, Jackie Robinson compiled a book of interviews entitled *Baseball Has Done It,* about the successful integration of the National Pastime. Most of the notable black ball players of the fifties and early sixties were interviewed, including Hank Aaron (who spoke quite absorbingly about James Baldwin), Larry Doby, Roy Campanella, Don Newcombe, Ernie Banks, Elston Howard, and Vic Power. Two prominent black players refused to be interviewed by Robinson: one was Maury Wills, the Los Angeles Dodgers shortstop, who was quoted as saying:

"I don't want to be involved in a controversy." This was said by Wills despite the fact that few of the black players had said anything that would have been considered shocking even in 1964. Players such as Banks and Howard, long known as models of self-effacing camaraderie, were positively and broadly accommodating—they tried so hard to be free of the remotest suggestion of complaint that they expressed no political consciousness at all. Perhaps Wills was right, in the end. Controversy *was* in the air, and those who tried the hardest to avoid it were actually confessing that they were drowning in it. Nonetheless, all the players spoke with a certain and earnest blend of honesty and caution, remembering, after all, that they were workingmen in a work world dominated by whites. This meant, in a richly ironic way, that they were precariously perched yet rooted in the twin tradition of both black and white baseball in America.

The other player who did not choose to be interviewed was Willie Mays. His refusal is understandable. Mays's huge and formidable myth—the exuberant Negro man-child, the Nigger Jim of American culture who went cruising with the white American male across the green, flat, achingly mystical expanse of center field in the Polo Grounds and Candlestick Park, locked in some impossibly intricate and gymnastic fox-trot called the pastoral romance, all of which he had so carefully and self-consciously constructed, as he had the myth of his speed by wearing a hat that was too large for him so that it would always come off—was at stake.

I remember as a boy seeing billboards in black neighborhoods with Mays's picture advertising Alaga Syrup. ("Alaga" is a portmanteau word combining the abbreviations of Alabama and Georgia.) "I was raised on Alaga Syrup—*This* Fielder's Choice is Always Alaga's *Real Cane* Flavor," read the sign. I suppose that only blacks used Alaga Syrup, as I never met a white who had ever heard of it and it could only be found in stores in black neighborhoods. A very thick, dark, molasseslike liquid, it was extremely sweet. I consumed gallons of it as a boy, not on pancakes but on biscuits. Many a morning my mother made me and my sisters a breakfast of biscuits that we covered or dipped with Alaga Syrup. At the time I thought these breakfasts to be a huge treat, and I remember eating whole trays of biscuits in a sitting. It was not until I was eighteen or nineteen years old and was told by a "dietetically conscious" Muslim friend that biscuits and syrup was "the breakfast of a sharecropper" that the poverty of my boyhood hit with a wave of shame. What I thought of as the homey ambrosia of my mother's strong, dark hands was nothing more than the malnutrition of degradation made palatable. For many years I could hardly think of biscuits and syrup without feeling ill. Since that day, I have never eaten Alaga Syrup again, although I sometimes think I would like to see a bottle of it. Probably because of his face on the advertisements I saw as a boy, I have always associated Willie Mays with Alaga

Syrup, as if his sweetness as an athlete was its sweetness, as if the nausea caused by its memory is precisely the nausea caused by the memory of him.

But it is impossible to talk about Willie Mays without talking about the man he rebuffed, Jackie Robinson. They were the first two black players to enter baseball's Hall of Fame on the basis of their accomplishments in the Major Leagues, not the Negro Leagues, which means they were among the earliest black ball players to achieve an official and eternal fame in American popular culture. They were both American Adams, natural men whose responses to the pastoral myth that engulfed them were disturbing: yet, Robinson hated the prolonged boyhood of professional athletics to the point where he adopted an almost depressive gravity; and Mays reveled in the conviction that eternal boyhood was all life had to offer an athlete. Mays's baseball career was twice as long as Robinson's.

The difference between the two men was akin to the difference between Pap Finn and Jim in *The Adventures of Huckleberry Finn* (1884). Both Pap and Jim were natural men, American Adams; Pap, however, was tormented by his marginality and yearned for status. Jim was satisfied with being outside because it was never his marginality alone that bothered him; Jim never wanted status, simply security. He never thought himself too good for his station in life; he only desired that his humility be respected. The difference between the two men as American Adams is underscored by their responses to codes: Pap was astonished and fearful when he discovered that Huck could read; Jim prided himself on being a master teacher and reader of signs. So Pap became, like Robinson, the most unnatural of natural men, and Jim, like Mays, became the idealization of humanity through nature.

"The only time I recall I ever worked," wrote Mays in his latest autobiography, *Say Hey* (1988), "was the night when I helped a friend of mine wash dishes in a restaurant. I didn't get home until six in the morning. My dad was having breakfast before going to work. He warned me never to come in that late again without telling him or Aunt Sarah." There are two important observations to make about this statement: First, Mays never considered his more than twenty years as a professional ball player to be work or labor. That is not surprising; it is indeed part of his myth as a natural man that he was for so long engaged in a kind of spirited adolescent play. Joe Louis had a similar attitude about his career as a boxer, and one is struck by how much alike Mays and Louis are. Both had very long and successful careers, much longer than the average in their sports; both served in the Armed Forces doing what they did as civilians, performing their sports; they both became greeters in Las Vegas after their athletic careers ended. And they were both celebrated by the white American public in much the same way and for the same reasons: they reminded whites that being a Negro was, in truth, quite a bit of wholesome and boyish fun. Whites were afforded the comfort of enjoying the romance of the unself-conscious black male without feeling burdened by any implications in denigrating him. Mays and Louis were never degraded; they were indulged.

Nothing makes this point clearer, about Mays being indulged, than a second observation about the above quotation. Mays apparently obeyed his father and never stayed out that late again. He also decided to let his family support him in his efforts to become a professional ball player, for his father's prohibition, in effect, made working impossible—the only type of job Mays could have worked as a teenager (when this dishwashing incident took place) would have forced him to come home very late at night, since he played sports for most of the afternoon and early evening. Mays's athletic talent was recognized when he was quite young and his family, as he tells us, freed him from the normal duties expected of a black boy reared in a working-class black family in the South during the thirties and forties. His uncle did his household chores for him; his aunt gave him ten dollars a week (a considerable sum at the time) for lunch money; and, most important, his father, a Negro league player, taught Mays how to play the game. This last point is especially significant. As Mays writes: "When I was sixteen, in 1947, Jackie Robinson broke into the major leagues. . . . I wouldn't say that Robinson was my idol. My father had always been that."

Robinson broke into white baseball when Mays was at an age susceptible to hero worship. Yet Robinson was never his idol. Robinson could never displace Mays's father. There may have existed between Mays and Robinson jealousy and even dislike, but never any "anxiety of influence." Mays never felt that Robinson was a hero he had to vanquish, because he could not afford to see him as a hero even before they became competitors. Yet, since they played for rival teams, one suspects that their competitive urges were fiercely expressed. Mays, however, had his own father as hero; then he adopted, by his own admission, his white father, manager Leo Durocher, under whom he began his career as a New York Giant. Mays describes Durocher's departure as manager of the Giants after the 1955 season as "my saddest moment in baseball." Elsewhere he writes: "I knew . . . that Leo and I had a relationship that never could be equaled. His departure was a source of regret that stayed with me for the rest of my big-league career." It is also intriguing that Mays married during the off-season between 1955, when Durocher left the Giants, and the start of the 1956 season. As he puts it: "Stickball would be behind me now, along with Leo and the carefree days in Harlem and the ball park." Did he get married because without Leo—or "Mister Leo," as Mays called him, conjuring up uneasy images of overwrought respect and endearing southern courtesy—Mays was really at a loss to find something better to do? The marriage was not successful. But the crucial difference between Mays and Robinson is precisely that: how each man saw the fathers in his life.

Jackie Robinson was high-spirited. He was perhaps known for being very little else once Branch Rickey told him, after two years in the major leagues, that he was free to be himself. Henry James warned us about people with that quality: "Of course the danger of a high spirit was the danger of inconsistency—the danger of keeping up the flag after the place has surrendered; a sort of behavior so crooked as to be almost a dishonour to the flat." That Robinson was a Republican and a conservative of sorts (he was, after his playing days, a business executive with Chock Full O'Nuts, so his conservatism was of the chamber-of-commerce type), should not be surprising since blacks as a group, especially the middle class, make very good philistines and fairly credible conservatives. (It must be admitted, however, that black conservatism and white conservatism are two very different things. For instance, government aid for minority businesses is a form of black conservatism but not, by any means, of the white variety.) There was a great deal of homely appeal in the conservative rhetoric of Booker T. Washington and Elijah Muhammad, which is strikingly similar to the current popularity of such "success-ethic" publications as *Black Enterprise* and the speeches of Louis Farrakhan (the former singer and dancer, once billed as the Calypso Kid). Perhaps Robinson never forgave himself his Republicanism simply because it was never quite stylish during the civil rights era—he had notable disagreements in his ghosted newspaper column with both Martin Luther King, Jr., and Malcolm X—which may explain why his militancy, while it may have striven unsuccessfully for sincerity, never lacked the vehemence of earnestness. But let us deal with the subject of fathers.

Robinson writes, in *I Never Had It Made* (1972):

> Some of the people who have criticized me have labeled me a black man who has been made by white people. They justify this by stating that I have had three fabulous, white godfathers—Mr. Rickey in baseball, Bill Black in business, and Nelson Rockefeller in politics.
>
> These critics overlook the fact that they are talking about three of the most hardheaded, practical men who ever lived. As capable as all three of these men may be of sentiment, not one of them did what they did out of misplaced emotionalism. Of the three, the closest to me was Mr. Rickey. But even though he was motivated by deep principle to break the barriers in baseball, Mr. Rickey was also a keen businessman. He knew that integrated baseball would be financially rewarding. His shrewd judgment was proven correct. (268)

Robinson's second paragraph seems to beg the question and ultimately ignores the fundamental theme of his autobiography: that Rockefeller, Rickey, and Black were "hardheaded, practical men" scarcely denies the possibility that they possessed some special feelings for Robinson, and it certainly does not speak to the more important issue of what Robinson felt about them. For instance, Robinson writes that the death of Rickey in 1965 "made me feel almost as if I had lost my own father. Branch Rickey, especially after I was no longer in the sports spotlight, treated me like a son." It must not be forgotten that Robinson's book is about lost and found fathers, denied and recognized sons. He tells in the beginning how he feels about his own father:

> To this day I have no idea what became of my father. Later, when I became aware of how much my mother had to endure alone, I could only think of him with bitterness. He, too, may have been a victim of oppression, but he had no right to desert my mother and five children. (16)

Unlike Mays, Robinson was an abandoned son, a son denied, and thus his autobiography becomes a quest for a father. He finds one for each of the major phases of his life: athletic, business, and political. The fact that his fathers are white is all the more fitting as a kind of justice (for it has been the white fathers who have denied the black fathers the right to fatherhood) and a kind of revenge (the inept, uncaring black father must pay for the pain he has caused). The autobiography ends with Robinson's tragic struggles with his own son, Jackie, Jr., who dies in an automobile accident after having fought to overcome drug addiction. The death of that son closes the book and the story possesses, as a result, a powerful symmetry: the dark son who succeeds haunted by the dark father who fails, and the dark father whose success haunts, oppresses, and finally destroys the dark son who fails. In the end, Robinson was obstinate and driven; Mays was driven as well (and often under stress, as his frequent fainting spells indicated), but he was never obstinate. Mays never forced an issue. It is doubtful whether he understood that any issue existed beyond playing the game.

Virtually all of Mays's autobiography is devoted to his career as a ball player; the afterlife is nothing more than a coda. More than half of Robinson's book is about his life after baseball. It is an indication not only of the length of the athletic careers of the two men but also of the shape and meaning of the two careers. Robinson could never really be satisfied by baseball; Mays could be satisfied by nothing else. Robinson describes his life as a series of clashes: as a child in California dealing with the racial taunts of white children; with white opponents while at the University of Southern California; with white officers while in the army; with white players, fans, and hotel and restaurant owners while a ball player; with militants, Uncle Toms, and dishonest white politicians while a businessman and a political

aide to New York Governor Nelson Rockefeller. Mays's life is always a resolution: there is no mention of racism in Mays's childhood; he and white children played together; he is not annoyed by the segregated accommodations
during his early days as a major league player; army life does not bother him.

Mays and Robinson are in such counterpoise that it is impossible to understand the black athlete as a cultural marvel without also understanding not
only the images of self-mythology that are afforded to black men in America
but the unique attraction of those images. What does it mean to Robinson
and to the rest of us that he was paradoxically the outsized rebel and the
symbol of capitulation? What does it mean to Mays that he was not only the
pastoral hero but also the symbol of an innocuous black manhood? Is professional athletics in America simultaneously both the triumph and the tragedy
of black male ambition, not success without meaning, but success flawed by
the very menacing limitations of its meaning? Few have bothered to inquire
into what ambition and achievement mean for black men, since black men
are usually studied and explained only for their inadequacies and failures.
Yet how else is a great athlete to be understood by his culture except as a
person consumed by ambition, pursuing a fabulous if narrow excellence, the
attainment of which is an achievement that demands nothing more than repetition?

Perhaps the sharp and telling edge of black male ambition is most de-
monstrably displayed and most intriguingly contemplated in the personality
of Frank Robinson (no relation to Jackie Robinson), who is a near contemporary of Mays (starting his minor league career two years after Mays had
started playing in the Major Leagues). It may be instructive to consider,
briefly, a black ball player who broke into the major leagues several years after the personalities of Willie Mays and Jackie Robinson had become the
stuff of popular culture—which means that in some ways Frank Robinson
was influenced by them. Frank Robinson divided his career between two
teams, the Cincinnati Reds in the National League and the Baltimore Orioles
in the American League. He won the Most Valuable Player Award in both
leagues (an incredible feat), was voted into the Hall of Fame after his retirement, and has served, on and off, as one of Major League baseball's few black
managers. Frank Robinson was one of the most hated players of his era; he
played with such manic intensity that he seemed excessively competitive,
much like Jackie Robinson. As he writes in his autobiography, *My Life Is
Baseball* (1968):

> I have, throughout my career, been called all kinds of names
> by opposing ballplayers. One guy said I was "deliberately vi-
> cious." Another accused me of "trying to maim people." A third

THE ECCO PRESS publishes poetry, fiction, essays, literary travel, biography, and cookbooks. Ecco also publishes the following series: THE DARK TOWER, NEGLECTED BOOKS OF THE TWENTIETH CENTURY, THE AMERICAN POETRY SERIES, MODERN EUROPEAN POETS, ECCO TRAVELS, THE ESSENTIAL POETS, and THE TALES OF CHEKHOV.

The Ecco Press is committed to publishing works, both new and old, of high literary merit. Our books are carefully designed and produced to last. If you would like to know more about us, please fill out and return this card.

We hope you are pleased with this book and thank you for your interest in The Ecco Press.

_____

NAME

_____

STREET

_____

CITY   STATE   ZIP

THE ECCO PRESS
100 WEST BROAD STREET
HOPEWELL, NJ 08525

said, "I hated his guts when I played against him." Okay, that's
their privilege. A lot of this, I think, came because the players
didn't know me. To get to know a player, you have to play with
him. But that never bothered me. I hate, too. I hate all the fellows
around the league who are wearing the other uniform. . . . I don't
like so much what's going on in baseball today, this friendliness
between opposing players. I think there's altogether too much of
it. Say a buddy of yours is playing shortstop for the other side and
you're going out to dinner with him after the game. Then, during
the game, you're on first base and a ground ball is hit and your
buddy is coming across to tag the bag. You're not going to knock
him down. You're not going to hit him to break up the double
play. You're just going to slide nicely, get up, dust off your pants,
and go back to the dugout. (8)

Later he explains why he has not been involved in politics, even when pressure has been applied by black activists for prominent blacks like himself to
speak out:

My life is baseball and I think it deserves all my attention.
It's the same even with my leisure. I go to the movies in season, I
attend pro and college basketball and football games in the off-
season because I love all sports. But I don't have any special interests that I think might distract me from the game. I don't read
books. I don't play golf. I don't hunt or fish. I simply don't want
to get involved in anything but baseball. (15–16)

A lot of Negro groups have criticized me for it, because when
they call me to lead marches and protests or to make personal appearances I have to tell them no. I sympathize with them, really.
They've done a great deal of good; I agree with them on some
points and there are some points I disagree with them. But I don't
think baseball should be a fight for anything but baseball. (16)

In effect, Frank Robinson combines the personalities of Jackie Robinson and Willie Mays, having the fervent, even overcompensating drive for
self-respect and achievement (like Jackie Robinson, Frank Robinson was a
fatherless boy whose family moved from the South, Texas in this case, to
California) coupled with an almost equally passionate provincialism that
expresses itself as a lack of political consciousness (he was the youngest child
and, like Mays, was indulged and pampered while growing up).

Some of this can be explained as typical of the working-class male's attitude toward work itself: the tremendous fear of and exaltation over rivalry;

hostility towards politics, particularly social-justice causes that smack of overt do-goodism, which always seems tainted with either "making trouble" or effeminacy; and an obsessive antiintellectualism that prides itself on being masculine. That participation in professional athletics should diminish a man's natural humanizing inclinations toward friendship and civic obligation is troubling (although Robinson's reluctance to have his fame exploited by civil rights organizations is certainly understandable). Moreover, that he should view baseball as a sphere of human activity that is politically neutral, when his very presence is both a political cause and effect, seems the wishful expression of our desire that sport be an image of man beyond politics.

The problem for the black male here—and it is an extremely important one, as athletics provides the only extensive field of survey for analyzing black male ambition in a context where its expression has had an enormous impact on American culture at large—is that while he is preoccupied, obsessed even, in exercising and empowering his manhood, the very nature of athletic endeavor requires that he prolong his adolescence almost in an act of stunting or thwarting his manhood. Frank Robinson's attitudes, his views toward life, are indeed those of an older adolescent male: laughingly bellicose, daringly vain, remarkably close-minded, insistently and uninterestingly self-absorbed. In Frank Robinson, the classic temperamental modes of Willie Mays and Jackie Robinson are flooded by a grandeur of expertise, tuned to a new pitch of passion, but distressingly unresolved, as if a giant potential remains unrealized.

There is an image we all have of Willie Mays and Jackie Robinson, and it is the same image: both are young men running on a baseball field on a bright afternoon, Robinson rounding the bases, Mays in the outfield chasing a fly ball. Their caps fly off; they seem graceful and free. But one must always be aware of the implication that if, in America, a black man is running then he is, to paraphrase a line from an Amiri Baraka poem, being chased by someone or something that hates him. Satchel Paige, the black pitcher whom Jackie Robinson never liked because he seemed so openly an Uncle Tom and whom Willie Mays admired as a "legend," put it best by inadvertently describing the dilemma of the black athlete: Don't look back; something might be gaining on you.

NOTES

1 It is interesting to note how much Nixon views his life and his "crises" in terms of adversative rhetorical encounters: debates (Kennedy, the Latin American Communists, Khrushchev); cross-examinations (Alger Hiss, the press during the slush fund episode); speeches before hostile audiences and judges (the slush fund speech, the speeches on the Latin American tour, the self-punishment of the entire 1960 campaign).

COLLECTING "THE ARTIFICIAL NIGGER"

Race and American Material Culture

I reckon I'll know a nigger if I see one.

—Nelson, the white boy, in Flannery O'Connor's
"The Artificial Nigger"

I

In the famous Flannery O'Connor story, when young Nelson, traveling with his grandfather, Mr. Head, on a train to Atlanta, for the first time in his life encounters a black man, who happens to be walking down the aisle, he, in his innocence, sees merely a man and nothing else:

"What was that?" [his grandfather] asked.

"A man," the boy said and gave him an indignant look as if he were tired of having his intelligence insulted.

"What kind of man?" [the grandfather] persisted, his voice expressionless.

"A fat man," Nelson said. He was beginning to feel that he had better be cautious.

"You don't know what kind?" [the grandfather] said in a final tone.

"An old man," the boy said and had a sudden foreboding that he was not going to enjoy the day.

"That was a nigger," [the grandfather] said and sat back.

Near the end of the story, when, on this disastrous trip, Nelson has been denied by his grandfather and their estrangement seems unhealable, they are finally brought together again:

> [The grandfather] had not walked five hundred yards down the road when he saw, within reach of him, the plaster figure of a Negro sitting bent over on a low yellow brick fence that curved around a wide lawn. The Negro was about Nelson's size and he was pitched forward at an unsteady angle because the putty that held him to the wall had cracked. One of his eyes was entirely white and he held a piece of brown watermelon. . . .
> Mr. Head breathed, "An artificial nigger!"
> It was not possible to tell if the artificial Negro were meant to be young or old; he looked too miserable to be either. He was meant to look happy because his mouth was stretched up at the corners but the chipped eye and the angle he was cocked at gave him a wild look of misery instead.
> "An artificial nigger!" Nelson repeated in Mr. Head's exact tone.

And so we learn from this story that "the artificial nigger," the common lawn statue of the black, was the wild caricature, the totem, by which whites unified around the idea of their whiteness. "The artificial nigger" was the alien, the other, elevated to the iconographic comic diminutive. But "the artificial nigger" in his damaged ambiguity represents both happiness and "misery," immunity and pain, triumph and tragedy. And the ultimate tragedy is that "the nigger" is both "artificial" and "real."

II

To be begin with the heart of the matter: The single feature that makes the hobby of black collectibles controversial, or at least uneasy, is the prominent and distressing existence in much, or a significant portion, of it of various degrading images of blacks—images I refer to collectively as "the Artificial Nigger." P. J. Gibbs, in her *Black Collectibles Sold in America,* puts the matter thus: "In one camp, most individuals feel that the existence of items which depict Blacks in a negative light should not be sold; on the other side, individuals feel that Black collectibles are an artifact of history and as such, should be sold in the same manner that other artifacts are sold." I suggest that a brief consideration of the relationship of some aspects of the image of "the Artificial Nigger" that is so characteristic of much black memorabilia to the historical development of American popular culture can teach us something essential about the nature of American culture as a whole and perhaps, at least partly, explain why black collectors, in particular, are attracted to the enterprise of owning and valuing these items.

American popular culture as we understand it today was largely created in the nineteenth century. We tend to think of popular culture today as a visual phenomenon (television, film, computer games) connected with erotic sensationalism; however, it is more proper to think of American popular culture, especially in the nineteenth century, as being indistinguishable from material culture and less connected with sensationalism (although there was the yellow press, to be sure) than with a feminized, nostalgic, or religious sentimentality. Popular culture must be understood not as the particular message of a medium but as the method of standardization of a mass society. The creation of popular culture is the creation of easily reproduced, cheaply available items and artifacts that appeal to large numbers of people. Before photography and visuals, before the phonograph and records, before mass advertising, popular culture was embodied in the book, and by mid-nineteenth century particularly it was the feminine, best-selling novel, the only kind of American book that would sell in America. *Uncle Tom's Cabin* was the most popular American book of the nineteenth century.

It is one of the curious paradoxes of American culture that Harriet Beecher Stowe's 1852 novel, *Uncle Tom's Cabin,* so sincerely and powerfully antislavery, should have so successfully trapped blacks in a series of images that so thoroughly discounted their humanity while so fervently pleading for their character. No American fiction of the nineteenth century so thoroughly and unambiguously condemned slavery on the slaveholder's own terms, yet few books from that era are as disliked by modern black readers. Despite the fact that most blacks today are still overwhelmingly Christian, the pious Uncle Tom is so hated by blacks that his name is an intraracial epithet. In a sense, although the denigrated comic darky character predates *Uncle Tom's Cabin* by twenty-odd years on the American stage, it is this grand American social protest novel, through its unimaginable popularity as both book and stage show, that sealed the white idea of blacks in American popular culture for roughly a hundred years.

In *Uncle Tom's Cabin* are two specific minstrel scenes, both associated with black children. The first occurs near the beginning of the book when young Harry, little son of mulatto slaves George and Eliza Harris, performs a bit of a show for his master, Shelby, and the slave trader, Haley, that includes impersonations of several stock stage Negro types—the pompous church elder and the aged "Uncle"—as well as "one of those wild, grotesque songs common among the negroes, in a rich, clear voice, accompanying his singing with many comic evolutions of the hands, feet, and whole body, all in perfect time to the music." Shelby calls the boy "Jim Crow," referring to that famous stage minstrel character who was the epitome of the plantation slave: lazy, childlike, fun-loving, and always in good humor. (Jim Crow's stage partner was Zip Coon, who was a well-dressed dandy and schemer, a teller of tall tales well sprinkled with malapropisms.)

Later in the novel, Augustine St. Clair buys a completely unregenerate and brutalized slave girl named Topsy for his New England cousin, Miss Ophelia, to reform. Upon St. Clair's command to "show us some of your dancing," she "struck up . . . an odd negro melody, to which she kept time with her hands and feet, spinning round, clapping her hands, knocking her knees together, in a wild, fantastic sort of time, and producing in her throat all those odd guttural sounds which distinguish the native music of her race, and finally, turning a summerset or two, and giving a prolonged closing note, as odd and unearthly as that of a steam whistle, she came suddenly down on the carpet, and stood with her hands folded." Unlike the handsome mulatto boy, Harry, Topsy, a full-blooded black, is a grotesque with "a white and brilliant set of teeth," "wooly hair . . . braided in sundry tails . . . stuck out in every direction," and a face that expresses "an odd mixture of shrewdness and cunning."

In these scenes, *Uncle Tom's Cabin* inadvertently joined a number of elements that were to solidify the image of the blacks in popular culture: the idea of the childishness of the race illustrated by the black child, an important image in much late-nineteenth- and early-twentieth-century black memorabilia such as advertising, playing-, and postcards as well as an image for commercial products. Thus, the grotesque childishness of the race and the childish grotesque of the child became interchangeable. It was Stowe's intention not necessarily to make the grotesque childishness of black slaves seem natural but rather the unfortunate result of the inhumanity of slavery. However, by the post–Civil War period, Topsy had become not only one of the most popular black characters in the stage play (second only to Uncle Tom himself) but was now clearly and purely a comic character who was to become the model for stage and film "picks" (pickaninnies) in the nineteenth and twentieth centuries.

In Victorian America, because children were identified with intense sentimentality and nostalgic yearnings (largely because of their vulnerability to sudden and early death), Stowe's association of "darky" stage antics with the black child did two damaging things: It strongly reinforced in the minds of whites, who already in the 1850s were waxing sentimental about "the old plantation," sentimentality and nostalgia for "darky" antics, by connecting them with children and childhood. It also, contrarily, distinguished black children as beings apart from white children, and thus separated the idea of black childhood from white childhood, linking black children to deviltry, mischief, silliness, and an intensely exhibitionist nature.

Uncle Tom's Cabin gave us a company of other black figures who were to become stereotypical images in material culture of "the Artificial Nigger." Some, like Sam, the "politician" and opportunist, and Andy, his sidekick, are nothing more than varieties of blackface minstrelsy. Others such as Uncle Tom's wife, Aunt Chloe, and Aunt Dinah, of St. Clair's plantation, give us the image of the overweight, greasy black, extraordinary cook and matriarch of the kitchen, who was to become both company icon (Aunt Jemima) and pop culture cliché in a range of manifestations from Tom and Jerry cartoons to Fannie Hurst's 1933 novel, *Imitation of Life,* and the films it spawned. With such black female stereotypes, white Americans made the association between nourishment, warmth, nurture, and a de-sexed black maternity that in no way made black women competitive threats to white women for the favors of white men.

Uncle Tom's Cabin, nineteenth-century America's most popular political novel, came along at a time when American popular culture was developing a consensus view about a number of American types: the Yankee as bargaining hustler, the southern planter as doomed aristocrat, the southern belle as spoiled but dutiful daughter, the white woman as true bearer of Christian virtues and as domestic light of the world, the westerner as tale-telling raw-boned barbarian, the dandy as the over-Europeanized fop. And into this mix came several ethnic types including the Jew, the Irish, the Indian, the German, and, most notably and most indelibly, the black. As technological innovations went apace in the nineteenth century, including better roads, improved travel with trains, the coming of the telegraph, the rapid urbanization and industrialization of the country with its attendant increase in leisure and in literacy, a vast array of popular culture mechanisms, from cheap, popular theater to city newspapers, from circuses to mass advertising to the mass commercialism of shopping and the growth of consumer culture to the organization and professionalization of sports, the image of the black American as "the Artificial Nigger" was enmeshed in an unstoppable historical moment (or series of moments) that made this intolerable image endurable and even, among whites, beloved.

In his article "Black Stereotypes as Reflected in Popular Culture, 1880–1920", J. Stanley Lemons asserts that blacks were most intensely caricatured, both on stage and in print advertisements during the 1840s, when northern opposition to antislavery was particularly violent, and during the 1890s, when, after Reconstruction, race relations in the country were at a low ebb and the most vicious forms of antiblack violence and legal strictures were carried out.[1] But the point Lemons misses is that during both the 1840s and the 1890s, the nation went through a period of expansion through conquest (the Mexican War, the Spanish-American War) and augmented population (European immigration) that was directly tied to how white America saw its mission and destiny in relation to darker races. In short, these particularly distressing periods occurred when whites were thinking about their own identity and the meaning of their race and nationality. Seeing themselves both as the advance guard of superior white civilization and members of an economically competitive, increasingly urban, and rapidly transforming society, native whites saw blacks as a refreshing nostalgic contrast: simple, rural, natural (to the point of sometimes resembling the missing link), noncompetitive, good-humored, and happy, in possession of a kind of folksy piety, and concerned only with basic appetites such as eating and sex. Indeed, blacks as "the Artificial Nigger" represented a kind of sentimental, if low-grade, pastoralism and, invariably, most of the images of blacks projected in the culture in the nineteenth and early twentieth centuries symbolized just these qualities. However, to whites "the Artificial Nigger" was not just a fiction or a figment of their imagination but a fact, a truth. Thus, from the very beginning of the creation of these caricatures, whites—from southern apologists for slavery like Josiah Nott and George Fitzhugh in their treatises to Harriet Beecher Stowe in her *Key To Uncle Tom's Cabin,* from Joel Chandler Harris in his creation of Uncle Remus's tales to D. W. Griffith's use of Woodrow Wilson's history texts to legitimate his 1 9 1 5 film, *The Birth of a Nation,* and to Freeman Gosden and Charles Correll's claims of extensive research in their characterizations of blacks in the popular radio (and later television) show, "Amos 'n' Andy"—have tried to argue that "the Artificial Nigger" of their imagination is in fact authentic. More than any other American ethnic group (except, arguably, Indians), blacks have had to battle for their identity in an arena where they have been not only pervasively caricatured across the entire range of the culture (from respected scholars like Ulrich Phillips to popular comic strips like "Moon Mullins" and "Mandrake the Magician") but where these caricatures and slurs have been so hotly and passionately defended as anthropologically accurate.[2]

III

There are two major reasons, one simple, the other complex, that many African Americans in the last twenty years or so have become so passionately engaged in the hobby of collecting black memorabilia (The National Black Memorabilia Collectors' Association has seven hundred members and thirteen local chapters in the United States). There is a national quarterly publication (*Black Ethnic Collectibles,* founded in 1 987), and several extensive collections including the Lewis and Blalock collection in Washington, D.C., Jeanette Carson's Black Ethnic Collectibles in Maryland, and the Black Archives Research Center and Museum at Florida A&M. The first explanation is simply economic: If the black underclass suffered in the 1 980s, the black middle class expanded and its overall wealth increased. Collecting memorabilia and antiques is, obviously and nearly exclusively, a middle-, upper-middle, upper-class pursuit. There are now a significant number of blacks with the income and the leisure to engage in this hobby to such a point as to make their presence, their aims, and their interests felt as a group. Moreover, in American culture collecting pop culture items has become a bourgeois investment pastime. For a people notoriously condemned for their lack of historical impulse, this junk-bin, attic subculture of collecting (especially of the mass-produced) on the part of Americans may, ultimately, become too much of a good thing. Preserving too much may give just as distorted a view of our past as saving too little. Moreover, there is the real fear that we may drown in our own junk at last, giving a false monetary value to things that really should bear no such weight. But it is good to know that blacks have crossed over sufficiently in the culture that they too may pursue hobbies formerly associated only with whites.

The second, more complex reason for black interest in black collectibles stems from their own quest for a usable past and a sense of identity. No group in America has been "thoroughly and deliberately dispossessed of both their identity and their heritage as have blacks. And it would only stand to reason that, especially among educated and wealthy blacks, a kind of national and spiritual, genealogical-group reclamation project would be both appealing and essential. In collecting black memorabilia, blacks come face to face with the dilemma of the meaning and the shape of their identities in the very terms of W.E.B. Du Bois's famous 1903 statement about "this double-consciousness," about "[their] two-ness—An American, a Negro," and how living in America "yields [the black] no true self-consciousness" as they are forced constantly to see themselves as others see them. Collecting black material culture offers two ways, heretofore unavailable to African Americans, of finding a true self-consciousness. First, since a significant portion of black collectibles are not degraded and denigrating stereotypical images in mass-produced items but the personal stuff of a group history, such as self-published autobiographies and histories, letters and personal papers, art objects and artifacts by black artists and artisans, blacks now have an opportunity to amass, classify, analyze, display, and preserve the very materials of their peoplehood in their own way and for their own ends, to think about how to use their own past as Americans. Second, with the degrading and denigrating images of "the Artificial Nigger," African Americans can begin to think, in their own terms, about what is authentic blackness and why, as a living and livable idea, it has been so alien yet so endearing, so frightening and yet so comforting to white America's conception of itself. These objects might also bring to mind the episode in Ralph Ellison's *Invisible Man* where Todd Clifton, former activist, becomes a pitchman for Sambo dolls and is ultimately murdered on the street by a white policeman. African Americans think about the ambiguous political meaning of these objects as a sign of oppression and defeat and as a sign of whites' need for constant vigilance and control against resistance. As a cultural object, the doll, for instance, is fraught with historical complexity for the black American, from the early-1920s campaigns of black newspapers like the *Amsterdam News* to get their readers to buy only black dolls at Christmas, to the Supreme Court decision in 1954 to integrate public schools, which was based in part on findings that black children, given the choice, preferred white dolls to black dolls, so low was their self-esteem.

If, as Ellison suggests, "the action of the early minstrel show . . . constituted a ritual of exorcism," perhaps this ritual of middle-class collecting, ironically, constitutes a necessary act of exorcism for blacks themselves. Finally, if this collecting of black memorabilia provides us with new ways of looking at the black American, and more importantly, a new and more compelling way for black Americans to look at themselves and each other, then perhaps we may have new things to say about the culture as a whole. As Ellison wrote, "And it is possible that any viable theory of Negro American culture obligates us to fashion a more adequate theory of American culture as a whole." For blacks, to collect the material stuff of their past may be the first step to fusing the schism between being black and being American.

NOTES

1 *American Quarterly* 29, no. 1 (spring 1977), 102–116.
2 Admittedly, Stowe's work is meant to authenticate her critique of slavery rather than to defend her delineation of blacks. Nonetheless, it is partly engaged in the task of showing that just the type of slaves she depicts—Tom, Topsy, etc.—do exist.

PULP AND CIRCUMSTANCE

The Story of Jazz in High Places

PROLOGUE: PLAIN DIRT

My master is sick outdoors.

—Shirley Caesar, recounting the story of Naaman in her sermon
"Go Take a Bath"

Sometime between 1966 and 1967, after she had left the Caravans for good, gospel singer and evangelist Shirley Caesar made a recording of her sermon entitled "Go Take a Bath," a fairly difficult record to find these days. In this twenty-five-minute homily, Caesar recounts the story of Naaman from the fifth chapter of Second Kings. Naaman is the captain of the army of Syria and "a great man with his master, and honorable" but Naaman is also a leper. During one of their battles with Israel, Naaman's company had captured an Israelite girl who tells Naaman's wife that Naaman can be cured of his leprosy by a great Israelite prophet, Elisha. Naaman goes forth to Israel to the house of Elisha and is told, not by Elisha but by a messenger, that he must wash in the Jordan River seven times if he wishes to be cured of his leprosy. The King James version continues the account in this manner.

> But Naaman was wroth, and went away, and said, Behold, I thought, he will surely come out to me, and stand, and call on the name of the Lord his God, and strike his hand over the place, and recover the leper.
> Are not Abana and Pharpar, the rivers of Damascus, better than all the waters of Israel? May I not wash in them, and be clean? So he turned and went away in a rage.

163

And his servants came near, and spake unto him, and said,
My father, if the prophet had bid thee do some great thing,
wouldst thou not have done it? how much rather then, when he
saith to thee, Wash, and be clean?

Then went he down, and dipped himself seven times in Jordan, according to the saying of the man of God: and his flesh came
again like unto the flesh of a little child, and he was clean.

And he returned to the man of God, he and all his company,
and came, and stood before him: and he said, Behold, now I know
that there is no God in all the earth, but in Israel; now therefore, I
pray thee, take a blessing of thy servant.

Elisha refused Naaman's offer of a gift. The essential message that Caesar conveys through her sermon, its moral, if you will, is that of the reduction of the pride of the mighty exemplified by Naaman's possessions (he left
Syria for Israel with "ten talents of silver, and six thousand pieces of gold,
and ten changes of raiment") and Naaman's attitude when Elisha refused to
cure him personally. But the story of the pride of the mighty being humbled
by the prophecy of the weak resonates and signifies particularly when one
considers that this sermon was delivered in the mid-sixties when the civil
rights battles, urban riots, and concerns about racial matters were at their
height and when one considers that this sermon was meant specifically for a
black audience that is both on the record responding to the sermon and the
consumer for whom the record is marketed. There is a double message and,
consequently, a layered complexity, in Caesar's message. She tells her black
audience that they must, like Naaman, go take a bath because, in one of her
many consumer-culture, womanly allusions, "Oxydol cannot make a soul
white."[1] This, of course, implies overtly that her audience must wash the leprosy of sin from their souls but also, as has always been the case when blacks
have had to mouth the cliché about being washed in the blood of the Lamb in
a culture that for so very long saw their blackness as the outward mark of
their inward depravity. There is nothing especially noteworthy in this, and
along with the sermon itself, it can be dismissed as the peculiar dilemma of
the Afro-Christian's struggle with theological rhetoric. But it must not be
forgotten that while Caesar is telling her black audience to take a bath, she is
telling the story of how the high and mighty Naaman was healed by the God
of a despised people, so, in effect, the sermon has two messages: the standard
cry for Christian salvation and repentance from the sinner and another covert
message that tells the tale of two peoples, one strong and the other weak, and
that would have a pointed significance in the mid-1960s era of race consciousness.

Caesar calls on God at the beginning of her sermon to "give us the Gospel" so that it might "root up and tear down," interesting language, indeed, in the days of Watts and the March on Selma. Some might say that the Gospel or its absence was certainly rooting up and tearing down a great deal of America's social fabric in those days. At the end of her sermon, she tells her audience of "the modern day bathroom. We got a face bowl, we got a shower, we got a bath tub." What is remarkable here is that it is in this modern bathroom that total transformation takes place, where one truly becomes clean, as the face bowl represents conversion, the shower sanctification, and the bathtub being washed in the blood of Jesus. It was on southern restrooms and public bathhouses that White and Colored signs were most commonly hung, and having the very type of modern indoor bathroom of which Caesar speaks was a mark of distinction that separated the rich from the poor in this country for a very long time. So it is greatly politically suggestive to speak of a major transformation of the soul taking place in the modern bathroom for, metaphorically, such a battle—between classes and between the races—for the transformation of the House of America was taking place in that very room.

Finally, and most important for her audience, when Caesar shouts what Elisha's servant tells Naaman, "Go wash, Go Wash, Go Wash down in the Jordan," to which the listeners shriek, the message is clearly that only the prophecy of the lowly can save the high from white leprosy. (Leprosy was often described in the Bible as a kind of whiteness; see the story of the leprosy of Miriam in Numbers 12:10: "Behold, Miriam became leprous, white as snow.") So to wash in the Jordan, in effect, washes the whiteness from Naaman while revealing to him the fundamental truth that the lowly Jordan is greater than the mighty rivers of Syria, and it is on this irony about the change that results from the act of washing, to become white or to become unwhite, that the true signifying power of Caesar's sermon depends. Since at least the early nineteenth century and certainly since the 1852 publication of Harriet Beecher Stowe's *Uncle Tom's Cabin,* the life of blacks, their presence, the very myth that has charged and inspired the nature of their condition have served as the spiritual waters of the Jordan in which whites have washed themselves clean of their whiteness, their civilization, their inhibitions, where, in fact, they have gone, from time to time, to refresh their consciousness. It is a truism in American cultural history that the African American is both a greater demon and a greater soul, from Stowe's Uncle Tom to Mailer's black prizefighters, from Fannie Hurst's Delilah to Margaret Mitchell's Mammy to Alice Walker's Shug Avery and Celie, is the authenticating consciousness that the white, trapped by a false whiteness, seeks. Blacks become the spiritual pools in which somehow the whites must transform their own souls. This myth has been nowhere so recurrent or so powerful in our country as in the making and performance of popular music. With only those few exceptions such as country and western or easy listening music in which whites do not share much performance space with blacks, virtually every popular music in this country is considered the authentic expression of blacks, and if whites play these forms of music they must somehow, like Naaman, wash themselves in the black Jordan to validate their right to play this music.

OLD ROCKIN' CHAIR'S GOT ME

In the entire history of jazz music, there have been two musicians who have become known to both their colleagues and their fans by the nickname Pops, signifying, for at least a certain time, the range of influence and the fervency of respect that each man generated. Oddly, one has become a permanent fixture in American popular music, his genius unquestioned, his popularity undiminished by the passage of time. The other is virtually forgotten nowadays, and when he is remembered it is largely thought that he had no genius and that his popularity was largely of the moment when his band enjoyed its heyday in the 1920s. The former is Louis Armstrong, the great black jazz musicians from New Orleans who so thoroughly reshaped American music in the 1920s. The other is Paul Whiteman, the white bandleader from Denver who also, in his way, thoroughly reshaped not American music so much as American musical taste with his very popular dance band. These are the twin father figures of American popular music, both reaching their stride and producing their most important work in the 1920s; both considered old heads in this business even when they were young, men without youths; both heavy and both popular as personalities as much as for their musical abilities. While we may speak of several mothers of American popular music—Bessie Smith and Ruth Etting, Ethel Waters and Sophie Tucker, Josephine Baker and Fanny Brice, Black Patti and Aretha Franklin—only one woman has ever been popularly called a mother in American music: (Gertrude) Ma Rainey, the Mother of the Blues. Perhaps it is fitting, since we see popular American music so much in terms of its influential male musicians, that it should have two fathers, one black and one white: Pops Armstrong and Pops Whiteman.[2]

POMP AND CIRCUMSTANCE; PULP AND CIRCUMSTANCE

> *The only thing that is different from one time to another is what is seen and what is seen depends upon how everybody is doing everything. This makes the thing we are looking at very different and this makes what those who describe it make of it, it makes composition, it confuses, it shows, it is, it looks, it likes it as it is, and this makes what is seen as it is seen. Nothing changes from generation to generation except the thing seen and that makes a composition. . . .*

Those who are creating the modern composition authentically are naturally only of importance when they are dead because by that time the modern composition having become past is classified and the description of it is classical. That is the reason why the creator of the new composition in the arts is an outlaw until he is a classic, there is hardly a moment in between and it is really too bad very much too bad naturally for the creator but also very much too bad for the enjoyer, they all really would enjoy the created so much better just after it has been made than when it is already a classic, but it is perfectly simple that there is no reason why the contemporaries should see, because it would not make any difference as they lead their lives in the new composition anyway.

—Gertrude Stein, "Composition as Explanation"

And whether there is Negro art or not, it is indisputable there is a certain spiritual something that has been deposited by the Negro in America, a certain buoyancy, spontaneity, and joy of living that has re-inspired the staid, mechanical, intellectualized Caucasian, stirring him to a merrier mood, and causing the blood to course with joyous rhythm through his veins. The Negro spirit, if I may use the phrase, practically dominates the amusement world in America and Europe today. Mr. Whiteman has brought out this art excellently, and given full justice to the Negro.

—J. A. Rogers, from his review of Whiteman's book, *Jazz,* in the December 1926 issue of *Opportunity*

On the evening of February 12, 1924, a major cultural event occurred in New York City. A concert was performed at the Aeolian Hall by Paul Whiteman, rotund band leader ("He trembles, wobbles, quivers—a piece of jazz jelly," wrote Olin Downes of the *New York Times*). Whiteman, like Jack Dempsey, the great heavyweight champion of this era, roared in from the west, Colorado being the birthplace of both men and San Francisco being the place of critical juncture in their careers, and succeeded in establishing not just one thriving dance band but, by the mid-twenties, a cohort of them. The Whiteman sound was the sound of the age, the sound of the 1920s. On February 12, Whiteman gave what he called a "jazz" symphonic concert. Whiteman was not without misgivings about the entire enterprise. Just an hour or so before the concert he felt this way according to his 1926 autobiography, *Jazz:*

I went back stage again, more scared than ever. Black fear simply possessed me. I paced the floor, gnawed my thumbs and vowed I'd give $5,000 if we could stop right then and there. Now that the audience had come, perhaps I had really nothing to offer after all. I even made excuses to keep the curtain from rising on schedule. But finally there was no longer any way of postponing the evil moment. The curtain went up and before I could dash forth, as I was tempted to do, and announce that there wouldn't be any concert, we were in the midst of it.

Whiteman, whose father was the supervisor of music education for the Denver public school system, was reared in a fairly strict, quite religious, and typically middle-class home where, of course, he received considerable instruction in music. He was a rather aimless and somewhat indolent young man which apparently infuriated his father, who decidedly and decisively pushed his son from the nest when he tired of his lack of ambition. Eventually, Whiteman became an indifferent viola player with, first, the Denver Symphony Orchestra and, later, the San Francisco Symphony Orchestra. But he had a great deal more ambition or more desire to be noticed and make money than could be accommodated by being an orchestra player whose meager pay often had to be supplemented by teaching. Whiteman began to investigate the possibilities of playing popular music and often went to dives and taverns around San Francisco to hear the locals play. And it was during these years, before World War I and before he formed his first band, that Whiteman first heard jazz music. Contrary to popular belief, jazz did not move up the river from New Orleans to Chicago in a straight line; some of the musicians went west, and the Barbary Coast became a very active hive of Dixieland or hot jazz music. Whiteman discovered, when he tried to play with a jazz band, that he could not play in the new idiom very well, but that if the music could be scored and played by better-trained musicians it could have broad appeal.

> "Jazz it up. Jazz it up," the conductor would snort impatiently at about this point in my reflections. And I would try, but I couldn't. It was as if something held me too tight inside. I wanted to give myself up to the rhythm like the other players. I wanted to sway and pat and enjoy myself just as they seemed to be doing. But it was no good.
>
> The second day the director fired me. . . .
>
> After many attempts, I finally worked out an orchestration and learned what I wanted to know about faking. Faking was what the early jazz orchestras relied upon. That is, they had no scores, each man working out his part for himself, "faking" as he went along. Up to that time, there had never been a jazz orchestration. I made the first and started into the jazz orchestra business.

Whiteman, not a terribly sophisticated or intellectual man, certainly no highbrow, was, due to his middle-class background, uneasy about playing a low-class music, a music, he goes to great pains to point out, that his father disapproved of, although his mother seemed to have liked it well enough; indeed, she used to sing the popular songs of the day to him when the father was out of the house. It was, obviously, not a conflict with his mother that Whiteman wanted both to resolve and to win by playing jazz music successfully, but an issue with his father. This is very important in understanding why Whiteman was attracted to the idea of jazz composition or highly arranged jazz music. Also, we know that Ferde Grofe was in San Francisco at the same time as Whiteman, writing arrangements for the Art Hickman band that people were describing as "new music." In 1915 the Hickman band was playing at the St. Francis Hotel and the Whiteman band at the Fairmount. Sometime after the war, before Whiteman took his band east, he hired Grofe as an arranger. As Whiteman writes: "For quite a while I did the arrangements and orchestrations, as well as the conducting, but it was too much for one man, so we took on Ferde Grofe, talented symphony player and composer." Although born in New York City, Grofe had played viola with the Los Angeles Symphony before turning to popular music. At the 1924 Aeolian Hall concert, the most important piece of music performed, George Gershwin's *Rhapsody in Blue,* was arranged—virtually shaped and molded—by Grofe, as Gershwin at that point knew very little about orchestrating music. As the story goes, Whiteman went from being a string player in a symphony orchestra to becoming, after the First World War, the highest paid dance band leader in the country, achieving both fame and money but not quite respect. A concert "to make a lady of jazz," as the critics put it, implying that jazz was actually no mere dame but an outright whore, would be an inevitable preoccupation to someone of Whiteman's background. As Gilbert Seldes, a critic and friend of Whiteman who helped write the program notes for the Aeolian Hall concert, said in his 1924 book, *The Seven Lively Arts,* "Paul Whiteman... wanted to 'elevate' jazz and thought the right way was to give a concert at Aeolian Hall."

In short, the source of Whiteman's motivation for holding a jazz concert in a symphony hall was the twin diseases of the American middle-class mind: self-consciousness and class anxiety. Throughout most of his life, Whiteman constantly suffered from stage fright, although seldom as severely as before the Aeolian Hall concert. His acute distress may have been the reason for his alcoholic and eating binges, which would last for weeks. The class anxiety is evidenced in other passages in his autobiography:

> To the Palais Royal [the New York club which Whiteman used as a base of operations during the height of his fame in the

1920s] came all the country's great names and foreign visitors of renown, too. Any night at all, we could look out and see Vanderbilts, Drexel Biddles, Goulds and the rest dancing to our music. Lord and Lady Mountbatten, cousins of the Prince of Wales, were among the distinguished guests one night. They had just arrived in this country to spend their honeymoon.

After that night, they came often, for they adored dancing. They were such a friendly, jolly pair that when they were in the room, we invariably played almost nothing but their favorite pieces. We had many conversations and Lord Mountbatten got to be friends with every boy in the band.

This is Whiteman's account of meeting the Prince of Wales during his band's first European tour:

The Prince had already arrived when I went into the room, but I was so nervous that I couldn't tell him from any of the others. I had a bad attack of stage fright and I wished I were somewhere else. Lord Mountbatten was disgusted with me. He is such a democratic, unassuming chap himself that he can't imagine anybody getting into what he calls a "funk" over a mere meeting with a prince. . . .

I hope I was natural, but if I wasn't at first, I was later; for the Prince put me instantly at ease with some flattering comment about the orchestra. He was wearing evening clothes and I thought I had never seen a man's shoulders look better in such dress. The Prince of Wales is really small, but for some reason, partly the way he carries himself, I suppose, you never realize it, even in his pictures.

I saw him many times after that evening. Sometimes we played for parties he or others gave at private houses; and whenever he wanted me, instead of sending an equerry to "command" my presence, he would come himself and ask in friendly fashion if it would be convenient for us to play.

We never accepted any pay from him.

Whiteman, like most of the middle class, is ambivalent in his feelings toward the aristocracy. There is always revealed the expressly astonished admiration that they, the royalty, are like everyone else, just ordinary-acting people; contrarily a great deal of pride is expressed that these quite extraordinary people, the royalty, are not above noticing a mere nobody, which, of course, is indicative, this act of noticing, that one is not a nobody after all.

("I didn't want you to think I was just some nobody," Gatsby tells Nick, but in the end he is actually what Tom Buchanan accuses him of being: "Mr. Nobody from Nowhere." In the age of the crystallization of modern mass culture, anonymity is a sin, the escape from it an obsession.) It is not that the aristocrats deign to acknowledge Whiteman's existence; what impresses Whiteman is that they seem truly pleased to meet him. Whiteman was sensitive about the idea of being a nobody, when his band was asked to play at "the home of a very rich, very well-known New Yorker" they were not permitted to mingle with the guests, were not in fact permitted to be seen as they were requested to play behind a screen, unlike in California where the band had played for and played with the rich and famous, especially the Hollywood crowd. Whiteman casually but cuttingly straightened the matter out with the host. But here is the class problem manifesting itself not simply because Whiteman is a popular bandleader but because he is a musician, which to many of the rich made him little better than a tradesman no matter what sort of music he played. Among the rich, to be a musician, black or white, especially a player of popular music, made one little better than a mere Negro domestic of the period. The fact that Whiteman never accepted any fee from the Prince of Wales only underscores this ambivalence of wishing to level class differences while using the existence of class differences to egoistic, if groveling, advantage. There was great pride for Whiteman in the fact that the Mountbattens came to hear his band for they were, after all, dancing to *his* music; but Whiteman was nervous in meeting the Prince, just as nervous perhaps as on the night of the Aeolian Hall concert. In the audience on the night of the concert were Damrosch, Godowsky, Heifetz, Kreisler, Stokowski, McCormack, Rachmaninoff, Rosenthal, and Stransky, all prominent classical musicians. (Walter Damrosch was to be so impressed by Gershwin's *Rhapsody* that he commissioned Gershwin to write the *Concerto in F* and conducted the New York Symphony in Gershwin's orchestration at the work's premiere, with Gershwin at the piano.) Also present were such noted writers as Fannie Hurst, Heywood Broun, Frank Crowninshield, S. J. Kaufman, Karl Kitchin, Leonard Liebling, O. O. McIntyre, Pitts Sanborn, Gilbert Seldes, Deems Taylor, and Carl Van Vechten. The striking similarity between Whiteman's response to meeting the Prince of Wales and his giving the Aeolian Hall concert is largely that he wanted to please both audiences as a sign of having made it, of being more than a mere parvenu socially or artistically. At the same time he wished to thumb his nose at convention, to level down, to democratize by bringing these European or Eurocentric aristocracies, one national and racial, the other critical and conformist, to his level, by making them dance to his music. It is an odd moment in the history of American popular culture that perhaps explains, more than any other, the precise nature of both rebellion and accommodation that is inherent in our music. Our popular artists become a sort of aristocracy for us while they seek audiences with the real aristocracy but still desire respect from legitimate or highbrow critical circles. Whiteman wanted to challenge and appease current social and critical conventions, as conflicted as the bourgeoisie has always been conflicted, with two relatively feeble weapons: first, his urge to democratize and second, his urge to cultural artifice that would make him acceptable to the aristocracies that torment the bourgeoisie by always making them aware that they, the middle classes, must sweat to live as much as the lower classes do. On the one hand, this explains why the concert took place on February 12, Lincoln's birthday, a day signifying both freedom and salvation and the triumph of the common man, in this case, specifically, the common midwestern man who had come east. (Of course, the February 12 date has a special significance to blacks as Lincoln himself bears a sort of mythical, if ambivalent, stature among blacks as the man who freed the slaves— Richard Wright used this date, for instance, as an important thematic device in his first novel, *Lawd Today,* written in 1936 but not published until 1963, three years after his death. The date for Whiteman's jazz concert would resonate in an ironic way for blacks since it is on this day that Whiteman, playing essentially a bowdlerized black, lower-class music, wishes to reinvent white bourgeois American music and white bourgeois American musical tastes.) On the other hand, that is why Whiteman had what must be, in some respects, a very unusual musical outfit: a jazz band with strings.

We all know what strings have come to mean for jazz and American popular music generally. Bebop alto saxophonist Charlie Parker's best-selling records were those he recorded with strings; in his later years, Louis Armstrong often sang pop songs against a string orchestra backdrop; Wynton Marsalis has not only recorded with symphony orchestras, he has also made a jazz album with strings entitled *Hot House Flowers;* horn players from Warren Vaché to Ornette Coleman, and the traditions they embody— and there is a tradition for every jazz taste—have recorded at least one record with strings; jazz guitarists ranging from Wes Montgomery to Earl Klugh and jazz pianists from Oscar Peterson to Errol Garner to McCoy Tyner to Keith Jarrett have made records with strings; the first, true rhythm and blues as Rock-and-Roll ballad record with strings (the Platters and Dinah Washington recorded with strings earlier but represent something different), the Drifters' 1959 *There Goes My Baby,* produced a veritable movement in both black and white popular music in which recordings with strings were meant to cut the barrier between easy listening and rock and roll. In this respect, Johnny Mathis becomes a more intriguing and suggestive crossover artist than Chuck Berry; his first string recordings, made just a few years after Berry's first successful records, suggest that ur-rock was not truly the political supersession of previous black American popular musics or that ur-rock was the music of the age of racial integration. The presence of strings is both aurally and symbolically a trip to both a pop culture and a high-culture heaven. The strings "sweeten" the music, as musicians so often put it, which means that the music can approach the generally understood idea among the populace of a sentimental and sentimentalized sound for music. But the strings not only popularize popular music, if such a redundancy can be acceptable; they also make it profound by making it a music that seems more Eurocentric, more closely associated with high-culture art music, requiring trained musicians to read a score. And a score was what Whiteman felt distinguished his music from ur-jazz or hot Dixieland jazz, which was almost exclusively a small combo music. "The greatest single factor in the improvement of American music has been the art of scoring. Paul Whiteman's orchestra was the first organization to especially score each selection and to play it according to the score." So wrote Whiteman supporter Hugh C. Ernst, in the program notes of the Aeolian Hall concert. We have currently in jazz the growing phenomenon of the jazz string quartet: the Kronos Quartet, the Turtle Island String Quartet, the Uptown String Quartet, this last being composed of four black women, led by jazz drummer Max Roach's daughter. Conceptually speaking, these groups are largely the offspring of two strains of jazz: the traditionalist string players such as violinist Joe Venuti, who early in his career played with Whiteman; Ray Nance, violinist, singer, and cornet player with the Duke Ellington Orchestra; Stephane Grappelli, the noted violinist who played with Gypsy guitarist Django Reinhardt during the thirties; and Snuff Smith, who combined both swing and country in his playing; and the new-school players such as cellist Doug Watkins, Ellington bassist Jimmy Blanton, Charles Mingus, Richard Davis, Jean-Luc Ponty, Michael White, and Billy Bangs. The particular branch of modern popular music known as jazz, in its search for respectability and its anguish to achieve a sound of European art music; may have finally achieved its end with this amalgam of small-group jazz and chamber string quartet. Whiteman missed the boat a little. We have not quite reached symphonic jazz jet, but we do have finally and literally classical jazz.

In regard to the presence of strings in Whiteman's band, nothing so underscores his ambivalence about the nature of the artistic revolt he was leading or at least "fronting" than his attitude toward classical music, the use of which was one of the major reasons Whiteman's band had strings:

> Until we went to Atlantic city, the only recognition we had won, aside from the approval of those who danced to our music, came from persons interested in our trick of jazzing the classics— that is, of applying our peculiar treatment of rhythm and color to well-known masterpieces.
>
> The notice this brought us was not always of the pleasantest.

Certain correspondents called us scoundrels and desecrators and one man described us as ghouls "bestializing the world's sweetest harmonies," rather a mixed metaphor, it seemed to me. A woman with a gift of epithet termed us "vultures, devouring the dead masters."

I don't get mad at these communications and I always read them. Sometimes I can even see justice in them. Besides, it's good to know the worst that people think of us. But of course I don't agree that we have done such very terrible things to the classics. I don't think we've even insulted them much.

I worship certain of the classics myself and respect them all. But I doubt it hurts Tschaikowsky or even Bach when we re-arrange what they have written—provided we choose appropriate compositions of theirs—and play to people who haven't heard good music before.

I have never had the feeling that I must keep my hands off the "dead masters," as people feel they must not speak the truth of the dead unless it is a complimentary truth. The masters are not dead to me. I think of the great writers of music, not as gods who finished their jobs forever in seven days, but as plain human men, as human as any of the rest of us. They were working on a job that will never be finished as long as human beings live, for music is as much a part of life as the heart beat. . . .

Not that I mean to imply that there was any real musical value in our jazzing the classics. Of course not. It was partly a trick and partly experimental work. We were just fooling around with the nearest material, working out our methods.

Here is Whiteman clearly thumbing his nose at the convention of apotheosizing European art composers. On the one hand, he suggests that existing compositions are made to be used and reinterpreted by musicians. On the other hand, "jazzing" the classics amounts for him to nothing more than a schoolboy's prank, rather like rearranging the periodic table—queer, quaint, humorous, but ultimately worthless. Whiteman believes this because he believes that jazz really is not music but only a modernistic technique of treating music and coloring composition. As he says elsewhere in *Jazz:* "With a very few but important exceptions, jazz is not as yet the thing said; it is the manner of saying it." (One of those exceptions would be George Gershwin's *Rhapsody in Blue.*) Jelly Roll Morton, the famous black New Orleans pianist who recorded some of his most important work in the 1920s, said much the same thing: "Ragtime is a certain type of syncopation and only certain tunes can be played in that idea. But jazz is a style that can be applied to any type of tune." When one hears such modern jazzers as Miles Davis, the Modern Jazz Quartet, and Chet Baker and Paul Desmond play the Adagio movement from Joaquin Rodrigo's *Concierto* or listens to the number of times Bach's music has been jazzed up (the Jacques Loussier trio and the John Lewis Group are the latest in this trend; Keith Jarret's un-jazzed-up *Goldberg Variations* and *Well-tempered Clavier* is a variant of the Benny Goodman school of the respectable jazzer playing classical music straight up), one thinks that on one level both Whiteman and Morton are right. But jazz is also rightly understood by such younger musicians as trumpeter Wynton Marsalis and saxophonist Christopher Hollyday as a demanding and tradition-laden discipline, a vision with certain accompanying sets of implementations. Whiteman and other noted jazz musicians of the era saw jazz not as an independent art form that proposed very specific solutions to the problem of creating composition and proposed very specific roles that the musician and the composer were to play not only in relation to the creation of this music but in relation to their audience and to the larger society in which they functioned, but largely as a way of spicing up dance music or making classical music more palatable to the hoi polloi. This ultimately blunts the political implication of jazz as an assault on Eurocentric cultural hegemony, which, as historian Cathy Ogren has pointed out in *The Jazz Revolution: Twenties America and the Meaning of Jazz,* is precisely what jazz in the twenties really was. Whiteman himself was at least partly aware of the revolutionary scope of the new music; he discussed in an early chapter in *Jazz* the makeup of his orchestra as something really new, not simply an amalgam of already existing musical configurations: "The usual jazz orchestra was no good for my purpose and neither were the more set-in-their-way symphony players. I needed musically trained youngsters who were ambitious, slightly discontented and willing to adventure a little." But Whiteman did not want to go so far as to propose turning the culture on its head and on its ear by questioning the very cultural assumptions that gave Eurocentric art and values their unquestioned validity. Few musicians, black or white, were ready to do that or even thought that by making a music called jazz they were doing so. (Indeed, few of the musicians thought of themselves as artists or of their work as art. It was not until the emergence in 1923 of drummer Dave Tough and the white Austin High that included Eddie Condon, Bud Freeman, Jimmy McPartland, and others that the idea of the jazz man as a romantic tragic artist began to be articulated. And with the mental breakdown of New Orleans Rhythm Kings' clarinetist Leon Roppolo in the mid-1920s, and the deaths of cornetist Bix Beiderbecke in 1931 of acute alcoholism and clarinetist Frank Teschemacher in 1932 in an auto accident—three promising careers cut short—jazz, by the mid-thirties, had the full-blown myth of the tragic white jazz artist. It was not until the 1950s, with the deaths of Charlie Parker, Billie Holiday, and Lester

Young, coinciding with the push for racial integration in this country, that jazz was to have a comparable black version of that myth.)

Whiteman's Aeolian Hall concert was apparently the first of its kind, and probably many people of the day found the term "symphonic jazz," which Whiteman seems to have made up, to be a contradiction, an oxymoron that could not fuse the chasm it appeared to create. Jazz, in whatever form, was not a completely respectable music in the twenties. In part, this attitude might be attributed to the music's lowly origins. As Whiteman reminds us on the very first page of his autobiography: "Jazz came to America three hundred years ago in chains. The psalm-singing Dutch traders, sailing in a man-of-war across the ocean in 1619, described their cargo as 'fourteen black African slaves for sale in his Majesty's colonies.' But priceless freight destined three centuries later to set a whole nation dancing went unnoted and unbilled by the stolid, revenue-hungry Dutchmen." Whiteman here is offering a re-statement of the original oxymoron in historical terms: the psalm-singing European and the rhythmic blacks, the masters above deck and the slaves below, fused in a commercial enterprise. That is, in part, what "symphonic jazz" as a concept means, the fusion of the black primitive and the white civilized. Jazz was suspect or disliked simply because its origins lie with a group of degraded and socially outcast people who performed this music in its inception in whorehouses or on streetcorners or at African-American parades. After all, most whites in the twenties who had heard of jazz at all were likely to know it only through Whiteman or through the Original Dixieland Jazz Band, the New Orleans Rhythm Kings, Vincent Lopez, or Jean Goldkette, all white bands that, in some sense or the other, were jazz bands. (To know black bands meant traveling to black neighborhoods to hear the music live in bars and clubs or to purchase black records, known in the twenties as "race records," from black record stores. Whites scarcely frequent black neighborhoods now and there is little reason to think, with Jim Crow as strong as it was, that they were any less reluctant to do so in the twenties.) Since jazz was understood in dominant white culture circles as at least in good measure a white artistic enterprise, race does not entirely or satisfactorily explain its status. Therefore, we must conclude that, in part, jazz was looked down upon because it was, as Whiteman points out, American: "Americans were ashamed of the upstart. They kept humming it absent-mindedly, then flushing and apologizing. Nothing so common could be esthetic, insisted the highbrows. Like everything else that was our own, its merits were, we thought, questionable. So it was left to Europe to discover the possibilities of our creature." The oxymoron acquires another distinct level: Symphonic jazz becomes the fusion of the European with the American. But there is more here than meets the eye: Americans disliked jazz because as rib-rock Protestant they were uncomfortable with the idea of music's existing for sensual pleasure, for the joy of the vulgarity that it symbolized and elicited. This fear transcended color; many blacks ostracized their brothers and sisters who played this music, and it was common for the believers to call jazz and blues "the devil's music." But if the lowbrow black or white heard jazz simply as "sin din," the highbrow heard it as "depraved dissonance." If the uncultivated Protestant heard jazz with disgust, the more intellectual Jew of the period heard it as despair, and in a kind of sweeping critical continuum jazz goes from trash to tragedy. In the 1927 film *The Jazz Singer,* the first feature-length talking film (the title alone is indicative of the popularity of both the term "jazz" and some form of popular music that went under that name), we have one form of fusion merging the Jew and the black, and the supposed linkage of minstrelsy and jazz (this latter being largely untrue as jazz was generally neither a music played by whites in blackface nor a music whites used to ridicule or parody blacks). Al Jolson plays a Jewish cantor's son who, when masked in blackface, becomes a successful blackface popular singer. What is interesting here is what Samson Raphaelson, author of "The Day of Atonement" and *The Jazz Singer,* the story and play upon which the film is based, said about jazz in explaining the title of his play in 1925:

> In seeking a symbol of the vital chaos of America's soul, I find no more adequate one than jazz. Here you have the rhythm of frenzy staggering against a symphonic background—a background composed of lewdness, heart's delight, soul-racked madness, monumental boldness, exquisite humility, but principally prayer.
>
> I hear jazz, and I am given a vision of cathedrals and temples collapsing and, silhouetted against the setting sun, a solitary figure, a lost soul, dancing grotesquely on the ruins. . . . Thus do I see the jazz singer.
>
> Jazz is prayer. It is too passionate to be anything else. It is prayer distorted, sick, unconscious of its destination. The singer of jazz is what Matthew Arnold said of the Jews, "lost between two worlds, one dead, the other powerless to be born."

This may have been the first time jazz was described as a kind of sacred music, but it was surely not to be the last. In effect, what Raphaelson is describing is not music of transcendence but an art form that mirrors the dysfunction and anguish of the culture that produced it. What Raphaelson defines is not a creative art form but a failed one that is incapable of articulating anything but its own inarticulation, its own inability to be art or to be religion. The highbrow criticism of jazz during these years supported the general idea that it was a dysfunctional art, a music that was both the sign and signifier of dysfunction. A variant of Raphaelson's observations on jazz was to become—and very much remain, ironically—the basis of jazz's critical acceptance among the highbrows as a profound art form: namely, jazz functions as holistic spirituality in a dysfunctional world, even if some of its finest players have themselves been unstable, depressed, or disturbed personalities. In the twenties, highbrows thought of jazz as simply symbolic of contemporary dysfunction; nowadays, according to the highbrow critic, jazz, like all great art, transcends dysfunction, even the dysfunctional tendency inherent in its process of creation. Today, jazz, like all accepted highbrow art, is a religion. The implications of Raphaelson's remarks were ahead of their time.

There had always been popular music in America since the inception of some form of theater in the eighteenth century, but jazz was particularly unnerving because it threatened completely to engulf the business, the aesthetic, the purpose, the very consciousness of music-making and music listening. With records, the beginnings of radio, and the urbanization of Americans, particularly blacks, jazz may have appeared more threatening and more pervasive than it really was. It was surely indicative of a frightening change, for if the rise of the nineteenth-century sentimental woman's novel could be called the feminization of American culture, the rise of jazz was in a real sense the primitivization of American culture. In early-twentieth-century highbrow culture criticism of American society, the terms "philistine" and "barbarian" were used interchangeably, in culture criticism terms, the 1920s was about the clash between the philistine and the barbarian. H. L. Mencken even continued to use these terms in the 1920s, although since the coming of jazz the two terms had come to signify quite distinct states of the American character. Once again, as had become the common cultural dialectic in American life since the middle of the nineteenth century, it was city versus small town, agrarian values versus urban trends. It was just these forces of opposition that clashed during the struggle over Prohibition in the late nineteenth and early twentieth centuries. In the instance of Prohibition, small town, agrarianism, and the conservative Christian reformism instinct won. In the case of jazz, it was the urban, secular, more liberal element of the culture that won. It is no accident that, of course, these two gigantic cultural movements should meet head-to-head in the 1920s, when jazz entered popular culture in a big way, largely through recordings and the burgeoning nightclub and speakeasy business (the latter made possible, in large part, by Prohibition), when the grandest social reform movement since abolitionism and Reconstruction was in effect. Symphonic jazz was not simply a bow to the highbrow culture that condemned jazz as unartistic noise but to the frightened small-towner, philistine and otherwise, who was alarmed by a secular music that seemingly had no restraints and no aim but seemed to possess enormous emotional and commercial power. Symphonic jazz was an attempt to make jazz less the cultural assault against white, middle-class, Christian, small-town taste than it appeared to be. There was a great fear of mongrelization among this very class of people, the small-town philistine; after all, during the Ku Klux Klan's resurgence as a political and social force in American life in the 1920s, it was just this mass group of Americans who were attracted to the insignias, the regalia, the idea of mythical American purity. The twenties symbolized acceleration (which is perhaps why a novel like *Gatsby* turns so much on the speed of automobiles): automobiles, airplanes, trains, telegraph, telephone, the era of instant communication. And what is jazz, in the end, but, as one musicologist told me, abrupt and explosive composing. (Cathy Ogren points out in her study of jazz in the 1920s that both detractors and admirers of the music often commented on how the music was both the cause and effect of the age of the motor and speed. She quotes Irving Berlin, who compared jazz to the "rhythmic beat of our everyday lives. Its swiftness is interpretive of our verve and speed and ceaseless activity. When commuters no longer rush for trains, when taxicabs pause at corners, when businessmen take afternoon siestas, then, perhaps jazz will pass." Ogren writes: "By indicating that jazz was a music of the city and industrial life, Berlin implied that it was clearly tied to increased mechanization.")

As early as 1917, in an article entitled "The Appeal of Primitive Jazz" that appeared in *Literary Digest,* "jazz" was defined by Walter Kingsley as an African word that meant "speeding things up. . . . In the old plantation days," Mr. Kingsley writes, "when the slaves were having one of their rare holidays and the fun languished, some West-Coast African would cry out, 'Jaz her up,' and this would be the cue for fast and furious fun." Considering the fact that jazz's black origin was the source of a great deal of the white critical contempt and discontent during the twenties, it is a sort of wild irony that a people normally associated with agrarianism and slowness (think of the Hollywood stereotypes of Stepin Fetchit and Willie Best as examples of the dominant cultural idea that blacks were slow in movement, slow in speech, and slow in thought) were now the creators of a music that symbolized machines and speed.

The musician has always been a charismatic being in Western culture, but with the coming of jazz he (gender specificity is important here because of the male dominance in music) becomes a magical primitive, in a sense, making music without a score, producing art without a text, based entirely upon his inspiration of the moment. Jazz was supposed to touch a more authentic, more primal core of creative consciousness. Jazz, in effect, has given us the newly stated old myth of the energetic barbarian, and the rest of the history of popular dance music in this country has simply reiterated this. Early jazzmen cashed in on this myth of the jazzer as the artist of the moment by often believing the fiction that learning to read music would ruin their ability to improvise. Symphonic jazz, with its emphasis on scoring, is at last the ultimate American oxymoron as it wishes to fuse both the past and the future, which was very much on the minds of intellectuals of the day. Consider T. S. Eliot's 1933 lecture on Matthew Arnold:

> What I call the "auditory imagination" is the feeling for syllable and rhythm, penetrating far below the conscious levels of thought and feeling, invigorating every word; sinking to the most primitive and forgotten, returning to the origin and bringing something back, seeking the beginning and the end. It works through meanings, certainly, or not without meanings in the ordinary sense, and fuses the old and obliterated and the trite, the current, and the new and surprising, the most ancient and the most civilised mentality.

Inasmuch as jazz was a primitive music (and it was certainly almost always referred to in that way by the white press and sometimes by the black press too), it could be seen as an artistic and cultural ritual meant to replicate a past, more primeval, archetypical consciousness in the modern world. Broadly considered, it was a new way to bring about a sort of racial syncretism by allowing whites to pretend that they were primitives of some sort, not through sight, not visually through picture imagination as blackface minstrelsy suggested, but through sound and one's response to the sound both as adventuresome musician and as adventuresome audience. It was during the jazz age of the twenties that blackface minstrelsy died as a mass form of American entertainment, died as America's most powerful theater. "Amos 'n' Andy" became a huge success on radio and when it was finally brought to a visual medium, television, black actors played the roles. When Jolson made *The Jazz Singer,* the blackface performer was already an anachronism. One white writer of the period wrote that "jazz differs from other music, as it wants to appeal to the eye as much as to the ear." But this was quite incorrect. Until the coming of rock, no popular American music was as vision-centered, as voyeur-obsessed as minstrelsy. Perhaps the Whiteman concert was both the sign and signifier, the deconstructive text of the auditory imagination.

In *The Great Gatsby* we have one of the few references that Fitzgerald, who named the twenties "The Jazz Age," ever made to jazz. The first time that Nick, the book's narrator, attends a grandiose Gatsby at-home he and the other guests are treated to some interesting music:

> There was the boom of a bass drum, and the voice of the orchestra leader rang out suddenly above the echolalia of the garden.

"Ladies and gentlemen," he cried. "At the request of Mr. Gatsby we are going to play for you Mr. Vladimir Tostoff's latest work, which attracted so much attention at Carnegie Hall last May. If you read the papers you know there was a big sensation." He smiled with jovial condescension, and added: "Some sensation!" Whereupon everybody laughed.

"The piece is known," he concluded lustily, "as Vladimir Tostoff's *Jazz History of the World.*"

Knowing that the *Gatsby* manuscript was not submitted to Scribner's until September 1924, nearly seven months after the Whiteman concert, and knowing how much notice the concert received, it is not unwarranted to suppose that Fitzgerald, even though he was abroad when he wrote most of his novel, had the Whiteman concert in mind when he made a reference to *Jazz History of the World*. The orchestra certainly has the same instrumentation as Whiteman or a Whiteman clone, "a whole pitful of oboes and trombones and saxophones and viols and comets and piccolos, and low and high drums." And certainly the Whiteman Aeolian Hall concert was, in effect, the Jazz History of the World. Starting from the earliest white jazz, *Livery Stable Blues* recorded by the Original Dixieland Jazz Band in 1917, the first jazz record, Whiteman's band worked its way in a clearly evolutionary manner to Victor Herbert's Serenades and George Gershwin's *Rhapsody in Blue*. The concert actually ended with Elgar's "Pomp and Circumstance" but Whiteman, even during this very first performance, thought the Elgar piece to be an anticlimax following Gershwin and in subsequent concerts "Pomp and Circumstance" was either deleted or moved to the middle of the program, thus emphasizing even more intensely the evolutionary nature of a program meant to display the growth of an American art form. As Whiteman wrote: "I still believe that 'Livery Stable Blues' and 'A Rhapsody in Blue' . . . are so many millions of miles apart, that to speak of them both as jazz needlessly confuses the person who is trying to understand modern American music." If, however, Whiteman's concert is a jazz history of the world or a history of the jazz world, it is a revisionist history that has excised the presence of blacks as creators of this music. There are no references to blacks in the entire concert. We know, of course, that *Gatsby* is a novel filled with theories of history, from Tom Buchanan's suggestion that the colored races are on the verge of overrunning the world to the European discovery of the New World being, in some measure, equivalent to or signifying Gatsby's own puerile idealism that is so compellingly represented by the *Hopalong Cassidy* novel with Gatsby's schedule for self-improvement printed inside the cover that is found among his effects after his death. In a novel obsessed with various geographical myths of America (southern belles, midwesterners, and westerners all meeting in the East), this boyhood novel with the printed schedule collapses east and west, as western cowboy hero meets Ben Franklin in what signifies not an evolution but a repetition. But there may be more in the theory of American culture history that Whiteman's concert tried to explicate and symbolize than simply easterner meets westerner or a falsified set of circumstances meant to signify progress and evolution.

After all, Whiteman was no more racist than other whites of his era and there is, indeed, evidence to indicate that he may have been less so. He wanted to hire black musicians to play in his band in the mid-twenties but was talked out of it by other band members and commercial sponsors. He did hire black arrangers William Grant Still and Don Redman before any other white band was known to do so. What Whiteman's 1924 concert was trying to establish was the idea that from its beginnings to its most fully realized form as symphonic concert music, jazz was and is an undeniable *American* music; and inasmuch as Whiteman wanted to convince himself and his audience that it was an American music, he was bound to convince both himself and others that it was, officially, a white music. Otherwise, history taught him that the only way he could perform black music would be in blackface or as a kind of minstrel. Whiteman, whatever his faults, did not want jazz to become another minstrel music and it is, in part, through his popularizing efforts that the music did not become that. As Neil Leonard pointed out in his *Jazz and the White Americans,* jazz signified, in its speeded-up rhythms, a rapid, almost dizzying change in American conventions. "This surprisingly quick change of taste resulted from the breakdown of traditional values, the esthetics needs jazz seemed to fulfill, its increased diffusion by new sound reproducing devices and the modifications that made it increasingly acceptable." Whiteman mediated a major shift in American culture. And while his concert could attempt to deny a mongrelized American cultural past, it could not ultimately deny a kind of racial syncretism that suggested that the sharing of art between black and white, from commercial co-option to friendly collaboration, would not be used exclusively as a method to further denigrate and oppress blacks within the culture. Whiteman's concert is evidence that whites felt no less threatened by black artistic expression and its charismatic power, but the whole business of how black artistic expression related to the dominant white culture changed and Whiteman, inadvertently symbolized that change.

People who have never heard Whiteman's band often ask if the music was good. Gunther Schuller probably provides the fairest analysis of the musical Whiteman:

> On purely musical terms . . . the Whiteman orchestra achieved much that was admirable, and there is no question that it was admired (and envied) by many musicians, both black and white. For it was an orchestra that was overflowing with excellent musi-

cians and virtuoso instrumentalists. Its arrangers—Lennie Hayton, Ferde Grofe, and particularly Bill Challis—wrote complex, demanding scores that took everything these musicians could give. It was not jazz, of course—or perhaps only intermittently so. Many of the arrangements were overblown technicolor potpourris, eclectic to the point of even quoting snatches of Petrushka and Tristram and Isolde. . . . But often enough—to make the point worth making—the arrangements were marvels of orchestrational ingenuity. They were designed to make people listen to music, not to dance . . . the resultant performances were often more than merely slick. Excellent intonation, perfect balances, and clean attacks do not necessarily equate with superficiality. There is in the best Whiteman performances a feeling and a personal sound as unique in its way as Ellington's or Basie's.

In an interview for the December 1936 number of *The Brown American,* a leading black magazine of the day, Duke Ellington, when asked what was his favorite band, said it was Paul Whiteman's.

EVERYBODY'S DOING IT NOW

Mumbo Jumbo is the god of jazz; be careful how you write of jazz, else he will hoodoo you.

—Walter Kingsley, "The Appeal of Primitive Jazz"

I feel like a whore in church.

—Trumpeter Harry James moments before the 1938 Benny Goodman Carnegie Hall Concert

But one night Helen {Oakley} came into the room and started talking about a concert. It seems she thought it would be a swell idea for people to get together and just listen to the band play, without a lot of waiters rattling dishes and people talking.
"Hell, no!" I said. "After all, this is just dance music. What's the use of trying to make something fancy and formal out of it.

—Benny Goodman, *The Kingdom of Swing*

The negro loves anything that is peculiar in music.

—James Reese Europe, 1919

But this analysis of the Whiteman concert has only scratched the surface; there are greater and more intricate complexities that we must confront if we are to come to some understanding of the connection between the meaning of popular music and the place where it is played and if we are to come to an understanding of how racial syncretism works in our culture. First, let us return to *The Great Gatsby* and Tom Buchanan's reference to a history book in a conversation he has with Nick Carraway:

> "Civilization's going to pieces," broke out Tom violently, "I've gotten to be a terrible pessimist about things. Have you read *The Rise of the Colored Empires* by this man Goddard?"
> "Why, no," I answered, rather surprised by his tone.
> "Well, it's a fine book and everybody ought to read it. The idea is if we don't look out the white race will be—will be utterly submerged. It's all scientific stuff; it's been proved."

The book Tom is referring to, as has been pointed out by several scholars, is Lothrop Stoddard's *The Rising Tide of Color Against White World Supremacy* published by Scribner's (Fitzgerald's publishing house) in 1919. While it may not be terribly surprising that the fictional Tom Buchanan—a selfish, racist, stupid, and brutal rich white man—is recommending the book, it may be a bit more remarkable that Hubert H. Harrison, one of the leading black nationalist intellectuals of the 1920s, was also recommending Stoddard's book—to black readers. Harrison, a fervent Marcus Garveyite, was both member and fellow traveler of the United Negro Improvement Association and one of the editors of *Negro World,* Garvey's paper, back during the early twenties, the peak days of Garvey's movement. In his *When Africa Awakes,* published in 1920 and a quite popular book in black circles, Harrison writes about Stoddard's work: "Here is a book written by a white man which causes white men to shiver. For it calls their attention to the writing on the wall. It proves that the white race in its mad struggle for dominion over others has been exhausting its vital resources and is exhausting them further." "Mr. Stoddard's thesis," Harrison continues, "starts from the proposition that of the seventeen hundred million people on our earth today the great majority is made up of black, brown, red, and yellow people. The white race, being in the minority, still dominates. . . . In the course of this dictatorship and domination the white race has erected the barrier of the color line. . . . But this barrier is cracking and giving way at many points and in the flood of racial self-assertion." He ends the chapter by recommending Stoddard's book, despite the fact that Stoddard is "an unreconstructed Anglo-Saxon," writing that "intelligent men of color from Tokio [sic] to Tallahassee" should read it. Of course, at least for Tom Buchanan and for the millions of other whites who either bought or read *The Rising Tide of Color Against White World Supremacy,* the fact that Stoddard was an unreconstructed Anglo-Saxon was the whole reason for the message of the book. To paraphrase Marshall McLuhan, in this instance, the messenger is the message. Nonetheless, we have this mad irony that gives us a fictional white racist and a black nationalist, one who never reads and the other who writes editorials in his black nationalist newspapers exhorting his people to "read, read, read," recommending a book by a white New Englander who wishes to warn the white world of its impending doom. This should not seem as unusual as it might at first glance. In the 1920s there was a conflict occurring about the racial origins and the racial future of the American self. It was largely a battle about authenticity and authenticating a glorious or at least praiseworthy heritage of achievement. This authenticating heritage became, in effect, an authenticating essence of some sort of national or racial peoplehood. Jazz became one of the major cultural happenings of the twenties in which this preoccupation with authenticating the American self in racial and national ways was most intense. Indeed, Fitzgerald himself was aware that, by 1925, there were clearly two competing theories of history or theories of authenticating the American racial and national self. One was the pseudoscience of pure racial origins espoused by Stoddard and the like and the other was satirized in the passage I quoted earlier about the jazz band playing a "Jazz History of the World." There were a number of people who were trying to authenticate something about the American racial and national character through the development of American popular music. But in order to understand this fully we must, within the flow of this discussion, examine some events that happened both before and after the 1920s, and we must look at art forms other than jazz.

Stoddard was simply the most popular of a line of white racist scientific theorists writing around the time of World War I. Madison Grant's *The Passing of the Great Race* (1916), Dr. Carl C. Brigham's *A Study of American Intelligence* (1923), Dr. William MacDougall's *Is America Safe for Democracy?* (1921) and Stoddard's book were all part of a larger overall assault (as were the creation of the intelligence quotient—the IQ—in 1912 by William Stern and the introduction of the Stanford-Binet intelligence test in 1916 by Lewis Terman) against the incursion of not only dark-skinned people in American life and culture but also an attempt to stop the further immigration of eastern and southern Europeans to this shore. The authentic American was the Anglo-Saxon or, as these writers designated, "the Nordic" (there were, according to these theorists, three classes of Europeans: the Nordic or highest class, the Alpine or next highest, and the Mediterranean or the lowest), and the Nordic American's hegemony must be protected and fortified against the hordes, so this scientific racist movement asserted. Stoddard's book is partic-

ularly interesting in this regard, for not only did he argue for the authentic
superiority of the Nordic over the other whites as well as over dark-skinned
peoples, he further argued that the downfall of the white race was rooted in
its acceptance of the doctrines of Jean-Jacques Rousseau, because through
Rousseau the white world embraced the concept of the noble savage and the
natural equality of all people. Certainly, Stoddard's argument has some validity when we think of the relationship of white and black in America,
where so often the white has looked upon the black as a kind of primitive alter ego; but the danger rested in the very idea of the primitive or uncivilized
nature of the black, for inasmuch as that nature represented a predating, pre-
historical, or primeval consciousness, it became a kind of undeniable and
compelling authentication of the human soul, the human essence. In a dangerous and ironic, yet mutually exploited, way, the black became the white's
authenticating self; thus the cultural rite of having periodic performances of
concerts called "The Jazz History of the World," which seem to be nothing
more, on one grand level, than to ask: Where is the Negro located in American popular culture, where is he located in the origins of the American self?

If, around the time of the war, many white intellectuals were engaged
in authenticating something called white history and the white historical
mission through science, blacks were concerned with authenticating themselves through the location and discovery of the history that had been denied
them. For whites this was expressed through a voracious and rampant deconstructive expropriation of everything that was called civilization during the
entire course of human history, while for blacks it was the hopeful archaeo-
logical hunt for anything that was black and civilized in the past, anything
that would support an ideological conception of blackness as something other
than a sign of degradation in the world. (It must be understood that this is
why the Harlem Renaissance occurred after the war. There was, finally, a
critical mass number of black intellectuals and a sufficiently literate black
bourgeois population to begin the engagement of this issue that the Negro
could authenticate himself through his past. Countee Cullen asked the most
relevant question of the age in his poem "Heritage": "What is Africa to me?"
Or as black bibliophile Arthur A. Schomburg put it, "The American Negro
must remake his past in order to make his future." The most important in-
tellectual/historical formation of this period for blacks was Garvey's and
DuBois's separate developments of Pan Africanism.) In 1915, Carter G.
Woodson formed the Association for the Study of Negro Life and History
and started *The Journal of Negro History*. During the Harlem Renaissance of
the 1920s, a spate of anthologies—some edited by blacks, others by whites—
were published in an attempt to authenticate the black history and cultural
contributions to America. Between 1922 and 1927, for instance, five anthologies of Negro poetry were published: James Weldon Johnson's *The Book of*

American Negro Poetry (1922), Robert T. Kerlin's *Negro Poets and Their Poems* (1923), White and Jackson's *An Anthology of Verse by American Negroes* (1924), Alain Locke's *Four Negro Poets* (1926), and Countee Cullen's *Caroling Dusk* (1927). What makes this even more striking is that before the decade of the twenties, excepting Arthur Schomberg's *A Bibliographical Check List of American Negro Poetry* (1916), which made these anthologies possible, no one ever attempted an anthology of black literature of any sort. There were also several collections of black music during this decade, including James Weldon Johnson and J. Rosamond Johnson's *The First Book of Negro Spirituals* (1925) and *The Second Book of Negro Spirituals* (1926), Howard W. Odum and Guy B. Johnson's *The Negro and His Songs* (1925), and *Negro Workaday Songs* (1926), Dorothy Scarborough's *On the Trail of Negro Folksongs* (1925), and Abbe Niles and W. C. Handy's *Blues* (1926). Just as Schomberg's pathbreaking work made the black poetry anthologies possible, so did Henry Edward Krehbiel's seminal 1914 study, *Afro-American Folksongs,* make the music books possible. Finally, the major anthologies of African-American literature and culture were Howard University professor of philosophy Alain Locke's *The New Negro,* published in 1925, and National Urban League Executive Director Charles S. Johnson's *Ebony and Topaz,* which appeared in 1927. This brief summary of anthologies of black life and culture in the 1920s certainly does not exhaust the list. Digging up the Negro's past became something of an obsession with both blacks themselves and many liberal white intellectuals.

The most important of all these anthologists was James Weldon Johnson, former school principal, Atlanta University graduate, popular songwriter, poet, former U.S. consul to Nicaragua and Venezuela, novelist, and, during the 1920s, field secretary of the NAACP. As early as 1905 Johnson and his brother Rosamond, composers of "Lift Every Voice and Sing," the song that became known as the Black National Anthem, were propagandizing for blacks as creators of American popular music in one of the most important and popular bourgeois magazines in America: *Ladies Home Journal.* Under the title, "The Evolution of Ragtime," *Ladies Home Journal* published four songs written by the Johnson brothers and Bob Cole that demonstrated the growth of a musical form. An interesting sign of that growth is that the first three songs in the series—"Lay Away Your Troubles," a minstrel song about plantation work, "Darkies' Delights," a minstrel tune about blacks eating possum, and "The Spirit of the Banjo!" a tune celebrating "the old-time banjo song of the cotton-fields"—have lyrics in dialect, while the final and best song, "Lindy: A Love Song," does not (Johnson, who wrote dialect song lyrics during the very early 1900s and who wrote dialect poetry for his first collection of poems, "Fifty Year and Other Poems," published in 1917 was to turn away from dialect in the 1920s and, indeed, in his writings, discourage other black writers from using it. In his 1927 book of poems, *God's Trombones,* Johnson had, like Langston Hughes and Sterling Brown, solved the problem of dialect by re-creating black speech through idiomatic expressions, syntax, and rhythm.) As early as January 1909, J. Rosamond Johnson, in an article in *The Colored American Magazine* entitled "Why They Call American Music Ragtime," wrote:

> The happy expressions of the Negro's emotions in music have been dubbed "ragtime," while his more serious musical expressions have been called "plantation" and "Jubilee" songs, and these two styles of his expressions in music are all that I can see that is distinctively American music. It is the only music that the musical centers of the world and great musicians of the world recognize as American music.

James Weldon Johnson went still further in promoting the range of influence blacks exercised in music in an earlier 1905 article in *Charities* entitled "The Negro of Today in Music" in which he discussed the works of serious black composers Samuel Coleridge-Taylor and Harry T. Burleigh as well as the show music of black minstrel Ernest Hogan, then the highest paid black performer on the American stage and composer of the song "All Coons Look Alike to Me," Black Patti, and Walker and Williams.[3] The black presence in contemporary music was ubiquitous; the black's magnetism was pervasive and encompassing. If whites were going to stereotype blacks through their so-called "natural" gifts of rhythm and song, black propagandists like the Johnson brothers, Du Bois, and others decided to make a virtue of a necessity and authenticate the black as a vital presence in American culture through music.

So, in reading the lengthy preface Johnson wrote for his anthology of American Negro poetry, probably one of the most important and, surely, one of the most brilliant cultural and historical evaluations of Black America ever written, a stunning manifesto of the African-American origins of the modern American self, there was really no surprise to any knowledgeable black reader of the 1920s who came across these passages:

> I make here what may appear to be a more startling statement by saying that the Negro has already proved the possession of these powers [of creating that which has universal appeal and influence] by being the creator of the only things artistic that have yet sprung from American soil and been universally acknowledged as distinctive American products.
>
> These creations by the American Negro may be summed up

under four heads. The first two are the Uncle Remus stories, which were collected by Joel Chandler Harris, and the spirituals or slave songs. . . .

The other two creations are the cakewalk and ragtime. We do not need to go very far back to remember when cakewalking was the rage in the United States, Europe and South America. . . .

The influence which the Negro has exercised on the art of dancing in this country has been almost absolute. For generations the "buck and wing" and the "stop-time" dances, which are strictly Negro, have been familiar to American theatre audiences. A few years ago the public discovered the "turkey trot," the "eagle rock," "ballin' the jack," and several other varieties that started the modern dance craze. These dances were quickly followed by the "tango," a dance originated by Negroes of Cuba and later transplanted to South America.

As for Ragtime, I go straight to the statement that it is the one artistic production by which America is known the world over. It has been all-conquering. Everywhere it is hailed as "American music. . . ."

The power of the Negro to suck up the national spirit from the soil and create something artistic and original, which, at the same time, possesses the note of universal appeal, is due to a remarkable racial gift of adaptability; it is more than adaptability, it is a transfusive quality.

Thus, in the 1920s, the battle was about locating a usable American past; the white racists argued that the American past was white and the black cultural promoters argued that the American past was, at least, significantly, black. The fact that Johnson and other blacks chose to argue the importance of the black presence through the very line of stereotype that had been used to denigrate the black in Western culture—the black as instinctive, pagan, sensual, imitative—was in some ways a stroke of genius; in other ways, it revealed the limitations of the black intellectual's ways of conceiving the cultural paradoxes and contradictions of American culture.[4] In effect, the black propagandists won a victory—that is, succeeded all too well in making the general population of this country think of the black as the noble savage of American music, the authenticating soul of American instinctive artistic expression—that was to prove the creation of the very matrix of confinement and dilemma that bedevils the black intellectual today.

The Whiteman concert, as a cultural phenomenon, was largely both a result and a cause of this quest for sources, an evolutionary spiral of history, a teleological authentication, and a politicization of culture as battle between

the oppressor and the oppressed. Whiteman's concert was the one supreme
moment of the authentication of white jazz and thus of a white hegemony
over American popular music and its sources. It was a false authentication in
some very important respects. And yet it was a true authentication because
the concert demonstrated so well how racial syncretism in American culture
works and why it works in the way it does that ultimately is acceptable to
both races.

"I have come back from France more firmly convinced than ever that
negroes [sic] should write negro music," said black bandleader James Reese
Europe in the *New York Tribune* in 1919. "We have our own racial feeling
and if we try to copy whites we will make bad copies. . . . Our musicians do
their best work when using negro material. Will Marion Cook, William
Tires, even Harry Burleigh and Coleridge-Taylor are not truly themselves in
the music that expresses their race. The music of our race springs from the
soil, and this is true with no other race, except possibly the Russians." Perhaps it is this view of hegemony through the artistic realization of a racial
consciousness that makes Europe, in the same article, give his version of the
origin of the word "jazz," which differs quite significantly than the earlier
version I quoted from white writer and stage performer Walter Kingsley:

> I believe the term "jazz" originated with a band of four pieces
> which was founded about fifteen years ago in New Orleans, and
> which was known as "Razz's Band." This band was of truly ex-
> traordinary composition. It consisted of a baritone horn, a trom-
> bone, a cornet, and an instrument made out of the china-berry
> tree. This instrument is something like a clarinet, and is made by
> the Southern negroes themselves. . . . The four musicians of Razz's
> Band had no idea at all of what they were playing; they improvised
> as they went along, but such was their innate sense of rhythm that
> they produced something which was very taking. From the small
> cafes of New Orleans they graduated to the St. Charles Hotel, and
> after a time to the Winter Garden, in New York, where they ap-
> peared, however, only a few days, the individual musicians being
> grabbed up by various orchestras in the city. [Black dance bands
> dominated popular music in the very early 1900s and there were
> scarcely enough musicians to go around. It would hardly be sur-
> prising that if these players were in any way competent they would
> be employed by the larger bands. In the 1920s, the star players of
> both black and white bands were constantly being recruited and
> wooed and earned unbelievable salaries, although most of them
> were virtually unknown to the record-buying public.] Somehow in
> the passage of time Razz's Band got changed into "Jazz's Band"
> and from this corruption arose the term "jazz."

Europe's etymology shows how the politicalization of American popular culture was moving apace: Here, the idea that jazz is connected with either Africa or slavery is eliminated. Jazz refers to something that is purely Negro-American and is purely unconnected with a degraded past. Here, jazz is not associated with bars and whorehouses and places of ill-repute; the places where the Razz Band played were all quite respectable venues. Europe realized, as did Whiteman, that the status of a particular form of music has little to do with what it is and much to do with where it is played.

Whiteman's band is considered the first to perform some sort of symphonic jazz concert in a hall known only for permitting the performance of classical European art music, but this is not actually so. James Reese Europe, organizer of New York's black musicians into something called the Clef Club, which someone remarked at the time to be an odd name as most of its members could not read music, led 125 black musicians in a concert of ragtime-based popular music at Carnegie Hall in May 1912. James Weldon Johnson described the concert in his history of Harlem, *Black Manhattan:*

> There were a few strings proper, the most of them being 'cellos and double-basses; the few wind-instruments consisted of cornets, saxophones, clarinets, and trombones; there was a battery of drums; but the main part of the orchestra was composed of banjos, mandolins, and guitars. On this night all these instruments were massed against a background of ten upright pianos. In certain parts the instrumentation was augmented by voices. New York had not yet become accustomed to jazz; so when the Clef Club opened its concert with a syncopated march, playing it with a biting attack and an infectious rhythm, and on the finale bursting into singing, the effect can be imagined. The applause became a tumult.

There is evidence that Europe may have performed more than one such concert at Carnegie Hall; there is a review of a Carnegie Hall concert by the Clef Club in the March 1913 issue of *The Craftsman* that would seem a bit late for a review of a concert that took place in May of the previous year. Europe, who often wore a white suit and matching white shoes, and small, round, wire-framed glasses, was doubtless the first black band leader to play symphonic jazz in a European art-music hall.[5] Indeed, he seems to have been the first American of any color to have done so. The fact that he did is virtually forgotten in the history of American popular music. The fact that Whiteman did is not. But there is one crucial difference, aside from the primary one of race, that must be kept in mind when considering Europe and Whiteman. It has been suggested that few members of Europe's band could read music (although Europe insisted on his musicians' being disciplined and dedicated; as he said, "It takes a lot of training to develop a sense of time and delicate harmony"), whereas it was almost impossible to be a member of Whiteman's band unless one could sight-read well.[6] (When Bix Beiderbecke joined Whiteman in 1927, he played his solos brilliantly but struggled with the often demanding ensemble parts because he was such a poor reader.) With Whiteman we cannot overlook his emphasis on scoring and composition as the essence of the new American popular music. However challenging and innovative Europe's music may have been, it could not have been, conceptually, a music that saw or realized its essence as a score. In this sense, Europe's music lacked a certain legitimating power that Whiteman's had. Thus, Whiteman's band was really and truly modern and Europe's was still a throwback to a kind of ur-jazz, primitive black music, although, apparently, Europe's music was far from sounding primitive and Europe himself, reared in the same black middle-class environs of Washington, D.C., that was later to produce Duke Ellington, was classically trained and came from a family of classically trained musicians.

Later, in 1914, Europe formed the Temp Club and played and wrote music for Irene and Vernon Castle for the next three years. (His associate, Ford Dabney, organized and directed a jazz orchestra featured at Florenz Ziegfeld's roof-garden shows.) It may have been that blacks, as James Weldon Johnson argued, invented the popular dances of the 1910s that took the country by storm, but a white upper-middle-class theatrical couple, the Castles, popularized them and helped to spread Europe's music to wider circles than those of New York High Society. Once again, an example of the racial syncretism of American popular music is illustrated by how the Castles and Europe were able to work together quite well and to their mutual benefit. Despite the fact that the Castles were white, they were still seen as threatening to many conservative, small-town Americans who feared the new dancing craze. There were cases of women being arrested for dancing in public and of being fired from jobs for dancing during their lunch breaks. When Edward Bok tried to run a series of dance instruction articles with accompanying photos of the Castles in his *Ladies Home Journal* in 1914, the outcry from his readers and segments of the general public was so great that he discontinued the feature after only one installment. If such significant pockets of the country were that resistant to white dancers performing quite respectable and chaste versions of black dances, how much more resistant would that public have been to black dancers trying to do the same thing? Here is the paradox: Blacks may very well have created most American forms of music and dance, but they certainly could not popularize them. This means, strictly speaking, that they never created American popular music and dance but rather contributed a lion's share of the ideas that helped to shape an American popular imagination. They constantly needed whites as brokers, intercessors, collaborators, and promoters in order to help introduce them to wider audiences and to make the music truly popular. This very idea that modern black art not only is created but in some vital senses is conceptualized as having its presence through the mediating patronage of whites is the informing and controversial message of Zora Neale Hurston's 1942 autobiography, *Dust Tracks on a Road,* and of her essay "The 'Pet Negro' System," which appeared in *The American Mercury* in May 1943. For Hurston, the political question of whites' ultimately exercising control over the nature and shape of black art was obviously of importance, but her point was that art was being created only partially for blacks themselves. It could reach its final if diminished realization only if it came to mean something for whites as well. In the way popular black arts developed, blacks may have had to share much with the whites who, in some instances, may not have contributed much to their creation, but the blacks ultimately gained immeasurably as well; so much so, in fact, that by the 1920s, there was a literary and artistic movement called the Harlem Renaissance in which blacks such as James Weldon Johnson spoke of the renovation of the black's political, social, and psychic status through the creation and acceptance of art.

"The music world is controlled by a trust, and the negro must submit to its demands or fail to have his compositions produced," James Reese Europe said in 1914. "I am not bitter about it. It is, after all, but a small portion of the price my race must pay in its, at times, almost hopeless fight for a place in the sun. Some day it will be different and justice will prevail." But the future brought no real change except the institutional and legal breakdown of segregation, and, despite that cataclysmic cultural change in America, the ties that bind blacks and whites and American popular artistic forms simply have become more intricate. We may conclude from this either that segregation as the operating ideology in this culture is not dead because whites or blacks or both do not wish it to die, or that how blacks and whites relate to each other as ritual, as anthropological reality, as psychokinetic construct, is far stronger than anything that was ever embedded in the codes created to govern that relationship.

Perhaps nothing better illustrates this problem of how black artists should relate to whites than the entire discussion that took place in the 1920s and earlier among blacks as to whether they should indeed be engaged in creating a race-based or racially conscious art. This is far too complex a topic for me to explore at length in this essay, but there are two relevant instances that need to be reviewed here. First, Europe, whom I have already quoted as expressing an interest in creating a distinctly "Negro music," was attacked by Will Marion Cook, whom Europe singled out in his comments on "serious" black composers, for creating a cheap commercial music that was insufficiently elevated. Cook himself, at the time of Europe's popularity, was lead-

ing a fifty-piece popular music band called the New York Syncopated
Orchestra and had provided music for Bert Williams's stage shows as well as
having written several pop standards including "I'm Coming Virginia,"
which became a favorite of Bix Beiderbecke in the 1920s. So, on one level,
the source of the criticism might seem a bit more than disingenuous; however, Cook had done rather over-Europeanized arrangements of Negro spirituals and had written extended scores using Negro folk themes. As Gunther
Schuller writes, Cook thought of "both Europe's band of brassy jazz and the
novelty bands on Broadway, which claimed to represent the Negro's music
from New Orleans, as unworthy reflections upon the dignity of Negro
music." But Cook was not alone. Other serious composers felt the same way:
Harry T. Burleigh, the British black musician Samuel Coleridge-Taylor,
even popular songwriter James Weldon Johnson, whose 1912 novel, *The
Autobiography of an Ex-Coloured Man,* is, in part, about a very light-skinned
black musician who hopes to elevate ragtime to a "serious" art through the
creation of elaborate scores. If there was to be a distinctive Negro music,
first, it would be scored and self-consciously composed and not just
intuitively created, indeed, it would require extremely well-trained, sight-
reading musicians. Second, it would be, in some sense, an amalgam of an
African sensibility with a Eurocentric method. In short, it would be some
sort of symphonic black music. Despite the symphonic pretensions of
Europe's Clef Club, it was not quite regarded, in some circles, as what black
music was aspiring to be.

In 1926, this controversy was articulated in another way between the
two leading young black literary figures of the day, Countee Cullen and
Langston Hughes. By then one of most celebrated literary figures of the Renaissance, Cullen, who wrote poetry of a strictly metered, well-schooled
Eurocentric form largely inspired by Keats, Shelley, Houseman, and Edna
St. Vincent Millay, reviewed Hughes's first volume of poetry, *The Weary
Blues,* in the February issue of *Opportunity,* one of the leading black magazines
of the day. In what was otherwise a very favorable review, he took Hughes to
task for writing jazz poems:

> I regard these jazz poems as interlopers in the company of the
> truly beautiful poems in other sections of the book. They move
> along with the frenzy and electric heat of a Methodist or Baptist
> revival meeting, and affect me in such the same manner. The re-
> vival meeting excites me, cooling and flushing me with alternate
> chills and fevers of emotion; so do these poems. But when the
> storm is over, I wonder if the quiet way of communing is not more
> spiritual for the God-seeking heart; and in the light of reflection I
> wonder if jazz poems really belong to that dignified company, that

select and austere circle of high literary expression which we call poetry.

Like Raphaelson earlier, Cullen connects jazz and religion. But in his case, the very atavistic, pagan quality of the jazz poems summons forth the more pagan, atavistic quality of black Christian worship that disturbs him—not from fear that the entire expression of jazz is dysfunctional, but that it is a kind of infantile obsession with something orgasmic that pulls the black writer away from the entire purpose of writing, from the script or the score, which demands permanency. The conflict between what Cullen felt were the pagan and Christian impulses of Black-American consciousness was the constant theme of most of his poetry. This is not surprising, as he was the foster son of Frederick A. Cullen, one of the most important African Methodist Episcopal ministers in 1920s Harlem.

In his famous June 1926 *Nation* article, "The Negro Artist and the Racial Mountain," Hughes, known for writing poems based on blues and jazz themes, supposedly responding to an article written the previous week by black conservative satirist George S. Schuyler called "The Negro-Art Hokum," was clearly responding directly to Cullen's criticism: "One of the most promising of the young Negro poets said to me once, 'I want to be a poet—not a Negro poet,' meaning, I believe, 'I want to write like a white poet'; meaning subconsciously, 'I would like to be a white poet'; meaning behind that, 'I would like to be white'." Of course, every black reader and some of the more knowledgeable white ones knew instantly that Hughes was referring to Cullen, who had, in nearly every public forum available to him, repeatedly said that he did not wish to be known as a Negro poet or purely as a racial poet. After dealing succinctly with what he felt to be Cullen's racial neurosis, Hughes discussed why he wrote jazz poems:

> Most of my own poems are racial in theme and treatment, derived from the life I know. In many of them I try to grasp and hold some of the meanings and rhythms of jazz. . . . What makes you do so many jazz poems? [Hughes is asked by his incredulous and sometimes unappreciative black public.]
>
> But jazz to me is one of the inherent expressions of Negro life in America; ;the eternal tom-tom beating in the Negro soul—the tom-tom of revolt against weariness in a white world, a world of subway trains, and work, work, work; the tom-tom of joy and laughter, and pain swallowed in a smile. Yet the Philadelphia clubwoman is ashamed to say that her race created it and she does not like me to write about it. The old subconscious "white is best" runs through her mind.

Hughes moves neatly from the opening image of the neurotic, inferior-feeling, assimilative black poet of the beginning of the piece—old Uncle Tom of the literary world—to the jazzman as race poet and the tom-tom of revolt. The piece, more cleverly designed than necessarily intellectually convincing, was an attack against the black bourgeois concept of a race-based or racially conscious art as being necessarily centered in some sort of recognizably mastered Eurocentric method or discipline. Yet the answer for blacks was never as simple as the Hughes-Cullen debate would suggest. As the symphonic jazz music movement continued beyond the 1920s, Duke Ellington became one of its leaders. One can scarcely imagine a more bourgeois-minded black artist: reared in a home of such conventionality that he heard little hot music or jazz, growing up adopting the same kind of mass bourgeois, popular taste as Paul Whiteman. Yet Ellington, in his blackness, was to have one of the most successful dance bands and swing music aggregations in the 1920s and the 1930s. Ellington was an almost completely unschooled musician; he never finished high school and never formally studied music, much like many of the ordinary lower-class black musicians of his day. He was indeed the least musically educated of the major black big band leaders and arrangers of the 1920s and 1930s, with the exception of Count Basie. He was certainly far less musically educated than Don Redman, Fletcher Henderson, Andy Kirk, Bennie Moten, and others. Yet he was to write, and have performed, more jazz concertos, symphonylike jazz compositions, ballets, and the like than virtually any other black or white jazz musician in the history of American popular music, and it was in these extended compositions that Ellington tended to be his most racially conscious. He symbolizes the paradox of the black artist in American popular culture and the contradictory and contrary idea of what a black art in relation to a larger white cultural framework really is.

There were two Jews whose parents were part of that mass that escaped the ghettos of Russia in the late nineteenth century to come to America whose spectacular success in popular music was part of the larger infusion of Russian and Eastern European Jews in the workings of American popular culture of the late nineteenth and early and middle twentieth centuries that so changed the entire course of the culture. The success of these two Jewish men in particular has a great deal to do with the entire business of white jazz and racial syncretism and our understanding of it. First, let us consider the case of clarinetist Benny Goodman, who became the extremely successful leader of a swing jazz band during the 1930s. Goodman, born in Chicago in 1909, had fewer than two years of formal musical instruction yet became one of the most compelling and accomplished hot jazz musicians of his generation. Forming his own band in March 1934 after an apprenticeship of nearly a dozen years as a sideman and studio player, Goodman struggled until, while on a national tour, the band clicked in California at the Palomar Club in 1935. Like Whiteman, when Goodman came back east he seemed like a triumphant, newfangled westerner. (Also like Whiteman, Goodman was to write his autobiography shortly after his Carnegie Hall concert, signifying that reaching that venue was a kind of pinnacle.) The band stopped in Chicago to play the Congress Hotel before going on to the legendary Paramount engagement in New York City in 1937, where the kids danced in the aisle, and finally to the swing concert at Carnegie Hall. Because the band had built its popularity in the West and the Midwest, there was a sense, once again, of the displaced westerner coming east, intensified by the fact that Goodman was from Chicago. But the fact that his ancestry was Eastern European added a reversed image to the myth, as he was also the easterner come west for freedom, and what better way to symbolize that quest than by playing an art form noted for its freedom of expression?[2]

The January 16, 1938, Carnegie Hall concert has always been seen as an analogue to the Whiteman concert that took place fourteen years earlier. And inasmuch as the former can be viewed as a major event in the history of American popular music, such a reading is actually correct—despite the fact that Vincent Lopez and His Orchestra performed a symphonic jazz concert at the Met on November 23, 1924, and included the work of black blues pioneer W. C. Handy, whose "St. Louis Blues" had been plugged by Lopez's band several years earlier; and despite the fact that Fats Waller performed James P. Johnson's *Yamekraw (Negro Rhapsody),* orchestrated by black composer William Grant Still, at Carnegie Hall with W. C. Handy conducting in 1928. The Goodman band was clearly the most popular and remarkable band to play a popular music concert at Carnegie Hall. It differed from all previous popular music concerts at classical European art halls in two ways: First, Goodman was not playing symphonic jazz but rather swing or hot jazz; second, his band was racially integrated, at least in the small group portion that featured Lionel Hampton on vibes and Teddy Wilson on piano. Unlike Whiteman, Goodman devoted only a portion of his concert to an evolutionary historical look at the development of jazz, and this portion was a mixture of songs associated with and written by both black and white musicians, including pieces by Will Marion Cook and Ford Dabney from the James Reese Europe era. Moreover, for several of these selections, Goodman was accompanied by black musicians from the Duke Ellington and Count Basie bands, therefore presenting the entire historical scope of the music as an integrated, openly racially syncretized art instead of as a subversively racially snycretized art. The article that ran in the *New York Times* magazine on the day of the concert entitled "Swing It! And Even in a Temple of Music" emphasized the comparison with the symphonic jazz concerts of an earlier day and saw a kind of evolution in the entire nature of popular music concerts at European art music halls: One might say, with Goodman at Carnegie Hall, that the country had officially gone "into the hot." As writer Gama Gilbert states:

> The occasion is a landmark in the growth and recognition of a species of music that was reborn after the halcyon days of symphonic jazz some ten years ago. . . .
>
> The salient impression of orchestra music and performance was one of order, decorum, and control. Jazz was congratulating itself, and receiving the congratulations of polite society, that it had shed every vestige of its uncouth and disreputable origins and had taken on the odor of respectability. It had disowned and erased from its memory its forebears and ancestral homes—the darky workers on the levees of the lower Mississippi, the hell-holes of New Orleans, the riverboat bands with Bix Beiderbecke, King Oliver and Stachelmouth Armstrong, Memphis and its blues, the sawdust and smoke-beery air of the Chicago joints. . . .
>
> But the germ of its undoing was implicit in its irreconcilable elements and in its flagrant artificiality. Divorced from the urgency of human emotion, lost to the lusty world from which it had exiled itself, its cleverly fabricated, sterile music began to ail and pall.

Clearly, this analogue recapitulates the concern that the culture had been expressing all along throughout the twenties: authentication. Jazz had lost its own authenticating voice by having, through the corruption of bourgeois, philistine appeasement, denied its own origins. Through Goodman, it had come back in a sort of loop to its own authority through its own primitiveness, its own lack of presumption or lack of unease about its disreputable origins. Yet there are a number of problems with this thesis: First, virtually all of the symphonic jazz bands, Europe's in some sense, Whiteman's, Lopez's, and others, were also dance bands playing arranged music that could only be played by highly skilled players, whether sight-readers or not. Indeed, the introduction of the saxophone as an innovative, virtuosic instrument in jazz can be credited not to black hot bands in New Orleans or on the Barbary Coast or in Chicago but to sophisticated black and white big dance bands, particularly Whiteman's, and was precisely what the Goodman band was. Moreover, the idea that the great musical theorists, organizers, and bandleaders were not concerned with composition, with achieving the entire range of musical effects and possibilities available through a highly arranged music executed with discipline, is false. In other words, symphonic jazz, as an extension of the American dance band tradition, was not an aberration but a serious if occasionally unsuccessful exploration of the possibility that dance music could be metamorphosed into an art music. Goodman's concert was the culmination of the acceptance of jazz music with whites as popularizers and blacks as cocreators, coperformers, and atavistic spiritual source. Goodman also made people listen to dance music and thus, even more than the beboppers who came later, he effected the transformation of hot jazz music to an art music and reoriented the public to accepting jazz as high art without the trappings of classical European art music. The irony is that Goodman elevated jazz while he himself, despite being white, was to the Anglo-Protestant public nothing more than a lower-class Eastern European Jewish immigrant, the very kind of ethnic who, along with the blacks, the white racist writers of the 1920s kept saying, was going to swamp American civilization. If Goodman's Carnegie Hall concert was any indication, the white racist theorists were right at last:

> That night at Carnegie Hall was a great experience, because it represented something—a group of musicians going on that stage and playing tunes by Gershwin and Berlin and Kern in arrangements by Fletcher and Edgar Sampson, getting up and playing the choruses the way they wanted to, each of them just being himself—and holding the attention of all those people for two hours and a half.
>
> When the thing was first put up to me, I was a little bit dubious about it, not knowing just what would be expected of us. But as soon as it was understood that we could handle the thing in our own way, and let the people listen to it as they would any other kind of music, the proposition really began to mean something. Certainly if the stuff is worth playing at all, it's worth playing in any hall that presents itself. I didn't have the idea of putting across a "message" or anything like that—I was just satisfied to have the kids in the band do what they always had done, and the way they did it was certainly wonderful. Personally, it was the thrill of my life to walk out on that stage with people just hemming the band in [some of the overflow audience sat on the stage], and hear the greeting the boys got. We were playing for "Bix" and the fellows on the riverboats, in the honky tonks and ginmills that night.

While the end of this passage from Goodman's autobiography sounds suspiciously as if it were lifted from the *New York Times* magazine article, one particular observation needs to be made: Goodman described the creative configuration of jazz as being the songs of Jewish Tin Pan Alley songwriters

(Berlin, Gershwin, Kern) and the arrangements of black arrangers (Fletcher Henderson and Edgar Sampson) who, apparently, could make the songs swing. This brings me to the other Jew we must consider, popular songwriter Irving Berlin. Born Israel Baline in Temun, Russia, in 1888, Berlin started his musical career as a singing waiter in the Bowery, making a name for himself at Nigger Mike Salter's Saloon and dance hall at 12 Pell Street in the heart of Chinatown. Nigger Mike was not black; he was, like Berlin, a Russian Jew whose dark skin earned him his extremely distasteful, if vivid, nickname. It was at Nigger Mike's that Berlin began his songwriting career and it was during the early stages of his career that his name underwent a change from Israel Baline to I. Berlin and, finally, Irving Berlin, "a Jew boy that had named himself after an English actor and a German city," so jocularly said George M. Cohan. Cohan said this at a banquet in honor of Berlin, who had, by the early 1910s, become the most prolific and the most successful songwriter in America. In 1911, Berlin had one of his biggest hits with "Alexander's Ragtime Band," which, for a time, was the song that he was known by, despite his other hits. The success of "Alexander's Ragtime Band" led to a spate of ragtime songs from Berlin: "That Mysterious Rag," "Whistling Rag," "The Dying Rag," "The Ragtime Jockey Man," "The Ragtime Soldier Man," "That International Rag," and the huge hit "Everybody's Doin' It Now." All of these songs were written between 1912 and 1917. Berlin is the linchpin that, finally, ties everything together, for his songs appeared on the bill of the two major jazz concerts at European art music halls between 1924 and 1938—Whiteman's 1924 Aeolian Hall concert and Goodman's 1938 Carnegie Hall concert. Berlin's music not only ties together both symphonic and swing or hot jazz, it also ties together virtually the entire era of American popular music from nearly the turn of the century to the Goodman concert, since Berlin's music and the musical traditions it represents—both African-American and East European Jewish as well as the ethnic song of the minstrel and Yiddish theaters—goes back that far. Berlin's music confirmed that any "serious" American art form, be it inspired by some symphonic form or the energy of the popular dance, was going to be based on the largely Jewish-created Tin Pan Alley song. (The apotheosis of the American popular song and its writer occurred shortly after Whiteman's concert, when drama critic Alexander Woolcott, of Algonquin Roundtable fame, wrote a biography of Berlin published in 1925 when Berlin was just thirty-six years old.) Certainly jazz has developed largely and recognizably as an art form built on the chord changes of the Tin Pan Alley song. For instance, modernist trumpeter Wynton Marsalis's symphonic jazz album, *Hot House Flowers,* is not a collection of concertos or European derived forms, but a series of string settings of a bunch of evergreen popular songs familiar to nearly everyone in America who is aware of show music. There are, of course, compositions by jazz composers from Jelly Roll Morton to Duke Ellington to Thelonious Monk that have become part of the stock repertoire of the jazz performer, but most frequently it is a specific group of Tin Pan Alley pop tunes that are called "standards," implying the very foundation upon which the art is built. And many compositions by noted jazz players have merely been variations of the chord changes of these standards.

It might be unnerving to some blacks and even some liberal whites that Whiteman was called the King of Jazz, that Berlin was called the King of Ragtime, and that Goodman was called the King of Swing. The titles, on the one hand, signify a kind of white cultural hegemony, a white cultural imperialism, some might argue. And while the story is, perhaps, as simple as that (for theft explains a great deal of the phenomenon of the popularization and racial politicalization of American popular art), it is in the end a great deal more complicated, too. The growth of syncopated rhythmic American popular music has been the growth of racially inclusive art, virtually the only racially inclusive art in America where whites, as a commonplace, acknowledge the work of blacks. Moreover, the impulse of this music was also to battle against the conventions of the day; the impulse of the music was always to bring the races and classes closer together even if, meeting the walls of commercialism and stubborn social and political customs, it did not succeed. Where else, other than in the popular culture arenas of sports and music, have the races really come together, really syncretized their being? And has it not been, in many compelling ways, that society has experienced its greatest changes for the better through just these avenues of marginalized popular culture suddenly taking center stage in the culture for one crucial moment? Popular culture has changed us and how we see ourselves, and how we relate to ourselves as blacks and whites and to each other, more than any other single force or combined forces in this country. Let us not forget that it is impossible for American culture, popular or otherwise (and in a real sense America has no other culture but popular culture), to authenticate *anything,* since American culture exists, from its very inception, to authenticate *everything.* As Kierkegaard argued about the relationship of paganism and Christianity, when whites in America tried to define the culture by their whiteness, it only intensified their realization that it must exclude blackness, and as it fought to exclude blackness, it only, paradoxically, continued to include it by recognizing it as a power, a symbol, a threat, a principal, that had to be excluded. In the end, Hubert H. Harrison more properly assessed Stoddard's book than Tom Buchanan ever did. American culture is the one human aggregate that will support any proposition you wish, because its energy is its willingness to try to sell anything at least once.[7] The King of Swing, the King of Ragtime, the King of Jazz—these titles are a sign of cultural hegemony, to be sure, but also of the racial syncretism that

gives American popular music its distinctiveness and its power. White guitarist Eddie Condon organized a jazz concert on January 14, 1942, at Carnegie Hall as a tribute to black jazzman Fats Waller, and the program included
many of the famous songs Waller composed and other songs he did not write
but made famous through performance, such as "I'm Gonna Sit Right Down
and Write Myself a Letter." It was the first concert in tribute to a black jazz
musician ever held at Carnegie Hall. Jazz had been reauthenticated through
its blackness and the entire cycle had moved fully around from Whiteman
and symphonic jazz and popular song in 1924 to Waller and Harlem stride
piano and the popular song in 1942. Waller had been drinking heavily both
before and during the concert and was a bit unsteady at times, and Condon
kept wondering why so many of the tunes played had snatches of Gershwin
in them.

It might be that Duke Ellington said it right in his 1931 song title: "It
Don't Mean a Thing, If It Ain't Got That Swing." But considering how
mongrelized our culture really is and how our popular music constantly cele-
brates the wonder and glory of our mixed-up selves, Berlin said it even better
in 1916: "Everything in America is Ragtime."

EPILOGUE: IT COULD HAPPEN TO YOU

> *The Carnegie concert was the biggest thing that ever happened to me.*

> —Billie Holiday, *Lady Sings the Blues*

Billie Holiday gave two concerts at Carnegie Hall. The first, which she describes in her autobiography, *Lady Sings the Blues,* took place on March 27,
1948, ten days after her release from prison, where she served nine and a half
months of a year and a day sentence for the possession of narcotics. It was a
midnight concert, the night before Easter, a bad night for business according
to Holiday, and it was the only time in her life that she fainted.

> Just before I was set to go on for the second set a big mess of
> gardenias arrived backstage. My old trademark—somebody had re-
> membered and sent it for luck. I took them out of the box and fas-
> tened them smack to the side of my head without even looking
> twice. I hadn't noticed, but there was a huge hatpin and I stuck it
> deep into my head. I was so numb from excitement I didn't even
> feel anything until the blood began running down in my eyes and
> ears.

It was, one supposes, as a result of this wound and the general excitement of
doing her "welcome back" concert at such a prestigious forum that Holiday

fainted, although she ultimately performed a show of twenty-one tunes and six encores.

Holiday's second and last Carnegie Hall concert took place nearly eight years later—on November 10, 1956, more than a year after the highly publicized drug death of Charlie Parker. Her autobiography had just been published and, between groups of numbers she sang, Gilbert Millstein, a writer for the *New York Times,* read lengthy though not profane excerpts from Holiday's book. (There is a recording of this concert available on Verve Records.) Perhaps the readings from the autobiography would have been more effective had Holiday read the book herself, or perhaps had any woman at all read it. The overall effect of hearing these passages between the songs is strange and dislocating, the sort of victory-in-defeat that was, at points, the hallmark of Holiday's life, the hallmark of the black jazzer's life, the singular triumph of vulgarity, bad taste, feminized artifice, politicized artifact, and profound art. At the second concert an excerpt from her book about her first Carnegie Hall concert was read, giving a tremendous sense of performance as both replication and reification. Jazz had, at last, acquired a text; it had become a narrative art, an epic. In both concerts, it was Holiday's life or rather the myth of her victimization as woman (her bad marriages and the publicly known fact that her drug addiction was caused by men she knew), artist (one of the reasons she was performing in Carnegie Hall was because she lost her cabaret card as a result of her arrest and imprisonment and could, therefore, no longer perform in nightclubs and bars in New York), and black (she was the victim of racism, segregation, limited life choices, and a bad education) as much as her art that was being celebrated. Holiday's concerts were the final public acceptance of jazz as an art form and of the black performer as artist: The life and the art had become interchangeable. And the life and the art had become a kind of voyeuristic tragedy for the audience and a self-conscious tragedy for the artist. Indeed, as embodied by Holiday, jazz had, ironically, ceased to be art while being swallowed by the weight of its artistic pretensions; jazz had now become a sort of postmodernist negritude, a stance, a stunt, which means that it had become both more and less than it had been, existing somewhere between Walt Whitman's "barbaric yawp" and an existential aria. If jazz had once symbolized the revolt of modernity, it had now come to symbolize modernity as absurd. Jazz had become a forlorn and fashionable pulp and Billie Holiday had become our greatest, most stirring pulp heroine. After all, only in America could someone sin so helplessly and yet be given a second chance, be granted the great buildup for the Grand Comeback. Billie Holiday, demonstrating at last the new and ultimate arrival of the black jazz artist in the mainstream and wanting so much to prove that she was loved in America and did not need to escape to Europe, showed that redemption of that sort could happen to anyone.

NOTES

1 Caesar makes other references that would be particularly striking and relevant for the
   women in her audience such as "They got all kinds of perfumes like Avon, Matchabelli,
   and Chanel No. 5 but none of them can reach where we're going tonight." And later, toward the very end of the sermon: "I saw something else on television. I'm always catch-
   ing things. One day I was sitting at home I saw a bald headed man come on the screen
   with one earring in his ear say my name is Mr. Clean and Mr. Clean hates dirt. But I
   wish he'd walk in here tonight so I can tell him that I know a man named Mr. Clean." I
   am not suggesting here that Caesar's sermon was feminist but clearly she expresses that
   salvation from God and thus empowerment by the holy spirit means rejecting the carnal-
   ity of this world and specifically for women the products that have defined their role and
   their spiritual (and, ironically for feminists and female evangelists alike, their earthly)
   enslavement.

   One other point that needs to be mentioned here is that Billie Holiday cowrote a
   song entitled "Don't Explain" inspired by discovering strange lipstick on her first husband's, Jimmy Munroe's, collar. "'Take a bath, man,' I said, 'don't explain,'" she writes
   as her reply to him in her autobiography, *Lady Sings the Blues.* So, Holiday the jazz singer
   gives us the profane rhetorical analogue to the sacred sermon on bathing by Caesar.

2 Earl Hines, the famous black pianist and bandleader from Pittsburgh who played in Chicago during the heyday of the 1920s and 1930s, was called Fatha, and Sonny was a not
   uncommon sobriquet for black men. Hines did not acquire the name under circumstances that are indicative of the sort of endearment that the Pops nickname suggests. See
   Stanley Dance's *The World of Earl Hines*—and despite his importance in the history of
   jazz, Hines does not have the same historical magnitude as either Armstrong or
   Whiteman.

3 In the same year, black writer and activist Mary Church Terrell wrote a piece on Samuel
   Coleridge-Taylor's tour of the United States for *The Voice of the Negro,* a short-lived but
   important black magazine of the period.

4 Harold Cruse develops this line of reasoning further in his seminal work, *The Crisis of the Negro Intellectual* (1967), and trying to negotiate the interpretive quagmire that the earlier
   black intellectuals such as Johnson and Du Bois stumbled into is largely what Ralph Ellison's *Shadow and Act* (1964) is all about.

5 Europe was apparently a very impressive man and his music was quite compelling. Arthur
   W. Little, in *From Harlem to the Rhine* (1936), his book on the Fifteenth Colored Infantry
   known as Harlem's Hell Fighters, describes the effect of Europe's band on an audience of
   hostile southern whites in Spartanburg, South Carolina. The regiment, of which Europe
   was a member, had been stationed in Spartenburg shortly after the famous race riot involving black troops (the 24th Infantry) in Houston, Texas.

> The talk which some of us overheard through that crowd, during the
> early stages of the concert, was by no means reassuring. At first it seemed, al-
> most, as if an error of judgment had been made in forcing the colored regi-
> ment into prominence at so early an hour after our arrival. But there must be
> something in the time-honored line about music and its charms; for, grad-
> ually, the crowd grew larger, but the noises of the crowd grew less and less,
> until finally, in that great public square of converging city streets, silence
> reigned. Lieutenant Europe conducted, as was his custom, with but a few sec-
> onds between numbers, and the program appeared to be short. When the final

piece had been played and the forty or fifty bandsmen had filed out of the stand in perfect order with the "Hep-Hep-Hep" of the sergeants as the only sound from their ranks, the flower of Spartanburg's citizenry looked at each other foolishly, and one could be heard to say:—"Is that all?" while another would say:—"When do they play again?"

Little, the white commander of the regiment, described both Europe and Noble Sissle as "artists of genius and of high musical education, and gentlemen, by instinct and by bearing," and he recounts how Europe maintained both his dignity and his common sense after both he and Sissle were verbally abused and assaulted by a white tavern owner in Spartanburg. Little reveals his respect for the two men by not having them speak in the rather overwrought Negro dialect he uses for the speech of most of the other black soldiers.

6 Whether Europe's musicians could generally read scores well is open to dispute. Irene Castle wrote: "He would not employ a man who could not read music and he would not tolerate dissipation or irresponsibility" (from "Jim Europe—A Reminiscence" in *Opportunity Magazine*, March 1930). Generally, her description of Europe matches that of Little. Ironically, she refers to him as "the Paul Whiteman of the colored race," revealing the closeness in both aesthetic vision and organizational abilities between the two men. Perhaps it would have been more apt to refer to Paul Whiteman as the James Reese Europe of the white race.

7 The obvious penalty for this is the wholesale justification of vulgarity as an art form that rock and roll music has given us. Here blacks stand uneasily, as they always have, as the symbolic basin or sink of vulgar expression from which whites can draw inspiration and through which they can justify their own preoccupation with vulgarity-as-freedom-expression and as the lowest common denominator of expression. Instead of symbolizing a sort of sophisticated stylization of art, the contemporary black rapper, for instance, is only the stylization of vulgarity now defined by white liberals, (not as symptomatic urge to profanity that afflicts culture generally), but as the special, charismatic, and skillful expressions of "ethnicity."

BLACK HERMAN COMES THROUGH ONLY ONCE EVERY SEVEN YEARS

Black Magic, White Magic, and American Culture

THE BOOK OF BLACK HERMAN

Just so the conjurer never reveals in advance the full nature of a trick that the spectator may not know where to center his attention.

—from "The Psychology of Conjuring" by Dr. Max Dessoir
and H. J. Burlingame, in Burlingame's *Herrmann the Magician,
His Life; His Secrets*

Although the books possess the same covers and deal with the same subject matter, there are a number of differences—both major and minor—between the 1934 Martin Publishing Company edition of *Black Herman's Easy Pocket Tricks Which You Can Do* and the 1938 Dorene Publishing Company edition of the same work. The Dorene edition has about twenty-eight fewer pages than the earlier one. Moreover, the earlier edition makes no claim to be "four volumes in one" as the later does, although there were apparently four distinct sections in every version of the book. These "volumes," or chapters really, are "The Life of the Great Black Herman," "The Study of Legerdemain," "The Signification of Dreams," and "The Story of Oriental Magic I Found in the Orient, An Ancient Practice." The earlier edition has these sections: "The Life of the Great Black Herman," "The Study of Magic," "Horoscope," and "The Signification of Dreams." The two books share most of their material except in three significant instances: the earlier edition is profusely illustrated and the later one is hardly illustrated at all; there is no section in the earlier book corresponding to "The Story of Oriental Magic I Found in the Orient, An Ancient Practice" in the 1938 edition; and finally, in the later book Herman worked out an elaborately complex number system for his interpretation of dreams that is absent from the earlier volume in which the dream section reads like any standard dream book for people who play the numbers (a popular, though illegal, lottery game among blacks in the 1920s). What is curious here is not only the nature of the revisions but the fact that the revisions even exist. Black Herman died in April 1934 in Louisville, Kentucky, at the age of forty-two from, as the *Chicago Defender* put it in its banner headline, Acute Indigestion. The immediate suggestion to some minds was that he was poisoned. This was precisely the kind of death that would have had many of his followers thinking that poor Black Herman had been hoodooed or had a met a conjuror more mighty than he. (In truth, Black Herman's death resembles in its unexpectedness and its strangeness the deaths of two of the most famous performers in the history of stage magic: Harry Houdini, who died in October 1926 of a ruptured appendix, and Alexander Herrmann the Great, who died in December 1896, apparently of a heart attack. Perhaps they were hoodooed too. Or perhaps famous magicians often die in ways that seem as though their deaths were caused by supernatural agents, that even in death, ambiguity and theatrics cast a certain surreal verisimilitude.) Still, one wonders who was responsible for the changes for the 1938 edition of Herman's book. Perhaps the 1938 edition was simply another earlier edition that was reprinted; nonetheless, there is no indication that it is a posthumous work or that Black Herman had died. Black Herman's funeral was held at the Mother A.M.E. Zion Church, and he was buried in Woodlawn Cemetery in New York, the same place, apparently, where Herrmann the Great was interred.

At the time of his death, Black Herman was the most famous black magician in American history, as evidenced by the prominence the report of his death received in black newspapers, where it was invariably a page one story. Even today, among people who know the subject of blacks and the history of performance magic, his name is still mentioned as among the most colorful and charismatic of American magicians. Over six feet tall, with a magnificent physique and a showman's flair for grabbing attention through the most flamboyant, if tawdry, kind of publicity, Herman was certainly a figure to be reckoned with. (For many, however, Herman was the archfraud of frauds whose technique left much to be desired. The article about his death that appeared in the April 28, 1934, issue of the *New York Amsterdam News* was, at times, more morosely arch than laudatory: The headline read "BLACK HERMAN REGULARLY RAISED THE 'DEAD' BUT THEY BURIED HIM LIKE ANY MORTAL MAN.") Herman was immortalized by Ishmael Reed in his 1971 novel about the New Negro or Harlem Renaissance, *Mumbo Jumbo,* as one of the book's two heroes. (I assume that Reed was also influenced in the creation of both the fictitious Black Herman and PaPa LaBas not only by Chester

Himes's Jones and Johnson but by the real-life Harlem detective of the twenties, Herbert Boulin, who frequently appeared in stories in the black New York press. Herbert Boulin's initials are, of course, the exact reverse of Black Herman's, just the sort of arcane symbolism that would appeal to Reed.)

Herman, as entrepreneur and great magician of color, must have had in mind the model of Richard Potter, the first great American-born conjuror, who also happened to be a mulatto. Potter, who was born in Frankland town near Boston in 1783, was the son of a British tax collector and one of his black slaves. The slight young man began a career as a performing conjuror in his mid-twenties, after having served as an apprentice to John Rannie, a noted Scottish magician. Potter was extraordinarily successful on his extended tours, where he was often mistaken for a Hindu or an American Indian. He eventually invested more than ten thousand dollars in about two hundred acres of New Hampshire farmland and became a rich landowner. In a novel based on the life of Potter entitled *Conjuror's Journal,* by Frances L. Shine (1978), the character is shown to be just as enterprising but haunted by his love for a white woman and by his rejection at the hands of his white father (neither of these are biographically accurate). In short, the character in the novel is, in effect, bedeviled, paradoxically, by the lack of acknowledgment of his blackness by his white father and by his need to assimilate because of the egoistic inadequacy of his blackness. However Potter's real life may have differed from the author's version, nonetheless the novel suggests a set of psychological problems associated with blackness (or the taint of it, as the case may be) that, in truth, may be of little concern for the pioneering black male who, in the end, learns to negotiate white fathers (real or surrogate) and white women as a sort of minor aside to the real business of taking a distinct disadvantage (his blackness) and transforming it to, if not a virtue, then certainly a decidedly neutralized necessity. Herman's opportunistic use of race pride and nationalism were simply ways for a black male with some sense of bourgeois ambition in a largely difficult and, at times, quite daunting social setting to get about the business of making an independent career that is a legal activity. If Herman knew about Richard Potter, the life of the early black magician may have suggested that there were ways to have a career as a black itinerant adept and, even, to make money.

Black Herman's most famous illusion or trick was burying a woman alive—and the trick was always performed with a woman as the fictive corpse—for a certain period of time and then resurrecting her unharmed. The time that the woman would remain buried varied, sometimes just a few hours, sometimes as long as six days. This trick had become so famous, such a signature, that each performance was something of a news event. For instance, in the July 4, 1923, issue of the *New York Amsterdam News* appears this story:

BLACK HERMAN TO BURY WOMAN 6 HOURS

At the Independence Day Jubilee and Aviation Carnival and Athletic Meet at Hasbrouck Heights aviator field, Hasbrouck Heights, New Jersey, Professor Black Herman, the magician, will hypnotize and bury a woman under six feet of earth at 11 o'clock and raise her at 4:45 p.m. Lieut. Herbert Julian will drop 4,000 feet in a parachute and alight exactly over the grave of the sleeping woman. In addition, there will be track races, boxing, baseball, tennis, cricket, a potato race, a three-legged race, etc. This promises to be an afternoon of thrills.

It is much to Black Herman's credit and a signal indication of how successfully he advertised himself as a mere harmless entertainer that he was able to perform a conjuring act at a black picnic. Especially among good Christian black folk, this sort of stuff by Herman normally would be considered the rankest form of the devil's work. Remember these lines from an old Negro spiritual: "De devil is a liar an' a conjuror too/If you don't look out he'll conjure you." The conjuror, the magician, was someone not to be trusted, yet many poor black folk found him irresistibly attractive. Herman asserted in his book that he performed in churches such as, for instance, St. Paul's A.M.E. and Metropolitan A.M.E. Zion Church, both in St. Louis, and that he was "a devoted Christian . . . [who] recognizes no man as his superior save God and Christ." This last clause about recognizing no superior in any man resonates with the kind of implicit nationalistic claim one could expect from a man whose very name suggested a deep race consciousness and who was proud to have played at Marcus Garvey's headquarters, Liberty Hall, when he first came to New York in March 1923—interestingly, around the time of the start of the Harlem Renaissance, according to most historians. In fact, Herman did a number of performances in connection with Garvey, and Herman's own entourage of fancy cars could be found among Garvey's Black Legion and other units in the UNIA's grand parades. Herman always seemed quite interested in wanting to politicize performance magic in ways that were subtle yet, ironically, cheaply blatant and sensational; to awaken a black woman—the life-bearer—from a simulated death was to symbolize Garvey's cry "Up, you mighty race." Herman, with this trick was literally uplifting the race from its spiritual death and confinement. Whenever Herman performed in schools he mentioned his friendship with Booker T. Washington, which was formed when he played at Tuskegee. Although it is said in several sources that Washington wrote an introduction for one of Herman's books, I have been unable to locate an extant copy of it. I suppose such a book did once exist as Herman always mentioned it. Whatever the

merit of Herman's claim of intimacy with Washington, it clearly suggests
two things: first, that Herman was an important or noteworthy performer
before 1915—the year of Washington's death—and that he was known in
important black circles long before he came to New York, which, of course,
is exactly what Herman claims in the brief autobiography in his book; and
second, that he possessed a political consciousness that invariably influenced
his art even if it was not apparent in any particular trick he performed. This
political consciousness was partly an idealized race nationalism and partly a
practical understanding of getting along and getting ahead in the world. He
melded, in a particularly fascinating way, the twin pillars of the black bourgeois dream-wish: race pride and self-sufficiency. Herman revealed Garvey's
influence by stating in the autobiographical section of his book that he was
"born five miles from a small town in the dark jungles of Africa" and suggesting that somehow his powers as a performer were tied to his origin. He
revealed Washington's influence by becoming—through the sale of his books
and extensive herb collection—one of the most successful black businessmen
of his age. He was Afrocentric mysticism incarnate and a hardheaded money-
getter, he was *homo faber* (the man who makes things and himself) and *homo
economicus* (the man who exploits his circumstances for control and gain) with
few peers. We know from the most ancient times that the juggler, the conjuror, has been not just a performer but a salesman as well. Black Herman
was purely and simply within the traditions of both the absolute conceit of
the charlatan and the pure hustle of the Yankee peddler. He was truly The
Magician.

Black Herman's success as a stage magician in black churches and at
black family affairs suggests that in a way he was able to de-theologize or de-
sanctify his act, which meant that he made magic as obvious or self-evident
trick; its fakery in short had been made explicit and intelligible by the very
context of acceptability in which the acts were being performed: in schools,
at churches, at picnics, in short, at respectable bourgeois social gatherings or
representations of bourgeois institutions. The tricks ceased to have any significance as rites or spiritual rituals as they became mere demonstrations of
technique, of a kind of secularized charisma, without the signification of
spirit control or spirit summons. In short, like the relentlessly mechanical
father of modern magic, clockmaker Robert-Houdin, or his neurotically ra-
tionalist and antispiritualist namesake, escapist and lock specialist Houdini,
Black Herman would have been considered a scientist, an inventor, an engineer, a tinkerer (in the spirit of the hero of Ellison's *Invisible Man* and Benjamin Franklin), and finally, just as he called himself in one of the sections of
his autobiography, a detective.

Ishmael Reed did not reinvent or reimagine Black Herman when he
made him a detective; he simply made him, as magic historian Milbourne

Christopher has noted, exactly what the magician in the modern world has become. Interestingly, in the mythology constructed by the Nation of Islam (the Black Muslims) the evil Yacub who invents white people is called a scientist and not a magician; yet as W. B. Yeats makes clear in the first part of his 1901 essay entitled "Magic," this archetype upon which the Frankenstein and Faust stories are based is in fact the tragic magician whose very insistent uncovering or discovering is the cause of his tragedy. The magician's tragedy, in truth, is the hubris of hardheaded knowledge and engineering dexterity, not of mysticism. The modern world has fused the scientific urge to explain with the magician's urge to dominate and command so that explanation as the modernist version of the magician's prophecy has indeed become a form of domination; formularized discourse as the modernist version of the magician's recipe or spell has become a form of control. Herman's book is not simply a book of formulas. It is a book of explanations, all obviously fake, from the pictures that show Herman with a collection of ventriloquist dummies that are plainly real children or with a supposed dead man in a coffin who is really alive, to the explanations of dreams that explain nothing, to often either incomplete or unclear explanations of simple tricks. Here is a cunning magician's book that offers explanation and formulas while thwarting the very possibility of explanation and formula, but which was accepted by his readership as containing, self-evidently, explanations and formulas of incredible power. His autobiography, itself a blatant narrative of lies, of fantastic escapades reminiscent of the memoirs of other famed magicians but even more closely linked to heavyweight champion Jack Johnson's 1927 autobiography, *In the Ring—and Out,* operates as a set of fictive recollections that simply thwart and question the very act of narrative memory, but which, again, his readership would accept as self-evidently the only life story Herman could have had. His acts of explanation become little more than virtuosic displays of the manipulation of obscurity.

Black Herman's magic was an outdoor vaudeville of entertainment and not an outdoor grandiose gesture of pure mysticism. As he writes in the very beginning of his book, "In offering to you my solution of the troubles and difficulties that beset your pathway, I wish to state so that there will no misunderstanding at any time, that I do not claim to be the possessor of any supernatural or unnatural power whatsoever, nor do I claim to be able to accomplish anything that is impossible to the average mind, were it to be devoted to specializing along these lines entirely." Here is the preachment of practice and discipline, of learning skills that characterized both Garvey and Washington. At his stage shows, Herman frequently denounced fortune-tellers and spiritualists. "If they can read your fortune," he would say with venom, "why don't they read their own and know when the cops are after them?" The trick for Herman is not mysticism but the irony of the detective

presenting the audience with a mystery that can only be solved through rational and deductive logic and an understanding of simple ingenuity but that
seems to defy both logic and ingenuity as the magic mystery offers itself as an
expression of the utterly inexplicable.

Burying someone alive and then resurrecting the person is a quite old illusion, some saying that Christ performed a variation of it at his entomb-
ment. It apparently originated with Indian fakirs; they are at least the most
famous performers of living burial as a signification of body discipline and
the power of the mind to display the height of its force through a simulation
of the very negation of that force. Yet I am inclined to think that Black Herman performed this trick in part because it was both an answer and a complement to the famous trick performed by both Alexander and Carl Herrmann,
German Jews who became very famous magicians and from whom Black
Herman may very well have taken his name (Herman never acknowledged in
his books that his real name was either Herman Rucker or Benjamin Rucker
as the newspapers variously asserted); the white Herrmann's trick was called
"The Creation." As told by Francis Joseph Martinka, an old intimate of the
Herrmanns and other magicians in a 1916 number of the *Brooklyn Eagle,* the
trick worked thus: "In this feat a [hypnotized] woman was folded in a coffin
and set afire. The audience plainly beheld the feminine form shrivel into a
skeleton. After a long moment of suspense, the woman would again appear
from behind a curtain at the other end of the stage. The machinery of this
trick involved days of ingenious plotting and combined illusions, and
brought in nearly $100,000 to Herrmann at the end of his tour." Black Her-
man wanted an act that was at least as grand as the Herrmann brothers', giving women—the life-bearers—the gift of life from an elaborately induced
death that could only occur through a pantomime of submission imitating
the gestures of hypnotism, the well-known tool for the psychoanalytic treatment of hysterical women. Aside from this obvious feminist interpretation of
symbolic sexual politics given a masculine metaphysical and theatrical veneer, the contrived display of which may have appealed to Herman and his
black audience, Black Herman was also very competitive, constantly com-
paring himself to the best magicians. He had to feel that his illusions were on
a par with theirs. If the white Herrmanns had a cremation, he would have a
burial.

Among blacks, the business of the fakery of the resurrection trick was
made even more explicit and more comic when 1950s rhythm and blues
singer Screaming Jay Hawkins of "I Put a Spell on You" fame decided to
open his act by rising from a coffin holding a skull. "He outraged the establishment by wearing wildly colored capes and turbans, kaleidoscope suit and
leopard-skin shoes, and using such props as fireworks, fuse boxes, coffins,
snakes, shrunken heads and, of course, his ever-faithful companion, Henry
the Skull," wrote rock critic Tony Burke. Hawkins conflated the images of

the magician, the conjuror, the hoodoo doctor, the spiritualist, the medium, and the vampire—the entire cast of necromantic wonder-workers that lurks in the Western (particularly, in this instance, the black Western) subconscious mind—into a pop culture parody of the arcane and the occult that was meant to make explicit the roots of black American showmanship while mystifying the implicit sexuality and authorial premises of male rhythm and blues singing.

The fact that Black Herman, an herbalist and astrologer in addition to being a standard magician, was often written about in black newspapers was not very unusual. During Herman's heyday in the 1920s, the doings of black magicians and conjurors seemed virtually to blanket such newspapers as, one supposes, they themselves blanketed black neighborhoods. These professors—only black ragtime piano players were so commonly referred to by this appellation of learning (and of course ragtime and magic occupied the same demi-twilight world of black vaudeville and nightclubs, the devil's world yet perceived as a world of learning and skill)—straddled both mysticism and science and yet were, in truth, paradoxically, the negation and essence of both. Ads for fortune-tellers and "spiritualists" such as Professor Edet Effrong, Native of Africa; Professor N. Phoenix, Spiritualist, Magician, Healer; Professor Ejo A. Mohammedan, Scientist; Professor J. Du JaJa, a Mohammedan Scientist; Professor S. Indoo; Professor Alpha Roktabija, Arabian Mystic Seer; Professor S. M. Haffaney; and Professor Akpan Aga, Wonderful Magician by Alchemy and Fire were common enough in major black newspapers whose readers would be attracted not only by the fortune-telling or spiritualism of these magicians but by the idea that they were physicians, healers who would often be more accessible, more sympathetic, and seemingly more powerful than many medical doctors. (It must be remembered, as Norton Smith notes in his *Jesus the Magician,* that Christ's charismatic authority stemmed largely from the fact that his miracles or tricks were mostly feats of healing among the poor.) Professor Joseph Domingo, "World's Wonder, African Spiritualist and Occultist [*sic*], and Mohammedan from Kano, West Coast, Africa," who also frequently advertised in black newspapers of the day, was twice arrested for fraudulent medical practice, and both instances were reported in front page stories in the *Amsterdam News.* This was certainly a common enough feature in newspapers that often ran stories about voodoo doctors, cult murderers, jailed boy healers, quack fortune-tellers, dishonest mediums, and the like, obviously because their readers wanted them. (Although most of these grotesque yet comic stories were written with a certain derisive dismissiveness, there was much coverage of the black vaudeville circuit where many magicians, wonder-workers, and spiritualists worked. For instance, Coy Herndon, who was featured at minstrel shows and circuses as one of the most extraordinary hoop rollers in the world and one of the great wonder workers of his time, wrote a regular gossip column for the Chicago Defender called "Coy Cogitates," mostly about black vaudeville but with a mystical tone.) Black Herman did not lack competitors, yet he seemed to have risen above them in some way. Not because he was, in the end, any less a charlatan or a quack or a confidence man but because he was something else, possibly something more, than merely a predator upon the ignorant and unlucky poor. His nationalistic pretensions and his business acumen had a distinct nobility. He was one of the few magicians who advertised himself not merely as a wonder-worker but as a sort of race hero. Of course, the others, with their Islamic trappings and African or Arabic pretensions, hinted at being race heroes as well. Herman's own claims were never really atavistic but synthetic. He may have claimed an African birthplace, but he was also a professed Christian of a very American, albeit black, nature. Nor, in the end, despite his claims to an African origin, did he try to mystify the concept of race. Like, say, black nationalist Hubert H. Harrison (a contemporary), Herman really tried to mystify *the power* while, paradoxically, demystifying *the act* of acquiring knowledge. When Herman spoke of knowledge as a discipline open to any of "average mind," he was truly undermining one of the assumptions upon which fake spiritualists make their claim to priestcraft. Herman was undoubtedly a hustler but possibly less a fraud than a shrewd fox.

There is one final distinction between the 1934 and 1938 editions of Black Herman's *Easy Pocket Tricks Which You Can Do.* His slogan is slightly altered. In the earlier work it reads: Black Herman Comes Through Only Once Every Seven Years; in the later edition it is: Black Herman Comes Through Once Every Seven Years—a very minor revision that does not really change the sense of the statement. His detractors said that Herman could come to a town only once every seven years because the uproar he would cause and the dissatisfied unhappy people he left behind virtually assured no return engagement in the near future. Perhaps this was true. But he was surely no worse than other local magicians and wonder-workers and probably a bit better than the many religious vultures who picked bones clean with their revivals. Who knows why the slogan was altered? Someone, perhaps Herman's ghost, realized that "only" was, after all, a redundancy.

TWO FILMS

> *"I want to be a detective, sar," he said.*
> *"What?" I thought that I hadn't heard him.*
> *"A detectives sar. Like the ones you see in the movies," he made himself* explicit.

—An account of a conversation between the author and a young African in Richard Wright's *Black Power: A Record of Reactions in a Land of Pathos*

From across the void of thirty-seven years, Ingmar Bergman's 1959 film, *The Magician,* and the 1922 film *The Man From Beyond,* which Harry Houdini wrote, produced, and starred in, seem to complement and actually speak to one another: the Victorian melodrama and the postmodernist comedy about life as imposture. They are two of the most striking films about magicians in the history of cinema.

Houdini does not really play a magician in *The Man From Beyond,* but a man who, after one hundred years, is found frozen alive in the Arctic. But in effect he plays no one else or, at least, no one other than himself, for his character, Howard Hillary, is simply a distillation and extension of his own fictive construct, Harry Houdini. In this film, Houdini is, in rapid succession, every pulp fiction hero imaginable: The scenes in the Arctic where he runs around in a loin cloth conjure up Tarzan (as does the entire movie) as well as Houdini's self-absorption with his own physique as image, his myth as the man who takes ice-water baths. His escape from confinement in a mental institution suggests his own escapist myth as well as the escapist myth of virtually every swashbuckling hero of old castle-and-costume epics. His uncovering of the mystery of the missing father in what proves to be a very father-obsessed film not only once again suggests Houdini's own myth as detective and uncoverer of chicanery and fraud in his famous investigations of mediums and the spirit world, but also brings to mind the Brooks Brothers–suited detective hero. His (literally) cliff-hanging fight with the villain is typical of the western hero; and his rescue of the leading lady from the rapids of Niagara Falls not only brings to mind both the jungle and the western hero but Houdini's own water escapes from the Chinese Water Torture Cell to the frozen Detroit River. In effect, Houdini collapsed his own outsized myth as escape artist/magician with that of the collective image of the B-movie pulp hero. Perhaps that is why his movies were never successful commercially; his own stage, in-person myth could never be tellingly or compellingly conveyed in movies; and he lost his ability to excite once his gestures became the standard clichés of any action hero. He simply burdened and camouflaged one kind of imposture as improbable magician and preposterous escape artist with another as preposterous and improbable movie hero. But one wonders, more importantly, if the whole film, as an exploration and revelation of Houdini's interest in reincarnation and the afterlife, is nothing more than a giant fraud, a cinematic experience designed to promote misreading. What has most profoundly misled many viewers is the ending, where Houdini's character is discovered by the leading lady in a garden reading a book on spiritualism by Sir Arthur Conan Doyle. Doyle, himself an ardent spiritualist and firm believer in the existence of a spirit world within reach of mortals, who had been a friend and adversary of Houdini for several years before the film was made, lavished praise upon *The Man from Beyond,* probably thinking that Houdini, the publicity-seeking archenemy of the spiritualists, had produced a parable about reincarnation and the possibility of spirit return. Houdini's 1924 treatise on the subject of spiritualism, *A Magician Among the Spirits,* which most fully develops his position on the subject of spiritualism, is vehemently opposed to most of Doyle's beliefs.

There are two points to be considered in evaluating *The Man from Beyond.* First, it must be understood that Houdini's was a contrary mind, a mind that searched constantly to repudiate, expose, and disillusion, even while as an entertainer and magician he spent most of his life engaged in creating illusion. His earlier books, *Miracle Mongers and Their Methods* (1920), *The Unmasking of Robert-Houdin* (1908), and *The Right Way to Do Wrong: An Exposé of Successful Criminals* (1906), all show a consistent pattern of obsession with exposing imposture and debunking spirituality or supernaturalism. Houdini may have been a divided, even deeply conflicted personality, as Bernard Meyer argues in his psychobiography of the famed magician. Especially convincing portions are Meyer's discussions concerning Houdini and his Jewishness—Houdini was never bar mitzvahed, and his wife was Catholic— and his demented preoccupation with escaping from every object imaginable, from coffins to carcasses to milk cans to prisons. Second, *The Man from Beyond* is about Houdini's own obsession with the fear of his imposture. Here we have a story not about spirit return and reincarnation but about an immature, sexually repressed eternal male love for an idealized woman. Houdini's character, who has been frozen, imprisoned in a block of ice for one hundred years, is freed only to search for the woman he loved, and he finds, unbelievably, a exact replication of her. This is not a belief in reincarnation—that the woman is the completely unchanged descendant of the sister of the original woman he loved is a device commonly used in pulp romances and gothic fiction—but rather a belief in the power of Houdini's character's imagination to keep the object and the objectification of his love alive despite imprisonment and competitive male jealousy. It has become common knowledge that Houdini worshipped his mother, believed her to be a saint, and became interested in spiritualism as an avenue of exposé only after his mother died. It is also well known that Houdini was a faithful and obedient husband, almost neurotically so, to his Bess. The film then becomes a clear revelation of Houdini's concern with his own virtues, a celebration of his own conventional morality, which is, after all, the true subject of this film. For Houdini is always the center of attention even when he is not on the screen. It is the force of his will and the power of his speech that convinces the descendant of his true love that he is sincere and courageous and not insane. (This, no less, during the middle of a wedding where she is about to marry another man.) His determination and ingenuity that uncover the sinister plot of villains and turns up his true love's father. Finally, the film is preoccupied with Houdini's body, from the time he is discovered in a block of ice to the film's end, when, presumably, he will finally marry his true love. Houdini's body is first considered as food by one of the desperate Arctic explorers who discovers him; he is imprisoned, tied up, and beaten. He swims, runs, fights, climbs, and squirms. The film presents Houdini, the mysterious if clichéd action hero, as the displaced but irresistible body that ultimately finds a conventional and respectable place within an essentially Victorian bourgeois social framework. The film wishes to deny the idea of the magician as impostor, although it concedes that his presence is troubling. The Magician, as Houdini represents him, is a relentless and insistently real physical presence who does not offer arcane or potentially subversive wisdom but a replication of conventional bourgeois social values.

The idea of the magician's body as both irresistible and displaced is also the main idea in Bergman's film *The Magician.* Max Von Sydow plays Vogler, an obviously disguised, seemingly mute leader of a rather inept magical company, who for one night confronts the arrayed heads of bourgeois authority and reason: the Judge, the Chief of Police, and the Medical Examiner. It is the Medical Examiner's wish to dissect Vogler, and that appears to happen in the film except that, through Vogler's misdirection, of course, the doctor performs the autopsy on the wrong man. The theme of imposture runs throughout the film: Vogler is not the mysterious and compellingly dark presence who provokes confession and evokes the dream-wishes of those around him, but a fair-haired second-rate performer who desperately desires approval and money; his dark male ward is his blond wife in disguise; their conjurors' elixirs are fake; the pillars of bourgeois society are exposed as petty, arrogant, and proud of their minor social status. Neither the viewers nor the characters in the film know where performance ends and real life begins. Like *The Man from Beyond,* Bergman's film insists that the magician is a relentlessly real and inescapable presence, but this outlaw (Vogler is disguised because he is trying to escape the police from another town) is a mutable figure, not a representation of either arcane wisdom or conventional bourgeois values but rather a projection and objectification of whatever his audience wishes him to be. Speech is an essential aspect of Houdini's powerful presence in *The Man from Beyond,* for not only is his past story locked in his ability to speak it to the others but his demonstrations of love, sincerity, and intelligence as well are prefaced or even displayed through speech. (Of course, for the stage magician, patter is often an important part of his act, a way to misdirect as well as to entertain.) However, in *The Magician,* Vogler denies himself the property of speech for most of the film, thus allowing virtually every other character to speak for him, to function as an instrument of expression for others. His seeming passivity is an appeal and an absolute attraction. (There have always been a number of magicians who performed their stagecraft without speaking a word to the audience, but these silent conjurors seem especially common today.) Does the magician, in the end, make the unreal seem real or does he make everything real unreal? Does it matter?

INTRODUCING THE METAMORPHOSIS

Magic is the hardest profession in the world in which to succeed.

—Black Herman

Coming forward and seating himself on the ground in his white dress and tight-ened turban, the chief of the Indian Jugglers begins with tossing up two brass balls, which is what any of us could do, and concludes with keeping up four at the same time, which is what none of us could do to save our lives, nor if we were to take our whole lives to do it in. Is it then a trifling power we see at work, or is it not something next to miraculous?

—William Hazlitt, "The Indian Jugglers"

On July 5, 1990, the second evening of the sixty-second annual convention of the International Brotherhood of Magicians, just before the presentation of the finalists for the gold medal competition in stage magic, a troupe of young magicians from Arkansas are introduced to the capacity audience at the Kiel Opera House in St. Louis. Winners of the junior stage magic competition, they are led by a personable blond kid, perhaps sixteen or seventeen, named Nathan Burton. Burton, I was told, is a regular at Tannen's Magic Camp, a place on Long Island where a lot of middle-class kids go for one week every summer to learn about and practice magic. Some very notable magicians have graduated from the Magic Camp, and Tannen's claims to be the largest magic distributor in the country. I have no idea if this is true, but I was told that "they certainly seem to have supplied nearly everybody's act." At the turn of the century, the big supplier for magicians was the Palace of Magic on Sixth Avenue in New York, where Francis Joseph Martinka and his wife supplied the likes of Harry Kellar, Alexander Herrmann, and Julius De Kolta. It was bought by the noted magician Charles Joseph Carter in 1916 and was eventually purchased by Houdini and some partners. I wonder if Tannen's had as rich a history.

Nathan Burton's troupe is given about ten minutes to perform two comic illusions, one of which has been the talk of the convention. They first perform a "Let's Cut Up" routine where Burton and several others begin throwing toilet paper all over the stage and blowing it by machine to the audience. A police officer comes to quell the situation but he is captured by the boys and stuffed head-first down a small toilet in a hoary but nonetheless well-executed effect reminiscent of a silent movie comedy reel. The message of this is clear: If we think authority figures are shit-heads, then let us literally make them that. And how many different puns can be generated by the idea of waste: the boys wasting time by scattering waste paper and finally wasting the authority figure by literally treating him as if he were waste.

The talked-about piece is called "The Tanning Bed of Death." Burton announces that he will perform an escape that would defy even David Copperfield and he is then manacled and placed in a blindingly bright tanning bed. Perhaps the performers are too nervous to remember their lines, their "patter," as the magicians call it, but Burton neglects to tell his evening audience what he told the judges in the contest on the previous afternoon: If he is not freed from the tanning bed in fifteen seconds, he will burn to death! Since everybody has been talking about the illusion, and many in the audience have already seen it performed in competition, there is, I suppose, no real need to explain the game-show-looking clock that stood beside the tanning bed. But without the explanation, without that bit of narrative suspense, the act seems a bit disjointed and unclear. For everyone in the audience knows that this illusion is nothing more than a version of the old metamorphosis trick, supposedly invented by Harry Houdini but apparently dating back as far as Robert-Houdin and the Herrmann Brothers. In Houdini's version, his wife stood on a trunk in which Houdini was encased, handcuffed in a cloth sack, and within a matter of seconds they would change places, Houdini free on top of the trunk and the wife, handcuffed and "bagged" within. The addition of the element of danger to this trick is not done simply to create suspense but actually to make the trick modern. Getting a tan is a risky business these days, especially for a fair-skinned person. This variation of the Houdini illusion signifies that within the very mundaneness of consuming artifices is a kind of ultrasurreal danger. The magic trick is a consuming artifice—magic, from fire eating to coin disappearing, is often, though not always by any means, about consumption; things do not really disappear in magic, they are absorbed—and so is the tanning bed contraption that consumes the magician. The trick loses some dimension of its modernistic cleverness without the movie-serial-cum-game-show patter of impending doom.

Nathan places himself in the tanning bed and the lid is closed. He stays beyond the fifteen seconds, the tanning bed begins to smoke, the assistants panic. They open the bed and billows of smoke puff out. Then, as the air clears, a figure emerges. It is a black boy, manacled, wearing what is supposed to represent burned clothing. This is not a clever joke; indeed, all of the act's cleverness is located elsewhere. But it is assuming that everyone in the audience had to be expecting just this dénouement—the black symboliz-

ing both immunity to sun and to skin color change and thus assumes a kind
of immutability that makes him the butt of jokes that do not seem to come at
his expense. (Take, for instance, the late Sammy Davis, Jr., in the sixties Rat
Pack classic, *Ocean's 11*, when, just before the gang is to pull off its caper of
robbing five Las Vegas casinos, they blacken their faces commando-style.
Davis laughs, saying he doesn't need the camouflage because he is, in effect,
permanently camouflaged.) The black also symbolizes superiority to the machine, for the real complexity of Nathan Burton's illusion lies in his variation: The metamorphosis, as Houdini invented it, was not meant to depict
the transformation of the magician into another being, but simply that the
magician could "dematerialize" and change places with an assistant. In
short, nothing could trap the magician, nothing could contain his material
essence. It is a trick of visibility. The magician can be present and absent on
the stage at the same time, but his visibility or invisibility determines everything else, makes everything else on the stage possible. What the magician
constantly manipulates on the stage is the idea that his presence or absence is
actually the entire illusion that is being created in the audience's mind, an illusion that corresponds to the distinction between shadow and act, between
skepticism and belief in something that can produce neither skepticism or
belief but a taut and elaborately tense amusement. It is precisely this manipulation, this inversion that Vogler so skillfully exploits at the end of the performance sequence in Bergman's film *The Magician,* that in fact turns upon
the metamorphosis being performed without the audience being aware of it,
without its being made explicit. But for Burton's trick to have signification,
the act must be explicit.

The stage magician is a tactician of the seemingly momentous disguised
as a bemusing triviality. That is what he mediates. Burton's variation of the
metamorphosis suggests the transformation of the magician into another being, the white becoming a black. But while the trick suggests this, it also
suggests its impossibility because, of course, everyone knows that the metamorphosis is a trick of dematerialization, not of transformation. But since we
know this, we know when the black emerges from the machines that he is
not its product, not a result of its processes but rather a being independent of
it entirely, since the tanning bed is not real and the danger suggested—that
the white can become black—is really a fiction, a pseudo-suspense that corresponds to, and collaborates with, a real suspense and a real tension in our collective American psyche. It is this ambiguity in Burton's trick that makes
the trick really quite brilliant, far more interesting than its technique, which
is rather limited.

When the act was performed in competition, the programmatic music
that is the magician's opera and soundtrack simultaneously, segued to some
sort of Michael Jackson or Prince song and the transformed magician danced

on stage. But the house band at the evening performance did not seem to know what to play, and the black boy simply wandered around on the stage with a rather lost look, shuffling a bit, looking for all the world with those rags and handcuffs like a slave, like a relic from the American theater's past who had, through the accident of some time warp, managed to find himself on a new stage. If the black boy's performance was meant to be so crudely stereotypical as to be amusing, then the fact that the band screwed up made the performance a failure because it became less funny than disturbing. What does this illusion tell but what we already know: first, that the American theater and significant portions of American popular culture have been built on this odd, provoking fantasy of blacks' and whites' being twins in perverse ways such as Twain in *Puddin' head Wilson* (1894), Charles Chesnutt in *The Marrow of Tradition* (1901), and Ralph Ellison in *Invisible Man* (1952) all suggest; second, that white and black are bound together through some device, some ghostly machine, a postmodernist umbilical cord like the cord that tied Queequeg and Ishmael in *Moby-Dick*. Who gave birth to whom? Or are they freaks of nature, Siamese twins, who both die if one dies?

There are three particular examples in American culture of the complexity of this idea about the bonding between black and white; in one of those instances, blacks and whites exchange places. First, there is Lee Falk's comic strip character Mandrake the Magician and his black African assistant, Lothar (which Falk discovered to his embarrassment was a German and not an African name). This nomadic pair go all over the world solving crimes and having adventures in what can only be likened to the relationship between Huck Finn and Jim, a kind of Tom Sawyer—like boy's fantasy life, freed from any real societal constraints, although of course they act and appear as if they are imprisoned by the social constraints of their roles—Mandrake with his tails and top hat, looking for all the world like a stereotypical stage magician, the unflappable mentalist and hypnotist, and Lothar the stereotypical jungle man, the muscular primitive, the faithful native. What the pair really seek in their adventures is not freedom but simply a certain idealized dimensionless consciousness that seems like an escape. "At first," Falk said, "[Lothar] was a body servant. The idea was that Mandrake was a mental giant and Lothar was the physical giant and he spoke in pidgin English and he wore the leopard skin." Despite some modifications in Lothar's character since his inception in 1934, including being given a girlfriend so that readers would not think the pair was homosexual (Mandrake always had a girlfriend, Princess Narda, but even her presence was insufficient to quell concern on this score, especially with a character whose name was so laden with sexuality); the pair operate, in effect, as one complete person, the id and the ego of American popular culture.

The second example of the bonding of white and black is the actual metamorphosis in the famous slave narrative *Running a Thousand Miles for Freedom or the Escape of William and Ellen Craft from Slavery* published in 1860. This story of how two slaves, a dark-skinned husband and a light-skinned wife, escaped slavery by disguising themselves as master and slave, the wife becoming the sick, pale, tragic southerner (an interesting reversal here since, in effect, the tragic southerner is the feminized southern man; the antebellum southerner commonly believed that the blacks were the female of the races) and the husband the stalwart and loyal body servant. This story was known throughout the antislavery circuit long before the book was published, as the Crafts had effected their escape in 1848 and had been lecturing about it for many years. Perhaps the right word here would be "performing," as one could scarcely imagine the pair reinventing their story before the audience without taking on the roles they played to better illustrate the drama and suspense. The illusion became so popular that Harriet Beecher Stowe used a variation of it in her book *Uncle Tom's Cabin* (1852).

The third example is the 1899 short story by Stephen Crane called "The Monster," in which Henry Johnson, a Negro, has his face burned away when he rescues his employer's son from a fire. The fact that his face is destroyed by exploding chemicals when he is in his employer's laboratory adds a kind of Frankenstein-like element to the story as the creation of Johnson-as-Monster, of Johnson as the burned, ruined, maimed man-cum-Negro is somehow the responsibility and fault of the white (a physician, in this case, but whose laboratory apparatus brings to mind both the scientist and the alchemist). The scene where Johnson is burned uses magical imagery and supernatural metaphors, reinforcing the connection between science, alchemy, and magic:

> Suddenly the glass splintered, and a ruby-red snakelike thing poured its thick length out upon the top of the old desk. It coiled and hesitated, and then began to swim a languorous way down the mahogany slant. At the angle it waved its sizzling molten head to and fro over the closed eyes of the man beneath it. Then, in a moment, with a mystic impulse, it moved again, and the red snake flowed directly down into Johnson's upturned face.
>
> Afterward the trail of this creature seemed to reek, and amid flames and low explosions drop like red-hot jewels pattered softly down it at leisurely intervals.

In the course of the story the Frankenstein-to-monster relationship is made even clearer when Dr. Trescott, Johnson's employer, and Judge Hagenthrope discuss the moral dilemma of saving Johnson's life at the psychic cost of the lives of both the doctor and Johnson, whose horrible face has not only unhinged him but cast him out of the human community:

Presently [Judge Hagenthrope] braced himself straightly in his chair. "He will be your creation, you understand. He is purely your creation. Nature has very evidently given him up. He is dead. You are restoring him to life. You are making him, and he will be a monster, and with no mind."

"He will be what you like, judge," cried Trescott, in sudden polite fury. "He will be anything, but, by God! he saved my boy."

In the context of the debate at the end of the nineteenth century among whites concerning Social Darwinism, whether in their own arrogantly superior way they had responsibility for the people of color who had been intentionally or inadvertently misused and maimed by them, the relevance of the dialogue between the doctor and the lawyer, those twin pillars of respectability and authority in industrialized bourgeois society, becomes plain. Watching the black boy on stage that night who seemed so maimed and lost, I was forced to ask not why he was there but, more tellingly, what would be his fate?—which, as it turned out, was to become white, when Burton reappeared in his place.

This reversal seems, in one respect, anticlimactic, necessary only to make the magician visible again for the audience's acclaim and approval. Burton had to reappear to bring the trick to closure, to make the audience understand that something, at last, had been revealed. But on another level what had been revealed was that the black boy had now become white, a metamorphosis that, at times, our country itself seems to wish for as one kind of solution: to make the black simply disappear or be forever concealed offstage.

The magician as tactician is the great mediator between concealment (how does he do his illusions?) and revelation (the magician seemingly manipulates reality as a sign that he can call things forth that have been concealed; that he does not explain his power always implies that the explanation is latent). Burton's act was without question the most intriguing of the night, though far from being the most technically accomplished.

THE MAGIC COMPETITION AND IDEAS OF POLITICAL CORRECTNESS

I was particularly interested to see James Brandon's act during the gold medal stage magic competition. I had met Brandon the night before; he is a New York magician, with a strikingly handsome appearance. Striking, I suppose, because it is so theatrical. He looks rehearsed as if he were a magician posing as someone posing as a magician, hip as only a young performer from New York can be. I first saw him in the upper level eating area of

Union Station theatrically twirling a tray while waiting for his order; he wore
a dark, cutoff jacket, matching trousers, and boots in what can only be described as a muted hybrid of a matador's attire and something from the Old
West, rather like the suit Robert Conrad used to wear in the old "Wild Wild
West" television series. Fortunately, it was not sequined, which is only to
say that Brandon did not look as garish as Liberace or Elvis Presley, but it did
have something of the appearance of a put-on, of a costume. "One of the first
things I learned from Harold D.," Karl Grice, an architect, a leading black
magician and one of the major behind-the-scenes presences at this convention, told me in speaking about one of the lessons he received from his
mentor, "was not to wear your performing clothes offstage. That's not professional. Offstage, you should dress like everyone else." Brandon was not
wearing his performing clothes offstage; he was simply being everlastingly
the thespian as were several others at the convention, dressed in black with
black carrying pouches across their middles, clothing striking the outsider as
being as individualistic as any clique's uniform. Brandon's dress, combined
with his pale face and long black hair, made him a particularly imposing,
mysterious figure. Also, it was more than 100 degrees on the afternoon I saw
him, and I could not imagine how he could tolerate being so overdressed. He
did not seem to mind sweating. He must have had an endless supply of such
suits; he wore a different one every night. He was explaining to Hiawatha,
my Virgil in this sometimes Dante-esque world of performance art, that he
had changed his act entirely from what it was a few years ago. He had com-
peted and won first prize in the stage magic competition with an act back in
1985 when IBM held its convention in Kansas City. Hiawatha was competing in the close-up magic competition that year, and they became admirers
of each other's work. Hiawatha had missed Brandon's act during the pre-
liminaries but Brandon, with the arrogant élan of the New Yorker, told
Hiawatha he could catch it onstage the following night as he was certain to
be one of the finalists. Now Brandon was competing again, trying to win the
gold medal, which is not awarded every year and which few have won.

"Brandon shouldn't be competing," Hiawatha told me. "He has nothing to prove. He has nothing to gain. The boy is crazy. You have to know
when to stop competing. He doesn't need to compete anymore."

Hiawatha stopped competing a few years ago. One of the leading black
magicians in the country and one-fourth of the quartet that makes up The
Phoenix, a black magician core group, Hiawatha does not believe in prolonged participation in the competitions at the International Brotherhood's
annual conventions. Any magician, from the upstart with a brand-new,
freshly purchased kit to David Copperfield, Penn and Teller, or Harry Black-
stone, can compete at the convention.

"You do it for a couple of years to get the exposure and then that's it,"

Hiawatha said of competing, "Brandon just wants to get the gold medal. But the more he competes, the less is his chance of getting it."

This is the advice Hiawatha gave Chris Broughton, the newest member of Phoenix and 1989 first-place winner of the stage magic competition with an amusing act he calls "homeboy magic." Chris, a handsome young man in his late twenties, is often accompanied by his mother, Theo, a pleasant and down-to-earth woman who is proud of her son's accomplishments in such an unusual field; he is from Detroit but currently lives in Los Angeles, where he hopes to launch a career as an actor and scriptwriter. He was annoyed throughout the convention because he was not allowed a technical rehearsal, so when he performed his act on the first night, things did not go as well as he would have liked. The act still went over well but he was bitterly disappointed and embarrassed and felt it was an awful performance. There is an understated feeling among all the members of Phoenix that the authorities running the IBM convention were trying to undermine Chris's act because he is black. His was the only act at the entire convention not to receive a technical rehearsal. He was the only black magician to perform at any of the stage shows. On the other hand, Chris is one of the main sound technicians for the Vaudeville 2000 show, the major stage show of the convention and, for some at least, evidence that blacks have made their presence felt at the IBM— certainly, all the members of Phoenix are justly proud of that. Chris has taken Hiawatha's advice; he does not compete anymore.

Hiawatha offers the same advice to his young white protégé, Mark Nathan Sicher, who won the close-up magic competition this year. An extremely talented magician in his early twenties, he met Hiawatha at Tannen's several years ago when Hiawatha was invited to teach there. He has been Hiawatha's student ever since, crediting him with all his success. "Hiawatha is a genius," Sicher says flatly. Hiawatha is right about the business of competing; exposure is everything, especially for unknown magicians who dream of playing the Mecca, the Magic Castle in Hollywood, where reputations are made and contracts to play Vegas and Europe are generated. The competitions at the IBM conventions provide excellent exposure, but there is a point of diminishing returns. Brandon has played the Magic Castle and continues to compete; Hiawatha has played the Magic Castle and does not compete. So what has Brandon gained? For some, obviously, the lure of the competitions is hard to resist. Sicher is thinking about trying for the Gold Cups, the equivalent in close-up magic to the gold medal for stage magic. "Only three other magicians have won it," Sicher says. This sense of epochal accomplishment is probably what drives a magician as established as Brandon who really does not need the competitions anymore. Both Brandon and Sicher are products of Tannen's Magic Camp. So, the two coasts become the Alpha and Omega of the professional American magician: He starts on

the east at the Magic Camp and hopes to culminate on the west, at the
Magic Castle.

Later, on the first evening of the convention, a group of us met Brandon
again. He asked if anyone was willing to go across the river to some strip
joints in Belleville. No one seemed very interested. It was certainly not prud-
ishness that inhibited the others. Hiawatha, who is from Lynchberg, Virginia (where, strangely yet appropriately, Black Herman spent a considerable
portion of his youth, has made several trips to St. Louis and two of his fellows
from Phoenix have taken trips across the river to the topless clubs. Perhaps
the idea of going in mixed racial company was inhibiting as there is a kind of
racial code that is followed at those places. Some people still feel a bit uncomfortable if a black man is looking at a naked white woman.) Or perhaps
everyone was a bit tired from the festivities of the first evening, although we
were going to the room of Harold D. Russell, an old black master magician
who lives in St. Louis, "the best coin man in the business," I am told, who
had invited us to share some time and wine with him. (In the magic fraternity people are often referred to or refer to themselves as "coin men," "bird
men," "scarf men," "card men," and the like, according to what constitutes
the main prop. Hiawatha hates this bit of specialization. "You're a magician
and that's it," he says with vehemence. "You should be able to learn from
and appreciate everybody. Instead, you got people going around saying, 'I'm
a bird man, I can only deal with a bird act. Or I'm a card man, so I'm only
interested in other card acts.' A good magician should be a generalist.") So
nobody was going to bed anytime soon. Hiawatha makes the excuse that he
is married, after all, and that those places are not appropriate for him even if,
as Brandon reminds him, he is away from home.

"Besides, I don't want to see any strippers," Hiawatha said.

"I don't want to watch them," Brandon said. "I want to date them."

We did not see Brandon again until the next evening.

Harold D., an elderly man with a gimp leg, glasses, and a taste for
bourbon, has been performing magic around St. Louis for many years at various children's parties and other social functions. He deserves a reputation as a
true black pioneer in twentieth-century stage magic on a par with Ellen
Armstrong, one of the few women to make it in magic; fire-eater Presto
Johnson; and Fetaque Sanders, a black magician from Tennessee. When architect Karl Grice decided when he was in college that he wanted to be a
magician, he went to Harold D., about whom he had read in a newspaper article. The first time they met Harold kept Karl at his home nearly the whole
night, showing him scrapbooks and performing tricks for him. Karl has become famous for his pyramid trick, an elaborate and intricate reworking of
some ideas he learned from Harold D. And Harold D. has been as proud of
Karl's success as if Karl had been a son. In his hotel room, Harold is operat-

ing an open bar and people come in and out, paying their respects to him and drinking the liquor that is being supplied by who knows whom. Another black magician in the corner, a young guy with greasy wet hair, eventually performs for me some nice moves with the ring and rope trick. He enjoys performing magic at bars because it helps him meet women. "It's an ice-breaker," he says. Harold D. performs several astonishing coin tricks for me that seem to tickle and entertain him nearly as much as they do me. After every trick, he shouts, "Bam! Zoom!" and laughs at my bewilderment. It is wonderful to be around such an infectiously happy man, so pleased with his work and with the pleasure he gives others. Using me as a prop, Hiawatha performs a new coin trick of his own devising that impresses Harold D. greatly. Then, Harold D., Hiawatha, and the other black fellow whose name I think was Derrick began to perform tricks one after the other. I alone am the privileged member of this private audience as everyone has cleared out because of the lateness of the hour. It is a fabulous display of marvels, each one more exciting than the one preceding it as each man, in a sort of magical cutting contest, tries to top the other. Before leaving, I ask Harold D. if he ever experienced racism during his years of performing. "No," he says, "magic is a pretty fair business and the race stuff doesn't really enter in. Only one time really stands out. I was supposed to be doing this party, had made all the arrangements with the wife, and I guess she didn't tell her husband about it. So, when I get there, he takes one look at me and then asks what I want. I told him I was the entertainment for the party. He then proceeds to take me down to the basement, goes upstairs, turns out the lights and leaves me there, in the dark and the cold. So, I'm just sitting there wondering what the hell is going on. I'm hearing these voices upstairs so I know the party is going on and everything but I don't know why the man put in the basement. Finally, his wife comes down there and sees me sitting there and did she hit the ceiling. She laid her husband's soul to rest for that and I came up and did my show. That happened a long time ago. That's the only thing I can think of that I felt was a real race thing."

Brandon's act, as it turns out, was very good. He came close to winning the competition. Admittedly, some of his competitors were less than slick and were still a ways from being the very best in their field. An Asian lad had some good effects but seemed too nervous and made far too many errors, dropping paraphernalia and mistiming some of his tricks. There was another troupe from Arkansas whose act was long on costumes and story line and short on magic. A magician from St. Louis danced so much that he seemed on the verge of consuming his entire act in unintentional parody. Brandon was a futuristic, dark, and menacing warrior. I suppose that menacing war-rior acts are far from original in magic these days, especially since the youn-ger magicians seem to draw many of their ideas from science fiction movies and rock albums, but Brandon performed well. His effects were imaginative and well executed, including a finale in which he made a dove appear on the end of a sword. Karl Grice thought Brandon's act was too similar to his earlier one of a few years ago. "He didn't really change it that much." Hiawatha, on the other hand, thought the act was significantly different: "He took out a lot of the wild stuff he had. People thought he was into Satan and devil worship before. But he's really cooled that out now. In the other act, he was drinking potions and changing into other things like a clown or a devil. But he has eliminated that now. His act is a lot tighter." Probably, as the judges' decision turned out, the truth about Brandon's act was somewhere in the middle. The act was different but not sufficiently different in concept from what had been seen from Brandon before. When Brandon was finished performing he received thunderous applause. However, the contestant who eventually won the contest received a standing ovation when she finished her act. The first place and gold medal winner was an Asian woman from San Francisco named Jade whose most dazzling effect was that popularized by New York magician and mime Vito Lupo (another Tannen's Magic Camp alum), "Snowstorm in China." In this effect, the magician dips some sort of paper towel or piece of paper into a solution, then removes the soaked paper and clenches it tightly in one fist. Then, using a Japanese hand fan for current, slowly, dry flakes are released from the magician's hand and fanned in the air for a swirling effect. With the proper lighting, this is a stupendous illusion for someone who has never seen it before, although it dates back many centuries in Asian culture. "That's getting real old," Hiawatha told me. "Everybody's doing 'Snowstorm in China.' It's getting to be as much of a cliché as the paper tear." I saw more than a few "Snowstorms in China" before the convention ended. I also saw more than a few paper tears, so many, in fact, that, dunce that I am, I finally figured out how it was done.

As last year's stage magic winner was a black, one supposes that the IBM is sending a message to its membership and to the world at large that magic is changing and no longer should it be perceived as a white man's art. (And of course there is the other political consideration too. Some suggested that because the Asian contingent at the IBM is so large and that the Japanese in particular give a great deal of money to the organization that it may have been expedient not only to make Jade the winner but to give her the gold medal as a kind of sop to the Asians. One never knows about this sort of thing and people are often eager to see self-serving conspiracies in the most well-intentioned acts. Nonetheless, being Asian and being a woman probably did not hurt Jade as it undoubtedly would have just a mere ten or fifteen years ago.) Brandon as the dark warrior, a pseudo, toned-down Satan, the dark man of the stage, was simply, in the end, not dark enough. Mandrake too was a dark white man—dark hair, dark clothing, a dark, impenetrable manner; the clichéd white magician is always dark, always mysterioso. In some ways, the old-fashioned tails and top-hatted magician has been superseded, but in some ways Brandon as the dark warrior is merely more of a changing same. Hiawatha may have been right when he said that Jade's act was "just status quo," but Brandon may have been more old-fashioned than he himself realized.

POSTSCRIPT: THE MAGIC KINGDOMS

—the Phantom of the Opera in a perfect image of our priest—

—Bob Dylan, "Desolation Row"

—architecture is always dream and function, expression of a utopia and instrument of a convenience.

—Roland Barthes, "The Eiffel Tower"

Upon entering Disney World—that complex and expansive resort in Lake Buena Vista right outside Orlando, Florida—one is constantly reminded that the place is, after all, a resort, which means it is not an everyday landscape but some special location of escape. One is reminded of this not only by the insistent demands for money—for spending money is a favorite middle-class American pastime when the American goes on vacation and can briefly play the role of having gold-imbued leisure as do the rich; one is also reminded of Disney World's otherworldliness by the constant use of the word "magic." There is "Disney Magic," "The Magic Kingdom," "Magical Attractions," "Mickey's Magical TV World," "Mickey's Magical TV Special," "motion picture magic," "Magic Journeys," "Magic Eye Theater," where one can see the George Lucas film *Captain EO,* starring Michael Jackson, and a "House of Magic." And this relentless reinforcement of the idea of the faraway resort is only, finally, to remind visitors that they are nothing more than tourists, yet it seems to suggest something richer and more profound: that one is a pilgrim and that Disney World is a conflation of both a landmark monument and an illusory ideal, that it suggests both a crass reality and a heightened spirituality. So, upon entering this fantasy, one becomes an oneiric tourist walking through a landscape as if one is Hansel and Gretel in the forest, Alice in Wonderland, or Dorothy in Oz. This sort of mass-induced dream-wish successfully hides the hideous expense, the long, insufferable lines, the interminable waiting to get on ordinary amusement park rides done up in Disney, the sheer emptiness of the place, of this Xanadu, that seems to keep one entranced by the sheer grandeur of its ever-receding and ever-shrinking promise of a good time. Perhaps what magic means in this resort is precisely what stage magic has become: an illusory diversion that suggests that technology and the spirit can exist side by side in a phantasmagoria of the wonder-working mimesis of animation and cinema. For Disney is built on the idea, the cult-assumption, of the implicit spirituality and morality of its omnipresent animation and cinema.

To get to the Magic Kingdom portion of Disney World one must take a tram from a parking lot that seems to extend outward like an endless prairie and then take either a ferry or a monorail—something clearly futuristic or something that harkens back to a stylized past. This juxtaposed rendering of the past and future, of the old-fashioned and the postmodern in a kind of seamless playground is really the essence of Disney World: to give patrons a past that never traumatizes and a future that seems assured in both its beneficence and its bounty. One walks down Main Street USA and discovers that this endless neighborhood of shops and restaurants got up in the style of a midwestern small town is not meant to be a re-creation of the Heartland values of Springfield, Illinois, or Springfield, Missouri, or Topeka, Kansas, but actually a re-creation of a movie set that only through a kind of weird verisimilitude suggests an overly stylized and depthless midwestern small-town street. What Disney World gives the visitor in its Main Street USA attraction is the conflation of the suburban shopping mall and Hollywood, of the circus and the holy shrine, where art meets commerce, where art and architecture is in fact commercialized as both a utopian gesture and a historical mythology. Every location in Disney World looks like a movie set, so much so that to go on the MGM-Disney studio tour or the Universal Studios tour is almost, but not quite, redundant.

All over Disney World, people take pictures and shoot video cameras not only at their children, relatives, and friends, but they take pictures of various objects in the park from the Eiffel Tower atop the French pavilion in the EPCOT Center to the pink flamingoes in front of the Odyssey Restaurant. In fact, the most insistent refrain one hears from attendants within the exhibits and rides is that "Flash photography is not permitted." This preoccupation of visitors with photographing Disney World brings to mind Roland Barthes's discussion of panoramic vision in his essay "The Eiffel Tower"; "The world ordinarily produces either purely functional organisms (camera or eye) intended to see things but which then afford nothing to sight, what *sees* being mythically linked to what remains *hidden* (this is the theme of the voyeur), or else spectacles which themselves are blind and are left in the pure passivity of the visible." So the visitor becomes a spectator and voyeur at Disney World in much the same way as at a stage magic show, continuously awed by the manipulations, by the transgressions of the seen and the hidden; and Disney World itself, like the Eiffel Tower, becomes that which com-

bines seeing and being seen; but unlike the tower this conflation is not concentrated in a point or structural location but, in keeping with the American
myth of frontier and the west, is centered in the idea of space. One does not
seek a view or panorama from Disney World, rather Disney World is the
view itself; it is its own panorama. Nothing makes this clearer, this mythology of Disney World as purely realized and realizable panoramic wonder,
than the several exhibits in the EPCOT Center that show Circle Vision 360
films, in a theater of screens that surround and entrap the audience with
images of vast spaces; or than the Future World Exhibit that also serves as
the landmark entrance to EPCOT, where a 180-foot-high "geo-sphere" that
resembles both Buckminster Fuller's geodesic dome and, as my children
pointed out, a giant golf ball on a tee, and which encases a highly atmospheric ride through the history of human communications that takes one
from the bottom to the top of the dome and down again. This stark monument has an interior that isn't explored as much as it is presented and displayed, an interior that resembles both an Egyptian tomb in its grandeur and
landmarks like the St. Louis Arch and the Eiffel Tower in its uselessness despite its vaunted claims of being educational (claims, one supposes, that the
Arch and the Eiffel Tower can make as well). This dome is not only the focal
point for the eye to structure the space of Disney World but is a representation of space itself as the dome brings to mind other technological dome-
wonders running the gamut from enclosed sports stadia to Fuller's geodesic
dome, which was meant to cover an entire city. But the fact that it purposely
looks like a golf ball also emphasizes another idea of space, bringing to mind
the bourgeois leisure space of the sculpted greens of a golf course.

Even as the visitors are cameras they are also encased within the camera
that is both Disney World and Universal Studios; for nearly every ride in
these two parks becomes virtually the same ride. Whether it is a ride involving simulated flight such as the E.T. Adventure at Universal or the Peter
Pan's Flight in the Magic Kingdom at Disney World, or rides that stimulate
motor vehicles such as the Funtastic World of Hanna-Barbera or Kongfronta-
tion at Universal or Journey into Imagination or Mr. Toad's Wild Ride at
the Magic Kingdom, or whether it is a water ride such as 20,000 Leagues
Under the Sea, It's a Small World, the Jungle Cruise or Pirates of the Carib-
bean at the Magic Kingdom, or the Living Seas, El Rio del Tiempo or the
Maelstrom at EPCOT, the rides all become the same atmospheric enclosure
in utter darkness, the same passive journey through well-lighted, exquisitely
designed rooms with loud music and moving mannikins that, paradoxically,
are meant to place the visitor in the center of an incredibly action-filled
adventure that involves some movie or television show that is part of our collective pop culture memory. In effect, each ride replicates the oneiric quality
of watching a film that has become our culture's mass-induced and mass-

directed way of participating in and understanding the phenomenon of fantasy. And, of course, watching a film brings to mind performance magic and the séance, the darkened stage or unlighted room from which sudden light and images burst forth. Special photographic effects, including Spirit Photography, magic lanterns, camera obscura, image projection, and the like, were first associated with the occult and magic performance. To enter the Disney Haunted House and see ghost projections flying around is to replicate similar, indeed nearly identical tricks of parlor mediums and stage magicians of the late nineteenth century. Magic and film have always been bound together. It is interesting to note this odd and amusing turning of the tables: At the annual dinner meeting of the Society of American Magicians, an organization founded by Houdini, his good friend Arthur Conan Doyle was invited to attend. Doyle and Houdini, who had been differing on the subject of the validity of spiritualism and psychic phenomenon, always had a somewhat tense if cordial relationship. At this dinner, Doyle showed some moving pictures of prehistoric monsters that were afterward incorporated in the film *The Lost World.* So realistically were the creatures rendered that the magicians, thinking this to be some sort of documentary footage or some powerful psychic materialization, were absolutely spellbound and puzzled by the viewing. Only later in a letter to Houdini did Doyle explain that "[the] Dinosaurs and other monsters have been constructed by pure cinema art of the highest kind," and that they were neither documentary nor supernatural. Houdini responded to Doyle by pointing out, naturally enough considering Houdini's publicity hound instincts, that the ruse generated a great deal of newspaper coverage for the meeting, for which he was thankful.

On Main Street USA, among the many shops and restaurants, is the House of Magic, a small dimly-lit store that sells cheap magic kits of standard card tricks or the Chinese linking rings and other paraphernalia that would largely be of interest to children. Here too there is a tie-in to a Disney film, namely, the Sorcerer's Apprentice episode in *Fantasia;* in a small bin near the register are buttons of Mickey in his sorcerer's regalia that sell for a dollar or so. I was sorely tempted to buy a small kit of tricks that cost about twenty dollars but finally left the store with my daughter without having made the purchase. Standing across the street, waiting for my other daughter to finish buying some book or trinket or memento of some sort and facing a glaring sun going down behind a man-made lagoon, squinting a bit as I do after I have left a movie or a magic show and entered the real world again, I was more than a little struck by a paradox: whether this small resistance to an even smaller temptation was an instance of being blinded or gifted by the light.

NOTES ON THE INVENTION
OF MALCOLM X

Wrestling with The Dark Angel

TOWARD A DEFINITION OF THE IDEA OF ANCESTRY

I

After my younger daughter gave me the book, I went to the living room to lie down on the sofa. I could not immediately remember how long it had been since I had read *The Autobiography of Malcolm X,* a book that once held a certain literary magnitude for me, the only thing I read as a boy that I felt was, undeniably, an epic written expressly for a black American male, and that even now still commands respect and admiration. As I thumbed the pages, stopping here to read of Malcolm's first process, or here to read of the confrontation with West Indian Archie, or flipping back to read about his mother's institutionalization, or ahead again to read about his reading in prison, I was still impressed by it as a piece of work. Many passages hold up well, although I was not so sure about the work as a whole. At least I was not so sure at that moment, as I reclined on the sofa, thumbing through it, thinking *I last taught this book about five years ago. I must teach it again soon.* Not because of the Spike Lee film, which I had been hearing about all spring and which I truly feared someone might ask me to review. I wanted to teach it again to talk to students about it. I hadn't taught it for five years because I felt it had nothing more to say to me after years of constant rereadings. The last time I read the *Autobiography* it left me, well, indifferent. The rhetoric seemed so out-of-date, the energy of the man seemed so contained in a vision that was as narrow as it was vivid. There was something about the nature of his raillery that left me unprovoked, something about his quest for humanity that left me unmoved. *It is age,* I thought simply at that time, *I am too old to read this book anymore.* But I suddenly realized, jerked from my sofa with a jolt of urgency, that I had something to say about it, something that my age entitled me to say, not about the book necessarily, but about the man himself, something to say to my students, something to say to my children, that I wanted them desperately to hear.

When it was publicly announced last spring that I would become, starting July 1, the new director of African and Afro-American Studies at my school, I was beset by a perplexing, even stunning response on the part of black students. I was furiously denounced and publicly pilloried by students, most of whom did not know me, and most of whom had never read anything I had written. Probably it was just as well they hadn't as, in this instance, being misinterpreted is far more distressing than being ignored. I was condemned for not being Afrocentric, which was rather akin to being criticized, to use 1960s argot, for "not being black enough." What was baffling was that I did not possess nay of "the social tokens" of being "insufficiently black": I do not have a white wife; I served on most of the university Affirmative Action committees; I was intellectually engaged in the study of black subject matter; I had never publicly criticized any black person connected with the campus during my entire ten-year stay. That these congeries of careerism, temperament, and personal preference should indeed be weighed at the bar is, without doubt, ludicrous, but they should have put me in good stead with black students. I could not understand why I should stand so discredited before them.

On the other hand, in their eyes, I had never done anything so heroic as to lead some sort of protest on behalf of blacks on campus, on behalf of their interest. "I haven't heard of Professor Early being out here doing anything for black students," was the common refrain of many. I had never signed a petition. I never led a protest march or even suggested that one should be held. I had never attended any of their meetings, feeling it was not my place to be a demagogue by exploiting my position of authority and influence. I had never, in short, shown any especial interest in their affairs.

Part of this standard teacher-student strife is inevitably generational and typical adversative fare, but still I was more than a bit pained to have been seen by younger blacks as someone who compromised, who shuffled, who slouched, someone who had not stood up and been counted when I should have been, as someone who had never done anything heroic for the race. I had felt that way about many of the older black adults I encountered when I was "an angry young man." For the young, a lack of demonstrable outsized heroism is a lack of commitment, and a lack of commitment is a lack of honor. "The only thing your generation gave the world," one disgruntled student told me, "was disco and administrating 'community relations' programs." Nothing had been learned from the recent past of the civil rights era except that what it had so brightly promised, the dream of an integrated America, seemed so false in its premise and so abject in its cynical thwarting. I was never more depressed and distressed than during the spring of 1992. I was never closer to quitting the entire enterprise of teaching.

Today, it is a rare black student indeed who has not read *The Autobiography of Malcolm X,* if not before reaching college, then certainly sometime during "the undergraduate adventure." It is, without question and with few exceptions, the most commonly taught and most frequently recommended book by a black American male in current American education. Perhaps I had been moved to pick it up on this day because I had seen of late so many X caps, perhaps even a few at this entirely unsuccessful meeting and, somehow, I linked my troubles to Malcolm X. *It was he who wrought these silly T-shirts of black consciousness, this ideological standard of African-ness,* I thought. I am now considered the enemy because I am a middle-class assimilationist. How rich, I thought, how utterly rich that I who grew up absorbing what my wife calls "a near fanatical hatred of all things middle-class," that I who probably feel the most un-integrated and most un-assimilable of men, a pure isolate, should be so cast; it was poignant (or pathetic) with irony.

When my younger daughter came home from school, she was surprised to find me home, more surprised to find me visibly upset.

"What's wrong?" she asked.

"The American Negro," I said sarcastically, as she made herself a snack, "goes through periodic bouts of dementia when he romantically proclaims himself an African, lost from his brothers and sisters. These tides of benighted nationalism come and go but this time it seems particularly acute." By now, my voice had become strident, my rage nearly uncontrollable.

"Never have I been subjected to more antiintellectual, proto-fascistic nonsense than what I have had to endure in the name of Afrocentrism. And this man," I said, shoving Malcolm's autobiography in my daughter's face, "is the architect of it all, the father of Afrocentrism. This idiot, this fool." I threw the book across the room. I slumped at the kitchen table, placing my forehead against the cool wood. I felt tired. The room was silent for a long time.

"But I thought you liked Malcolm X," she said suddenly. And then she handed me the book.

II

It was about 1966 that my oldest sister, then a college student, joined the local chapter of SNCC. I suppose that was inevitable considering the nature of the times and my family: As young women, several of my aunts began wearing Afros in the early 1960s after seeing Cicely Tyson in the TV series "East

Side, West Side." Some adopted the Yoruba religion, and even married
Africans. The men were never as "culturally inclined," so to speak. These
changes were not without their dislocations, as my family were largely either
high-church Episcopalians or Jehovah's Witnesses. My sister joined SNCC
at the time it became a much more radical, more Marxist-oriented, more
militant group. I remember her conversation was now sprinkled with phrases
like "the white power structure," "the man," "black power" and "self-
determination for oppressed people." One day she brought home a recorded
Malcolm X speech entitled "Message to the Grassroots." I had heard of Malcolm, of course, indeed, had seen him on television news shows and was always thoroughly arrested by his rhetoric. It seemed exciting, thrilling to the
bone, to hear a black person say what he was saying in public. I heard men in
barbershops say many of the same things but they would never say around
whites what they said among themselves.

I was immediately intrigued by my sister's Malcolm X record and soon
contrived a way to listen to it when she was not around. Hearing it for the
first time was a shock and a revelation: its power and humor, the sheer gigantic humanity of the speech, and the grandeur of the man himself, of his vision of a redeemed black world. I laughed and laughed at his words but I felt
each word burn with the brightness of a scalding truth that was utterly new
to me yet so deeply, profoundly familiar, as if I had always known what he
was saying before anyone had ever uttered it, as if it had always existed as
precisely the way he expressed before it had ever been expressed. It was the
greatest speech, the greatest oral statement, I had ever heard; Malcolm spoke
for me. Every day, whenever I had the chance, I would play the record over
and over. In a few days, I had memorized the entire speech, every vocal
nuance, every turn of phrase. I could deliver the speech just as Malcolm had.
I was proud of myself. The speech was the first thing I can remember ever
having consciously memorized—at least the first thing that was not from The
Bible. I never looked at the world the same way after experiencing that
speech. And what was my world? I lived, was related to, and grew up among
what Martin Kilson calls the black "tertiary elite." I knew a small number of
underclass or desperately poor black people, most of whom I did not like. I
was certainly not middle class by any means; my world was made up of the
working poor and blue-collar blacks: maids, janitors, hospital workers, meat
packers, fruit stand laborers, day laborers for construction sites, barbershop
owners, beauticians, door-to-door salesmen. The most prestigious jobs I
knew through personal interaction with those who did the work were being a
policeman and clerking for a department store. Archie Epps, in his introduction to *Malcolm X: Speeches at Harvard,* is right: It was to the black people
from this world that Malcolm X spoke most vehemently and whom he
reached more often than not. I was from this world and I felt, with every

word I heard from him, that Malcolm spoke for me as a big brother or uncle might. Malcolm did not understand the pride of the people from this world. I don't think Malcolm ever understood that black people could ever have pride in *what they were*. But he understood their aspiration and, further, their sense of humiliation, their sense of righteous and justified complaint. He never understood their sense of pride but he understood their sense of honor.

Not all of the tertiary elite responded enthusiastically to Malcolm X. I often heard in the barbershop men making statements like: "All that Malcolm X does is talk. In fact, that's what all them Muslims do is talk. Just another nigger hustler." But in my enthrallment I did not hear the nay-sayers. Within a matter of months from the time I first heard Malcolm's "Message to the Grassroots," I had not only read his autobiography but had heard other speeches such as "The Ballot or the Bullet" and "Malcolm X on Afro-American History" and had become conversant with such topics as the Congo, Patrice Lumumba, the Bandung Conference, and the leadership of the civil rights movement, which were hardly of interest to any other boys my age.

One day a friend I will call Gary, whose mother was a school cafeteria worker, became very angry with me because I called him black.

"Don't call me black, man. I don't like that. I ain't black," he said vehemently.

"We are all black people," I said. "You've been brainwashed by the white man to hate your color. But you're black and you've got to accept that."

"I said don't call me black," he shouted. "Am I the color of the street or a pencil point? I ain't no tarbaby. What wrong with you, anyway? You sound like you been hanging out with them Muslims and militants. What are you anyway, one of them Malcolm X guys? He was a phony just like all the rest of them Muslims. You sound like you snappin' out or something. I don't know what your problem is but don't call me black again or I'll slide you."

"You're black, black, black," I said angrily. I hated the fact that he insulted Malcolm X, who, at that time, was my hero, the man who gave the greatest speech ever in America. "Malcolm X was a great man who tried to free black people. What 've you ever done to free black people or what's your mother done other than dishing out food in a lunch room? You're black and I'll call you black anytime I want to, you dumb nigger."

He hit me so hard in the chest that I fell down in the street, stunned and hurt from the blow that literally lifted me off my feet, and embarrassed because our other friends just snickered at me.

"Don't call me that," he said, walking away.

Over the years, I was never sure (and I never bothered to ask him after we made up) whether Gary hit me because I called him "black" or because I called him a "nigger" or because I insulted his mother. It took a long time before we became friends again and we were never as close as we were before that argument. There was a wall of shame, recognized yet unacknowledged, that separated us even as, as a joint construction, it bonded us together.

MALCOLM X, YOUTH CULTURE, AND THE RISE OF AFROCENTRISM

I

There he stands in our collective imagination, the lonely outsider, a kind of intellectual-looking prince, estranged and embattled, perpetually frozen in a high-noon posture of startled and doomed confrontation. And how do we yet account for this figure in the American carpet? Can it be said that Malcolm X is an important figure in American cultural history because he was merely a charismatic black nationalist? Hubert H. Harrison, Henry McNeal Turner, Richard B. Moore, Martin Delany, David Walker, Elijah Muhammad, Alexander Crummell, Edward Wilmot Blyden, and Ron Karenga have all been charismatic black nationalists of some sort in the nineteenth and twentieth centuries but none is held in the same regard as Malcolm. Indeed, most are not even remembered as distinct personages except by historians of African-American life and culture. Black nationalistic thinking, whether it be Ethiopianism, Back-to-Africa, Black Judaism, the Black Moors, Pan-Africanism, the Black Aesthetic, Afrocentrism, or something else, has existed for well over two hundred years in America. Like Martin Luther King, Malcolm, fierce debater, compelling public speaker, and man of considerable intellectual agility though he was, was hardly an original thinker. Nearly all of his ideas had been circulating in the national black community for a long time. Perhaps that is the essence of his appeal—the comforting familiarity of a set of ideas that, for the black mind, are both utterly banal and classically enduring. A sense surrounds Malcolm's basic idea—millenarian race-based cultural nationalism culminating in a worldwide race war that would overturn European dominance forever—that, like the Puritanism of Jonathan Edwards, was already anachronistic even when it seemed most current. But, as Edwards did with Calvinism, Malcolm popularized ideas about black nationalism, a universal African identity, and black self-determination, reinvigorating them for the American intellectual mainstream. Indeed, his historical importance, in part, lies in the fact that he gave these ideas a presence in American intellectual circles that they never had before. Yes, Malcolm X's charismatic black nationalism—that stark intersection of medieval energy and a Manichean imagination—does account for his hold on the black American mind but only if we understand both the specificity of his magnetism and his moment. But why now has he become a pop culture icon and his ominous phrase, "by any means necessary," become a kind of cant among the young, especially young blacks?

Had Malcolm not written or had written by Alex Haley (or by Betty Shabazz, Malcolm's wife) his *Autobiography,* which mythologized his presence and being forever, he would have died a negligible curiosity on the American political landscape in much the same way that, say, George Lincoln Rockwell or Father Divine did. I remember being quite surprised when I read many years ago Robert F. Williams's 1962 classic militant work, *Negroes With Guns,* and discovered that Malcolm—despite his considerable fame at the time and despite the fact that he most insistently advocated black self-defense—is never mentioned in the text (although Elijah Muhammad and the Black Muslims are). Malcolm was not, during his lifetime, nearly as important a radical political organizer or strategist as, say, either Eugene Debs or A. Philip Randolph. As a pure demagogue he does not come close to being as striking or compelling a figure as Huey Long and he never had anywhere near the audience of Father Coughlin. He did less during his lifetime for the cause of Pan-Africanism than NAACP founder and *Crisis* editor W.E.B. Du Bois or UNIA founder and black nationalist Marcus Garvey or Cheikh Anta Diop, the French African intellectual whose translated works have become the cornerstone for Afrocentrism, or Ron Karenga, who gave us the Kawaida principles, the Kwanzaa holiday, and an *Introduction to Black Studies.* So, we are drawn to the man through the filter of his own myth, his culminating act of public confession, the self-determined meaning of a black man's public career.

His *Autobiography,* a considerable literary accomplishment that borrowed freely and innovatively from Augustine's *Confessions,* the slave narrative tradition, and the bildungsroman tradition of Fielding and Goethe, has generated and sustained him in our collective American imagination. The book has sold over three million copies and is a staple on many college syllabi. The endurance of the *Autobiography* indicates that Malcolm as a literary and mythological presence continues to speak to readers, particularly young, educated, black, middle-class readers, even today. It is the black middle class from which some of the most vehement endorsements of Afrocentrism emanate. Thus, it is not surprising, since Malcolm has never left the black public consciousness (or, to a lesser degree, the white public consciousness either since the Hollywood powers have talked about making a Malcolm X film bio since the late 1960s), that he would be rediscovered by a new generation, as new generations are always apt to recast and redefine old heroes according to their lights or indeed to make old figures into heroes. Spike Lee's *Do The Right Thing,* which made much of the ideological differences between

Martin Luther King and Malcolm X, did not repopularize Malcolm as much as it reflected a popularity that already existed among the young—the very people who go to films and the very people for whom Lee marketed his product. Lee simply reaffirmed and validated Malcolm as a figure worthy of black popular adulation.

The key is that Malcolm, a man who dramatized and mythologized the particular circumstances of his own identity crisis, has become popular at this time because young black America, especially, is going through a massive identity crisis, more severe than the identity crisis of the 1950s and 1960s that produced Malcolm in the first place. This time the identity crisis is more severe because there is no framework of heroic public action or expression of public dissatisfaction as the civil rights movement in its most heady days provided, no common set of aims among blacks, no true consensus understanding of what the official breakdown of one type of segregation and the undisguised persistence of another means to any interpretation of the black past or to any direction for a black future. An awful fear lurks that black folk do not even constitute a viable community anymore in America. Malcolm provides for many black folk today a certain set of attractive, if often bemusingly flawed, answers, a way for black folk still to maintain a sense of community.

The fact that Malcolm represented something purely black and argued, throughout his public life, for a purely black political movement remains one of the strongest aspects of his appeal. Malcolm was driven by the idea of racial purity, in part, because he himself was so obviously of mixed racial lineage. What disturbed Malcolm nearly as much as the black American's oppression at the hands of the whites was the black's sense of ambiguity, the precarious state of his identity. Through Elijah Muhammad, Malcolm solved this problem by insisting on a blackness that corresponded to the "unspotted" whiteness of the whites but which was, paradoxically, a blackness that was far more inclusive than the white's whiteness, as it took in all people of pronounced or announced black descent. Here was an aesthetic invention that redeemed a bastardized people and provided them with a positive impetus for unity.

In the days of segregation, anything that was all-black—from a church to a social club to a Boy Scout troop—was seen as a badge of inferiority, as a mark of oppression because all-blackness was not a choice or option but a constant reminder that blacks were not wanted by, nor were they considered in any way part of, the white world (which for most blacks growing up during those days was something like the real world, that is, the world where things happened that seemed to matter). I cannot count the number of times as a child I heard phrases from black folk like "You know anything niggers do is second-rate" and similar sentiments. Malcolm, reemphasizing and reinventing Garvey of the 1920s, changed that thinking. All-blackness became a source of honor and accomplishment, not of degradation and shame.

To today's middle-class young blacks, Malcolm's espousal of all-blackness is even more crucial to their sense of identity because they have grown up, by and large, in an integrated world. Most of the black students who attend the standard, prestigious, private, research-oriented universities are the offspring of a mixed marriage or black professional parents, have lived most of their lives in mixed or largely white neighborhoods, or have attended white prep schools or predominantly white public schools. In arriving at a university with an African and Afro-American Studies program, they expect the formation of an all-black community that they have never experienced before, a sort of intellectual "nation within a nation," to borrow W.E.B. DuBois's term. Many have spent their entire lives integrating public or private educational institutions, an integration that has occurred largely on white terms—that is, largely in a way that would not make whites feel uncomfortable or threatened. Even more troubling for these black students is the contradictory terms of the integration they experienced: They were expected to be different (providing diversity and a rationale for their skin color) yet the same (for how else could they appreciate the opportunity they were being given without fundamentally having the same values as the whites who surround them which, much to the young black students' own confusion, they did). Perhaps the black students themselves are unsure of what their own terms should be, but, like Malcolm, they wish to rid themselves of their sense of ambiguity, their sense of precarious belonging. For many of them, and they are certainly not unjustified in feeling this way, integration is the badge of degradation and dishonor, shame and inferiority that segregation was for my generation.

It is, naturally, not hard to understand Malcolm's appeal to many black middle-class college students today in his advocacy of all-blackness. It is a reflection, among other considerations, of the intense state of unease among blacks—especially middle-class blacks—about race mixing, particularly about interracial sex. It must be remembered that the civil rights movement coincided with the sexual revolution of the 1960s—something that LeRoi Jones dramatized quite tellingly in his 1964 play, *Dutchman*—a movement that concentrated on the freeing of the black male politically and was contemporaneous with a movement to free the white woman sexually, so when the Muslims spoke vehemently against interracial sex during the 1950s and 1960s they were largely voicing one symbolic fear of integration that blacks and whites still secretly share today. A mother who belongs to the middle-class, all-black social organization Jack and Jill, which attempts to bring together black children in various extracurricular cultural activities and of which many black college students are a product, told my wife that she

joined the group because she was concerned about her sons when they become of dating age: "They should know some nice, respectable black families
with nice daughters," she said. Of course, my wife joined for much the same
reason. "They don't meet enough black kids," she says, accurately enough.
This concern is not to be taken lightly as it is part of an overall distrust that
many blacks have about "decadent" white life and "'white values" as being
destructive for the black mind. If, as the Afrocentrics argue, white racism is
the pathological result of the European's fear of being genetically "obliter-
ated" through interracial sex—blacks being "genetically inferior," cursed as
they are with weak, recessive genes—blacks today have virtually the same
fear of being, if not genetically annihilated, certainly culturally erased, an
idea that propelled Malcolm furiously: the fear of varieties of genocide.
When one thinks about the high incidence of drug and alcohol abuse, the
persistence of teen pregnancy, the extraordinary high-school dropout rate,
the terrifyingly high number of felonious crimes, the abysmally bad schools
that all exist within today's black community, sometimes one is inclined
to think that black writer Toni Cade Bambara might be right in saying,
"There's a race war going on and blacks sure didn't declare it." Or, put
another way, black fears of genocide or deliberately induced dysfunction are
not entirely the paranoid fixations of the oppressed. Simply considered,
Afrocentrism is the pure romanticization of black fear, loathing, and anger.
And Malcolm was, as he called himself, "the angriest man in America."

This explains the matching component of the enduring appeal of Malcolm X: his call for black unity as a way to preserve the race; an ancient call,
indeed, this has been upon these shores. Sometimes this concern drove Malcolm to absurdity. He praised white racism for its leveling-down effect on
blacks: "Actually, there is no such thing as an upper-class Negro, because he
catches the same hell as the other class Negro. All of them catch the same
hell, which is one of the things that's good about this racist system—it
makes us all one." Here Malcolm gives us all-blackness as the reductionist
urge to remove any sort of individualized distinctions among blacks. It is
common today still to hear among blacks any urges toward individuality
condemned as "being white," individuality being the creation of the European, while the holy and whole "community"—the creation of the African
and other dark-skinned peoples—is prized above everything else. Race-as-
community, race-as-invisible-church can be a form of stifling conformity,
and the urge for it reveals that some aspects of Afrocentrism or all-blackness,
as Malcolm popularized them and as they are preached in some quarters today, are far from imaginative or innovative; are, in fact, utterly prosaic and
philistine in their vision. Paradoxically, we have a rhetorically aggressive call
for self-determination that ultimately expresses itself at times as the kind of
repressive, crotchety conservatism that has from time to time afflicted

blacks for generations. Part of this is revealed in many blacks' adopting a "cultural diet" that abstains from "whiteness," the avoidance of white contamination. That Malcolm thought in this analogous way is not surprising as he condemned pork-eating—good Muslim that he was—in most of his public addresses and stressed the idea of a "clean," undefiled, presumably "unslavish" diet. Nothing reveals him as being more American as we, in this country, for at least 150 years, have been fascinated by diet cures—from graham crackers to the radical vegetarianism of Jethro Kloss—and the decontamination of our "nourishment." It is the ultimate form of American quackery.

Afrocentrism, in its attempts to reinvent segregation, has exhibited a kind of sentimentality and nostalgia that seems, frankly, quaint. One has only to read a book such as Nelson George's *The Death of Rhythm and Blues,* which argues that blacks enjoyed their best days as an empowered community during the 1940s and 1950s, to know that integration, and, in many instances, the havoc that it has caused among blacks in maintaining their sense of community, has evoked a reactionary impulse to reestablish a segregated black life. It is, of course, another indication of how truly American Afrocentrism is, this urge to romanticize and reinvent the past.

II

There is a story from my childhood that I have told my daughters on more than one occasion, a story that I think important although they find it scarcely even tolerable; it is always likely to come up when I feel that they are growing up "too white," getting too cozy with whites at school, when they seem too utterly middle-class and need to know that what they take for granted these days was not always so. So untouched are they by any blatant form of racism that I fear they are likely never to understand that it existed and continues to exist. Sometimes I feel estranged from my children; I do not fully understand their experience nor they mine. For instance, when we moved to an affluent white suburb they clamored for a golden retriever, largely because a neighbor down the street had a very attractive one. I adamantly refused to consent, thinking it just another concession to white, middle-class taste, getting the friendly, Leave-It-to-Beaver, Rover-and-Spot-type dog. "I don't like dogs," I said childishly before I finally relented. I tolerate the dog but I have no real affection for him. Let us call my story the black parent's jeremiad, a warning about the declension of the new generation. And Malcolm X as a kind of presence or even deus ex machina seemed central to it, and the aforementioned episode involving me and Gary is the prelude. The story goes something like this:

It was perhaps six months after Gary and I had our run-in about "blackness" that something quite unusual happened. Customarily, our walk from school took us through an Italian neighborhood and it often happened, especially in warm weather, that several Italian boys—actually older teens— would chase a group of us for several blocks with their Doberman pinschers. Once we hit the border of the black neighborhood, around Sixth Street, they would turn around and go back. They called this game "chasing the coons" or "spooking the spooks," and it sometimes resulted in a black kid being bitten by one of their dogs and demands from black parents for "police protection" for us. To which the Italians, at community center meetings, would always respond: "We're the ones who need police protection from you and your gangs and your thieving jungle habits." The black kids never did anything in return, never fought back. On occasion, they would retaliate later by jumping a lonesome Italian kid or two and beating him to a pulp, but this happened quite rarely because it always caused a severe police crackdown on blacks in the neighborhood. We simply ran for all we were worth and then cursed the Italian boys, rhetorically wreaking all manner of vengeance upon them.

On this particular afternoon, Gary and I had bought sodas and doughnuts, as we usually did on our way home, and were strolling along when we suddenly heard some voices cry out, "Get those niggers." We turned to see about five or six Italian boys and an unleased Doberman coming after us. We started running like beings possessed. We were comfortably ahead and could have easily avoided any risk of being caught when Gary abruptly pulled up and caught my arm.

"I'm tired of running from them guys. I ain't running anymore and neither are you."

"Hey, man," I said frantically. "Are you crazy or something? They can't catch us. What are we gonna do? Fight 'em? You must be crazy. There's about six of 'em, plus they got a dog. I'm getting out of here."

"You ain't going nowhere," he said angrily through his teeth. "It's time we stood up for ourselves. I'm tired of having them white bastards chase me and laugh at me, the old scared nigger. If they beat us up, well, I guess that's one ass-whipping we got to take. But I ain't running."

Gary turned his soda bottle over in his hand like a weapon and I reluctantly did the same. He picked up a brick from the street and I did the same and we waited for the Italian boys to come. The boys themselves looked almost bewildered that we had stopped. They stood perhaps twenty feet from us. Surprisingly, they called the dog back just as it was about to attack; it growled at us as if it wanted to pull our guts out. The Italian boys understood that we were standing our ground and that we would have fought the dog if it had attacked. Perhaps that is why they called it off. For several moments, except for the growling dog, everyone was silent. Then one of the Italian boys spoke:

"What you niggers doing walking through our neighborhood? We got a hunting season on jungle bunnies." The Italian boys began to move a few steps closer.

"We ain't causing no trouble," Gary said, "we just minding our own business. And if you come another step closer, I guarantee I'll put your ass in the hospital."

We all stood for what seemed the longest time as if frozen in some sort of still life. I was gripping the brick and bottle so hard my hands ached. Suddenly, feeling my blood pounding, I wanted to fight and, yet, just as suddenly, I realized we wouldn't have to. The Italians, I sensed, were going to back off.

And that is exactly what happened. One Italian boy mumbled something like "Watch yourselves next time," and they all began to drift off. As they were retreating, Gary shouted:

"And we ain't no niggers. We're black. Don't ever call us niggers again."

At this, I was more than slightly startled but very proud, as if I had made a convert. For one brief moment, two anonymous black boys in an anonymous big-city neighborhood stood up for something that made them, at least for that moment, slightly more than the ciphers they were. I recalled something I had heard Malcolm X say on television, something like this: "The so-called Negro has to stop the sit-in, the beg-in, the crawl-in, asking for something that is by rights already his. The so-called Negro has to approach the white man as a man himself." We felt like men, grown-up men or what we felt grown-up men must feel like when they have been tested and found themselves up to their moment.

We continued to go through the Italian neighborhood just as always in going to and from school. We were never bothered again.

Never once have I told this story in any way that impressed my daughters. My youngest usually says, "Are you finished now, Daddy?" They know the moral is something to the effect that it is good to be black and that it is something for which we have to stand up all together. "Yeah," my youngest says, "it's good to be black but it's better to not have to spend all your time thinking about how good it is to be black." They always complain, whenever I tell them of my youth, that I wish to live in the 1960s as if the times had not changed.

III

No amount of professed or contrived unity in the world can save black folk from the viciousness of their peculiar form of generational conflict, of youth against the aged. Generational conflict has always been strong among blacks because each new generation looks with suspicion upon the elders, thinks them to have been failures, people who compromised and accommodated themselves to survive among the whites. "The anxiety of influence" is an almost murderous impulse among blacks as each generation, in some way, wishes to free itself of the generation that produced it. Blacks, like all other Americans, worship youth.

There was a quality of magic in Malcolm's youth at a time when several American public political figures—Kennedy and King—enthralled the public in this way. Malcolm's rise coincided with the coming of rock and roll, the entire youth culture phenomenon, and the advent of television, which disseminated his ideas—in part, because of his serious youthfulness—far more effectively than those of any previous black nationalist. Malcolm's virility and youth made him an attractive alternative to the elderly and sickly Elijah Muhammad. Black nationalist and separatist ideas coming from Elijah Muhammad seemed cranky, cultlike, backwaterish, and marginal. The same ideas coming from Malcolm seemed revolutionary, hip, and vibrant. In the 1960s, Malcolm's youthfulness—both framing and disguising the essential reactionary politics of the Muslims—symbolized a kind of masculinity and force that seemed all the more compelling because the leadership of the civil rights movement was made, through its comparative conservatism, to seem even older than it was, more cowardly than it was, more of a sellout. Malcolm skillfully emphasized both political and age differences simultaneously by referring to the members of the black civil rights establishment, even Martin Luther King, who was, in fact, younger than he, as Uncle Toms or as Uncles, associating them with the conflated popular image of Uncle Remus and Uncle Tom—fictional characters created by white writers: aged black men (in popular culture) who "loved their white folks," as the expression goes. In this sense he has become for young blacks the kind of figure that Thoreau, who espoused the overturning of generations and the uselessness of elders in *Walden,* was for young whites in the late 1960s. Malcolm took advantage of his times and exacerbated a generation gap among blacks. Nothing reveals this better than the generational parable of the Chinese revolution that Malcolm told his black audience in 1963:

> When I was in prison, I read an article in *Life* magazine showing a little Chinese girl, nine years old; her father was on his hands and knees and she was pulling the trigger because he was an Uncle Tom Chinaman. When they had the revolution over there, they took a whole generation of Uncle Toms and just wiped them out. And within ten years that little girl became a full-grown woman. No more Toms in China. And today it's one of the toughest, roughest, most feared countries on this earth—by the white man. Because there are no Uncle Toms over there.

In short, revolution for Malcolm was black patricide bathed in the justifying beatific light of black brotherhood. Malcolm's own murder, his own fratricidal victimization, even further underscored his youth in an age when many—the Kennedys, Martin Luther King, young civil rights workers—died the tragic death of political martyrs, the kind of death that underscored loss, unrealized gifts, utter waste, unkept promises.

Malcolm had the imprimatur of prison (the mark of a revolutionary) and the street (the mark of the proletariat) upon him, but he was also a firm believer in the bourgeois concept of racial uplift, thus making him romantic and even gallant—a strikingly apt figure, by the late 1960s, for a black hero, for middle-class blacks and intellectuals have tended, like many bourgeois westerners, to romanticize the "authenticity" of lower-class life. After his death, Malcolm became the patron saint of black nationalism for SNCC and for the organization that emerged from it, the Black Panther Party, the leading black radical youth groups of the middle and late 1960s.

IV

I am convinced that the rise in interest in Malcolm X as a public icon, as a figure in popular culture, can be traced to the descent of Muhammad Ali as a public figure after the early 1980s. Because they were both militant Muslims, and because they were friends for a time who fell out rather distastefully, I believe they are always yoked together in the public's mind: the two public troublemakers, disturbers of the peace. But Ali's stance against the Vietnam War, combined with his flair and artistry as a champion boxer, an occupation that granted him a splendor more remarkable than might normally be expected in a public figure, made him a more potent symbol for an immense heroism. Here was a man who was throwing away his youth—his only asset—for his beliefs.

It was, I think, an extremely hot late spring day in 1969 when I was a high-school senior that rumors started flying around the city that Ali—then banned from boxing because of his draft conviction—was really going up to Joe Frazier's North Philadelphia gym to fight the new heavyweight champion in his gym, right then and there. That morning Ali made remarks to that effect on the "Sonny 'Mighty Burner' Hopson Show," a local soul radio program, but at first people gave it little credit, figuring it to be another Ali hoax. When Ali actually arrived at Frazier's that afternoon and started to strip as if they were actually going to fight, thousands of people appeared from nowhere. Traffic was backed up for miles. Along with some friends, I skipped school and headed straight for Cloverlay Gym. The crowd was such that Ali starting walking toward Fairmount Park, away from the gym, saying he would fight Frazier in the open air where there was more room. I will never forget getting a glimpse of Ali as he moved through the crowd, all of us feeling very much like the fancy must have felt trailing the fighters, during the days of bare-knuckle fighting in Regency England. Moving there, pouring sweat on this insufferably hot day, surrounded as he was, he seemed for all the world like a god in his glory. Someone in the crowd mentioned Malcolm's name, probably because there had been recently or was about to be in the community a small, homemade celebration of Malcolm's birthday, May 19, something that had become common after his death. "Yeah," a voice said, "Malcolm's cool. But Ali's the man." Naturally enough, there was no fight that day. Just another Ali hype.

Malcolm X and Ali are America's two most famous Muslims, both oddly sacrificed. Those of us who lived through the 1960s have returned to thinking about Malcolm because he is intellectually a man worthy of greater attention, a man who can tell us more about being an American Muslim and a race leader because we are not distracted by his having been something else. But also we return to Malcolm because we are unnerved by Ali now, by the brain damage he has suffered in the ring, by the way he has aged. Malcolm remains now frozen forever in his stern youthfulness almost immortal, like a saint, while Ali is the mirror of our own aging and mortality, a busted-up, broken-down hero.

V

What does it mean to blacks today that Malcolm X was a Muslim, that he tried to be something explicitly non-Western? How did this inform his charismatic black nationalism and what sort of authority did this most dramatic set of conversions—from unsaved to Black Muslim and from Black Muslim to orthodox Muslim—give him?

In some ways, it is almost standard Americanism to be drawn to the East as novelty, from the mid-nineteenth-century Transcendentalists and their "orientalism" to the unrelenting interest in both the nineteenth and twentieth centuries in Egyptology, to the sitar-playing rock stars and yoga-practicing middle-class whites of the late 1960s. Always this appeal of anti-Westernism in the form of the "Holy East" is particularly strong with the young who decry the West's lack of spirituality. Malcolm's climactic vision of the East as spiritual and racial paradise is the overlong, self-serving account of his hajj to Mecca in the *Autobiography,* which has become a kind of black paradigm of self-discovery, the reinvention of conversion for the American Negro. Through the historical and cultural authority of Islam he made blackness mythical, inclusive, and, finally, intelligible.

Because Malcolm, through his conversions to Islam, suggested to blacks that it is possible to be different from and to be better than the whites, his popularity is self-evidently clear. In the age of a muddled and halfhearted integration that forces both whites and blacks to dissemble as they joust in unequal rivalry, Malcolm's Islam is a natural extension of his black nationalism, suggesting an alternative way for blacks to be a group, an entry, to have an empowered identity. The question for many blacks now, a question that Malcolm made real in a way that no one had done since Garvey, is not "How can I assimilate?" but rather "Why should I want to?"

Malcolm, in connection with this Western fantasy about the East, developed two distinct but related beliefs: that blacks are not Americans and that they are really Africans, both ideas having a long and complicated history among blacks in relation to their identities, psychologically considered, and, more important, in relation to their sense of eschatology and political mission. Malcolm refined the arguments of Elijah Muhammad concerning the black American as the "lost-found nation." "You nothing but an *ex-slave*," Malcolm said. "You don't like to be told that, but what else are you?" [emphasis mine]. Black "social death," to borrow Orlando Patterson's concept, is precisely what the term "ex-slave" means; blacks exist as neither fully empowered citizens nor entirely discounted aliens.

Malcolm—as obsessed by a "Lost Eden" pastoralism as most industrialized westerners are—saw the remedy for the social death of the black in America as, not surprisingly, other earlier black nationalists such as David Walker or Martin Delany have seen it or as today's Afrocentrics see it: the romantic reunification with mythological Africa. "We are just as much African today as we were in Africa four hundred years ago, only we are a modern counterpart of it," said Malcolm X at Harvard in 1964. "When you hear a black man playing music, whether it is jazz or Bach, you still hear African music. The soul of Africa is still reflected in the music played by black men. In everything else we do we still are African in color, feeling, everything. And we will always be that whether we like it or not."

What Malcolm X asserted has, for blacks today, a positive importance despite its pedestrian and romantic qualities: that blacks are indeed, as DuBois argues, a people of double consciousness; that is to say, that both blackness and American-ness are, to use William James's term, live choices, each having meaning only when measured against the other. Malcolm would not have argued with such passion and virulence against the validity of any kind of black *American* experience if he were not convinced that assimilation, that being American, was not truly a rooted desire, if not fulfilled reality, for most blacks. Yet he also knew that black folk in America cannot think about what their American-ness means without thinking about what it means to be of African descent: The two are inextricably bound together. As historian Sterling Stuckey has argued, black people did not acquire a sense of what being African was until they came to America and were forced, ironically, in becoming American to invent a collective sense of an African memory and an African self. This process is similar to that of other immigrants who have come here, but for blacks the stakes are so much higher, the cause of psychic redemption is absolutely more vital, because of the intensity of the oppression they have suffered and because of the precariousness of their perch on the American family tree. For any black, Africanness has no meaning except within a context of understanding what it means, finally, to be American as both a history of negation and creation, of denial and affirmation. Black Americans' dilemma is that they are bound by the prison of self-consciousness about the meaning of their once having been African, while realizing that they can never be African again.

THE END OF GENEALOGY

I nearly joined the Black Muslims when I was eighteen, living in San Francisco and virtually surrounded by them, a wonderful community of saints. How Mr. P. helped me get a job at the Presidio because he "believed in helping young brothers" and how R. and H., two civil rights veterans in their mid-twenties who had converted, would drive me to the mosque to hear the lesson and how I was always given a suit jacket to wear as I certainly did not own proper clothing then to go to anyone's church. Both R. and H. would take me to their apartment where, after the Muslim service, they would dump their paid-for copies of *Muhammad Speaks* in a closet, break out some marijuana and play jazz records all night, laughing at my ignorance of joint-smoking and jazz. They were very good to me and I was quite fond of them. They were students at Berkeley but they never attended a class. They simply stopped on campus to pick up a check. "The white devil's gonna pay to have me here, so I'm just gonna take the devil's money and be about my business. It's reparations, man." I thought how much I would like to do that. And my view on Malcolm had changed. As Mr. P. told me: "Malcolm left the Nation because he wanted to be with the white man, because he felt he was too advanced for us backward, storefront niggers with our ignorant, fornicating Messenger. But it was the Messenger who gave him a message, not the other way around. It was the Messenger who gave Malcolm morals when he didn't have any, not the other way around. Then he wants to say when he left that he made the Muslims. Why, what would he have been if it weren't for the Muslims? Some old two-bit hustling, white woman–loving nigger. The Nation didn't kill Malcolm. Malcolm committed suicide going over there to them death-loving devils who was telling him he was so great and so important and sticking microphones in his face and all that stuff." I, too, as a Muslim fellow-traveler, denounced Malcolm. And yet when I returned to Philadelphia I was filled with shame and disgust as I learned how the mosques were shaking down black businesses, distributing drugs in the community, murdering apostates and drug rivals, and generally instituting a reign of terror. "The devil's paper accuse us of being the Black Mafia and all that but why don't they write about the Vatican and the real Mafia," one Muslim told me, and I was even more ashamed of such a feeble answer. I knew and have always continued to believe that had Malcolm taken over the Muslims that horrible saturnalia of crime and corruption would not have happened.

And I thought that it was something like this I wanted to say to my daughter, about how I have felt much shame over the years taking the money of whites, simply being paid because I was black and expected to make "black statements" in order to be praised by whites for my Negro-ness. I felt much as if I were doing what the black domestics in white homes do, that James Baldwin described so well in *The Fire Next Time,* taking money and items from whites that the whites expected to be taken, wanted to be taken, because it reenforced their superiority and our own degradation. For to allow the whites to purchase my "specialness" through Affirmative Action is not reparations but a new form of enslavement. It was from Malcolm, and his integrity, that I learned this needful shame.

Is Malcolm a hero these days because he seemed more his own man than Martin Luther King, because he was more "militant," because he did not speak to love and peace but of war and apocalypse? In this age of integration, when whites seem, in some way, to have taken hold of everything black as into some massive commercial/cultural maw, young blacks may feel particularly attracted to Malcolm because he spoke so insistently to black people, because he did not seem to crave and desire—as so many other blacks have— the approval and rewards of whites, because Malcolm never was and never has become a comfortable figure for whites. In any effort to claim him as a hero, I believe blacks, through their Afrocentrism, wish, as black artists used to do in periodically re-Africanizing black music, to make him virtually unclaimable for whites. King, many blacks feel, can be claimed by whites, is, in fact, as much a white hero as a black one, and every January several thousand whites can shed tears about a "dream" and reminisce about marches they participated in, freedom schools they helped to run, bail money they sent to free demonstrators, and church sermons they gave on behalf of civil rights. Blacks want no white tears or white memories for Malcolm. Blacks want him to themselves, without white nostalgia, white sympathy, or white interpretation.

I would like to say to my black students some words, not of wisdom, which God knows I scarcely possess, but of witness, to tell them of my witness, to reach out across the generational lines, to tell them how important it is to me for them to know what I had seen and heard. For the execration I may endure from younger blacks is tolerable only if they themselves are forced to acknowledge my entire being and if they, in the end, in that fullness, choose to condemn it and not to evade—through Mother Africa romances and self-conscious militant gestures—what I myself, and they, must confront: the explicit honest witness of our own lives that, painfully but surely, collected strenuously bit by bit, is what our blackness truly means.

It was Malcolm who said that the white man was "the earth's number-one hypocrite," who exposed so publicly the "white scribes and pharisees," who denounced, as Hannah Arendt put it, "the vice through which corruption becomes manifest." The rest of us attended the marvel of hearing a black man say to the world what we all wanted to say. To hear the demand for an uncompromised and unbargained-for freedom, a freedom unconditional and complete, was a kind of energizing thrill and, in effect, reminded all black people that we could never acquiesce to injustice or accept any kind of barter for our sense of dignity as a people.

Yet he gave black people a sense of being African at the complete expense of their own American selves, a love of the misty past at the cost of our lives, our triumphs, our sufferings in the New World and as modern people. In this way, Malcolm merely increased our anxiety, further fueled our sense of inadequacy, and intensified our self-hatred and failure by providing us with a ready excuse: America is the white man's country, and the whites don't want you here and will never give you equal citizenship. But it must always be remembered that our blood is here, our names are here, our fate is here, in the land we helped to invent. It is more than the fact that blacks were forced to give America free labor; other groups have built this and other countries for free or for nominal wages. We have given America something far more valuable than labor: We have given her an identity, indeed, the only identity that she has ever had. No black person should care what the whites want or don't want. It is they who must learn to accept, to live as committed equals with their former slaves. Our profound past of being African, which we must never forget, must be balanced by our complex fate of being American, which we can never deny, or worse, evade. For we must accept the fact of who and what we are and the forces and conditions that have made us this, not as defeat or triumph, not in shame or with grandiose pride, but as the tangled, strange, yet poignant and immeasurable record of an imperishable human presence.

MALCOLM X AND THE FAILURE
OF AFROCENTRISM

It comes as no surprise that Malcolm X is such a popular figure in America these days. Whatever may be said about his virtues or lack thereof as a black hero, it is clear that he is conveniently a multiculturalist's dream-come-true. For those who view history as a debate, here stands a man who publicly and fiercely debated, from Harvard to talk radio to Harlem street corners, against civil rights leaders, against liberal and conservative whites, against virtually anyone willing to oppose him, throughout his career as a race leader. For those who wish to see western civilization denounced as white, Eurocentric, exploitative, racist, as a civilization of liars, cheaters, thieves, rapists, and murderers, here was a man who, in fact, relentlessly accused white America (and, by extension, western civilization) of all these in relation to blacks. As he said with typical millenarian fervor in a speech at Harvard in 1961: "God has come to close out the entire old world, the old world where for the past six thousand years most of the earth's population has been deceived, conquered, colonized, ruled, enslaved, oppressed, and exploited by the Caucasian race." This type of talk is commonplace in America today, especially among multiculturalists, with or without the theological overlay, but in the early 1960s, only Malcolm X as representative of the Nation of Islam, was saying anything like this in the popular media.

There are a few immediate observations that come to mind about African American history, multiculturalism and Malcolm's ideology of racial separatism, black nationalism, and millennialistic race war, embraced today by many in the typical, mistakenly ahistorical manner in which Americans grab hold of anything in the fit of a fad.

First, that the central concern of the multiculturalist, and of Malcolm and the Afrocentric mind that he represents, is exposing the corruption of

western civilization through revealing its hypocrisy. As Malcolm said in a
speech in 1964, "[The white man] is the earth's number one hypocrite."
Hannah Arendt points out in her *On Revolution* that tearing away the mask of
the oppressors and revealing them as hypocrites has become the fashion of the
revolutionary-minded since the French Revolution (and there is a striking,
almost uncanny resemblance between the rhetoric of Malcolm X and that of
French Revolutionists like Robespierre). Of course, the danger is that the
revolutionists will become so obsessed with the rooting out of hypocrisy that
they will begin to accuse each other of it. Such was the case with Malcolm
and his religious leader Elija Muhammad. Malcolm left the Nation of Islam
accusing his elderly leader of hypocrisy, as he explicitly states in his
Autobiography, while in his *The Fall of America,* written several years after
Malcolm's death, Muhammad accuses Malcolm of the exact same crime.

Second, in refining the arguments of Elija Muhammad concerning
black Americans as the "lost-found nation," Malcolm gave us the view, common amon multiculturalists today, that there is no African American history
unless filtered through the lenses of Africa that the black American is, in essence, not a westerner. "You are not American citizens or members of the
white man's world," writes Muhammad, "The only American citizens are
the white people who are originally from Europe. So why fight a losing battle
by trying to be recognized as something you are not and never will be."

In Malcolm's rhetoric, the black American as westerner becomes a universal emblem for alienation, loneliness, unfulfilled human longing, a
blasted anonymous identity, as signified by Malcolm's own X and by this
idea which is repeated over and over to many of his black audiences, "You
nothing but an ex-slave. You don't like to be told that, but what else are
you?" Black "social death," to borrow Harvard sociologist Orlando Patterson's concept, is precisely what the term "ex-slave" means, a world where
blacks exist as neither fully-empowered citizens or entirely discounted aliens.
It is revealing of the depth of the schism, and the depth of the shame that
created the schism, in Malcolm X's own mind and heart about being American and being black that he would say in a speech on Negro history:

> They give us the impression with Negro History Week that we
> were cotton pickers all of our lives. Cotton pickers, orange
> growers'mammies, and uncles for the white man in this country—
> this is our history when you talk in terms of Negro History Week.

Malcolm is, after all, castigating an event created by black historian Carter
G. Woodson, from whose works Malcolm learned virtually everything he
knew about black history, even the central idea he is trying to express in the
passage, and in the speech itself: that blacks are miseducated and psychologi-

cally damaged because they are not properly taught their history. It is, of course, the position of the multiculturalist and the Afrocentric that this rampant and conspiratorial denial of self-knowledge has destroyed the black American's mind, and that an inexorable and completely admirable sense of victimology—ironically framed in the expansively "empowering" set of notions that the African and his civilization has created virtually everything in the world worthy of the name civilization—is the most remarkable and essential feature of the black American's psycho-history.

Not surprisingly, in some ways Malcolm saw the remedy for the social death of the black in America as other earlier black nationalists such as David Walker or Martin Delany have seen it, or as today's Afrocentrics see it: the romantic reunification with mythological Africa.

"We are just as much African today as we were in Africa four hundred years ago, only we are a modern counterpart of it," said Malcolm X at Harvard in 1964. "When you hear a black man playing music, whether it is jazz or Bach, you still hear African music. The soul of Africa is still reflected in the music played by black men. In everything else we do we still are African in color, feeling, everything. And we will always be that whether we like it or not."

After the bombing of his home in February 1965, he had this to say to the press: "One of the things that made the Black Muslim movement grow was its emphasis upon things African. This was the secret to the growth of the Black Muslim movement. African blood, African origin, African culture, African ties. And you'd be surprised—we discovered that deep within the subconscious of the black man in this country, he is still more African than he is American."

In another speech, given in 1964, he said: "Right now, in this country, if you and I, 22 million African-Americans—that's what we are—Africans who are in America. You're nothing but Africans. Nothing but Africans. In fact, you'd get farther calling yourself African instead of Negro. Africans don't catch hell."

The most obvious contradiction in all this is that Malcolm wishes to argue that American blacks are the most oppressed and abject people in the world, totally transformed by the blighting experience of slavery ("You must remember: The condition of America's twenty million ex-slaves is uniquely pitiful," he said.) Then, on the other hand, that they have remained incredibly and indelibly African despite 400 years of the most convulsive changes any group of people on this planet have ever experienced. Because blacks have remained separated from the mainstream of American life, Malcolm, for political reasons, thought he could construct an argument that they are simply a battered, refugee people in exile. That so many black Americans believe something like this today indicates Malcolm's ideas, through multicultural-

ism, have succeeded all too well and African-American history has become a
void of utter negation (slavery) that can only be corrected (cured) by the set
of African achievements (whether real or imagined) from which all history
emanates.

Despite the fact that many perspectives of our society must be recognized and understood, I am afraid the greatest disservice of such multiculturalism is to give us history as an attitude and expression of utter resentment and negation: offering the simplistic and dangerous moralism in which
one side is utterly wrong and the other side the beatific victim whose lamp
shall be the light for our feet. What has the multiculturalist wrought for us
who have a past of oppression but a nightmarishly Freudian historiography of
j'accuse, wrapped in the piety of our victimization and the holiness of our ethnicity.

I remember distinctly at least part of her answer when I asked my eldest
daughter one afternoon last summer if she wanted a Malcolm X t-shirt or
cap. This was after we had gone for a trip through the mall, browsing
through various stores. One of the stores was a "black" or ethnic shop: the
sort of place that sells African-styled clothing, black board games, a great
deal of jewelry and incense, a few books of the sort written by Yusef Ben-
Jochannan (Dr. Ben as we called him at Cornell), Frances Welsing, Ivan Van
Sertima, and some hot title by the Nation of Islam, *The Secret Relationship Between Blacks and Jews,* showing that blacks can give as good as they get in the
hate literature department. In short, it had that collection of stuff we might
call the black nationalist revision of American "patriotic gore," the grand
merchandising of black American history and black American psychotherapy. There were also many Malcolm X caps, t-shirts, and the like. I noticed
as we perused the merchandise how indifferent my daughter was, how bored
she looked.

"I don't want to make statements about being black with my clothes,"
she said. "And I don't want to say something I don't mean."

"Besides," she said after a pause, "he talked a lot of race stuff and, well,
maybe, that was good when you were a kid but it just doesn't interest me
much. I don't want to be clobbered with race stuff. Then you have to start
wondering about everything you like, and if you 'talk white,' and if you have
too many white friends and all that kind of stuff. I just don't want all that,
well, weight on me. It's like making your skin color some kind of prison." I
listened and remembered that Malcolm X once said, "Our skin became a
trap, a prison," but he meant something else.

On an evening shortly after a piece I wrote on Malcolm X was published
in *Harper's,* I spoke before a group at Washington University about Spike
Lee's film bio of the famous Muslim leader. It was not very long into the pro-

ceedings when a group of young black men, all connected with a local black store (not the one mentioned above) came in. Certainly their intention was clear to me, if not readily apparent to the others present. I was about to, as one of them later put it, "have my feet put to the fire" about the Malcolm piece, largely because it had little good to say about Afrocentrism and was insufficiently hagiographic. This is the nature of the "debate" about African American history as it exists among blacks today, an ominous atmosphere of fear, loathing, and intimidation as "truth squads" seek to put the heretics and apostates in their places by exposing them for the "race traitors" they supposedly are. After this confrontation ended, one of the young men handed me a letter which read in part:

Mr. Early:
Have you reasoned/thought Blackly lately or does all the literary, romantic, mythological understanding you have emanate from European novels, learning models, point of view, anti-culture?

Mixing Jay Gatsby and Afrocentricity/Malcolm X! They don't mix. African captives and Amerikkkanism? Thats the equivalent of putting a European-inundated, so full of European feces-constipated, objective (not Black minded) person, say a Gerald Early type, in charge of an African and Afro-American studies program. A great move for whites who would like to hoodwink more Blacks to attend their so-called prestigious attempt at a university.

Your reference to Malcolm as an idiot, fool is perhaps the greatest sign of your Amerikkkaness. Mr. Early, what little Africanity you had was probably replaced in computer-brain space with a whole lot of "Lost in Space," Marxism, Darwinism, Thoreauism, and Waldenism. Perhaps you thoroughly studied all of these "isms" because of your hate for yourself coupled with your blind faith and love for your "massa," the white race.

The letter goes on in this venomous vein for a few more paragraphs. That it is poorly written, completely misreads my article, exhibits discredited race-thinking that is, ironically, European (indeed, nineteenth-century Germanic in origin), makes no substantive argument of any sort, is nothing more than a lot of immature name-calling, is precisely one aspect of the point I wish to make. Not merely is the letter an angry insult directed at me, but it is an extraordinary example of how the "debate" over African American history, over the interpretation of black historical figures, has become murderously personal among blacks, how the lack of any attempt to form consensus in the black community has led to the attempt to stifle the act of critical inquiry and serious self-examination itself. The problem with Afrocentrism is not only its inability to recognize it is not an intellectual movement, but, that it is, in fact, almost exclusively a fundamentalist *religious sentiment*. This certainly explains its intolerance, and its astonishing preoccupation with being both charismatically spiritual and arrogantly self-righteous. Understood as such, the letter from the young man is perfectly comprehensible, if deeply distressing: I am being attacked not on intellectual but on *doctrinal* grounds. Black people and the meaning of their history have come to a pretty pass: we possess an orthodoxy not in search of a school, but a church, or more aptly put, a theater, for in the end, Afrocentricity is a philistine form of theatrical engagement, of mask-wearing and self-conscious gestures.

This leads to the second aspect of my point: the letter demonstrated exactly what my piece in *Harper's* was arguing: that blacks foolishly waste their time condemning other blacks, with whom they do not agree, as being "insufficiently black," making the whole idea of being black a cross between a McCarthy loyalty oath and joining an exclusive clique. It was Malcolm X who popularized this form of criticism when he began blasting civil rights leaders for being Uncle Toms and sell-outs. It has now become, among blacks, a virtual saturnalia of recriminations and denials, a carnival of accusations of hypocrisy and deception.

We blacks must learn history is the quest for consensus, and the essence of that consensus is discipline. To be black in America, no matter one's political persuasion or how one sees this or that black figure, is to have learned and exercised this discipline, this stern tempering in the fires of adversity, hypocrisy, freedom and enslavement in this strange democratic leviathan; to have learned a kind of precarious balancing and an extraordinary sort of carriage in a world where one misstep, one mistimed moment of revelation, can be so exceedingly costly. It is within this discipline, as unkind and unforgiving as a jam session, that blacks have sculpted their traditions in this country and have earned their humanity. This is what our history must tell: the story of the shaping of this discipline, disdainful of self-pity and victimology; of how it informed our survival and growth and flourishing; of its tough demand for a true consensus where all voices are included and all individuality respected and blackness is recognized in all its shades. For there is no paradigm of black authenticity except as it is understood that through our unique and common experiences we each hold some infinitely small portion of a large, collective truth. Our history has nothing to do with who is blacker than whom or with Afrocentric wonderlands. Our history is the stuff of the blues, as American as that, finally: the explicit honest witness of our own lives which, painfully but surely, collected strenuously bit and bit, is what our blackness truly means.

III

LIFE WITH DAUGHTERS

DUMBO'S EARS OR HOW WE BEGIN

(for Linnet, my daughter)

there is always talk among the knowing kind
if you are last to do a certain thing or anything or everything

that you are a slow one, as slow as the time
it takes to say anything twice or more

that you helplessly do not see the plainest
sights to be seen anywhere by anybody plainly

that you are as ungainly as Dumbo's ears, as
clumsy as a childish elephant with floppy ears

but there's always been a kind of pleasure
in a certain kind of slowness like a gait

that sort of ambles a bit through the park
of shuffles along the street sort of stopping

and not quite knowing where it's going because
what with stones and leaves and silver rabbits

and silken insects and all manner of infinite trash
and voices and echoes and signs and the wide sky

well, who could help but be subverted in one's quickness
if one is really a sky lover and likes to watch the earth too

so there is no real reason to go anywhere in particular
except the somewhere that anywhere can lead easily

along some way or other until another more
outright way comes, a way that is more a gift

that would make the gait even slower and more stately
like a meandering stream's or a balloon ascent

or a blues saxophone's or the words of a wedding or
the reading of any text worth the wait or water

evaporating in a glass—all a kind of awful slowness
that seems, like our gait together, to say wait awhile

and which, like the whiling tortoise, always starts the race
after the quick and the hares, gate open, in their blind rush, begin

LIFE WITH DAUGHTERS

Watching the Miss America Pageant

The theater is an expression of our dream life—of our unconscious aspirations.

> —David Mamet, "A Tradition of the Theater as Art,"
> *Writing in Restaurants*

Aunt Hester went out one night,—where or for what I do not know,—and happened to be absent when my master desired her presence.

> —Frederick Douglass, *Narrative of the Life of Frederick Douglass*

Adults, older girls, shops, magazines, newspapers, window signs—all the world had agreed that a blue-eyed, yellow-haired, pink-skinned doll was what every girl child treasured.

> —Toni Morrison, *The Bluest Eye*

It is now fast become a tradition—if one can use that word to describe a habit about which I still feel a certain amount of shamefacedness—for our household to watch the Miss America contest on television every year. The source of my embarrassment is that this program remains, despite its attempts in recent years to modernize its frightfully antique quality of "women on parade," a kind of maddeningly barbarous example of the persistent, hard, crass urge to sell: from the plugs for the sponsor that are made a part of the script (that being an antique of fifties and sixties television; the show does not remember its history so much as it seems bent on repeating it) to the constant references to the success of some of the previous contestants and the reminders that this is some sort of scholarship competition, the program has all the cheap earnestness of a social uplift project being played as a musical revue in Las Vegas. Paradoxically, it wishes to convince the public that it is a common entertainment while simultaneously wishing to convey that it is more than mere entertainment. The Miss America pageant is the worst sort of "Americanism," the soft smile of sex and the hard sell of toothpaste and hair dye ads wrapped in the dreamy ideological gauze of "making it through one's own effort." In a perverse way, I like the show; it is the only live television left other than sports, news broadcasts, performing arts award programs, and speeches by the president. I miss live TV. It was the closest thing to theater for the masses. And the Miss America contest is, as it has been for some time, the most perfectly rendered theater in our culture, for it so perfectly captures what we yearn for: a low-class ritual, a polished restatement of vulgarity, that wants to open the door to high-class respectability by way of plain middle-class anxiety and ambition. Am I doing all right? the contestants seem to ask in a kind of reassuring, if numbed, way. The contest brings together all the American classes in a show-biz spectacle of classlessness and tastelessness.

My wife has been interested in the Miss America contest since childhood, and so I ascribe her uninterrupted engagement with America's cultural passage into fall (Miss America, like college and pro football, signifies for us as a nation the end of summer; the contest was invented, back in 1921, by Atlantic City merchants to prolong the summer season past Labor Day) as something mystically and uniquely female. She, as a black woman, had a long-standing quarrel with the contest until Vanessa Williams was chosen the first black Miss America in September 1983. Somehow she felt vindicated by Williams for all those years as a black girl in Dallas, watching white women win the crown and thumb their noses at her, at her blackness, at her straightened hair, her thick lips, her wide nose. She played with white Barbie dolls as a little girl and had, I suppose, a "natural," or at least an understandable and predictable, interest in seeing the National White Barbie Doll chosen every year because for such a long time, of course, the Miss America contest, with few exceptions, was a totemic preoccupation with and representation of a particularly stilted form of patriarchal white supremacy. In short, it was a national white doll contest. And well we know that every black girl growing up in the fifties and early sixties had her peculiar love-hate affair with white dolls, with mythicized white femininity. I am reminded of this historical instance: everyone knows that in the *Brown versus Topeka Board of Education* case (the case that resulted in the Supreme Court decision to integrate public schools) part of the sociological evidence used by the plaintiffs to show the psychological damage suffered by blacks because of Jim Crow was an account by Kenneth Clarke of how, when offered a choice between a black doll and a white doll, little black girls invariably chose the white doll because they thought it "prettier."

On the front page of the January 6, 1962, *Pittsburgh Courier,* a black weekly, is a picture of a hospitalized black girl named Connie Smith holding a white doll sent to her by Attorney General Robert Kennedy. Something had occurred between 1954, when the Supreme Court made its decision, and 1962 that made it impossible for Kennedy to send the girl a black doll, and this impossibility was to signal, ironically, that the terms of segregation and the terms of racial integration, the very icon of them, were to be exactly the same. Kennedy could not send the girl a black doll, as it would have implied, in the age of integration, that he was, in effect, sending her a Jim Crow toy, a toy that would emphasize the girl's race. In the early sixties such a gesture would have been considered condescending. To give the black girl a white doll in the early sixties was to mainstream the black girl into the culture, to say that she was worthy of the same kind of doll that a white girl would have. But how can it be that conservatism and liberalism, segregation and integration, could produce, fantastically, the same results, the identical iconography: a black girl hugging a white doll because everyone thinks it is best for her to have it? How can it be that at one time the white doll is the sign of the black girl's rejection and inferiority and fewer than ten years later it is the sign of her acceptance and redemption? Those who are knowledgeable about certain aspects of the black mind or the collective black consciousness realize, of course, that the issues of segregation and integration, of conservatism and liberalism, of acceptance and rejection, of redemption and inferiority, are all restatements of the same immovable and relentless reality of the meaning of American blackness; that this is all a matter of the harrowing and compelling intensity that is called, quaintly, race pride. And in this context, the issue of white dolls, this fetishization of young white feminine beauty, and the complexity of black girlhood becomes an unresolved theme stated in a strident key. Blacks have preached for a long time about how to heal their daughters of whiteness: in the November 1908 issue of *The Colored American Magazine,* E. A. Johnson wrote an article entitled "Negro Dolls for Negro Babies," in which he said, "I am convinced that one of the best ways to teach Negro children to respect their own color would be to see to it that the children be given colored dolls to play with. . . . To give a Negro child a white doll means to create in it a prejudice against its own color, which will cling to it through life." Lots of black people believed this and, for all I know, probably still do, as race pride, or the lack thereof, burns and crackles like a current through most African-American public and private discourse. Besides, it is no easy matter to wish white dolls away.

A few years ago I was thumbing through an album of old family photographs and saw one of me and my oldest sister taken when I was four and she was nine. It struck me, transfixed me really, as it was a color photo and most of the old family pictures taken when I was a boy were black-and-white because my mother could not afford to have color pictures developed. We, my sister and I, are sitting on an old stuffed blue chair and she is holding a white doll in her hand, displaying it for the picture. I remember the occasion very well, as my sister was to be confirmed in our small, all-black Episcopal church that day, and she was, naturally, proud of the moment and wanted to share it with her favorite toy. That, I remembered, was why these were color pictures. It was a special day for the family, a day my mother wanted to celebrate by taking special pictures. My mother is a very dark woman who has a great deal of race pride and often speaks about my sisters' having black dolls. I was surprised, in looking at the picture recently, that they ever owned a white one, that indeed a white one had been a favorite.

My wife grew up—enjoyed the primary years of black girlhood, so to speak—during the years 1954 through 1962; she was about five or six years younger than my oldest sister. She lived in a southern state, or a state that was a reasonable facsimile of a southern state. She remembers that signs for colored and white bathrooms and water fountains persisted well into the mid-sixties in Texas. She remembers also Phyllis George, the Miss America from Denton, Texas, who went on to become a television personality for several years. She has always been very interested in George's career, and she has always disliked her. "She sounds just like a white girl from Texas," my wife likes to say, always reminding me that while both blacks and whites in Texas have accents, they do not sound alike. George won the contest in 1971, my wife's freshman year at the University of Pennsylvania and around the time she began to wear an Afro, a popular hairstyle for young black women in the days of "our terrible blackness" or "our black terribleness." It was a year fraught with complex passages into black womanhood for her. To think that a white woman from Texas should win the Miss America title that year! For my wife, the years of watching the Miss America contest were nothing more, in some sense continue to be nothing more, than an expression of anger made all the worse by the very unconscious or semiconscious nature of it. But if the anger has been persistent, so has her enormous capacity to "take it"; for in all these years it has never occurred to her to refuse to watch because, like the black girl being offered the white doll, like all black folk being offered white gifts, she has absolutely no idea how that is done, and she is not naïve enough to think that a simple refusal would be an act of empowerment. Empowerment comes only through making demands of our bogeymen, not by trying to convince ourselves we are not tormented. Yet, paradoxically, among blacks there is the bitter hope that a simplistic race pride will save us, a creed that masks its complex contradictions beneath lapping waves of bourgeois optimism and bourgeois anguish; for race pride clings to the opposing notions that the great hope (but secret fear) of an African-American future is, first, that blacks will always remain black and, second, that the great fear (but secret hope) of an African-American future is that blacks will not always remain black but evolve into something else. Race pride, which at its most insistent argues that blackness is everything, becomes, in its attempt to be the psychological quest for sanity, a form of dementia that exists as a response to that form of white dementia that says blackness is nothing. Existing as it does as a reactive force battling against a white preemptive presumption, race pride begins to take on the vices of an unthinking dogma and the virtues of a disciplined religious faith, all in the same instance. With so much at stake, race pride becomes both the act of making a virtue of a necessity and making a necessity of a virtue and, finally, making a profound and touching absurdity of both virtue and necessity. In some ways my wife learned her lessons well in her youth: she never buys our daughters white dolls.

My daughters, Linnet, age ten, and Rosalind, age seven, have become staunch fans of beauty contests in the last three years. In that time they have watched, in their entirety, several Miss America pageants, one Miss Black America contest, and one Miss USA. At first, I ascribed this to the same impulse that made my wife interested in such events when she was little: something secretly female, just as an interest in professional sports might be ascribed to something peculiarly male. Probably it is a sort of resentment that black girls harbor toward these contests. But that could not really be the case with my daughters. After all, they have seen several black entrants in these contests and have even seen black winners. They also have black dolls.

Back in the fall of 1983 when Vanessa Williams became Miss America, we, as a family, had our picture taken with her when she visited St. Louis. We went, my wife and I, to celebrate the grand moment when white American popular culture decided to embrace black women as something other than sexual subversives or fat, kindly maids cleaning up and caring for white families. We had our own, well, royalty, and royal origins means a great deal to people who have been denied their myths and their right to human blood. White women reformers may be ready to scrap the Miss America contest. (And the contest has certainly responded to the criticism it has been subjected to in recent years by muting some of the fleshier aspects of the program while, in its attempts to be even more the anxiety-ridden middle-class dream-wish, emphasizing more and more the magic of education and scholarly attainments.) It is now the contest that signifies the quest for professionalism among bourgeois women, and the first achievement of the professional career is to win something in a competition. But if there is a movement afoot to bring down the curtain finally on Miss America, my wife wants no part of it: "Whites always want to reform and end things when black people start getting on the gravy train they've been enjoying for years. What harm does the Miss America contest do?" None, I suppose, especially since black women have been winning lately.

    Linnet and Rosalind were too young when we met Vanessa Williams to recall anything about the pictures, but they are amazed to see themselves in a bright, color Polaroid picture with a famous person, being part of an event that does not strike a chord in their consciousness because they cannot remember being alive when it happened. I often wonder if they attach any significance to the pictures at all. They think Vanessa is very pretty, prettier than their mother, but they attach no significance to being pretty—that is to say, no real value; they would not admire someone simply because he or she was good-looking. They think Williams is beautiful, but they do not wish that she were their mother. And this issue of being beautiful is not to be taken lightly in the life of a black girl. About two years ago Linnet started coming home from school wishing aloud that her hair was long and blond so that she could fling it about, the way she saw many of her white classmates doing. As she attends a school that is more than 90 percent white, it seemed inevitable to my wife that one of our daughters would become sensitive about her appearance. At this time Linnet's hair was not straightened and she wore it in braids. Oddly, despite the fact that she wanted a different hairstyle that would permit her hair to "blow in the wind," so to speak, she vehemently opposed having it straightened, although my wife has straightened hair, after having worn an Afro for several years. I am not sure why Linnet did not want her hair straightened; perhaps, after seeing her teenaged cousin have her hair straightened on several occasions, the process of hair straightening seemed distasteful or disheartening or frightening. Actually, I do not think Linnet wanted to change her hair to be beautiful; she wanted to be like everyone else.[1] But perhaps this is simply wishful thinking here or playing with words because Linnet must have felt her difference as being a kind of ugliness. Yet she is not a girl who is subject to illusion. Once, about a year earlier, when she had had a particularly rough day in school, I told her, in a father's patronizing way with a daughter, that I thought she was the most beautiful girl in the world. She looked at me strangely when I said that and then replied matter-of-factly: "I don't think I'm beautiful at all. I think I'm just ordinary. There is nothing wrong with that, is there, Daddy? Just to be ordinary?" "Are you unhappy to be ordinary?" I asked. She thought for a moment, then said quietly and finally, "No. Are you?"

    Hair straightening, therefore, was not an option and would not have been even if Linnet had wanted it, because my wife was opposed to having Linnet's hair straightened at her age. At first, Linnet began going to school with her hair unbraided. Unfortunately, this turned out to be a disastrous hairdo, as her hair shrank during the course of a day to a tangled mess. Finally, my wife decided to have both Linnet and Rosalind get short Afro haircuts. Ostensibly, this was to ease the problem of taking swim lessons during the summer. In reality, it was to end Linnet's wishes for a white hairstyle by, in effect, foreclosing any possibility that she could remotely capture such a look. Rosalind's hair was cut so that Linnet would not feel that she was being singled out. (Alas, the trials of being both the second and the younger child!) At first, the haircuts caused many problems in school. Some of the children—both black and white—made fun of them. Brillo heads, they were called, and fungus and Afro heads. One group of black girls at school refused to play with Linnet. "You look so ugly with that short hair," they would say. "Why don't you wear your hair straight like your mom. Your mom's hair is so pretty." Then, for the first time, the girls were called niggers by a white child on their school bus, although I think neither the child nor my daughters completely understood the gravity of that obscenity. People in supermarkets would refer to them as boys unless they were wearing dresses. Both girls went through a period when they suffered most acutely from that particularly American disease, that particularly African-American disease, the conjunction of oppression and exhibitionistic desire: self-consciousness. They thought about their hair all the time. My wife called the parents of the children who teased them. The teasing stopped for the most part, although a few of the black girls remained so persistent that the white school counselor suggested that Linnet's and Rosalind's hair be straightened. "I'm white," he said, "and maybe I shouldn't get into this, but they might feel more comfortable if they wore a different hairstyle." My wife angrily rejected that bit of advice. She had them wear dresses more often to make them look unmistakably like girls, although she refused out of hand my suggestion of having their ears pierced. She is convinced that pierced ears are just a form of mutilation, primitive tattooing, or scarring passing itself off as something fashionable. Eventually, the girls became used to their hair. Now, after more than a year, they hardly think about it, and even if Linnet wears a sweat suit or jeans, no one thinks she is a boy because she is budding breasts. Poor Rosalind still suffers on occasion in supermarkets because she shows no outward signs of sexual maturity. Once, while watching Linnet look at her mother's very long and silken straight hair, the hair that the other black girls at school admire, always calling it pretty, I asked her if she would like to have hers straightened.

"Not now," she said. "Maybe when I'm older. It'll be something different."

"Do you think you will like it?" I asked.

"Maybe," she said.

And in that "maybe," so calmly and evenly uttered, rests the complex contradictions, the uneasy tentative negotiations of that which cannot be compromised yet can never be realized in this flawed world as an ideal; there is, in that "maybe," the epistemology of race pride for black American women so paradoxically symbolized by their straightened hair. In the February 1939 issue of *The Atlantic Monthly,* a black woman named Kimbal Goffman (possibly a pseudonym) wrote an essay entitled "Black Pride" in which she accused blacks of being ashamed of their heritage and, even more damningly in some of her barbs obviously aimed at black women, of their looks:

> Why are so many manufacturers becoming rich through the manufacture of bleaching preparations? Why are hair-straightening combs found in nearly every Negro home? Why is the following remark made so often to a newborn baby, when grandma or auntie visits it for the first time? "Tell Mother she must pinch your nose every morning. If she doesn't, you're gonna have a sure 'nough darky nose."

According to Goffman, blacks do not exploit what society has given them; they are simply ashamed to have what they have, tainted as it is with being associated with a degraded people, and long to be white or to have possessions that would accrue a kind of white status. In the essay, blacks in general receive their share of criticism but only black women are criticized in a gender-specific way that their neurotic sense of inferiority concerning physical appearance is a particularly dangerous form of reactionism as it stigmatizes each new generation. According to Goffman, it is black women, because they are mothers, who perpetuate their sense of inferiority by passing it on to their children. In this largely Du Boisian argument, Goffman advises, "Originality is the backbone of all progress." And, in this sense, originality means understanding blackness as something uncontrolled or uninfluenced by what whites say it is. This is the idealism of race pride that demands both purity and parity. Exactly one year later, in the February 1940 issue of *The Brown American,* a black magazine published in Philadelphia, Lillian Franklin McCall wrote an article about the history of black women beauty shop owners and entrepreneurs entitled "Appointment at Seven." The opening paragraph is filled with dollar signs:

> The business of straightening milady's insistent curls tinkles cash registers in the country to the tune of two million and a half dollars a year. And that covers merely the semi-monthly session with the hairdresser for the estimated four million of Eve's sepia adult daughters by national census. Today there is a growing trend to top off the regular, "Shampoo and wave," with a facial; and, perhaps, a manicure. New oil treatments and rinses prove a lure, too, so milady finds her beauty budget stepped up from approximately $39 yearly for an average $1.25 or $1.50 "hair-do," to $52.00 per

year if she adds a facial to the beauty rite, and $10 more, for the manicure.

In a Booker T. Washington tone, McCall goes on to describe how the establishment of a black beauty culture serves as a source of empowerment for black women:

> Brown business it is, in all its magnitude for Miss Brown America receives her treatments from the hands of Negro beauticians and her hair preparations and skin dreams come, usually from Negro laboratories.

She then tells the reader that leading companies in this field were founded by black women: Madam C. J. Walker, Mrs. Annie Turbo Malone, Madame Sara Spencer Washington. And one is struck by the absences that this essay evokes, not only in comparison to Goffman's piece but also to Elsie Johnson McDougald's major manifesto on black women, "The Task of Negro Womanhood," that appeared in Alain Locke's seminal 1925 anthology of African-American thought, *The New Negro*. In McDougald's piece, which outlines all the economic status and achievements of black women at the time, there is absolutely no mention of black beauty culture, no mention of Madame C. J. Walker, although her newspaper ads were among the biggest in black newspapers nationwide during the twenties. (And why did McDougald not mention black women's beauty workers and businesspeople along with the nurses, domestics, clerks, and teachers she discusses at length? It can scarcely be because she, as a trained and experienced writer on black sociological matters, did not think of it.) It is not simply money or black woman's industry or endeavor that makes the black woman present or a presence; it is beauty culture generally that finally brings her into being, and specifically, her presence is generated by her hair. What for one black woman writer, Goffman, is an absence and thus a sign of degradation, is for another a presence and a sign of economic possibilities inherent in feminine aesthetics.

What did I see as a boy when I passed the large black beauty shop on Broad and South streets in Philadelphia where the name of its owner, Adele Reese, commanded such respect or provoked such jealousy? What did I see there but a long row of black women dressed immaculately in white tunics, washing and styling the hair of other black women? That was a sign of what culture, of what set of politics? The sheen of those straightened heads, the entire enterprise of the making of black feminine beauty: Was it an enactment of a degradation inspirited by a bitter inferiority or was it a womanly laying on of hands where black women were, in their way, helping themselves to live through and transcend their degradation? As a boy, I used to watch and wonder as my mother straightened my sisters' hair every Saturday night for church on Sunday morning. Under a low flame on the stove, the hot comb would glow dully; from an open jar of Apex bergamot hair oil or Dixie Peach, my mother would extract blobs and place them on the back of one hand, deftly applying the oil to strands of my sisters' hair with the other. And the strange talk about a "light press" or a "heavy press" or a "close press" to get the edges and the ends; the concern about the hair "going back" if caught in the rain. Going back where, I wondered. To Africa? To the bush? And the constant worry and vigil about burning, getting too close to the scalp. I can remember hearing my sisters' hair sizzle and crackle as the comb passed through with a kind of pungent smell of actually burning hair. And I, like an intentional moth, with lonely narrow arcs, hovered near this flame of femininity with a fascinated impertinence. Had I witnessed the debilitating nullity of absence or was it the affirmation of an inescapable presence? Had I witnessed a mutilation or a rite of devotion? Black women's hair is, I decided even as a boy, unintelligible. And now I wonder, is the acceptance of the reigns of black women as Miss America a sign that black beauty has become part of the mainstream culture? Is the black woman now truly a presence?

We, I and my wife and our daughters, sat together and watched the latest Miss America contest. We did what we usually do. We ate popcorn. We laughed at all the talent numbers, particularly the ones when the contestants were opera singers or dancers. We laughed when the girls tried to answer grand social questions—such as "How can we inspire children to achieve and stay in school?" or "How can we address the problem of mainstreaming physically disadvantaged people?"—in thirty seconds. In fact, as Rosalind told me after the show, the main reason my daughters watch the Miss America pageant is that "it's funny." My daughters laugh because they cannot understand why the women are doing what they are doing, why they are trying so hard to please, to be pleasing. This must certainly be a refreshing bit of sanity, as the only proper response for such a contest is simply to dismiss it as hilarious; this grandiose version of an elocution, charm school, dance and music recital, which is not a revelation of talent but a reaffirmation of bourgeois cultural conditioning. And this bit of sanity on my daughters' part may prove hopeful for our future, for our American future, for our African-American future, if black girls are, unlike my wife when she was young, no longer angry. When it was announced that Miss Missouri, Debbye Turner, the third black to be Miss America, was the winner, my children were indifferent. It hardly mattered to them who won, and a black woman's victory meant no more than if any other contestant had prevailed. "She's pretty," Linnet said. She won two dollars in a bet with my wife, who did not think it possible that another black Miss America would be chosen. "Vanessa screwed up for the whole race," she told me once. "It's the race burden, the sins of the one become the original sins of us all." Linnet said simply, "She'll win because she is the best." Meritocracy is still a valid concept with the young.

For me, it was almost to be expected that Miss Turner would win. First, she received more precontest publicity than any other contestant in recent years, with the possible exception of the black woman who was chosen Miss Mississippi a few years ago. Second, after the reign of Vanessa Williams, one would think that the Miss America powers that be very much wanted to have another black win and have a successful reign so that the contest itself could both prove its good faith (to blacks) and forestall criticism from white feminists and liberals (who are always put in a difficult position when the object of their disapproval is a black woman). As with the selection of Williams, the contest gained a veneer of postmodernist social and political relevance not only by selecting a black again but by having an Asian, a kidney donor, and a hearing-impaired woman among the top ten finalists. This all smacks of Affirmative Action or the let's-play-fair-with-the-underrepresented doctrine, which, as Miss Virginia pointed out after the contest, smacks of politics. But the point she missed, of course, is the point that all people who oppose Affirmative Action miss. The selection process for the Miss America contest has always been political. Back in the days when only white college women, whose main interest in most instances was a degree in MRS, could win, the contest was indeed just as political as it is now, a clear ideological bow to both patriarchal ideals and racism. It is simply a matter of which politics you prefer, and while no politics are perfect, some are clearly better than others. But in America, it must be added, the doctrine of fair play should not even be graced with such a sophisticated term as "political." It is more our small-town, bourgeois Christian, muscular myth of ethical rectitude, the tremendous need Americans feel to be decent. So Miss Turner is intended to be both the supersession of Vanessa Williams—a religious vet student whose ambitions are properly, well, postmodernist Victorianism, preach do-goodism, evoke the name of God whenever you speak of your ambitions, and live with smug humility—and the redemption of the image of black women in American popular culture, since the Miss America contest is one of the few vehicles of display and competition for women in popular culture.

And if my daughters have come to one profound penetration of this cultural rite, it is that the contest ought to be laughed at in some ways, as most of the manifestations of popular culture ought to be for being the shoddy illusions that they are. For one always ought to laugh at someone or a group of someones who are trying to convince you that nothing is something—and that is not really the same as someone trying to convince you that you can have something for nothing, because in the popular culture business, the price for nothing is the same as the price for something; this "nothing is something" is, in fact, in most cases what the merchandising of popular culture is all about. (But as my mother reminded me as a boy: Nothing is nothing and something is something. Accept no substitutes!) For my children, the contest can be laughed at because it is so completely meaningless to them; they know it is an illusion despite its veneer as a competition. And it is that magical word "competition," which is used over and over again all night long by the hosts and hostesses of the Miss America show (a contest, like most others these days, from the SATs to professional sports, that is made up of a series of competitions within the framework of larger competitions in such a pyramid that the entire structure of the outside world, for the bourgeois mind, is a frightful maze, a strangulating skein of competitions), that is the touchstone of reality, the momentous signifier that the sponsors of the pageant hope will give this extravaganza new significance and new life. For everything that we feel is important now is a matter of competition, beating out someone else for a prize, for some cheap prestige, a moment of notice before descending to cipherhood again; competition ranging from high culture (literary prizes, which seem to be awarded every day in the week, and classical music competitions for every instrument in a symphony orchestra, because of course for high culture one can never have enough art) to mid-culture (the entire phenomenon of American education, from academic honors to entrance requirements for prestigious schools, because of course for the middle class one can never have enough education or enough professionalism) to low culture (playing the lottery and various forms of gambling, because of course for the lower class one can never hope enough for money). And the most stringent and compulsively expressed the competition is (and the Miss America contest has reached a new height of hysteria in both the stridency and compulsion of the competition), the more legitimate and noteworthy it is.

Everyone in our culture wants to win a prize. Perhaps that is the grand lesson we have taken with us from kindergarten in the age of the perversions of Dewey-style education: Everyone gets a ribbon, and praise becomes a meaningless narcotic to soothe egoistic distemper. And in our bourgeois coming-of-age, we simply crave more and more ribbons and praise, the attainment of which becomes all the more delightful and satisfying if they are gotten at someone else's expense. Competition, therefore, becomes in the end a kind of laissez-faire psychotherapy that structures and orders our impossible rages of ambition, our rages to be noticed. But competition does not produce better people (a myth we have swallowed whole); it does not even produce better candidates; it simply produces more desperately grasping competitors. The "quality" of the average Miss America contestant is not significantly better now than it was twenty-five years ago, although the desires of today's contestants may meet with our approval (who could possibly disapprove of a black woman who wishes to be a vet in this day of careerism as the expression of independence and political empowerment), but then the women of twenty-five years ago wanted what their audiences approved of as well. That is not necessarily an advance or progress; that is simply a recognition that we are all bound by the mood and temper of our time. So, in this vast competition, this fierce theatrical warfare where all the women are supposed to love their neighbor while they wish to beat her brains out, this warfare so pointedly exposed before the nation, what we have chosen is not the Royal American Daughter (although the contest's preoccupation with the terminology of aristocracy mirrors the public's need for such a person as the American princess) but rather the Cosmopolitan Girl. As the magazine ad states:

> Can a girl be too busy? I'm taking seventeen units at Princeton, pushing on with my career during vacations and school breaks, study singing and dancing when I can, try never to lose track of my five closest chums, steal the time for Michael Jackson and Thomas Hardy, work for an anti-drug program for kids and, oh yes, I hang out with three horses, three cats, two birds and my dog Jack. My favorite magazine says "too busy" just means you don't want to miss anything. . . . I love that magazine. I guess you can say I'm That Cosmopolitan Girl.

When one reads about these women in the Miss America contest, that is precisely what they sound like: the Cosmopolitan Girl who knows how to have serious fun, and she has virtually nothing with which to claim our attention except a moralistic bourgeois diligence. To use a twenties term: she sounds "swell." She is an amalgam of both lead characters portrayed by Patty Duke on her old TV show: the studious, serious kid and the "typical" wacky but good-hearted suburban teenager, or, to borrow Ann Douglas's concept, she is the Teen Angel: the bourgeois girl who can do everything, is completely self-absorbed with her leisure, and has a heart of gold. Once again, with the Miss America contest we have America's vehement preoccupation with innocence, with its inability to deal with the darkness of youth, the darkness of its own uselessly expressed ambition, the dark complexity of its own simplistic morality of sunshine and success, the darkness, righteous rage, and bitter depth of its own daughters. Once again, when the new Miss America, victorious and smiling, walks down the runway, we know that runway, that victory march, to be the American catwalk of supreme bourgeois self-consciousness and supreme illusion. We are still being told that nothing is something.

Nonetheless, the fact that Miss Turner won struck both my wife and me as important, as something important for the race. We laughed during the contest, but we did not laugh when she was chosen. We wanted her to win very much; it is impossible to escape that need to see the race uplifted, to thumb your nose at whites in a competition. It is impossible for blacks not to want to see their black daughters elevated to the platforms where white women are. Perhaps this tainted desire, an echoing "Ballad of the Brown Girl" that resounds in the unconscious psyche of all black people, is the unity of feeling that is the only race pride blacks have ever had since they became Americans; for race pride for the African American, finally, is something that can only be understood as existing on the edge of tragedy and history and is, finally, that which binds both together to make the African American the darkly and richly complicated person he or she is. In the end, both black women magazine writers quoted earlier were right: race pride is transcending your degradation while learning to live in it and with it. To paraphrase an idea of Dorothy Sayers, race pride must teach blacks that they are not to be saved *from* degradation but saved *in* it.

A few days after the contests I watched both my daughters playing Barbies, as they call it. They squat on the floor on their knees, moving their dolls around through an imaginary town and in imaginary houses. I decided to join them and squatted down too, asking them the rules of their game, which they patiently explained as though they did not mind having me, the strange adult, invade their children's world. I told them it was hard for me to squat and asked if I could simply sit down, but they said that one always plays Barbies while squatting. It was a rule that had to be obeyed. As they went along, explaining relationships among their myriad dolls and the several landscapes, as complicated a genealogy as anything Faulkner ever dreamed up, a theater as vast as the entire girlhood of the world, they told me that one particular black Ken doll and one particular black Barbie doll were married and that the dolls had a child. Then Rosalind held up a white doll that someone, probably a grandparent, had given them (my wife is fairly strict on the point of our daughters' not having white dolls, but I guess a few have slipped through), explaining that this doll was the daughter of the black Ken and Barbie.

"But," I said, "how could two black dolls have a white daughter?"

"Oh," said Rosalind, looking at me as if I were an object deserving of only her indulgent pity, "we're not racial. That's old-fashioned. Don't you think so, Daddy? Aren't you tired of all that racial stuff?"

Bowing to that wisdom which, it is said, is the only kind that will lead us to Christ and to ourselves, I decided to get up and leave them to their play. My knees had begun to hurt and I realized, painfully, that I was much too old, much too at peace with stiffness and inflexibility, for children's games.

NOTES

1 Richard Wright tells a story in his 1956 account of the Bandung conference, entitled *The Color Curtain,* that emphasizes the absence of the black woman. He relates how a white woman journalist knocks on his hotel room door during the course of the conference and confides the strange behavior of her roommate—a black woman journalist from Boston. Her roommate walks around in the middle of the night and the white woman often covertly spies her in "a dark corner of the room . . . bent over a tiny blue light, a very low and a very blue flame. . . . It seemed like she was combing her hair, but I wasn't sure. Her right arm was moving and now and then she would look over her shoulder toward my bed." The white woman thinks that the black woman is practicing voodoo. But Wright soon explains that the black woman is simply straightening her hair.

> "But why would she straighten her hair? Her hair seems all right" [the white woman journalist asks].
> "Her hair is all right. But it's not straight. It's kinky. But she does not want you, a white woman, to see her when she straightens her hair. She would feel embarrassed—"
> "Why?"
> "Because you were born with straight hair, and she wants to look as much like you as possible. . . . "
> The woman stared at me, then clapped her hands to her eyes and exclaimed:
> "Oh!"
> I leaned back and thought: here in Asia, where everybody was dark, the poor American Negro woman was worried about the hair she was born with. Here, where practically nobody was white, her hair would have been acceptable; no one would have found her "inferior" because her hair was kinky; on the contrary, the Indonesians would perhaps have found her different and charming.

The conversation continues with an account of the black woman's secretive skin-lightening treatments. What is revealing in this dialogue, which takes on both political and psychoanalytic proportions is the utter absence of the black woman's voice, her presence. She is simply the dark, neurotic ghost that flits in the other room while the black male and the white female, both in the same room, one with dispassionate curtness and the other with sentimentalized guilt, consider the illness that is enacted before them as a kind of bad theater. Once again, the psychopathology of the black American is symbolized by the black woman's straightened hair, by her beauty culture.

LIFE WITH DAUGHTERS

The Cakewalk with Shirley Temple

Frieda brought her four graham crackers on a saucer and some milk in a blue-and-white Shirley Temple cup. She was a long time with the milk, and gazed fondly at the silhouette of Shirley Temple's dimpled face. Frieda and she had a loving conversation about how cu-ute Shirley Temple was. I couldn't join them in their adoration because I hated Shirley. Not because she was cute, but because she danced with Bojangles, who was my friend, my uncle, my daddy, and who ought to have been soft-shoeing it and chuckling with me. Instead he was enjoying, sharing, giving a lovely dance thing with one of those little white girls whose socks never slid down under their heels. So I said, "I like Jane Withers."

—Toni Morrison, *The Bluest Eye*

What is the use of discrimination in a world where anything can happen?

—David Mamet

Of course, no one can take seriously the statement of Toni Morrison's character, Claudia. It is impossible to like Jane Withers in any movie in which she played or would have played with Shirley Temple. She is an utterly contemptible child. In the 1934 classic *Bright Eyes,* for example, Withers plays a spoiled rich brat who, because she is so much bigger than Temple, seems menacing, a pure threat to Shirley even when they do not share a scene together. Shirley is poor and, as always in her films, winds up parentless midway through when her mother is killed by a bus. (Her father, an aviator, is killed before the start of the film in a plane crash, and so this film, as with so

278

many others that Temple starred in during her heyday, is an archaic quest for
family, exploiting the child viewer's precarious status in the adult world by
showing Temple as a child who can, in fact, get adults to like her obsessively.) In the course of the film, Shirley wins over everyone except Jane
Withers's character and her parents. The antagonism went beyond the camera, according to Temple's autobiography, *Child Star:*

> A very clever girl, Withers then started mimicking me to
> whoever would listen offstage. Put on the defensive by all this self-
> confident, noisy humiliation, both Mother and I tried politely to
> sidestep Withers's mother and, whenever possible, Withers herself
> by always having something else to do. . . .
>
> As cast, Withers was noisy, arrogant, and rich, constantly
> humiliating me as the shy, stubborn poor girl. For props we were
> each issued a doll, mine modest and frumpy, befitting my role,
> and hers a giant glorious Lenci from Italy with dangling blond
> curls and exquisitely costumed in ruffles and a velvet bonnet gar-
> landed with lifelike flowers. Offstage I admired the clothing, and
> following her stage role, Withers became possessive, denying me
> even a peek, clutching it and turning away. Ultimately it devel-
> oped into a quiet offstage competition for something she really did
> want, but I did not. [1]

So, even offscreen, these children remained strangely in character, which
meant that, in effect, they were not really acting on screen at all but, in some
sense, simply being themselves. It is this kind of claim to naturalism that
gives Temple's movies their appeal: It was not that she was a child star (after
all, in the thirties and forties there were plenty of those, from Jackie Cooper
and Mickey Rooney to Dickie Moore and Edith Fellows to Elizabeth Taylor
and Judy Garland to all the children of the Our Gang and Dead End Kids
comedies, none really as persistently memorable as Temple), but that she was
a child, period. She was the child every adult wanted, not because she was
famous or talented but because she was the kind of child that adults under
stress would want: On the one hand, she was self-reliant, determined, preco-
cious, and endearing; on the other hand, she was good, kind, obedient, loving, willing to share, sentimental, and moral—these last being odd things,
really, for a child to be. I do not recall, as a child, that I was particularly
moral or particularly sentimental, although I remember being, at times,
quite emotional and filled with very deep yearnings. I cannot remember any
other children I grew up with being either sentimental or moral either. In
the film, Shirley winds up getting parents and ultimately, one supposes, the
fortune that was to be Withers's as Withers's rich grandfather (or perhaps it

was a rich uncle, I am not sure) also goes off in the sunset of family happiness with Shirley. Withers, in the final scene of the film, is slapped hard across the face by her scheming mother when she says that she is happy that Shirley will not be living with them anymore. The mother realizes as Withers does not that Shirley has just walked away with all the dough. When I watched this film with my daughters, they laughed when Withers was slapped at the end. They were glad that she finally got what she deserved. It is quite strange what a Shirley Temple movie can do to children; normally, my children would have been disturbed seeing an adult strike a child in that manner.

It was two years ago, the summer that my daughters gave up their Afros and had their hair straightened, that I decided to watch every Shirley Temple film available on video with them. This included nineteen 20th Century Fox films that were made during her heyday, from 1934 to 1938 (she was, at the time, the hardest-working actor in Hollywood) and several Baby Burlesque short features that Temple made around 1932 and 1933. Her breakthrough film, *Little Miss Marker* (1934), is not currently on video, although my children and I were able to see it one afternoon on television. I am not quite sure why I did this. I do not like Shirley Temple movies. I did not like them much as a child with one exception. But my daughters, after having seen a colorized version of *Our Little Girl,* a perfectly wretched Temple vehicle (Temple herself admits this in her autobiography) on the Disney channel one evening, very much wanted to do this summer project. We watched each of the films at least three times. Perhaps I associate my children's change in hairstyle with our Shirley Temple summer because so much was made of Temple's hair, her curls, during her years of stardom. My daughters liked Temple's hair very much.

I have taken my daughters to the theater many times over the last several years to see movies. I have done this much more frequently than my wife, whose tolerance for children's films is lower than mine. Since so few films for young children are even made, I doubt if I have missed many in the last six or seven years. In the darkness I have seen the Care Bears and the Muppets and Sesame Street and various Disney productions, from *Fantasia*— which Linnet and Rosalind and virtually every kid in the theater found boring because it was not really a children's movie but an effort by middle-class parents to try to ram culture down their children's throats—to *Oliver and Company,* and even Spielberg's *An American Tail.* Somewhere around the middle of the proceedings, I usually fall asleep. Sometimes I just close my eyes and drift.

Once I began to recall when my mother sent me to the movies with my sisters on a Saturday afternoon. They were never very willing to take their younger brother but of course the ultimatum was either to take me or not go to the movies at all. It was a shabby theater called the Palace where all the black children went in my South Philadelphia neighborhood. The Italian children went to the Italia and the Irish and Jews went to the Strafford. I never went to the movies with a white until I was in college; I rarely went to a downtown theater to see a movie during my youth. The very earliest time I can recall going to the movies with my sisters was to see two horror movies: *Frankenstein 1970* starring Boris Karloff and *Queen from Outer Space* starring Zsa Zsa Gabor and Eric Fleming. I was probably about six or seven years old, as these movies were released in 1958 or 1959. I cringed in my chair and cried because I was so frightened by what I saw on the screen; I was having a perfectly miserable time. And so were my sisters. Lenora, the oldest, was completely exasperated and kept telling me to hush. Instead of crying, I whimpered, "I want to go home." We did not have much money for candy and popcorn, so my sisters could not bribe me or distract me to silence. When we left the theater Lenora would not even walk near me. Going ahead, she said simply, "I'm gonna tell Mom just how you acted in the theater and I'm never taking you again." My other sister, Rosalind, felt a bit more sympathy for me. I told her I was scared when the Queen in *Queen from Outer Space* removed her mask and showed her horrible face. "It was just cold cream and jelly on her face," Lenora said. "He's little," Rosalind said. "He doesn't know any better." "He's a little sissy," Lenora said. "I am not a sissy," I said, pouting. But I recall going to the movies with my mother to see a movie called *All the Young Men,* a Korean War racial drama starring Sidney Poitier and Alan Ladd, and being scared out of my wits when coming attractions for a horror film called *The Village of the Damned* were shown. "You have to be a man," my mother said sternly. "It's just a movie. It's not real." The real horror was that it was a movie about children but they were monstrous children. It does no good to tell children that a movie is not real, because they are bound by the alchemy of their own psychology to think the thing to be absolutely and unutterably real because it so closely resembles the fantasies and dreams that are the reality of children. (Suddenly, while watching Disney's *The Black Cauldron,* I am awakened when my daughter, Rosalind, at one of the film's dark parts, whimpers to me, "I'm scared, Daddy." And I am amazed to find that I am no longer a child being taken to the theater by women but an adult taking my own girls. I almost start to say, "It's not real," but I check myself and take Rosalind in my lap and then Linnet, who is afraid and jealous now as well. "Well, that is pretty scary," I say. "Cover your eyes and don't look." And two little girls press their heads against my chest. And there I sit, holding them, like Tiresias, "an old man with wrinkled female breasts.")

Sprawled on the floor with a big bowl of popcorn and cans of pop we spent most of July and August that year at home watching Temple movies nearly every afternoon. I would make lunch as my sister, Rosalind, did when we were home from school for the summer. The only memory I have of Shirley Temple from my youth is watching *Captain January* on some rainy, cool afternoon, eating tuna fish sandwiches that my sister made and curling our stockinged feet together under an old blanket. I remember nothing about the film but because it was one of the most pleasant afternoons I ever spent in my life, I was under the impression for a very long time that *Captain January* was one of my favorite films.

We started with Temple's Civil War films, strictly in the Hollywood mode of southern apologia: *The Little Colonel, The Littlest Rebel,* and *Dimples.* The first two featured the famous black dancer Bill "Bojangles" Robinson, one of her most remarkable and effective male leads.[2] (Temple films were built around strong male leads.) The mother/women figures in Temple films were always weakly drawn because the films were always about the psychosexual tensions of father figures and daughters in bourgeois culture, not simply revelations about male nurturing but also about its limits, which is why the films always had epithalamiumlike endings.)[3] In both films, Robinson is an affectionate teacher, a dignified character quite distinct from either the black kitchen maids in *The Little Colonel* or a young Willie Best in *The Littlest Rebel* who were the buffoons.[4] (It would be instructive to compare Bill Robinson with Arthur Treacher, who played the British equivalent to Robinson's character in several Temple films such as *Stowaway, The Little Princess,* and *Heidi.*) *Dimples,* while not directly about the Civil War, as it places Temple in the New York Bowery of the 1850s, does feature an interesting play-within-a-play bit that ends the film: a performance of Harriet Beecher Stowe's *Uncle Tom's Cabin* in which Frank Morgan plays Uncle Tom and Temple plays Little Eva, a perfectly fitting role as Temple was, in many respects, America's Little Eva or the perfect realization of a Victorian child, for it was the sentimentality and nostalgia that she evoked that made her films appealing. But in this film, as in other Hollywood antebellum or Civil War movies, there is no tension about the impending conflict, no sense of anything political for which a war could have been fought; indeed *Uncle Tom's Cabin* is rendered as a comedy and even Eva's death, which is still presented as something tragic (or at least as something well-acted as the audience responds with great cheering), fails because Temple as the new American Eva is not really expected to die. She is not a martyr; she has an undying, puerile American optimism. We know *Uncle Tom's Cabin* was reduced to rubbish as a stage show after the Civil War and know that there was a popular effort to minimize the political conflicts of the war in the popular culture of the late nineteenth century, but this film, in its revisionist reactionism to the Depression, minimizes everything even before the war started, which does not simply whitewash American history but actually renders it meaningless.

During that summer as we watched these films together, my relationship with my daughters changed. At first, I saw the films merely as vehicles for parental instruction, black parental instruction, I should say; for I had prepared to give a history of black actors in Hollywood in the 1930s and provide information on the lives of Bill Robinson, Hattie McDaniels, and some of the other blacks who appeared in Temple films. I was never given much of an opportunity.

"I don't want to hear your old lectures, Daddy," Linnet said. "We want to watch the movies. This isn't school. You make being black seem like a lesson."

When they laughed uproariously at some graceless thing that Stepin Fetchit or Willie Best did, Rosalind turned to me, knowing that I was aghast, and said:

"Don't worry, we know they aren't real black people."

"But do you know what you're laughing at?" I asked, chagrined.

"Yeah," Rosalind said, "clowns, not black people."

Eventually, I was told that if all I wanted to do was talk about the movies or analyze them, then I would not be permitted to watch. Besides, they were more than capable of judging the films themselves. Some, like *The Little Colonel* and *Little Miss Broadway,* they liked immensely; others such as *Wee Willie Winkie* and *Dimples* they thought to be wretched. *Poor Little Rich Girl* and *Curly Top* were so-so. So, I grew quiet as the summer went on. I did not want to be banished.

It was during this summer that they abandoned their Afro hairstyles for good. They had had a hard time of it in school the previous year, were the subject of jokes and taunts from both black and white children. Moreover, I suppose they wanted straightened hair like their mother's. For Linnet, I think it was a particularly hard year; having been classified as learning disabled and feeling herself to be a plain girl, she felt the school year to be one long battle against the contempt of her classmates.

When they burst through the door that evening with their hair newly straightened, beaming, looking for all the world like young ladies, like my sisters when they were children, I was so taken aback in such horror that I could only mutter in astonishment when they asked: "How do you like it?" It was as if my children were no longer mine, as if a culture that had convinced them they were ugly, had taken them from me. I looked at my wife as if to say, "This is your doing. If only you would wear your hair as you did when we first met, this would not have happened." My wife's response would have been: "They wanted their hair straightened and they thought they were old enough for it. Besides, there is no virtue in wearing an Afro. I don't believe in politically correct hair. Who was the last white woman you saw who didn't have something done to her hair? Most white women don't wear their hair the way God put it on their heads. It's been dyed, moussed, permed, teased, spiked, shagged, curled, and coiffed. What do you think, Shirley Temple was born with those curls? I've got news for you. Her mom had to work like heck to get those curls set just right. I want the same privilege to do to my hair what white women can do to theirs. It's my right to self-expression."

Right after this happened, late in the summer, I began to find excuses not to watch the Shirley Temple movies with my daughters. More and more, I began to rent videos for them, Shirley Temple or anything else for children, and simply left them to the television set. After about two or three weeks of this, Linnet, who was particularly upset by my lack of approval, asked me why I would not watch the movies with them anymore. I said that I thought the films were for children, not adults, that I was, in effect, intruding. Besides, I had work to do. Eventually, we got around to her new hairstyle.

"I like my hair like this," she said. "This is the way I want to wear it."

"Do you care if I like it?" I asked.

She paused for a moment. "No," she said, bravely. "I want to wear my hair the way I like."

"To get the approval of other people?" I asked unkindly.

"Well," she said, "a little. I don't like to be called dumb. I don't like to be called ugly. I want to be like everybody else. I wear my hair some for me and some for other people. I don't think I'm Shirley Temple or a white girl but I want to look like a girl, not like a boy. When you write, Daddy, don't you want approval from other people too?

"I wish you would watch the movies with us. It's more fun when you watch too."

About two weeks after this, the weekend before the start of school, I received in the mail a Shirley Temple video we hadn't seen, some early shorts that mimicked adult genre movies in which she and the other toddlers went around dressed in diapers: *Kid in Africa, War Babies, Pollytix in Washington*. I thought this might make a good truce and so I brought them to my daughters' room and offered to watch with them. Just before the video started I made a gesture that surprised even me: I stood above Linnet, bent over, and smelled her hair. It had just been washed and freshly straightened ("touched up," my wife said) and it smelled a bit like shampoo, a bit like pressing oil, and very slightly burned, much like my mother's, my sisters', and my aunts' hair smelled during my childhood. It was a smell that I had, in some odd way, become fond of because, I suppose, it was so familiar, so distressingly familiar, like home. The priest André Malraux quotes in his *Anti-Mémoires* was right: There is no such thing as a grown-up person.

NOTES

1 Jane Withers gives a different version of her relationship with Temple during the filming of *Bright Eyes*. In Dick Moore's retrospective interviews with former child stars, *Twinkle, Twinkle, Little Star* (1984), Withers states: "When the shooting ended, they had a little party. I wasn't even invited to it. But when an actress [Lois Wilson] finished her part in the film, she brought their beautiful doll to Shirley. I'm sure she didn't realize what it would do to another child, but we were both there, you know." Withers goes on to mention that she and her mother found it impossible to make friends with Shirley and her mother: "We weren't friends as children. We did one film together and that's all. We didn't socialize at all. . . . I was not permitted to talk to Shirley at all. I was told to go and wash my hands before I went into a scene with her. That upset Mother a lot."

2 Temple writes in her autobiography that the great director D. W. Griffith wrote Fox head Winfield Sheehan proposing: "There is nothing, absolutely nothing, calculated to raise the goose-flesh on the back of an audience more than that of a white girl in relation to Negroes." It was shortly after receiving this, in 1935, that Sheehan contracted Bill Robinson for *The Little Colonel*.

3 The late Graham Greene got into serious trouble in his 1937 review of *Wee Willie Winkie* for suggesting that "In *Captain January* she wore trousers with the mature suggestiveness of a Dietrich; her neat and well-developed rump twisted in the tap-dance; her eyes had a sidelong searching coquetry. Now in *Wee Willie Winkie*, wearing short kilts, she is a complete totsy. . . . Her admirers—middle-aged men and clergymen—respond to her dubious coquetry, to the sight of her well-shaped and desirable body, packed with enormous vitality, only because the safety curtain of story and dialogue drops between their intelligence and their desire." He further suggests that real childhood ended for Temple in *The Littlest Rebel*, which was also the last film that she and Bill Robinson shared real intimacy. In *The Little Colonel* they presumably slept in the same house and apparently Robinson had access to Temple's bedroom. In *The Littlest Rebel* he was her guardian and they, in fact, traveled together to Washington, D.C., to beseech President Lincoln to spare her captured rebel father. When Robinson was featured in later Temple films, when she was much bigger, *Rebecca of Sunny Brook Farm* and *Just Around The Corner*, Robinson was a more peripheral character. Greene and the magazine for which he wrote this review, *Night and Day*, were sued in 1938 by Temple and 20th Century Fox, who won a judgment that put the magazine out of business.

Of course, Temple's films constantly suggested incest. In a nightclub scene in *Little Miss Marker* Temple is tossed from one set of male arms to another as they try to guess her weight while female lead Dorothy Dell voices her disapproval. In the same film, Adolph Menjou undresses Temple and she hops into his bed. He, naturally enough, decides to sleep on a chair. In *Captain January*, Slim Summerville and Guy Kibbee begin undressing themselves in front of Temple to show off their tattoos when a female truant officer enters the room with a disapproving look.

4 Robinson liked Temple greatly and even bought her a little motor car to ride around the 20th Century lot. He kept a shrine of her pictures on his dresser. According to Temple, he even threatened her first husband, John Agar: "If you ever hurt this girl, I'm gonna cut you." One can never be sure, of course, if toting around razors (Robinson was more known for carrying a pistol) was in keeping with Robinson's fast life as an inveterate gambler or a stereotype of any popular Negro vaudevillian.